Frontend Development Projects with Vue.js 3

Learn the fundamentals of building scalable web applications and dynamic user interfaces with Vue.js

Maya Shavin

Raymond Camden

BIRMINGHAM—MUMBAI

Frontend Development Projects with Vue.js 3

Group Product Manager: Pavan Ramchandani
Publishing Product Manager: Aaron Tanna
Senior Editor: Hayden Edwards
Content Development Editor: Abhishek Jadhav
Technical Editor: Simran Ali
Copy Editor: Safis Editing
Project Coordinator: Sonam Pandey
Proofreader: Safis Editing
Indexer: Manju Arasan
Production Designer: Aparna Bhagat
Marketing Coordinator: Nivedita Pandey

First published: November 2020

Second edition: March 2023

Production reference: 2100523

Published by Packt Publishing Ltd.
Livery Place
35 Livery Street
Birmingham
B3 2PB, UK.

ISBN 978-1-80323-499-1

www.packtpub.com

*To my husband, Natan, for always supporting my career in high tech,
and for being my strength and my best buddy in this life.*

– Maya Shavin

*To my wife, Lindy, for being my rock, my best friend, my partner in LEGO,
and the best part of every day.*

– Raymond Camden

Contributors

About the authors

Maya Shavin is a senior software engineer at Microsoft, working extensively with JavaScript and frontend frameworks, and is based in Israel. She holds a BSc in computer sciences, a BA in business management, and an International MBA from Bar-Ilan University, Israel.

She has worked with JavaScript and the latest frontend frameworks, such as React, Vue.js, and so on, to create scalable and performant frontend solutions at companies such as Cooladata and Cloudinary, and currently Microsoft. She founded and is currently the organizer of the VueJS Israel Meetup Community, helping to create a strong playground for Vue.js lovers and like-minded developers.

Maya is also a published author, international speaker, and an open source library maintainer of frontend and web projects. She can be reached on her blog (`https://mayashavin.com`), on Twitter at @mayashavin, or via email.

Raymond Camden is a senior developer evangelist for Adobe. He works on the Acrobat Services APIs to build powerful (and typically, cat-related) PDF demos. He is the author of multiple books on web development and has been actively blogging and presenting for almost 20 years. Raymond can be reached at his blog (`www.raymondcamden.com`), at `http://bit.ly/3KaN4Fr` on Mastodon, or via email at `raymondcamden@gmail.com`.

About the reviewer

Andrea Koutifaris has a passion for programming, which he likes to say is in his DNA. At the age of 13, he began using his father's laptop to write his own programs. After graduating high school, he enrolled, without a second thought, at the University of Florence, Faculty of Computer Engineering. After being a Java developer for several years, Andrea gradually moved to frontend development, which is still his passion today. Having spent too much time fixing messed-up code, he is obsessed with good programming and test-driven development, which, in his opinion, is the only way to write production-quality code.

Table of Contents

Part 1: Introduction and Crash Course

1

Starting Your First Vue Project   3

2

Working with Data   77

3

Vite and Vue Devtools   125

Part 2: Building Your First Vue App

4

Nesting Components (Modularity)   147

5

The Composition API   197

6

Global Component Composition   249

7

Routing   289

8

Animations and Transitions   353

Part 3: Global State Management

9

The State of Vue State Management   399

10

State Management with Pinia   425

Part 4: Testing and Application Deployment

11

Unit Testing   449

12

End-to-End Testing   501

13

Deploying Your Code to the Web   539

Preface

Are you looking to use Vue.js 3 for web applications, but don't know where to begin? *Frontend Development Projects with Vue.js 3* will help build your development toolkit and get ready to tackle real-world web projects, helping you get to grips with the core concepts of this JavaScript framework with practical examples and activities.

In this book, you'll work on mini projects, including a chat interface, a shopping cart and price calculator, a to-do app, and a profile card generator for storing contact details. These realistic projects are presented as bitesize exercises and activities, allowing you to challenge yourself in an enjoyable and attainable way.

Here, you'll discover how to handle data in Vue components, define communication interfaces between components, and handle static and dynamic routing to control the application flow. You'll also work with Vite and Vue Devtools and learn how to handle transition and animation effects to create an engaging user experience. Later, you'll discover how to test your app and deploy it to the web.

By the end of this book, you'll gain the skills to start working like an experienced Vue developer, build professional apps that can be used by others, and have the confidence to tackle real-world frontend development problems.

Who this book is for

This book is designed for Vue.js beginners. Whether this is your first JavaScript framework or you're already familiar with React or Angular, this book will get you on the right track. To understand the concepts explained in this book, you must be familiar with HTML, CSS, JavaScript, and Node package management.

What this book covers

Chapter 1, Starting Your First Vue Project, helps you understand the key concepts and benefits of Vue. js, how to set up the project architecture using the terminal (or command line), and how to create a simple Vue component with local data following the component fundamentals.

Chapter 2, Working with Data, enables you to monitor, manage, and manipulate data from various sources in your Vue.js components. You will learn how to utilize Vue's powerful data reactivity and cache system through computed properties and how to set up advanced watchers to observe components' data changes.

Chapter 3, Vite and Vue Devtools, introduces you to Vite and shows you how to debug these computed properties and events using Vue Devtools.

Chapter 4, Nesting Components (Modularity), helps you discover how to modularize a Vue application using component hierarchies and nesting. This chapter introduces concepts such as props, events, prop validation, and slots. It also covers how to use refs to access DOM elements at runtime.

Chapter 5, The Composition API, teaches you how to write isolated composables (or custom hooks) to reuse in multiple components using the Composition API with the `setup()` method, and how to build a scalable component system for your Vue project beyond using the classic Options API.

Chapter 6, Global Component Composition, helps you to organize your code using mixins and plugins, achieve global composition, and keep the code DRY (following the **Don't Repeat Yourself** (**DRY**) principle) in any project. You will also understand the advantages and drawbacks of global composition, thus deciding the right approach to maximize your component's flexibility.

Chapter 7, Routing, guides you through how routing and Vue Router work. You will learn how to set up, implement, and manage the routing system in your app with Vue Router.

Chapter 8, Animations and Transitions, helps you explore the essentials of Vue transitions and how to create your transition, including single-element animation and group-of-elements animation, and how to combine them with external libraries for further customization. You will also learn how to create full-page animations with transition routes.

Chapter 9, The State of Vue State Management, helps you understand how to manage the state (data) in a complex Vue application.

Chapter 10, State Management with Pinia, teaches you how the Pinia library makes managing the state easier.

Chapter 11, Unit Testing, introduces you to testing Vue components.

Chapter 12, End-to-End Testing, provides an explanation of **End-to-End** (**E2E**) testing and how it differs from Unit tests, as well as many examples of adding it to your Vue project.

Chapter 13, Deploying Your Code to the Web, helps you take a deep look into actually getting your Vue project live on the internet.

To get the most out of this book

Software/hardware covered in the book	Operating system requirements
Node Package Manager (npm)	Windows, macOS, or Linux
Yarn Package Manager (`yarn`)	
Visual Studio Code (VS Code) IDE	

If you are using the digital version of this book, we advise you to type the code yourself or access the code from the book's GitHub repository (a link is available in the next section). Doing so will help you avoid any potential errors related to the copying and pasting of code.

Download the example code files

You can download the example code files for this book from GitHub at `https://github.com/ PacktPublishing/Frontend-Development-Projects-with-Vue.js-3/tree/ v2-edition`. If there's an update to the code, it will be updated in the GitHub repository.

We also have other code bundles from our rich catalog of books and videos available at `https:// github.com/PacktPublishing/`. Check them out!

Download the color images

We also provide a PDF file that has color images of the screenshots and diagrams used in this book. You can download it here: `https://packt.link/kefZM`.

Conventions used

There are a number of text conventions used throughout this book.

`Code in text`: Indicates code words in text, database table names, folder names, filenames, file extensions, pathnames, dummy URLs, user input, and Twitter handles. Here is an example: "An example of using the `this` instance is shown here: "

A block of code is set as follows:

```
export default {
  data() {
    return {
      yourData: "your data"
    }
  },
  computed: {
    yourComputedProperty() {
      return `${this.yourData}-computed`;
    }
  }
}
```

When we wish to draw your attention to a particular part of a code block, the relevant lines or items are set in bold:

```
// header.vue
<script>
    import logo from 'components/logo.vue'

    export default {
        components: {
            logo
        }
    }
</script>
```

Any command-line input or output is written as follows:

```
node -v
```

Bold: Indicates a new term, an important word, or words that you see onscreen. For instance, words in menus or dialog boxes appear in **bold**. Here is an example: "We can do this by checking that it is called when clicking the **Close** button."

> **Tips or important notes**
> Appear like this.

Get in touch

Feedback from our readers is always welcome.

General feedback: If you have questions about any aspect of this book, email us at customercare@ packtpub.com and mention the book title in the subject of your message.

Errata: Although we have taken every care to ensure the accuracy of our content, mistakes do happen. If you have found a mistake in this book, we would be grateful if you would report this to us. Please visit www.packtpub.com/support/errata and fill in the form.

Piracy: If you come across any illegal copies of our works in any form on the internet, we would be grateful if you would provide us with the location address or website name. Please contact us at copyright@packt.com with a link to the material.

If you are interested in becoming an author: If there is a topic that you have expertise in and you are interested in either writing or contributing to a book, please visit authors.packtpub.com.

Share Your Thoughts

Once you've read *Frontend Development Projects with Vue.js 3*, we'd love to hear your thoughts! Scan the QR code below to go straight to the Amazon review page for this book and share your feedback.

https://www.amazon.in/review/create-review/error?asin=1803234997

Your review is important to us and the tech community and will help us make sure we're delivering excellent quality content.

Download a free PDF copy of this book

Thanks for purchasing this book!

Do you like to read on the go but are unable to carry your print books everywhere? Is your eBook purchase not compatible with the device of your choice?

Don't worry, now with every Packt book you get a DRM-free PDF version of that book at no cost.

Read anywhere, any place, on any device. Search, copy, and paste code from your favorite technical books directly into your application.

The perks don't stop there, you can get exclusive access to discounts, newsletters, and great free content in your inbox daily

Follow these simple steps to get the benefits:

1.   Scan the QR code or visit the link below

https://packt.link/free-ebook/9781803234991

2.   Submit your proof of purchase

3.   That's it! We'll send your free PDF and other benefits to your email directly

Part 1:
Introduction and Crash Course

In this part, we will be introduced to the Vue framework by building Vue components and running live projects. We will find out how easy it is to control data using Vue's two-way binding directives syntax, understand event life cycles and reactivity in Vue, and become comfortable creating complex forms.

We will cover the following chapters in this section:

- *Chapter 1, Starting Your First Vue Project*
- *Chapter 2, Working with Data*
- *Chapter 3, Vite and Vue Devtools*

1

Starting Your First
Vue Project

In this chapter, you will learn about the key concepts and benefits of **Vue.js** (**Vue**), how to set up the project architecture using the terminal (or command line), and how to create a simple Vue component with local data following the component fundamentals.

This chapter will cover the following topics:

- Understanding Vue as a framework
- Setting up a Vite-powered Vue application
- Exploring `data` properties as a local state
- Writing components with `<script setup>`
- Understanding Vue directives
- Enabling two-way binding using `v-model`
- Understanding data iteration with `v-for`
- Exploring methods
- Understanding component lifecycle hooks
- Styling components
- Understanding CSS modules

By the end of this chapter, you will be able to describe the fundamentals of Vue lifecycle hooks and expressions and use various styling approaches and HTML syntax flavors to control the HTML template competently.

Technical requirements

The Node version has to be below v20 (preferable Yarn 1.22 and Node version above 16 and up to 19.x, and npm up to version 9.x).

The complete code for this chapter is available on GitHub at: `https://github.com/PacktPublishing/Frontend-Development-Projects-with-Vue.js-3/tree/v2-edition/Chapter01`

Understanding Vue as a framework

Developers in the industry must resolve frontend development problems quickly with minimal impact on existing workflows or backend architecture. In many cases, developers tend to overlook the UI until the end of a project, which can happen because of a lack of resources, ever-evolving product requirements, or the existing attitude that the frontend is the easy bit.

However, companies such as Apple and Google have proven that thinking through the design of the frontend is key to a solid product or platform that will excite and engage users, leading to a higher return on investment and a more successful business.

If you know Vue, you may have also come across other frontend frameworks that, at face value, solve the same problems, such as Ember, Angular, or React. At a surface level, they attempt to make reactive frontend development more reliable and introduce patterns that make it easier. However, there are significant differences in how a Vue project might play out compared to an Angular or React project. Let's investigate them.

Angular versus Vue

Angular is a **Model-View-ViewModel** (**MVVM**) framework built by Google and has built-in support for TypeScript. The Angular ecosystem includes **Ahead-of-Time** (**AoT**) rendering, a router, and a CLI tool. However, it fails to deliver a simplified system for global state management; developers would need to learn how to use Flux or adopt NgRx.

Vue takes Angular's core robustness and provides a better development experience by removing the restriction of an enforced code style for developers. Vue also simplifies common Angular patterns, such as HTML directives, and eliminates a variety of Angular's project structures, such as injectables, components, pipes, modules, and so on. From Vue 3.0 onward, it provides excellent support for TypeScript and typing without the drawbacks of Angular-enforced coding styles.

Vue is more flexible, developer-friendly, efficient, and straightforward to set up and learn to use than Angular in many cases.

Next, let's look at how Vue and React differ.

React versus Vue

First released in 2013 and backed by Meta (previously known as Facebook), React rapidly gained popularity in the developer community. React introduces the **JSX pattern** to write HTML syntax directly with JavaScript. With JSX, React increases the amount that new developers are required to learn about both JavaScript and component-based architecture.

Both React and Vue share the same component-driven development approach, allowing developers to build applications in a modular way. Each component contains its functionalities and lifecycle. Vue takes these core concepts of modular coding and offers flexibility to developers in choosing which approach to use to write their components: JSX or the traditional style, in which HTML, CSS, and JavaScript are separated.

Vue uses the **Single-File Component** (**SFC**) approach to leverage this modular structure into a single file while keeping the separation readable and understandable for developers.

Advantages of using Vue for your project

Vue has a gentler learning curve and a vibrant ecosystem. This gentle learning curve helps reduce overhead and cost for any team onboarding developers to a new Vue project.

One key benefit of Vue is its approachability for both new and veteran developers:

- Out of the box, developers can use a well-optimized and performant framework on which to build scalable, dynamic frontend applications.
- The SFC format pattern offers a modular and flexible blueprint that provides an enjoyable experience to developers. SFCs allow Vue to be genuinely versatile. You can implement basic functionalities and incrementally adopt pieces of a static site into Vue rather than overhaul your entire website.

As powerful as Redux and NgRx, Vuex (and lately Pinia) proves to be an outstanding official global state management tool that is flexible enough to meet most development needs.

Thanks to its stable performance; well-defined tools such as Vue Router, Pinia, Vuex, and so on; and a supportive community, developers can save time and money by choosing Vue for their development stack.

The following section explores the essential Vue architecture before deep-diving into the SFC pattern and template syntax.

Working with Vue

To learn about the Vue architecture, we will start by importing the Vue package into our coding playground. One straightforward way is to import the Vue package through the official **Content Distribution Network** (**CDN**). We can do so by creating an index.html file and adding a <script> tag to load the Vue CDN within the <head> section of the HTML template, as demonstrated in the following code block:

```
<!DOCTYPE html>
<html>
<head>
    <title>Vue.js project with CDN</title>
    <script src="https://unpkg.com/vue@3"></script>
</head>
</html>
```

The browser will also load the Vue package using the CDN defined in the `script` tag when loading the page. Once completed, you can utilize the Vue functions and start writing Vue code.

But first, let's look at the Vue instance.

Understanding the Vue instance

In general, each Vue application consists of *only one* root Vue instance, which can be created using the `Vue.createApp` method:

```
const vm = Vue.createApp({
   // options
})
```

The Vue class constructor accepts an `options` object for the configurations and behavior of components. We call this approach Options API and we can use it for all corresponding Vue components. However, all of them are considered nested Vue instances, with their own options and properties.

> **Note**
>
> vm is a term commonly used to refer to a **View Model**, which is an abstraction of the view that describes the state of the data in the model. Binding a Vue instance to vm helps you to keep track of your Vue instance in a block of code.

For the Vue engine to render the application instance, in our `index.html` file, we declare an `<div>` element within the `<body>` tag using a unique class name, ID, or data attribute as the main entry point for the application accordingly:

```
<body>
  <div id="vue-app"></div>
  <script>
    const vm = Vue.createApp({
    //Options
    })
  </script>
</body>
```

To render the Vue application in the browser, we need to trigger `vm.mount()` to mount the root component to the targeted HTML element using a unique selector. In this example, it is an `id` with a value of `vue-app`:

```
<body>
  <div id="vue-app"></div>
```

```
<script>
  const vm = Vue.createApp({
              //Options
              })
  vm.mount('#vue-app')
</script>
</body>
```

Now, you bind the `<div>` element with `id="vue-app"` to the new Vue instance.

Next, let's define text with a value of `"Start using Vue.js today!"` and add it as a property of the `return` value for the `data` method in the application options:

```
const vm = Vue.createApp({
   data() {
     return {
       text: 'Start using Vue.js today!'
     }
   }
})
```

In the preceding code example, `data` is a function that returns an Object instance containing the local state (or local variables) of a component. We will discuss this further in an upcoming section of this chapter.

To render the content of `text` to the DOM, we use Vue template syntax, represented by double curly braces (`{{ }}`) wrapped around the reactive content. In this case, we use `{{ text }}`, as shown in the following code:

```
<div id="vue-app">{{ text }}</div>
```

The Vue engine will replace the data property labeled `text` and the curly brace placeholder with the `Start using Vue.js today!` string.

The output of the preceding code will be as follows:

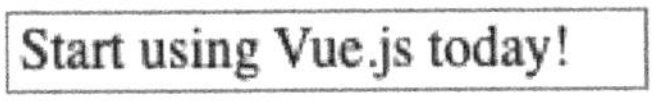

Start using Vue.js today!

Figure 1.1 – Displaying "Start using Vue.js today!" using a local data property

In the <head> tag, we can also use the DOM API to construct a Vue application instance and bound it to our target element (with the ID selector as #vue-app):

```
<head>
  <title>Vue.js CDN</title>
  <script src="https://unpkg.com/vue@3"></script>
  <script>
    document.addEventListener('DOMContentLoaded', function
    () {
     Vue.createApp({
       data(){
         return {
           text: "Start using Vue.js today!"
         }
       }
     }).mount('#vue-app')
    })
  </script>
</head>
<body>
 <div id="vue-app">{{text}}</div>
</body>
```

The output is the same for both approaches. However, we strongly recommend *not* using DOMContentLoaded.

While working with a CDN is very portable, we recommend using package managers as the installation method for Vue. From Vue 3 and above, Vue projects use Vite (or Vite.js) to initialize and bundle the code. You can access it here: https://vuejs.org/guide/quick-start.html#creating-a-vue-application.

Using a bundling management tool is very helpful for managing other third-party libraries and building an optimized code package for production. In the next section, we will explore a package-controlled example.

Setting up a Vite-powered Vue application

A Vue project is structured similarly to a lot of modern node-based apps and contains the following:

- A package.json file

- A node_modules folder in the root of your project

- Various other configuration files are usually contained at the root level, such as vite.config. js and .eslintrc.js, since they will generally have an effect across your whole project.

The following screenshot displays a default Vue app folder structure:

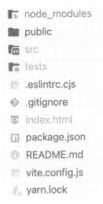

Figure 1.2 – Default Vue application folder structure

By default, there is an `index.html` file at the root level that serves as a placeholder for loading the Vue application. You can modify this file to include `header` and `footer` scripts, such as Google Fonts or third-party JavaScript libraries that are not included as a part of your bundle.

The Vue project structure follows a pattern where you manage most of your source code within the `/src` directory. You can subdivide your Vue files into various folders, for example, using a `components` folder to store reusable Vue components. By default, Vite will create `assets` and `components` folders to code-split the default files. For beginners, it is good to follow this pattern until you get more comfortable:

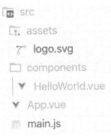

Figure 1.3 – Default Vue application src folder structure

The `public` folder is a special directory containing files that need to be transferred directly to the output location. The following screenshot displays how this folder will look:

Figure 1.4 – Default Vue application public folder

At this point, you should be somewhat familiar with how a Vue project structure looks. Next, we discuss Vue's unique pattern – the SFC architecture.

Vue's SFC architecture

Components are the building blocks of most modern frameworks. In general, splitting your code into component-specific chunks ensures code readability and facilitates the **Don't Repeat Yourself** (**DRY**) principle. Vue's SFC pattern follows this approach closely.

The SFC architecture centralizes the responsibility of both appearance and behavior into a single file, thus simplifying the architecture of your project. You now can refer to your HTML, CSS, and JavaScript logic without switching files. Your default .vue file structure will be as follows:

```
<template>
  <div>
    <!-- Write HTML syntax here -->
  </div>
</template>

<script>
  export default {
    // Write javascript here
  }
</script>

<style>
  /* Write styling here */
</style>
```

Figure 1.5 – Default .vue file structure

A general good practice is to ensure your components file doesn't contain more than 500 lines of code. If you encounter this situation, it's recommended to split them into smaller reusable components. For example, in the header of your application, you may have a logo element that is reused on other pages. You would create a component such as logo.vue:

```
// logo.vue
<template>
  <img src="myLogo.png" />
</template>
```

In header.vue, you import the logo component into the script section and then include it as a nested component of the header component. You can achieve this by declaring it as a property of the components field:

```
// header.vue
<script>
    import logo from 'components/logo.vue'

    export default {
        components: {
            logo
        }
    }
</script>
```

In the template section, you can use the logo as a normal HTML element, as shown here:

```
<template>
    <header>
        <a href="mywebsite.com">
            <logo />
        </a>
    </header>
</template>
```

The output will be a header with the logo image rendered – and you can reuse the logo component in any other component when needed.

Very soon, you will have lots of these semantically structured files, which use small chunks of a reusable syntax that your team can implement across various application areas.

In the next exercise, you will practice creating your first Vue component and displaying it in another component.

Exercise 1.01 – building your first component

We are going to build our first component, Exercise1.01, inside of a Vue project and import it to use it in the App.vue component using ES6 module syntax.

To access the code file for this exercise, refer to https://github.com/PacktPublishing/ Front-End-Development-Projects-with-Vue.js/tree/v2-edition/Chapter01/ Exercise1.01.

> **Note**
>
> Your app will hot-reload when you save new changes, so you can see them instantly.

To get started, execute the following steps:

1. Use the application generated with npm init vue@3 as a starting point, or within the root folder of the code repository, navigate into the Chapter01/Exercise1.01 folder by using the following commands in order:

    ```
    > cd Chapter01/Exercise1.01/
    > yarn
    ```

2. Run the application using the following command:

    ```
    yarn dev
    ```

3. Go to https://localhost:3000.

4. Open the exercise project in VS Code (by using the code . command within the project directory) or your preferred IDE.

5. Open the src/App.vue file, delete everything in that file, and save.

6. In your browser, everything should be a blank, clean state to start working from.

7. The three primary components that make up a single-file component are the <template>, <script>, and <style> blocks. Add the following code blocks as our scaffolding for a Vue component:

    ```
    /** src/App.vue **/
    <template>
    </template>
    <script>
    export default {
    }
    ```

```
</script>
<style>
</style>
```

8. Create another file in the `components` folder called `Exercise1-01.vue` and repeat the same step for scaffolding the Vue component:

```
// src/components/Exercise1-01.vue
<template>
</template>
<script>
export default {
}
</script>
<style>
</style>
```

9. Within our `Exercise1-01.vue` component, compose a set of `<div>` tags, with an `<h1>` element and a heading inside the `<template>` tags:

```
<template>
  <div>
    <h1>My first component!</h1>
  </div>
</template>
```

10. Inside the `<style>` block, add some styling as follows:

```
<style>
  h1 {
    font-family: 'Avenir', Helvetica, Arial,
    sans-serif;
    text-align: center;
    color: #2c3e50;
    margin-top: 60px;
  }
</style>
```

11. Import our component into App.vue by using the ES6 import method and defining the component inside the components object in the <script> block. We can now reference this component inside the HTML by using its name in camelCase or kebab-case (both will work):

```
<template>
  <Exercise />
</template>
<script>
import Exercise from './components/Exercise1-01'
export default {
  components: {
    Exercise,
  }
}
</script>
```

When you press *Ctrl* + *S* (or *Cmd* + *S* on macOS), https://localhost:3000 should reload and look amazing:

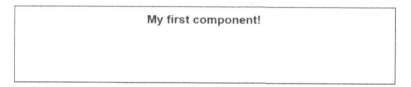

My first component!

Figure 1.6 – localhost output for Exercise 1.01

In this exercise, we saw how to structure Vue components using template tags, and scaffold basic Vue components using Vetur. We also created a new Vue component and reuse it in App.vue using ES6 syntax and property field components.

In the next section, we will gain an understanding of how to define the local state data of a component using data properties.

Exploring data properties as a local state

One of the most used terms and reactive elements used when constructing Vue components is data properties. These manifest themselves within the data() function of a Vue instance:

```
<script>
  export default {
    data() {
```

```
        return {
          color: 'red'
        }
      }
    }
</script>
```

You can use the `data()` function to create a local data object to essentially store any information you want to use within your Vue templates. This local object is bound to the component and we call it the local state data of the component. When any property of this local object is updated or changed, it will reactively update in the corresponding template.

Once we have defined our local data, we need to bind it to the `template` section to display its values in the UI, which is called **data interpolation**.

Interpolation is the insertion of something of a different nature into something else. In the Vue context, this is where you would use *mustache* syntax (double curly braces) to define an area in which you can inject data into a component's HTML template.

Consider the following example:

```
<template>
  <span> {{ color }}</span>
</template >
<script>
export default {
  data() {
    return {
      color: 'red'
    }
  }
}
</script>
```

The `data` property of `red` is bound to Vue.js reactive data and will update during runtime, depending on state changes between the UI and its data.

At this point, we should look at how to define and bind local data in the most classical Vue way. With Vue 3.0, we enjoy a shorter and simpler approach to writing and importing components. Let's explore it next.

Writing components with script setup

Starting from Vue 3.0, Vue introduces a new syntactic sugar setup attribute for the <script> tag. This attribute allows you to write code using Composition API (which we will discuss further in *Chapter 5, The Composition API*) in SFCs and shorten the amount of code needed for writing simple components.

The code block residing within the <script setup> tag will then be compiled into a render() function before being deployed to the browser, providing better runtime performance.

To start using this syntax, we take the following example code:

```
// header.vue
<script>
    import logo from 'components/logo.vue'

    export default {
        components: {
            logo
        }
    }
</script>
```

Then, we replace <script> with <script setup>, and remove all the code blocks of export default.... The example code now becomes as follows:

```
// header.vue
<script setup>
    import logo from 'components/logo.vue'
</script>
```

In <template>, we use logo as usual:

```
<template>
    <header>
        <a href="mywebsite.com">
            <logo />
        </a>
    </header>
</template>
```

To define and use local data, instead of using `data()`, we can declare regular variables as local data and functions as local methods for that component directly. For example, to declare and render a local data property of `color`, we use the following code:

```
<script setup>
const color = 'red';
</script>
<template>
  <div>{{color}}</div>
</template>
```

The preceding code outputs the same result as the example in the previous section –`red`.

As mentioned at the beginning of this section, `<script setup>` is the most useful when you need to use Composition API within SFCs. Still, we can always take advantage of its simplicity for simple components.

> **Note**
>
> From this point onward, we will combine both approaches and use `<script setup>` whenever possible.

In the following exercise, we will go into more detail about how to use interpolation and data.

Exercise 1.02 – interpolation with conditionals

When you want to output data into your template or make elements on a page reactive, interpolate data into the template by using curly braces. Vue can understand and replace that placeholder with data.

To access the code file for this exercise, refer to `https://github.com/PacktPublishing/Frontend-Development-Projects-with-Vue.js-3/tree/v2-edition/Chapter01/Exercise1.02`:

1. Use the application generated with `npm init vue@3` as a starting point, or within the root folder of the code repository, navigate into the `Chapter01/Exercise1.02` folder by using the following commands in order:

    ```
    > cd Chapter01/Exercise1.02/
    > yarn
    ```

2. Run the application using the following command:

    ```
    yarn dev
    ```

3. Open the exercise project in VS Code (by using the `code` . command within the project directory) or your preferred IDE.

4. Create a new Vue component file named `Exercise1-02.vue` in the `src/` `components` directory.

5. Inside the `Exercise1-02.vue` component, let's add data within the `<script setup>` tags by adding a function called `data()`, and return a key called `title` with your heading string as the value:

```
<script>
export default {
  data() {
    return {
      title: 'My first component!',
    }
  },
}
</script>
```

6. Reference `title` by replacing your `<h1>` text with the interpolated value of {{ `title` }}:

```
<template>
  <div>
    <h1>{{ title }}</h1>
  </div>
</template>
```

When you save this document, the data title will now appear inside your h1 tag.

7. In Vue, interpolation will resolve any JavaScript that's inside curly braces. For example, you can transform the text inside your curly braces using the `toUpperCase()` method:

```
<template>
  <div>
    <h1>{{ title.toUpperCase() }}</h1>
  </div>
</template>
```

8. Go to `https://localhost:3000`. You should see an output like the following screenshot:

Figure 1.7 – Display of an uppercase title

9. Interpolation can also handle conditional logic. Inside the data object, add a Boolean key-value pair, `isUppercase: false`:

```
<template>
  <div>
    <h1>{{ isUppercase ? title.toUpperCase() : title }}</
h1>
  </div>
</template>
<script>
export default {
  data() {
    return {
      title: 'My first component!',
      isUppercase: false,
    }
  },
}
</script>
```

The preceding code will generate the following output:

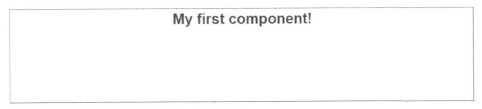

Figure 1.8 – Exercise 1.02 output after including the inline conditional statement

10. Add this condition to the curly braces and when you save, you should see the title in sentence case. Play around with this value by changing `isUppercase` to `true`:

```
<script>
export default {
  data() {
    return {
      title: 'My first component!',
      isUppercase: true,
    }
  },
}
</script>
```

The following screenshot displays the final output generated upon running the preceding code:

MY FIRST COMPONENT!

Figure 1.9 – Displaying the uppercase title

11. Now, let's replace `<script>` with `<script setup>` and move all the local data declared within the `data()` function to its own variable names respectively, such as `title` and `isUpperCase`, as shown here:

```
<script setup>
const title ='My first component!';
const isUppercase = true;
</script>
```

12. The output should remain the same as in *Figure 1.9*.

In this exercise, we were able to apply inline conditions within the interpolated tags ({{ }}) by using a Boolean variable. The feature allows us to modify what data to display without overly complicated situations, which can be helpful in certain use cases. We also learned how to write a more concise version of the component using `<script setup>` in the end.

Since we are now familiar with using interpolation to bind local data, we will move on to our next topic – how to attach data and methods to HTML element events and attributes using Vue attributes.

Understanding Vue directives

All Vue-based directives start with a v-* prefix as a Vue-specific attribute:

- v-text: The v-text directive has the same reactivity as with interpolation. Interpolation with {{ }} is more performant than the v-text directive. However, you may find yourself in situations where you have pre-rendered text from a server and want to override it once your Vue application has finished loading. For example, you can pre-define a static placeholder text while waiting for the Vue engine to eventually replace it with the dynamic value received from v-text, as shown in the following code block:

  ```
  <template>
    <div v-text="msg">My placeholder</div>
  </template>
  <script setup>
  const msg = "My message"
  </script>
  ```

- v-once: When used, it indicates the starting point of static content. The Vue engine will render the component with this attribute and its children exactly once. It also ignores all data updates for this component or element after the initial render. This attribute is handy for scenarios with no reactivity needed for certain parts. You can combine v-once with v-text, interpolation, and any Vue directive.

- V-html: Vue will parse the value passed to this directive and render your text data as a valid HTML code into the target element. We don't recommend using this directive, especially on the client side, due to its performance impact and the potential security leak. The script tag can be embedded and triggered using this directive.

- v-bind: This directive is one of the most popular Vue features. You can use this directive to enable one-way binding for a data variable or an expression to an HTML attribute, as shown in the following example:

  ```
  <template>
    <img v-bind:src="logo" />
  </template>
  <script setup>
  const logo = '../assets/logo.png';
  </script>
  ```

The preceding code demonstrates how to bind the logo data variable to image's src. The img component now takes the source value from the logo variable and renders the image accordingly.

You can also use it to pass a local data variable as props to another component. A shorter way is using the :attr syntax instead of v-bind:attr. Take the preceding example, for instance. We can rewrite the template as follows:

```
<template>
  <img :src="logo" />
</template>
```

- v-if: This is a powerful directive you can use to conditionally control how elements render inside a component. This directive operates like the if...else and if...else if... conditions. It comes with supporting directives, such as v-else, standing for the else case, and v-else-if, standing for the else if case. For example, we want to render different text when count is 2, 4, and 6. The following code will demonstrate how to do so:

```
<template>
<div v-if="count === 2">Two</div>
<div v-else-if="count === 4">Four</div>
<div v-else-if="count === 6">Six</div>
<div v-else>Others</div>
</template>
```

- v-show: You can also control the visible state of HTML elements by using v-show. Unlike v-if, with v-show, the Vue engine still mounts the element to the DOM tree but hides it using the display: none CSS style. You can still see the content of the hidden element visible in the DOM tree upon inspecting it, but it is not visible on the UI to end users. This directive does not work with v-else or v-else-if. If v-show results in a true Boolean, it will leave the DOM element as is. If it resolves as false, it will apply the display: none style to the element.

- v-for: We use the v-for directive to accomplish the goal of list rendering based on a data source. The data source is an iterative data collection, such as an array or object. We will dive deeper into different use cases for this directive in a separate section within this chapter.

We have gone over the most common directives in Vue. Let's review and experiment with how to use these directives with the following exercise.

Exercise 1.03 – exploring basic directives (v-text, v-once, v-html, v-bind, v-if, v-show)

More complicated components will use multiple directives to achieve the desired outcome. In this exercise, we will construct a component that uses several directives to bind, manipulate, and output data to a template view.

To access the code file for this exercise, refer to `https://github.com/PacktPublishing/Frontend-Development-Projects-with-Vue.js-3/tree/v2-edition/Chapter01/Exercise1.03`.

Let's start the exercise by performing the following steps:

1. Use the application generated with `npm init vue@3` as a starting point, or within the root folder of the code repository, navigate into the `Chapter01/Exercise1.03` folder by using the following commands in order:

    ```
    > cd Chapter01/Exercise1.03/
    > yarn
    ```

2. Run the application using the following command:

    ```
    yarn dev
    ```

3. Open the exercise project in VS Code (by using `code .` command within the project directory) or your preferred IDE.

4. Create a new Vue component file named `Exercise1-03.vue` in the `src/components` directory.

5. Inside `Exercise1-03.vue`, compose the following code to display the `text` content:

    ```
    <template>
      <div>
        <h1>{{ text }}</h1>
      </div>
    </template>
    <script setup>
    const text = 'Directive text';
    </script>
    ```

6. Replace the `{{ }}` interpolation with the `v-text` attribute. The output should not change:

    ```
    <template>
      <div>
        <h1 v-text="text">Loading...</h1>
      </div>
    </template>
    ```

Figure 1.10 displays the output of the preceding code:

Directive text

Figure 1.10 – Same output for v-text and the interpolation method

7. Add the v-once directive to the same element. This will force this DOM element to only load the v-text data once:

```
<template>
  <div>
    <h1 v-once v-text="text">Loading...</h1>
  </div>
</template>
```

8. Underneath the h1 element, include a new h2 element that uses the v-html attribute. Add a new local data called html that contains a string with HTML formatting in it, as shown in the following code block:

```
<template>
  <div>
    <h1 v-once v-text="text">Loading...</h1>
    <h2 v-html="html" />
  </div>
</template>
<script setup>
const text = 'Directive text';
const html = 'Stylise</br>HTML in<br/><b>your data</b>'
</script>
```

Running the preceding code will generate an output as follows:

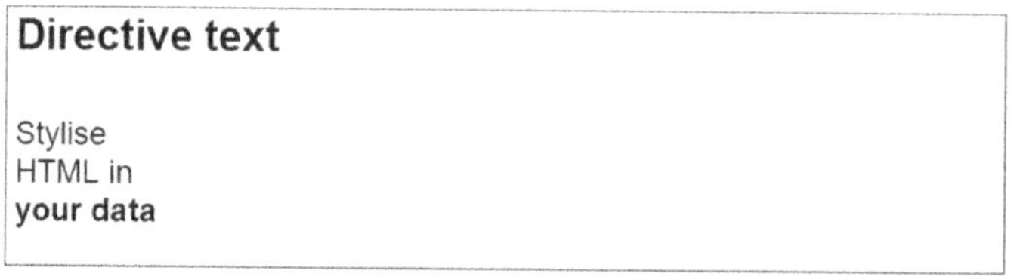

Directive text

Stylise
HTML in
your data

Figure 1.11 – Rendering HTML elements from a string using v-html

9. Add a new local `link` object that contains a bunch of information such as the URL, target, title, and tab index. Inside the template, add a new anchor HTML element and bind the `link` object to the HTML element using the `v-bind` short syntax – for example, `:href="link.url"`:

```
<template>
  <div>
    <h1 v-once v-text="text">Loading...</h1>
    <h2 v-html="html" />
    <a
      :href="link.url"
      :target="link.target"
      :tabindex="link.tabindex"
      >{{ link.title }}</a>
  </div>
</template>
<script setup>
const text = 'Directive text';
const html = 'Stylise</br>HTML in<br/><b>your data</b>'
const link = {
  title: "Go to Google",
  url: https://google.com,
  tabindex: 1,
  target: '_blank',
};
</script>
```

The following screenshot displays the output:

Figure 1.12 – Output on binding the reactive data from the Vue instance to any HTML attribute

10. Apply `v-if="false"` to the h1 element, `v-else-if="false"` to h2, and `v-else` to the a tag like this:

```
<template>
  <div>
    <h1 v-if="false" v-once v-text="text">Loading...
    </h1>
    <h2 v-html="html" v-else-if="false" />
    <a
      v-else
      :href="link.url"
      :target="link.target"
      :tabindex="link.tabindex"
      >{{ link.title }}</a>
  </div>
</template>
```

You should only see the `<a>` tag on the page since we have set the main conditional statements to `false`.

The `v-else` condition will display the following:

Go to Google

Figure 1.13 – false v-if statements hiding the whole HTML element from the DOM

11. Change the template to use `v-show` instead of the `v-if` statements, remove `v-else` from the `<a>` element, and change the value of `v-show` in h1 to `true`:

```
<template>
  <div>
    <h1 v-show="true" v-once v-text="text">Loading...
    </h1>
    <h2 v-html="html" v-show="false" />
    <a
      :href="link.url"
      :target="link.target"
      :tabindex="link.tabindex"
```

```
        >{{ link.title }}</a>
    </div>
  </template>
```

The output of the preceding code will be as follows:

Directive text

Go to Google

Figure 1.14 – Changing v-show to true will display the main directive text

When you open the `Elements` tab of your browser Devtools, you should be able to observe that the h2 display state is set to `none` as follows:

```
<!DOCTYPE html>
<html lang="en">
 ▶<head>…</head>
 ▼<body data-gr-c-s-loaded="true">
   ▶<noscript>…</noscript>
   ▼<div data-v-d9ee5bac>
       <h1 data-v-d9ee5bac>Directive text</h1>
  ···  ▶<h2 data-v-d9ee5bac style="display: none;">…</h2> == $0
       <a data-v-d9ee5bac href="https://google.com" target="_blank"
       tabindex="0">Go to Google</a>
     </div>
     <!-- built files will be auto injected -->
     <script type="text/javascript" src="/js/chunk-vendors.js">
     </script>
     <script type="text/javascript" src="/js/app.js"></script>
   </body>
 </html>
```

Figure 1.15 – h2 has "display: none" for the false condition

In this exercise, we learned about the core Vue directives to control, bind, show, and hide HTML template elements without requiring any JavaScript outside of adding new data objects to your local state.

In the next section, we will learn how to achieve two-way binding with the help of Vue's `v-model`.

Enabling two-way binding using v-model

Vue achieves two-way data binding by creating a dedicated directive that watches a data property within your Vue component. The `v-model` directive triggers data updates when the target data property is modified on the UI. This directive is usually useful for HTML form elements that need to both display the data and modify it reactively – for example, input, textarea, radio buttons, and so on.

We can enable two-way binding by adding the v-model directive to the target element and binding it to our desired data props:

```
<template>
    <input v-model="name" />
</template>
<script>
    export default {
      data() {
        return {
          name: ''
        }
      }
    }
</script>
```

In *Figure 1.16*, the output generated by running the preceding code will be as follows:

Figure 1.16 – Output for the v-model example

> **Note**
> Binding a huge amount of data using v-model can affect the performance of your application. Consider your UI and split the data into different Vue components or views. Vue data in the local state is not immutable and can be redefined anywhere in the template.

In the next exercise, we are going to build a component using Vue's two-way data binding and experiment with what it means to bind data in two ways.

Exercise 1.04 – experimenting with two-way binding using v-model

The context for this type of data model is usually forms or wherever you expect both input and output data. By the end of the exercise, we should be able to utilize the v-model attribute in the context of a form.

To access the code file for this exercise, refer to https://github.com/PacktPublishing/ Frontend-Development-Projects-with-Vue.js-3/tree/v2-edition/Chapter01/ Exercise1.04.

Let's start the exercise by performing the following steps:

1. Use the application generated with npm init vue@3 as a starting point, or within the root folder of the code repository, navigate into the Chapter01/Exercise 1.04 folder by using the following commands in order:

    ```
    > cd Chapter01/Exercise 1.04/
    > yarn
    ```

2. Run the application using the following command:

    ```
    yarn dev
    ```

3. Open the exercise project in your VS Code (by using the code . command within the project directory) or your preferred IDE.

4. Create a new Vue component file named Exercise1-04.vue in the src/components directory.

5. Inside Exercise1-04.vue, start by composing an HTML label and bind an input element to the name data prop using v-model inside the template area:

    ```
    <div class="form">
       <label>
         Name
         <input type="text" v-model="name" />
       </label>
    </div>
    ```

6. Complete the binding of the text input by returning a reactive data prop called name in the <script> tag:

    ```
    <script>
    export default {
      data() {
    ```

```
      return {
        name: '',
      }
    },
  }
</script>
```

7. Next, compose a `label` and selectable HTML `select` tied to the `language` data prop using `v-model` inside of the `template` area:

```
<div class="form">
  <label>
    Name
    <input type="text" v-model="name" />
  </label>
  <label>
    Preferred JavaScript style
    <select name="language" v-model="language">
      <option value="Javascript">JavaScript
      </option>
      <option value="TypeScript">TypeScript
      </option>
      <option value="CoffeeScript">CoffeeScript
      </option>
      <option value="Dart">Dart</option>
    </select>
  </label>
</div>
```

8. Finish binding the `select` input by returning a reactive data prop called `language` in the `<script>` tag:

```
<script>
export default {
  data() {
    return {
      name: '',
      language: '',
    }
```

```
      },
    }
  </script>
```

9. Below the `form` fields, output the name and language inside of an unordered list structure (`<ul>` and `<li>`) by using curly braces such as {{ name }}:

Your code should look as follows:

```
<template>
  <section>
    <div class="form">
      <label>
        Name
        <input type="text" v-model="name" />
      </label>
      <label>
        Preferred JavaScript style
        <select name="language" v-model="language">
          <option value="JavaScript">JavaScript
          </option>
          <option value="TypeScript">TypeScript
          </option>
          <option value="CoffeeScript">CoffeeScript
          </option>
          <option value="Dart">Dart</option>
        </select>
      </label>
    </div>
    <ul class="overview">
      <li><strong>Overview</strong></li>
      <li>Name: {{ name }}</li>
      <li>Preference: {{ language }}</li>
    </ul>
  </section>
</template>
```

10. Add styling inside the `<style>` tag at the bottom of the component:

```
<style>
.form {
  display: flex;
  justify-content: space-evenly;
  max-width: 800px;
  padding: 40px 20px;
  border-radius: 10px;
  margin: 0 auto;
  background: #ececec;
}

.overview {
  display: flex;
  flex-direction: column;
  justify-content: space-evenly;
  max-width: 300px;
  margin: 40px auto;
  padding: 40px 20px;
  border-radius: 10px;
  border: 1px solid #ececec;
}

.overview > li {
  list-style: none;
}
.overview > li + li {
  margin-top: 20px;
}
</style>
```

11. Go to `https://localhost:3000`. Your output should look as follows:

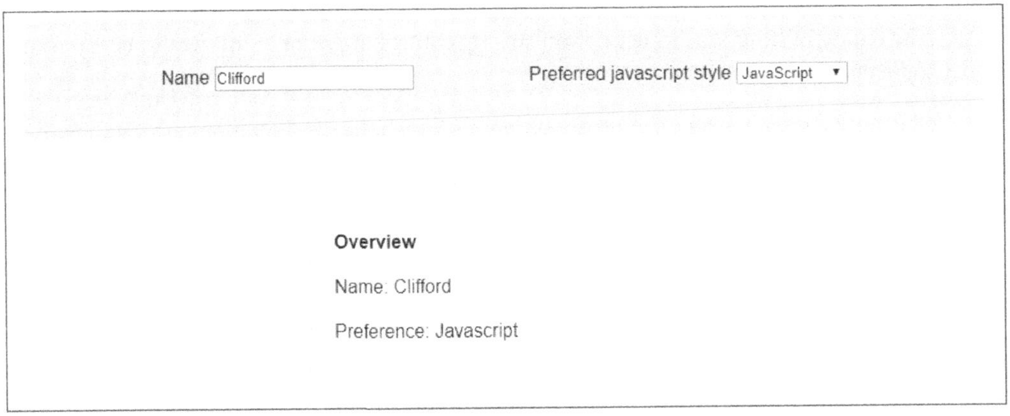

Figure 1.17 – Displaying the final form after the data is updated

When you update the data in the form, it should also update the overview area synchronously.

In this exercise, we used the `v-model` directive to bind the name and JavaScript-style drop-down selection to our local state's data. When you modify the data, it will reactively update the DOM elements to which we output its value.

Next, we will discuss our `v-for` directive further and different approaches to handling iterative data collection in Vue.

Understanding data iteration with v-for

To loop over HTML elements in Vue, you use the `v-for` loop directive directly on the target elements. When Vue renders the component, it will iterate the target to use and render the data being parsed into the directive, with the same concept as a normal JavaScript `for` loop.

Basic iteration using v-for

The basic syntax of `v-for` is as follows:

```
v-for="(item, index) in items" :key="index"
```

The preceding syntax example indicates that we are iterating through a list of `items`. We have access to a single `item` and its appearance `index` in the list in each iteration. `:key` is a required attribute, acting as the unique identifier of each iterating element rendered for the Vue engine to keep track.

When the `key` or `item` content changes, either programmatically or due to user interactions, the Vue engine triggers an update of the changed item on the UI. If you have multiple loops in one component, you should randomize the `key` attribute with extra characters or context-related strings to avoid `key` duplication conflicts.

There are various use cases for this direction. One straightforward use case is to perform **anonymous loops**, in which you can define a number, X, as a symbolic list, and the loop will iterate that X times. This can be handy in situations in which you strictly control the number of iterations you want or render some placeholder content.

In the following example, we see an anonymous loop in which the total iterations are 2 and we define key with a loop-1 prefix:

```
<template>
<div v-for="n in 2" :key="'loop-1-' + n">
    {{ n }}
</div>
<template>
```

You can also use template literals (with `` `` `` backticks) to compute strings without +:

```
<template>
<div v-for="n in 5" :key="`loop-2-${n}`">
    {{ n }}
</div>
<template>
```

The output of the preceding code in both approaches should look as follows

Figure 1.18 – Output of anonymous loops example

Now that we have covered how to handle basic loops by using v-for, we will utilize this function in the next exercise.

Exercise 1.05 – using v-for to iterate through an array of strings

In this exercise, we are going to create an anonymous loop using Vue's v-for directive. This will be familiar to those who have used for or forEach loops in JavaScript before.

To access the code file for this exercise, refer to https://github.com/PacktPublishing/Frontend-Development-Projects-with-Vue.js-3/tree/v2-edition/Chapter01/Exercise1.05.

Perform the following steps to complete the exercise:

1. Use the application generated with npm init vue@3 as a starting point, or within the root folder of the code repository, navigate into the Chapter01/Exercise1.05 folder by using the following commands in order:

    ```
    > cd Chapter01/Exercise1.05/
    > yarn
    ```

2. Run the application using the following command:

    ```
    yarn dev
    ```

3. Open the exercise project in VS Code (by using code . command within the project directory) or your preferred IDE.

4. Create a new Vue component file named Exercise1-05.vue in the src/components directory.

5. Inside Exercise1-05.vue, we compose a new component with an <h1> element to render the static title of Looping through arrays, and an <ul> element containing an empty <li> tag:

    ```
    <template>
    <h1>Looping through arrays</h1>
    <ul>
       <li></li>
    </ul>
    </template>
    ```

6. In the script section, let's add a setup attribute to the script tag. Then, let's declare an array of interests containing some strings as follows:

    ```
    <script setup>
    const interests = ['TV', 'Games', 'Sports']
    </script>
    ```

7. Now, let's go back to the template section and add the v-for directive on the <li> tag to iterate through interests. For each iteration, we get a combination of (item, index) from the interests, in which item outputs the string of the array, and index is the loop index. We map the key attribute to index, and display the value of item as shown in the following code block:

    ```
    <template>
    <h1>Looping through arrays</h1>
    <ul>
    ```

```
        <li v-for="(item, index) in interests"
            :key="index">{{ item }}</li>
    </ul>
    </template>
```

8. Go to `https://localhost:3000`. The following output is as follows:

Looping through arrays

- TV
- Games
- Sports

Figure 1.19 – Output of iterating through an array of strings

In this exercise, we learned how to iterate through a specific array of strings, outputting the string value or index of an array. We also learned that the key attribute needs to be unique to avoid DOM conflicts and forces the DOM to re-render the component properly.

Next, let's experiment with iterating a collection of objects.

Iterating through an array of objects

In most practical scenarios, we work with data as objects, especially when iterating through an array of objects. Vue makes it easy to control various data states through its directive syntax. Like iterating through an array of strings, the directive syntax remains the same:

```
v-for="(item, index) in items" :key="index"
```

The `item` you receive is now an Object, with various properties. You can bind each property using what you have learned so far to display its value. For example, assume in `item`, we will have `id`, `title`, `description`, and another array, `characteristics`, containing some strings. We can display the `title` and `description` information for each `item` like so:

```
<template>
  <ul>
    <li v-for="(item, index) in items" :key="item.id">
      <h2>{{ item.title }}</h2>
      <span>{{ item.description }}</span>
    </li>
  </ul>
</template>
```

Note here we don't use an index as the key; instead, we use id as the unique identifier for key. It is considered a more secure approach to use id or any other unique identifier and we also don't need to include index in the syntax in this case since we don't use it.

Since characteristics is an array, we display its values by using a v-for directive again for characteristics. You don't have to use the same name, item, that the syntax example shows. Instead, you can give it a different name depending on how you want your variable to be.

In the following example, we use str for each element in the item.characteristics array:

```
<template>
  <ul>
    <li v-for="item in items" :key="item.id">
      <h2>{{ item.title }}</h2>
      <span>{{ item.description }}</span>
      <ul>
          <li v-for="(str, index) in item.characteristics"
            :key="index">
              <span>{{ str }}</span>
          </li>
      </ul>
    </li>
  </ul>
</template>
```

And in the script section, we define items as follows:

```
<script setup>
const items = [{
  id: 1,
  title: "Item 1",
  description: "About item 1",
  characteristics: ["Summer", "Winter", "Spring", "Autumn"]
}, {
  id: 2,
  title: 'Item 2",
  description: 'About item 2",
  characteristics: ["North", "West", "East", "South"]
}]
</script>
```

The preceding code will output as shown in *Figure 1.20*:

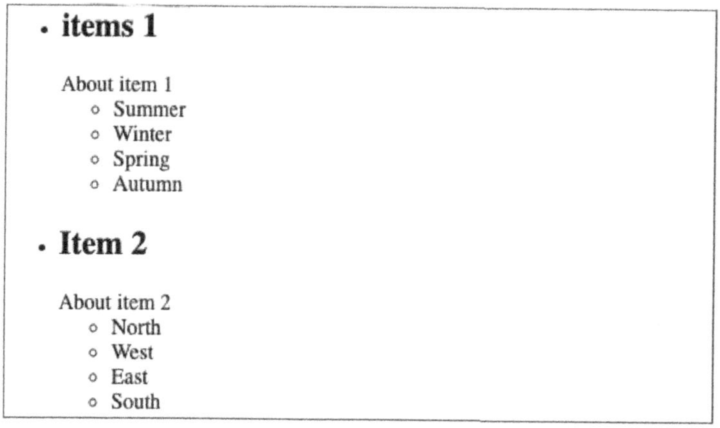

- **items 1**

  About item 1
    - Summer
    - Winter
    - Spring
    - Autumn

- **Item 2**

  About item 2
    - North
    - West
    - East
    - South

Figure 1.20 – Output of iterating through an array of object items

Understanding how to loop through collections of objects with `v-for` is essential and useful for handling data, especially with external data. In the next exercise, you will combine `v-for` and `v-if` to display a list of objects conditionally.

Exercise 1.06 – using v-for to iterate through an array of objects and using their properties in v-if conditions

In this exercise, we will be controlling a Vue data array and iterating through the objects inside of it.

To access the code file for this exercise, refer to `https://github.com/PacktPublishing/ Frontend-Development-Projects-with-Vue.js-3/tree/v2-edition/Chapter01/ Exercise1.06`.

Let's start the exercise by performing the following steps:

1. Use the application generated with `npm init vue@3` as a starting point, or within the root folder of the code repository, navigate into the `Chapter01/Exercise1.06` folder by using the following commands in order:

    ```
    > cd Chapter01/Exercise1.06/
    > yarn
    ```

2. Run the application using the following command:

    ```
    yarn dev
    ```

3. Open the exercise project in VS Code (by using the code . command within the project directory) or your preferred IDE.

4. Create a new Vue component file named `Exercise1-06.vue` in the `src/components` directory.

5. Inside `Exercise1-06.vue`, create an array of data objects, `interests`, as local data. Each interest contains a `title` string and a `favorites` array of strings:

```
<script setup>
const interests = [
    {
        title: "TV",
        favorites: ["Designated Survivor",
                    "Spongebob"],
    },
    {
        title: "Games",
        favorites: ["CS:GO"],
    },
    {
        title: "Sports",
        favorites: [],
    },
];
</script>
```

6. In `template`, we loop over `interests` and display the `title` for each `item` in the `interests` array:

```
<template>
  <div>
    <h1>Looping through array of objects</h1>
    <ul>
      <li v-for="(item, n) in interests" :key="n">
        {{ item.title }}
      </li>
    </ul>
  </div>
</template>
```

7. Go to `https://localhost:3000` and the output of the preceding code will be as follows:

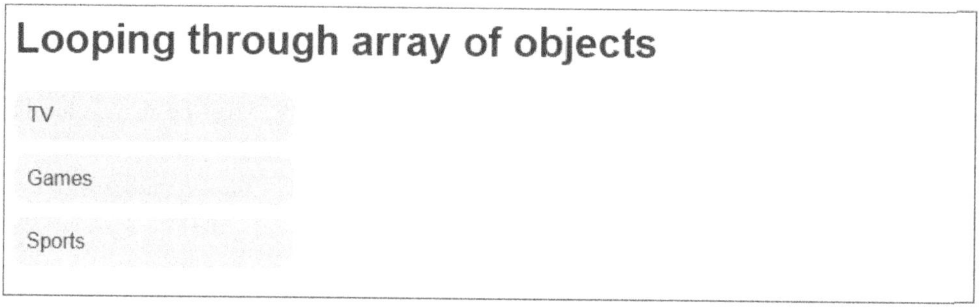

Looping through array of objects

TV

Games

Sports

Figure 1.21 – You should now see a list of titles in the browser

8. Let's create a second `v-for` loop to iterate through a `favorites` list for each `item`. Note that we use different names – `fav` and m – for our nested loop:

```
<template>
  <div>
    <h1>Looping through array of objects</h1>
    <ul>
      <li v-for="(item, n) in interests" :key="n">
        {{ item.title }}

        <ol>
          <li v-for="(fav, m) in item.favorites"
            :key="m">
            {{ fav }}</li>
        </ol>
      </li>
    </ul>
  </div>
</template>
```

Figure 1.22 displays an output where looping is performed through an array of objects:

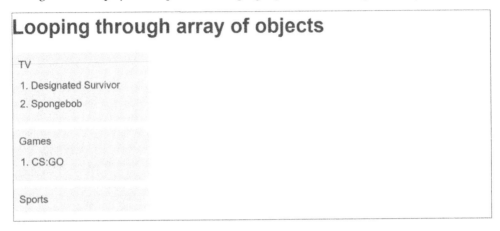

Figure 1.22 – Nested ordered list detailing your favorites

9. When inspecting the DOM elements (press *Ctrl + F12* or open **Developer Tools**), you can see there are some empty elements as in *Figure 1.23*. This is because the Vue engine still renders the `<ol>` element even though `favorites` is an empty array:

```
▼<ul data-v-d999cea6>
   ▶<li data-v-d999cea6>…</li>
   ▶<li data-v-d999cea6>…</li>
   ▼<li data-v-d999cea6>
        " Sports "
...        <ol data-v-d999cea6></ol> == $0
      </li>
   </ul>
```

Figure 1.23 – Displaying empty DOM elements in your virtual DOM

10. Now, we need to hide that empty `<ol>` element after applying it. We will check whether the `favorites` array is empty (`length > 0`) and then display the ordered list HTML element. Let's add a `v-if` directive to `<ol>` with the `item.favorites.length > 0` condition:

```
<ol v-if="item.favorites.length > 0">
  <li v-for="(fav, m) in item.favorites" :key="m">
    {{ fav }}
  </li>
</ol>
```

This won't make a difference to the visuals of your page, but when you inspect the DOM tree in your browser, you'll notice an HTML comment in dev mode that allows you to understand where a `v-if` statement might be `false`. When you build for production, these HTML comments won't be visible in your DOM tree:

```
▼<li data-v-d999cea6>
      " Sports "
...      <!----> == $0
   </li>
</ul>
```

Figure 1.24 – Output displaying no HTML comment in production builds

In this exercise, we have iterated through complex arrays of objects, outputting the nested keys for these objects and controlling the view state of DOM elements based on length conditions.

Next, let's experiment with iterating through a keyed collection (or Object).

Iterating through a keyed collection (Object)

We can generally use `v-for` for looping through any iterative data collection type. Object in JavaScript is a key-value data collection, and we can iterate through its properties using `v-for`.

The syntax example is like the previous syntax example for arrays of objects and strings, with a tiny difference. Here, we change the naming convention from (`item, index`) to (`value, key`), in which `key` is the object's property, and `value` is that `key` property's value. Vue also exposes one more parameter – `index` – to indicate that property's appearance index in the target object. Thus, the syntax now becomes the following:

```
v-for="(value, key, index) in obj"
```

Here, `obj` is our target object to iterate.

For example, assume we have the following object named `course`, which contains a title, a description, and the name of the lecturer(s):

```
<script setup>
const course = {
  title: 'Frontend development with Vue',
  description: 'Learn the awesome of Vue',
  lecturer: 'Maya and Raymond'
}
</script>
```

In our template, we iterate through the course's properties and output their value in the `<index>.<key> : <value>` format as shown in the following code block:

```
<template>
  <ul>
    <li v-for="(value, key, index) in course" :key="key">
      {{index}}. {{key}}: {{value}}
    </li>
  </ul>
</template>
```

The output will be as shown in *Figure 1.25*:

- 0. title: Frontend development with Vue
- 1. description: Learn the awesome of Vue
- 2. lecturer: Maya and Raymond

Figure 1.25 – Iterating and displaying values of the course's properties

Looping through the properties of an object is also a joint development practice. It is the same concept as winding through any keyed collection type, such as a hash-map (mapping according to key), lookup dictionary (it is also an object), and so on. Since the syntax stays consistent between both array and object iteration, it helps reduce the need for refactoring or data conversion.

Next, you will practice how to write basic looping for Object properties.

Exercise 1.07 – using v-for to loop through the properties of Object

In this exercise, we will be controlling a Vue data object and iterating through the properties inside of it.

To access the code file for this exercise, refer to `https://github.com/PacktPublishing/Frontend-Development-Projects-with-Vue.js-3/tree/v2-edition/Chapter01/Exercise1.07`.

Let's start the exercise by performing the following steps:

1. Use the application generated with `npm init vue@3` as a starting point, or within the root folder of the code repository, navigate into the `Chapter01/Exercise1.07` folder by using the following commands in order:

```
> cd Chapter01/Exercise1.07/
> yarn
```

2. Run the application using the following command:

    ```
    yarn dev
    ```

3. Open the exercise project in VS Code (by using the `code` . command within the project directory) or your preferred IDE.

4. Create a new Vue component file named `Exercise1-07.vue` in the `src/components` directory.

5. Inside `Exercise1-07.vue`, let's compose `information` for the local data within `<script setup>` as follows:

    ```
    <script setup>
    const information = {
            title: "My list component information",
            subtitle: "Vue JS basics",
            items: ["Looping", "Data", "Methods"],
        }
    </script>
    ```

6. In the `<template>` section, we will loop through `information` and display the values of its properties:

    ```
    <template>
        <div>
          <div v-for="(value, key) in information"
            :key="key">
            {{key}}: {{ value }}
          </div>
        </div>
    </template>
    ```

7. Go to `https://localhost:3000` and the output will be as follows:

    * title: My list component information
    * subtitle: Vue JS basics
    * items: ["Looping", "Data", "Methods"]

Figure 1.26 – Output using v-for on the information object

8. Note that Vue renders the value for items, which is an array of strings, the same as how we declared using JavaScript. To render it in a better format, we use the built-in JavaScript `toString()` function to export all the elements' values into a string with comma separation automatically:

```
<template>
    <div>
        <div v-for="(value, key) in information"
            :key="key">
            {{key}}: {{ value.toString() }}
        </div>
    </div>
</template>
```

9. The final output will render the list as follows:

- title: My list component information
- subtitle: Vue JS basics
- items: Looping,Data,Methods

Figure 1.27 – Output using v-for and toString() on values

Understanding iterations (or loops) is key to not only working with Vue but also with JavaScript in general. Now that we have covered how to handle loops by using the `v-for` directive and the importance of the `key` property for proper reactivity enhancement, we will explore how to use, write, and trigger methods in a component.

Exploring methods

In Vue 2.0, Vue defines component methods inside the `methods` object as part of a Vue instance. You compose each component method as a normal JavaScript function. The Vue method is scoped to your Vue component and can be run from anywhere inside the component it belongs to. It also has access to the `this` instance, which indicates the instance of the component:

```
<script>
  export default {
    methods: {
        myMethod() { console.log('my first method'); }
    }
  }
</script>
```

From Vue 3.0 onward, with `<script setup>`, as with local data, you can define a method as a regular function and it will work the same way as with the traditional approach. Hence, we can rewrite the preceding code as follows:

```
<script setup>
  const myMethod = () => { console.log('my first method'); }
</script>
```

You then can bind the methods to HTML events of an element as its event listeners in the `template` section. When binding events to HTML elements in Vue, you would use the @ symbol. For example, `v-on:click` is equivalent to `@click`, as shown in the following code block:

```
<template>
    <button id="click-me" v-on:click="myMethod">Click me
    </button>
    <button id="click-me" @click="myMethod">Click me
        shorter</button>
</template>
```

Clicking on both buttons triggers the same `myMethod()` method and generates the same result.

Let's build a component with some methods.

Exercise 1.08 – triggering methods

In this exercise, we are going to build a component that uses Vue's methods API. Consider how similarly these Vue methods can be written to your own named functions in JavaScript, as they behave in a very similar way. By the end of the exercise, we should be able to use methods and trigger them from the HTML template.

To access the code file for this exercise, refer to `https://github.com/PacktPublishing/Frontend-Development-Projects-with-Vue.js-3/tree/v2-edition/Chapter01/Exercise1.08`

We will build a list of different elements. For each element, we bind an `onClick` event with a component method, and alert users about the index of the clicked element by performing the following:

1. Use the application generated with `npm init vue@3` as a starting point, or within the root folder of the code repository, navigate into the `Chapter01/Exercise1.08` folder by using the following commands in order:

    ```
    > cd Chapter01/Exercise1.08/
    > yarn
    ```

2. Run the application using the following command:

    yarn dev

3. Open the exercise project in VS Code (by using the `code` . command within the project directory) or your preferred IDE.

4. Create a new Vue component file named `Exercise1-08.vue` in the `src/components` directory.

5. Inside `Exercise1-08.vue`, within the `<script setup>` section, let's define a method, `triggerAlert`, that receives an index and displays an alert informing users which index has been clicked:

```
<script setup>
const triggerAlert = (index) => {
    alert(`${index} has been clicked`)
    }
</script>
```

6. In the `template` section, set up an anonymous `v-for` loop on an HTML list and add a `button` element inside the list element. Set the loop to iterate 5 times, and display the `index` value as each button's label:

```
<template>
  <div>
    <h1>Triggering Vue Methods</h1>
    <ul>
      <li v-for="index in 5":key="index">
        <button>Trigger {{index}}</button>
      </li>
    </ul>
  </div>
</template>
```

7. Add the `@click` directive, referencing the `triggerAlert` method, and pass the value of `index` as an argument:

```
<template>
  <div>
    <h1>Triggering Vue Methods</h1>
    <ul>
```

```
        <li v-for="index in 5" :key="index">
          <button @click="triggerAlert(index)">Trigger
            {{ index }}</a>
        </li>
      </ul>
    </div>
</template>
```

8. Add a margin between each button for readability:

```
<style>
button {
   margin: 10px;
}
</style>
```

9. Your page should feature a list of buttons that when clicked, trigger an alert with a message that contains the button number you clicked, as follows:

Triggering Vue Methods

- Trigger 1
- Trigger 2
- Trigger 3
- Trigger 4
- Trigger 5

Figure 1.28 – Outputting a list of triggers

The following prompt is displayed when a trigger is clicked:

Figure 1.29 – Displaying a browser alert with the index number in it

> **Note**
>
> While you can add an event listener to any HTML element, we suggest applying them to native HTML interactive elements such as anchor tags, form input, or buttons to help with browser accessibility.

At this point, you can utilize the Vue methods API to define and trigger methods from the HTML template, and parse arguments into each method dynamically. In the next exercise, we will explore how to return data with Vue methods within a Vue component.

Exercise 1.09 – returning data using Vue methods

Often, in a web application, we want elements to appear on the page depending on whether a condition is met or not. For instance, if our product is not in stock, our page should display the fact that it is out of stock.

So, let's figure out how we conditionally render these elements depending on whether our product is in stock or not.

To access the code file for this exercise, refer to `https://github.com/PacktPublishing/Front-End-Development-Projects-with-Vue.js/tree/v2-edition/Chapter01/Exercise1.09`.

We will build a list of different elements and demonstrate adding different quantities to a cart. Then, we will display the updated cart's total value in a currency format by performing the following:

1. Use the application generated with `npm init vue@3` as a starting point, or within the root folder of the code repository, navigate into the `Chapter01/Exercise1.09` folder by using the following commands in order:

   ```
   > cd Chapter01/Exercise1.09/
   > yarn
   ```

2. Run the application using the following command:

   ```
   yarn dev
   ```

3. Open the exercise project in your VS Code (by using the `code .` command within the project directory), or your preferred IDE.

4. Create a new Vue component file named `Exercise1-09.vue` in the `src/components` directory.

5. Inside `Exercise1-09.vue`, within the `<script>` section, we set up two data objects, `totalItems` and `totalCost`, which will be updated when a user clicks on our shop's buttons:

```
<script>
export default {
  data(){
    return {
      totalCost: 0,
      totalItems: 0
    }
  }
}
</script>
```

6. In the `template` section, we display the value of `totalItems` and `totalCost` accordingly:

```
<template>
 <div>
   <h1>Returning Methods</h1>
   <div>Cart({{ totalItems }}) {{ totalCost }} </div>
 </div>
</template>
```

7. Within the `script` section, let's create an `addToCart` method, which will update `totalCost` and `totalItems` for the current component based on the received number, n, by using `this.totalCost` and `this.totalItems`:

```
<script>
export default {
  data() {
    /*...*/
  },
  methods: {
    addToCart(n) {
      this.totalItems = this.totalItems + 1
      this.totalCost = this.totalCost + n
    },
  },
}
</script>
```

8. Let's iterate through a random amount to create buttons for adding a quantity to the cart. The quantity is the button's index. Then, we bind the addToCart method to each button, with its index as the function's input argument:

```
<template>
  <div>
    <h1>Returning Methods</h1>
    <div>Cart({{ totalItems }}) {{ totalCost }} </div>
    <ul>
      <li v-for="n in 5" :key="n">
        <button @click="addToCart(n)">Add {{ n }}
        </button>
      </li>
    </ul>
  </div>
</template>
```

9. Add a 10px margin to the button element for readability:

```
<style>
button {
  margin: 10px;
}
</style>
```

10. Go to https://localhost:3000 and the output is as follows:

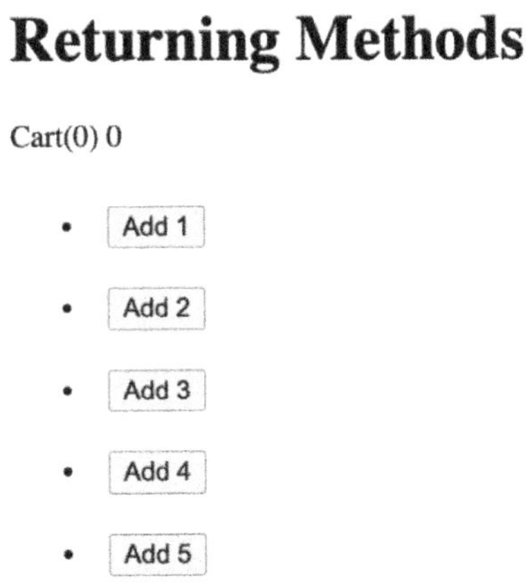

Returning Methods

Cart(0) 0

- Add 1

- Add 2

- Add 3

- Add 4

- Add 5

Figure 1.30 – Pressing any of the buttons will demonstrate the cart logic

When you click on the buttons, the `totalItems` counter should increment by 1, but `totalCost` will increment by the n value, which should demonstrate a normal cart functionality. For example, when clicking Add 2, then Add 5, the output will be as follows:

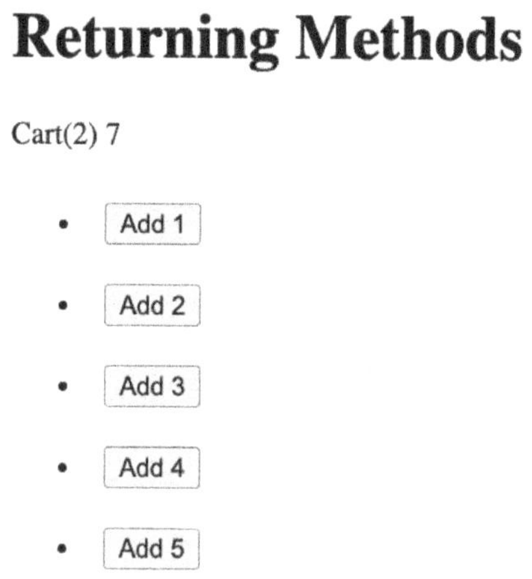

Returning Methods

Cart(2) 7

- Add 1

- Add 2

- Add 3

- Add 4

- Add 5

Figure 1.31 – Output displaying Returning Methods after increments of 2 and 5

11. Now, let's format `totalCost`. Create a method called `formatCurrency`, which accepts one argument. We will return the same value after giving it two decimal points and a $ symbol:

```
<script>
export default {
  data() {
    /*...*/
  },
  methods: {
    addToCart(n) { /*...*/},
    formatCurrency(val) {
      return `$${val.toFixed(2)}`
    },
  },
}
</script>
```

12. To use this method in the template, add it to the interpolated curly braces and pass the value that was there as an argument inside the method instead:

```
<template>
  <div>
    <h1>Returning Methods</h1>
    <div>Cart({{ totalItems }}) {{
      formatCurrency(totalCost) }}
    </div>
    <ul>
      <li v-for="n in 5" :key="n">
        <button @click="addToCart(n)">Add {{
          formatCurrency(n) }}</button>
      </li>
    </ul>
  </div>
</template>
```

The following screenshot displays the output of the preceding code:

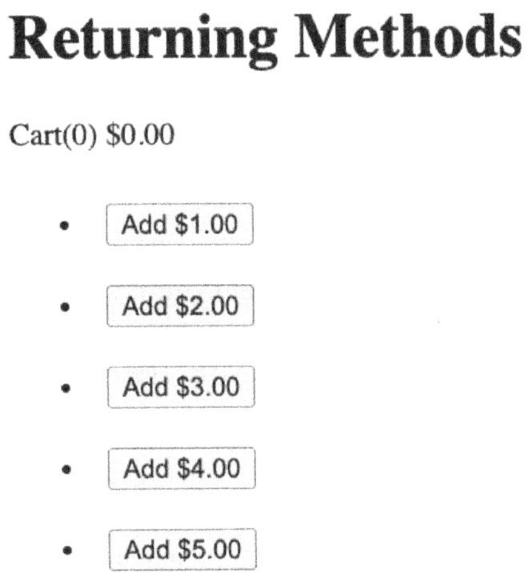

Returning Methods

Cart(0) $0.00

- Add $1.00
- Add $2.00
- Add $3.00
- Add $4.00
- Add $5.00

Figure 1.32 – All the values now are in currency format while retaining the cart counter

In this exercise, we were able to utilize Vue's methods API to parse arguments into methods, return modified values, and use methods to update the local data state in a life-like scenario.

In the next section, we will explore a significant part of a component – the lifecycle and available component hooks in Vue.

Understanding component lifecycle hooks

The Vue component lifecycle events happen during a component's lifecycle, from creation to deletion. They allow us to add callbacks and side effects at each stage of the component's life when necessary.

Vue executes the events in order, as follows:

- `setup`: This event runs before all other hooks, including `beforeCreate`. It doesn't have access to this instance since the instance has not yet been created at this point. It is mainly for using Composition API and is treated in the same way Vue treats `script setup`. We will discuss this event more in *Chapter 5, The Composition API*.

- `beforeCreate`: This runs when your component has been initialized. `data` has not been made reactive and events are not set up in your DOM.

- `created`: You will be able to access reactive data and events, but the templates and DOM are not mounted or rendered. This hook is generally good to use when requesting asynchronous data from a server since you will more than likely want this information as early as possible before the virtual DOM is mounted.

- `beforeMount`: A very uncommon hook, as it runs directly before the first render of your component and is not called **Server-Side Rendering**.

- `mounted`: Mounting hooks are among the most common hooks you will use since they allow you to access your DOM elements so that non-Vue libraries can be integrated.

- `beforeUpdate`: This runs immediately after a change to your component occurs and before it has been re-rendered. It's useful for acquiring the state of reactive data before it has been rendered.

- `updated`: It runs immediately after the `beforeUpdate` hook and re-renders your component with new data changes.

- `beforeUnMount`: This is fired directly before unmounting your component instance. The component will still be functional until the `unmounted` hook is called, allowing you to stop event listeners and subscriptions to data to avoid memory leaks. Note this event is called `beforeDestroy` in Vue 2.x.

- `unmounted`: All the virtual DOM elements and event listeners have been cleaned up from your Vue instance. This hook allows you to communicate that to anyone or any element that needs to know this has been done. This event in Vue 2.x is called `destroyed`.

Let's do a small exercise to learn how and when to use Vue's lifecycle hooks, and when they trigger.

Exercise 1.10 – using a Vue lifecycle to control data

In this exercise, we will be learning how and when to use Vue's lifecycle hooks, and when they are triggered by using JavaScript alerts. By the end of the exercise, we will be able to understand and use multiple Vue lifecycle hooks.

To access the code file for this exercise, refer to `https://github.com/PacktPublishing/ Frontend-Development-Projects-with-Vue.js-3/tree/v2-edition/Chapter01/ Exercise1.10`.

We will build a list of different elements demonstrating adding different quantities to a cart. Then, we will display the updated cart's total value in a currency format by performing the following:

1. Use the application generated with `npm init vue@3` as a starting point, or within the root folder of the code repository, navigate into the `Chapter01/Exercise1.10` folder by using the following commands in order:

    ```
    > cd Chapter01/Exercise1.10/
    > yarn
    ```

2. Run the application using the following command:

    ```
    yarn dev
    ```

3. Open the exercise project in VS Code (by using the `code .` command within the project directory) or your preferred IDE.

4. Create a new Vue component file named `Exercise1-10.vue` in the `src/ components` directory.

5. Inside `Exercise1-10.vue`, we start by creating an array of data to iterate through in a list element, set the key to n, and output the `{{item}}` value inside of the `<li>` element using curly braces:

    ```
    <template>
      <div>
        <h1>Vue Lifecycle hooks</h1>
        <ul>
          <li v-for="(item, n) in list" :key="n">
            {{ item }}
          </li>
        </ul>
      </div>
    </template>
    ```

```
<script>
export default {
  data() {
    return {
      list: [
        'Apex Legends',
        'A Plague Tale: Innocence',
        'ART SQOOL',
        'Baba Is You',
        'Devil May Cry 5',
        'The Division 2',
        'Hypnospace Outlaw',
        'Katana ZERO',
      ],
    }
  }
}
</script>
```

6. Add `beforeCreated()` and `created()` as properties below the `data()` function. Set an alert or console log inside these hooks so that you can see when they are being triggered:

```
<script>
export default {
  data(){ /*…*/ },
  beforeCreate() {
    alert('beforeCreate: data is static, thats it')
  },
  created() {
    alert('created: data and events ready, but no
          DOM')
  },
}
</script>
```

7. When you refresh your browser, you should see both alerts before you see your list load on the page:

Figure 1.33 – Observing the beforeCreate() hook alert first

8. The following screenshot displays the `created()` hook alert after the `beforeCreate()` hook:

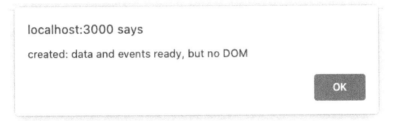

Figure 1.34 – Observing the before() hook alert after the beforeCreate() hook

9. Define `beforeMount()` and `mounted()` in the same way as in *step 6*. Set an alert or console log inside of these hooks so that you can see when they are being triggered:

```
<script>
export default {
  data() { /*...*/ },
  /*...*/
  beforeMount() {
    alert('beforeMount: $el not ready')
  },
  mounted() {
    alert('mounted: DOM ready to use')
  },
}
</script>
```

10. When you refresh your browser, you should also see these alerts before you can see your list load on the page:

localhost:3000 says

beforeMount: $el not ready

OK

Figure 1.35 – Observing the beforeMount() hook alert after the create() hook

11. The following screenshot displays the mounted() hook alert after the beforeMount() hook:

localhost:3000 says

mounted: DOM ready to use

OK

Figure 1.36 – Observing the mounted() hook alert after the beforeMount() hook

12. Add a new button element inside your <li> element that renders the item output. Use a @click directive to bind this button to a method called deleteItem and pass the item value as an argument:

```
<template>
  <div>
    <h1>Vue Lifecycle hooks</h1>
    <ul>
      <li v-for="(item, n) in list" :key="n">
        {{ item }}
        <button @click="deleteItem(item)">Delete</button>
      </li>
    </ul>
  </div>
</template>
```

13. Add a method called `deleteItem` into a `methods` object above your hooks but below the `data()` function. Inside this function, pass `value` as an argument and filter out items from the `list` array based on this value. Then, replace the existing list with the new list:

```
<script>
export default {
  data() { /*…*/ },
  /*…*/
  methods: {
    deleteItem(value) {
      this.list = this.list.filter(item => item !==
        value)
    },
  },
}
</script>
```

14. Add `beforeUpdate()` and `updated()` as functions same as in *step 9* and set an alert or console log inside them:

```
<script>
export default {
    /*...*/
  beforeUpdate() {
    alert('beforeUpdate: we know an update is about to
      happen, and have the data')
  },
  updated() {
    alert('updated: virtual DOM will update after you
      click OK')
  },
}
</script>
```

When you delete a list item by clicking on the **Delete** button in your browser, you should see these alerts. For example, when deleting the first item in the list, beforeUpdated will trigger:

Figure 1.37 – BeforeCreated is called first after clicking on any delete button

Then, updated triggers, as shown in the following screenshot:

Figure 1.38 – updated is called when the Vue engine finishes updating
the component before rendering to the DOM

15. Continue adding beforeUnmount() and unmounted() to the component options as function properties. Set an alert or console log inside these hooks so that you can see when they are being triggered:

```
<script>
export default {
  /*...*/
  beforeUnmount() {
    alert('beforeUnmount: about to blow up this
      component')
  },
  unmounted() {
    alert('unmounted: this component has been
      destroyed')
  },
}
</script>
```

16. Add a new string to your `list` array – for example, `testing unmounted hooks`:

```
<script>
export default {
  data() {
    return {
      list: [
          'Apex Legends',
          'A Plague Tale: Innocence',
          'ART SQOOL',
          'Baba Is You',
          'Devil May Cry 5',
          'The Division 2',
          'Hypnospace Outlaw',
          'Katana ZERO',
          'testing unmounted hooks',
        ],
      }
    },
```

17. You should see the unmount alerts according to this order: `beforeUnmount` – `beforeCreated` – `created` – `beforeMount` – `unmounted` – `mounted`. An example output screen displaying the alert for `beforeUnmount` is shown here:

Figure 1.39 – Alert displays when a component is about to be unmounted

> **Note**
> `mounted` and `created` lifecycle hooks will run every time a component is initialized. If this is not the desired effect, consider running the code you want to run once from the parent component or view, such as the `App.vue` file.

In this exercise, we learned what Vue lifecycle hooks are, when they trigger, and in what order they trigger. This will be useful in combination with triggering methods and controlling data within your Vue components.

Next, we will discuss how we style our Vue components using the `<style>` section.

Styling components

When using Vue components, the Vite compiler allows you to use almost any frontend templating language style. The easiest way to enable these expressive library plugins in your Vue templates is to install them when you initialize your project, or by using npm install (or yarn add) for the package.

When using the `style` tag inside of a Vue component, you can specify a language using the `lang` attribute, provided that you have installed that specific language plugin.

For example, if you chose to install the Stylus preprocessor, first you need to install the `stylus` package in your project as a dependency by performing the following command:

```
npm add -D stylus
#OR
yarn add -d stylus
```

Then, you can add the `lang="stylus"` attribute to the `style` tag to begin using Stylus:

```
<style lang="stylus">
ul
  color: #2c3e50;
  > h2
  color: #22cc33;
</style>
```

Another benefit of using Vue is scoping the style with the `scoped` attribute. This is a useful way to create isolated and component-specific CSS stylings. It also overrides any other CSS global rules, according to the CSS rule of specificity.

It is not recommended to scope global styles. A common method for defining global styling is to separate these styles into another style sheet and import them into your App.vue file.

Now, let's practice importing SCSS, a pre-processor plugin for CSS, to use in your application, and write some scoped stylings with the following exercise.

Exercise 1.11 – importing SCSS into a scoped component

In this exercise, we will be utilizing the `style` tag to add SCSS preprocessed styles to a component and importing external stylesheets.

To access the code file for this exercise, refer to `https://github.com/PacktPublishing/Frontend-Development-Projects-with-Vue.js-3/tree/v2-edition/Chapter01/Exercise1.11`.

Let's start by performing the following steps:

1. Use the application generated with `npm init vue@3` as a starting point, or within the root folder of the code repository, navigate into the `Chapter01/Exercise1.11` folder by using the following commands in order:

    ```
    > cd Chapter01/Exercise1.11/
    > yarn
    ```

2. Run the application using the following command:

    ```
    yarn dev
    ```

3. Open the exercise project in VS Code (by using the `code .` command within the project directory) or your preferred IDE.

4. Create a new Vue component file named `Exercise1-11.vue` in the `src/components` directory.

5. Inside `Exercise1-11.vue`, let's write some HTML that can be styled using SCSS. Let's keep practicing the interpolation method:

    ```
    <template>
      <div>
        <h1>{{ title }}</h1>
        <h2>{{ subtitle }}</h2>
        <ul>
          <li>{{ items[0] }}</li>
          <li>{{ items[1] }}</li>
          <li>{{ items[2] }}</li>
        </ul>
      </div>
    </template>
    <script>
    export default {
      data() {
    ```

```
            return {
              title: 'My list component!',
              subtitle: 'Vue JS basics',
              items: ['Item 1', 'Item 2', 'Item 3']
            }
          },
        }
      </script>
```

6. Add the `sass` SCSS package as a project dependency:

    ```
    npm add -D sass
    ```

7. Add the `lang` attribute to the `style` tag and add the `scss` value to enable SCSS syntax inside the `style` block:

    ```
    <style lang="scss"></style>
    ```

8. Create a folder inside the `src/` directory called `styles`. Inside this new folder, create a file called `typography.scss`:

    ```
    src/styles/typography.scss
    ```

9. Inside `typography.scss`, add some styling for the template you composed in your component, such as defining color variables (`green`, `grey`, and `blue`) to reuse in different areas of related CSS rules, and some CSS styles for h1, h2, and the list elements:

    ```
    /* typography.scss */
    $color-green: #4fc08d;
    $color-grey: #2c3e50;
    $color-blue: #003366;
    h1 {
      margin-top: 60px;
      text-align: center;
      color: $color-grey;

      + h2 {
        text-align: center;
        color: $color-green;
      }
    }
    ```

```scss
ul {
  display: block;
  margin: 0 auto;
  max-width: 400px;
  padding: 30px;
  border: 1px solid rgba(0,0,0,0.25);

  > li {
    color: $color-grey;
    margin-bottom: 4px;
  }
}
```

In SCSS, you can use standard CSS selectors to select elements in your component.

`ul > li` will select every `<li>` element inside of an `<ul>` element for styling. Similarly, using the addition symbol (+) means that the elements placed after the first element will be styled if they match the condition. For example, `h1 + h2` will dictate that all h2 elements after h1 will be styled in a certain way, but h3 will not. You can understand this better through the following example:

In CSS, you would present this code as follows:

```css
h1 + h2 {
  /* Add styling */
}
ul > li {
  /* Add styling */
}
```

In SCSS, the same code can be represented as follows:

```scss
h1 {
  + h2 {
    // Add styling
  }
}
ul {
  > li {
    // Add styling
  }
}
```

10. In your component, import these styles by using the SCSS `@import` method:

```scss
<style lang="scss">
@import '../styles/typography.scss';
</style>
```

This will generate an output as follows:

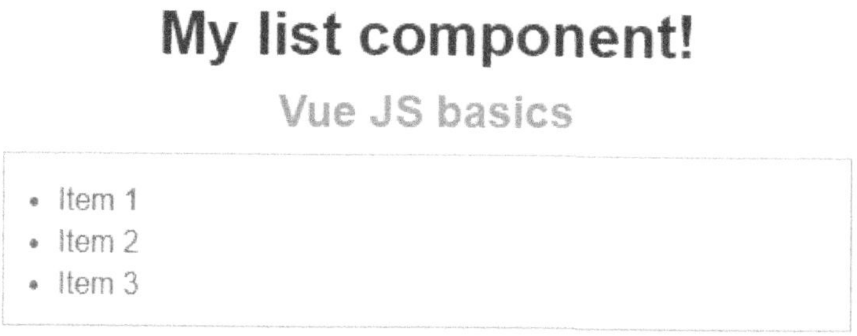

My list component!
Vue JS basics

- Item 1
- Item 2
- Item 3

Figure 1.40 – When you save and reload, your project should have the style imported

11. Add the `scoped` attribute to your `<style>` tag to only apply these styles to this component instance. Use the variable from the `$color-blue` imported stylesheet:

```scss
<style lang="scss" scoped>
@import '../styles/typography';
h1 {
  font-size: 50px;
  color: $color-blue; // Use variables from imported
stylesheets
}
</style>
```

The output of the preceding code is as follows:

My list component!
Vue JS basics

- Item 1
- Item 2
- Item 3

Figure 1.41 – The outcome of scoping styles

12. Inspect the DOM and you will notice that at runtime, that scoping has applied v-data-*
    attributes to your DOM elements specifying these specific rules.

    The **Elements** tab of your browser Devtools also shows the following after expanding the
    <head> and <style> tags:

```
▼<style type="text/css">
    /* typography.scss */
    h1[data-v-da7b46b6] {
      margin-top: 60px;
      text-align: center;
      color: #2c3e50;
    }
    h1 + h2[data-v-da7b46b6] {
      text-align: center;
      color: #4fc08d;
    }
    ul[data-v-da7b46b6] {
      display: block;
      margin: 0 auto;
      max-width: 400px;
      padding: 30px;
      border: 1px solid rgba(0, 0, 0, 0.25);
    }
    ul > li[data-v-da7b46b6] {
      color: #2c3e50;
      margin-bottom: 4px;
    }
    h1[data-v-da7b46b6] {
      font-size: 50px;
      color: #003366;
    }
  </style>
</head>
▼<body>
  ▼<div id="app" data-v-app>
    ▼<div data-v-da7b46b6>
        <h1 data-v-da7b46b6>My list component!</h1>
        <h2 data-v-da7b46b6>Vue JS basics</h2>
      ▶<ul data-v-da7b46b6>…</ul>
```

Figure 1.42 – How the virtual DOM uses data attributes to assign scoped styles

13. Create a new style sheet called global.scss in the styles folder, containing only stylings
    for the main body element:

```
/* /src/styles/global.scss */
body {
    font-family: 'Avenir', Helvetica, Arial,
```

```
       sans-serif;
    margin: 0;
  }
```

14. Import this stylesheet into your App.vue:

```
<style lang="scss">
@import './styles/global.scss';
</style>
```

Our app should render the same as before; only the font family for all elements should change to Avenir and there should be no margin for the main body, as follows:

My list component!

Vue JS basics

- Item 1
- Item 2
- Item 3

Figure 1.43 – Properly scoped styles for Exercise 1.03

In this exercise, we interpolated data that originated from an array and learned about some basic SCSS syntax. Then, we styled our component using forms of scoped SCSS, which can either exist inside the <style> tag or be imported from another directory into our project.

In the next section, we are going to experiment with how to write dynamic CSS for a component using Vue 3 features.

Setting up state-driven dynamic CSS in Vue 3

Vue 3.x introduces a new CSS function, v-bind(), to use within the style section of a Vue SFC. We use this function to create a one-way link between local data and a CSS value.

Under the hood, the Vue engine uses CSS custom properties (or CSS variables) to compute the dynamic stylings received from v-bind(). For each v-bind(), it generates a hashed custom property (with the -- prefix) and adds it to the component's root element. All the custom properties are added as inline static styles and will be updated whenever the linked local data's value changes.

For example, let's have a component that prints out a `title` and contains a local data property, headingStyles. The `headingStyles` data object contains several fields such as `marginTop`, `textAlign`, and `color`, indicating the relevant CSS properties:

```
<template>
<h1>{{ title }}</h1>
</template>
<script>
export default {
  data() {
    return {
      title: 'Binding with v-bind example',
        headingStyles: {
          marginTop: '10px',
          textAlign: 'center',
          : '#4fc08d',
        }
      }
    }
  }
}
</script>
```

At this point, the output does not have a custom style and will be as follows:

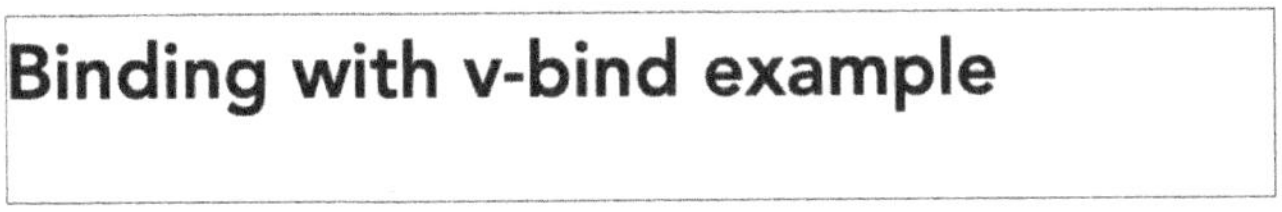

Binding with v-bind example

Figure 1.44 – Displaying the title without using v-bind() and custom CSS

We now can bind headingStyles to the CSS stylings of h1 in the `<style>` section, by applying v-bind() accordingly:

```
<style>
h1 {
  margin-top: v-bind(headingStyles.marginTop);
  text-align: v-bind(headingStyles.textAlign);
  color: v-bind(headingStyles.color);
}
</style>
```

The output will now have custom CSS enabled:

Figure 1.45 – Output with v-bind() and custom CSS applied

If you open **Developer Tools** and inspect this h1 element in the **Elements** tab, you will see it has inline styles, as shown in *Figure 1.47*:

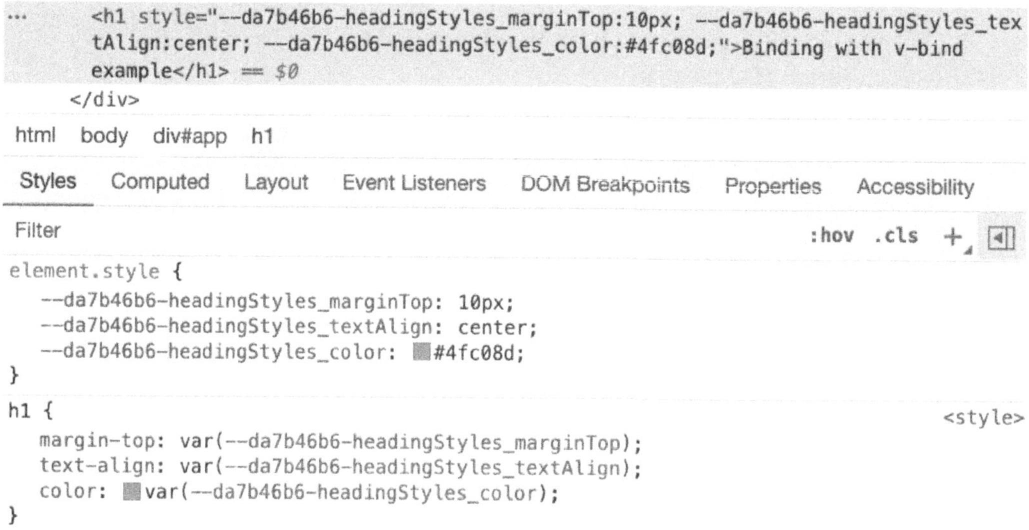

```
...        <h1 style="--da7b46b6-headingStyles_marginTop:10px; --da7b46b6-headingStyles_tex
           tAlign:center; --da7b46b6-headingStyles_color:#4fc08d;">Binding with v-bind
           example</h1> == $0
        </div>
```

html   body   div#app   h1

Styles   Computed   Layout   Event Listeners   DOM Breakpoints   Properties   Accessibility

Filter   :hov   .cls   +   ◀

```
element.style {
    --da7b46b6-headingStyles_marginTop: 10px;
    --da7b46b6-headingStyles_textAlign: center;
    --da7b46b6-headingStyles_color: ■#4fc08d;
}

h1 {                                                                         <style>
    margin-top: var(--da7b46b6-headingStyles_marginTop);
    text-align: var(--da7b46b6-headingStyles_textAlign);
    color: ■var(--da7b46b6-headingStyles_color);
}
```

Figure 1.46 – Devtools inspection shows the inline styles with hashed custom properties generated

Since v-bind() is a Vue 3.x feature, it also supports local variables defined using script setup out of the box. You can re-write the code in the script setup standards, and the outputs stay the same.

v-bind() also support JavaScript expressions. To use JavaScript expressions, you need to wrap them in quotes. For example, we can take headingStyles from the previous example and re-define marginTop as a number only:

```
headingStyles: {
  marginTop: 10,
  textAlign: 'center',
  color: '#4fc08d',
}
```

In the `<style>` section, let's compute `margin-top` for the h1 selector with the addition of 5px and add the px suffix:

```
<style>
h1 {
  margin-top: v-bind('`${headingStyles.marginTop + 5}px`');
  text-align: v-bind(headingStyles.textAlign);
  color: v-bind(headingStyles.color);
}
</style>
```

The output now has a margin top of 15px as shown in *Figure 1.48*:

```
element.style {
    --da7b46b6-___headingStyles_marginTop___5_px_: 15px;
    --da7b46b6-headingStyles_textAlign: center;
    --da7b46b6-headingStyles_color: ▇#4fc08d;
}

h1 {
    margin-top: var(--da7b46b6-___headingStyles_marginTop___5_px_);
    text-align: var(--da7b46b6-headingStyles_textAlign);
    color: ▇var(--da7b46b6-headingStyles_color);
}
```

Figure 1.47 – Generated custom property for margin-top is 15px

Using `v-bind()` is very beneficial for defining theming dynamically and programmatically. However, it provides only one-way binding from the local data to the styling, not vice versa. In the next section, we will explore the opposite binding direction using CSS modules.

Understanding CSS modules

A recent pattern that has become popular in the reactive framework world is CSS modules. Frontend development always faces the issue of conflicting CSS class names, ill-structured BEM code, and confusing CSS file structures. Vue components help to solve this by being modular and allowing you to compose CSS that will generate unique class names for the specific component at compile time.

Using CSS modules in Vue exports CSS styles from the `style` section into JavaScript modules and uses those styles in the template and logic computing.

To enable this feature in Vue, you will need to add the `module` attribute to the `style` block, and reference as classes using the `:class` and `$style.<class name>` syntax, as shown here:

```
<template>
    <div :class="$style.container">CSS modules</div>
</template>
<style module>
.container {
  width: 100px;
  margin: 0 auto;
  background: green;
}
</style>
```

Once you have enabled the CSS module, the Vue engine exposes the `$style` object containing all the defined selectors as objects for use within the `template` section, and `this.$style` to use within the component's JavaScript logic. In the preceding example, you are binding the CSS stylings defined for the `.container` class selector to `div` using `$style.container`.

If you inspected the DOM tree, that class would be called something such as `.container_ABC123`. If you were to create multiple components that had a semantic class name such as `.container` but used CSS modules, you would never run into style conflicts again.

Now, let's practice using CSS modules to style a Vue component.

Exercise 1.12 – styling Vue components using CSS modules

To access the code file for this exercise, refer to `https://github.com/PacktPublishing/Frontend-Development-Projects-with-Vue.js-3/tree/v2-edition/Chapter01/Exercise1.12`.

Let's start by performing the following steps:

1. Use the application generated with `npm init vue@3` as a starting point, or within the root folder of the code repository, navigate into the `Chapter01/Exercise1.12` folder by using the following commands in order:

    ```
    > cd Chapter01/Exercise1.12/
    > yarn
    ```

2. Run the application using the following command:

    ```
    yarn dev
    ```

3. Open the exercise project in VS Code (by using the `code` . command within the project directory) or your preferred IDE.

4. Create a new Vue component file named `Exercise1-12.vue` in the `src/components` directory.

5. Inside `Exercise1-12.vue`, compose the following code:

```
<template>
  <div>
    <h1>{{ title }}</h1>
    <h2>{{ subtitle }}</h2>
  </div>
</template>
<script>
export default {
  data() {
    return {
      title: 'CSS module component!',
      subtitle: 'The fourth exercise',
    }
  },
}
</script>
```

6. Add the `<style>` block and add `module` as an attribute instead of `scoped`:

```
<style module>
h1,
h2 {
  font-family: 'Avenir', Helvetica, Arial, sans-serif;
  text-align: center;
}
.title {
  font-family: 'Avenir', Helvetica, Arial, sans-serif;
  color: #2c3e50;
  margin-top: 60px;
}
.subtitle {
  color: #4fc08d;
```

```
        font-style: italic;
    }
    </style>
```

7. To use CSS modules in your template, you need to bind them to your HTML elements by using the :class syntax, which is the same as the v-bind:class directive:

```
<h1 :class="$style.title">{{ title }}</h1>
<h2 :class="$style.subtitle">{{ subtitle }}</h2>
```

When you save it, your project should look something like this:

CSS module component!

The fourth exercise

Figure 1.48 – Output using CSS modules

8. If you inspect the virtual DOM, you will see how it has applied unique class names to the bound elements:

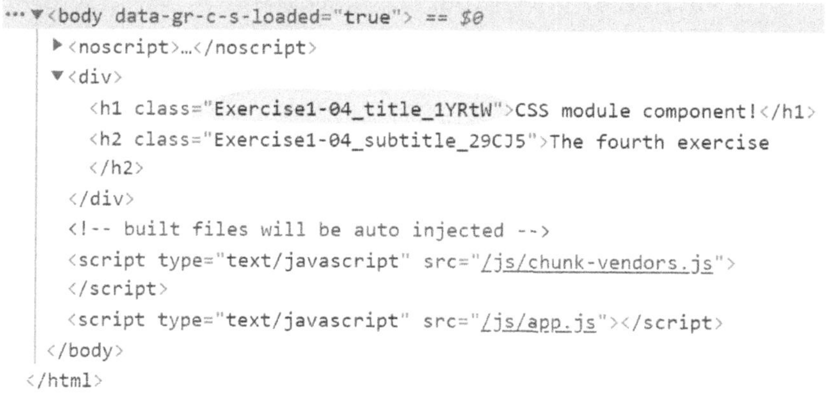

```
••• ▼<body data-gr-c-s-loaded="true"> == $0
    ▶ <noscript>…</noscript>
    ▼<div>
        <h1 class="Exercise1-04_title_1YRtW">CSS module component!</h1>
        <h2 class="Exercise1-04_subtitle_29CJ5">The fourth exercise
        </h2>
    </div>
    <!-- built files will be auto injected -->
    <script type="text/javascript" src="/js/chunk-vendors.js">
    </script>
    <script type="text/javascript" src="/js/app.js"></script>
</body>
</html>
```

Figure 1.49 – Generated CSS module class

In this exercise, we saw how to use CSS modules in your Vue components and how it works differently from CSS scoping.

In combination with file splitting and importing SCSS, using CSS modules is the preferred method for scoping component styling here. This safely ensures that individual component styles and business rules do not risk overriding each other and do not pollute global styling and variables with component-specific styling requirements.

Readability is important. The class name also hints at the component name as opposed to the v-data attribute, which can be good when debugging large projects.

In the next section, you will apply what you have learned in this chapter to build a dynamic shopping list app by combining directives, loops, two-way data, and method declaration for a Vue component together, with scoped CSS styling.

Activity 1.01 – building a dynamic shopping list app using Vue

To access the code file for this activity, refer to `https://github.com/PacktPublishing/Frontend-Development-Projects-with-Vue.js-3/tree/v2-edition/Chapter01/Activity1.01`

This activity aims to leverage your knowledge thus far about the basic features of an SFC, such as expressions, loops, two-way binding, and event handling.

This application should let users create and delete individual list items and clear the total list in one click.

The following steps will help you complete the activity:

1. Build an interactive form in one component using an input bound to `v-model`.

2. Add one input field to which you can add shopping list items. Allow users to add items by using the *Enter* key by binding a method to the `@keyup.enter` event.

3. Users can expect to clear the list by deleting all the items or removing them one at a time. To facilitate this, you can use a `delete` method, which can pass the array position as an argument, or simply overwrite the whole shopping list data prop with an empty array, `[]`.

   The expected outcome is as follows:

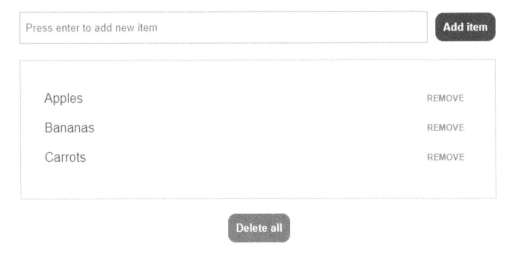

Figure 1.50 – Expected output of Activity 1.01

Summary

In this chapter, you learned how to create and run a Vue project using the command prompt with Vite. You also learned how to create basic Vue components. Within these Vue components, you can scaffold templates that use Vue's unique directives and HTML syntax sugar to loop over data or control DOM states with conditional statements. The key concepts of reactive data using data props and the v-model binding were explored and demonstrated as useful through real-life examples that utilized Vue methods and lifecycles.e

In the next chapter, we will learn about more advanced reactive data concepts that will build upon this first chapter: using computed props and watchers and fetching asynchronous data from an external source.ssssssse

2

Working with Data

In the previous chapter, you learned about the essentials of the Vue API and how to work with single-file Vue components. Building on these foundations, this chapter further explores different approaches to controlling data within a Vue component.

You will learn how to utilize Vue's powerful data reactivity and cache system through computed properties and how to set up advanced watchers to observe the component's data changes. You will also learn how to utilize asynchronous methods to fetch and handle data for your Vue components. By the end of this chapter, you will be able to watch, manage, and manipulate data from various sources in your Vue.js components.

So, in this chapter, we will cover the following topics:

- Understanding computed properties
- Understanding computed setters
- Exploring watchers
- Watching nested properties
- Exploring async methods and data fetching
- Comparing methods, watchers, and computed props

Technical requirements

In this chapter, you need to set up a basic Vue project following the instructions in *Chapter 1*, *Starting Your First Vue Project*. You can create a single file Vue component to easily practice the examples and concepts mentioned.

The Node version has to be below v20 (preferable Yarn 1.22 and Node version above 16 and up to 19.x, and npm up to version 9.x).

You can find this chapter's source code here: `https://github.com/PacktPublishing/Frontend-Development-Projects-with-Vue.js-3/tree/v2-edition/Chapter02`.

Understanding computed properties

Computed properties are unique data types that will reactively update only when the source data used within the property is updated. By defining a data property as a computed property, we can perform the following activities:

- Apply custom logic on the original data property to calculate the computed property's value

- Track the changes of the original data property to calculate the updated value of the computed property

- Reuse the computed property as local data anywhere within the Vue component

By default, the Vue engine automatically caches the computed properties, making them more performant at updating the UI than using the property of the returned value of data, or using a Vue component's method.

The syntax of a computed property is like writing a component method *with a return value*, nested under the computed property of the Vue component:

```
export default {
  computed: {
    yourComputedProperty() {
      /* need to have return value */
    }
  }
}
```

Within the computed property's logic, you can access any component's data property, method, or other computed property using the this instance, which is the reference to the Vue component instance itself. An example of using the this instance is shown here:

```
export default {
  data() {
    return {
      yourData: "your data"
    }
  },
  computed: {
    yourComputedProperty() {
      return `${this.yourData}-computed`;
```

```
      }
   }
}
```

Let's look at some examples of where you should consider using a computed property:

*   **Form validation**: In the following example, we have an `input` field, which attaches to the `name` data property, and `error` is a computed property. If `name` contains a `falsy` value (which means `name` is an empty string, `0`, `undefined`, `null`, or `false`), `error` will be assigned a value of `"Name is required"`. Otherwise, it will be empty. The component then renders the value of the `error` property accordingly:

```
<template>
  <input v-model="name">
  <div>
    <span>{{ error }}</span>
  </div>
</template>
<script>
export default {
  data() {
    return {
      name: '',
    }
  },
  computed: {
    error() {
      return this.name ? '' : 'Name is required'
    }
  }
}
</script>
```

The error computed property updates itself whenever the name value is modified by the user. Hence when name is empty, the output will be as follows:

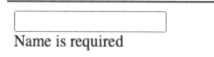

Figure 2.1 – Output of the error computed property

And when name is valid, the output will display just the filled input field:

Figure 2.2 – Output of error when name contains a valid value

- **Combining data props**: You can use computed props to combine multiple data properties to generate a single computed property. Take the following code for instance. We combine two pieces of data – title and surname – into one computed string, formalName, and render its value using template:

```
<template>
    <div>{{ formalName }}</div>
</template>
<script>
    export default {
        data() {
            return {
                title: 'Mr.',
                surname: 'Smith'
            }
        },
        computed: {
            formalName() {
                return `${this.title}
                    ${this.surname}`;
            }
        }
    }
</script>
```

This will generate the following output:

```
Mr. Smith
```

- **Calculating and displaying complex information**: Sometimes there is a need to perform an extra calculation or to extract specific information from one large data object source. Computed properties help to achieve this goal while keeping our code readable.

Take a large data object, such as `post`. This data object has a nested `fields` property, which contains several additional information objects, such as the full name of `author` and an array of `entries` objects. Each entry in `entries` contains further information, such as `title`, `content`, and a `feature` flag indicating whether the entry should be featured:

```
data() {
  return {
    post: {
      fields: {
        author: {
          firstName: 'John',
          lastName: 'Doe'
        },
        entries: [{
          title: "Entry 1",
          content: "Entry 1's content",
          featured: true
        },
        {
          title: "Entry 2",
          content: "Entry 2's content",
          featured: false
        }]
      }
    }
  },
```

In this scenario, you need to perform the following steps:

1. Display the full name of the post's `author`.

2. Calculate and display the total number of `entries` included.

3. Display a list of entries that have the feature flag turned on (feature: true).

4. By using computed properties, we can decouple the previous post object into several computed data properties while keeping the original post object unchanged, as follows:

-   fullName for combining firstName and lastName of post.fields.author:

```
fullName() {
  const { firstName, lastName } =
    this.post.fields.author;
  return `${firstName} ${lastName}`
},
```

-   totalEntries contains the length of the post.fields.entries array:

```
totalEntries () {
  return this.post.fields.entries.length
},
```

-   featuredEntries contains the filtered list of post.fields.entries based on the feature property of each entry, by using the filter built-in array method:

```
featuredEntries() {
  const { entries } = this.post.fields;
  return entries.filter(entry => !!entry.featured)
}
```

You then use the simplified and semantic computed properties to render the information in your component's template. The full code is shown here:

```
<template>
  <div>
    <p>{{ fullName }}</p>
    <p>{{ totalEntries }}</p>
    <p>{{ featuredEntries }}</p>
  </div>
</template>
<script>
  export default {
    data() {
      return {
        post: {
```

```
          fields: {
            author: {
              firstName: 'John',
              lastName: 'Doe'
            },
            entries: [{
              title: "Entry 1",
              content: "Entry 1's content",
              featured: true
            },
            {
              title: "Entry 2",
              content: "Entry 2's content",
              featured: false
            }]
          }
        }
      }
    },
    computed: {
      fullName() {
        const { firstName, lastName } =
          this.post.fields.author;
        return `${firstName} ${lastName}`
      },
      totalEntries () {
        return this.post.fields.entries.length
      },
      featuredEntries() {
        const { entries } = this.post.fields;
        return entries.filter(entry => !!entry.featured)
      }
    }
  }
</script>
```

This will generate the following output:

John Doe

2

[{ "title": "Entry 1", "content": "Entry 1's content", "featured": true }]

Figure 2.3 – The computed name output

Computed properties are very valuable to Vue developers when creating performant components. In the next exercise, we will explore how to use them inside a Vue component.

Exercise 2.01 – implementing computed data into a Vue component

In this exercise, you will use a computed property to help cut down the amount of code you need to write inside your Vue templates by concisely outputting basic data.

To access the code for this exercise, refer to https://github.com/PacktPublishing/ Frontend-Development-Projects-with-Vue.js-3/tree/v2-edition/Chapter02/ Exercise2.01.

We are going to implement a component that receives the user's first name and last name input, and displays the user's full name accordingly, by performing the following steps:

1. Use the application generated with npm init vue@3 as a starting point, or within the root folder of the code repository, navigate to the Chapter02/Exercise2.01 folder, by using the following commands in order:

    ```
    > cd Chapter02/Exercise2.01/
    > yarn
    ```

2. Open the exercise project in your **Visual Studio** (**VS**) Code (by using the code . command within the project directory), or your preferred **integrated development environment** (**IDE**).

3. Let's create a new Vue component called Exercise2-01 by adding the Exercise2-01. vue file to the ./src/components/ folder:

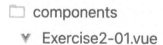

Figure 2.4 – The components directory hierarchy

4. Open `Exercise2-01.vue` and let's create the code block structure for the Vue component, as follows:

```
<template>
</template>
<script>
export default {
}
</script>
```

5. In `<template>`, create an `input` field for the first name, and use `v-model` to bind the data prop, `firstName`, to this field:

```
<input v-model="firstName" placeholder="First name" />
```

6. Create a second `input` field for the last name, and use `v-model` to bind the `data` prop, `lastName`, to this field:

```
<input v-model="lastName" placeholder="Last name" />
```

7. Include these new `v-model` data props in the Vue instance by returning them in the `data()` function:

```
data() {
    return {
        firstName: '',
        lastName: '',
    }
},
```

8. Create a computed data variable called `fullName`:

```
computed: {
    fullName() {
        return '${this.firstName} ${this.lastName}'
    },
},
```

9. Underneath your `input` fields, output the computed data using the h3 tag:

```
<h3 class="output">{{ fullName }}</h3>
```

10. Finally, run the application using the following command:

```
yarn dev
```

11. Upon visiting `http://localhost:3000` in the browser and keying the input `John` for first name, and `Doe` for last name, the page will generate the following output:

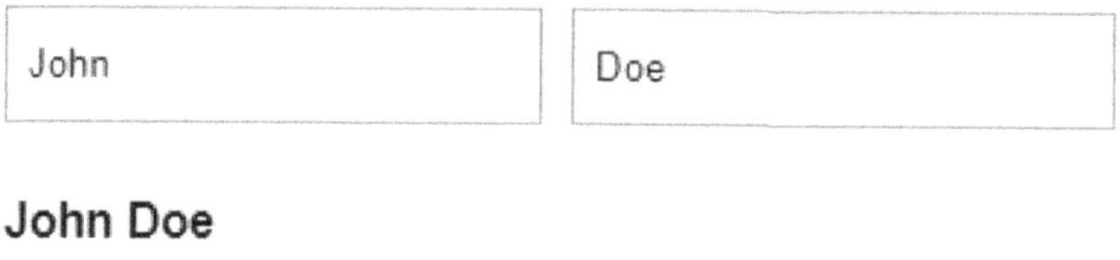

John	Doe

John Doe

Figure 2.5 – Output of the computed data will show the first and last name

This exercise demonstrates how we can write an expression inside a computed data property using data received from `v-model`, and then combine the first name and last name into a single output variable with the `fullName` computed property that can be reused within the component.

We now understand how a computed property works and how to write a declarative, reusable, and reactive computed property. Next, we will look at how to intercept the mutation process of a computed property and add additional logic with the computed setter feature.

Understanding computed setters

By default, computed data is a getter only, which means it will only output the outcome of your expression. In some practical scenarios, when a computed property is mutated, you may need to trigger an external API or mutate the original data elsewhere in the project. The function performing this feature is called a **setter**.

Using a setter in a computed property allows you to reactively listen to data and trigger a callback (setter) that contains the returned value from the getter, which can optionally be used in the setter.

But first, let's look at JavaScript ES5's getter and setter. Starting from ES5, you can use the built-in getter and setter to define Object accessors, such as the following:

- `get` to bind the Object property to a function that returns a value for that property whenever it is looked up, as shown here:

```
const obj = {
  get example() {
    return 'Getter'
  }
}
console.log(obj.example) //Getter
```

- `set` to bind the specific Object property to a function whenever that property is modified:

```
const obj = {
  set example(value) {
    this.information.push(value)
  },
  information: []
}
obj.example = 'hello'
obj.example = 'world'
console.log(obj.information) //['hello', 'world']
```

Based on those features, Vue.js provides us with similar functionalities, `get()` as the getter and `set()` as the setter, for a specific computed property:

```
computed: {
  myComputedDataProp: {
    get() {}
    set(value) {}
  }
}
```

To understand how setter and getter work, let's perform the following steps:

1. Define the returned value of `myComputedDataProp` to be `this.count + 1` whenever `myComputedDataProp` is looked up:

    ```
    myComputedDataProp: {
      get() {
        return this.count + 1
      }
    },
    ```

2. Then, whenever `myComputedDataProp` is modified, use the setter to update the `count` data prop to its new value, and then call a method within the component called `callAnotherApi` with this new `this.count` value:

    ```
    myComputedDataProp: {
      set(value) {
        this.count = value - 1
        this.callAnotherApi(this.count)
      },
    ```

With count and `callAnotherApi` is the component's local data and method, respectively.
The full example code is as follows:

```
data() {
  return {
    count: 0
  }
},
method: {
  callAnotherApi() { //do something }
},
computed: {
    myComputedDataProp: {
      get() {
        return this.count + 1
      },
      set(value) {
        this.count = value - 1
        this.callAnotherApi(this.count)
      },
    },
  },
}
```

Here the computed myComputedDataProp prop will output 1 in your Vue component.

You will find out exactly how to use computed data as both getters and setters in the following exercise.

Exercise 2.02 – using computed setters

In this exercise, you will use a computed prop as a setter and a getter, which will both output expressions and set data when triggered by a user's input.

The complete code can be found at https://github.com/PacktPublishing/Frontend-Development-Projects-with-Vue.js-3/tree/v2-edition/Chapter02/Exercise2.02.

We are going to implement a component that contains an `input` field that receives a number from the user, calculate the half value of the input, then display both values on the UI, by performing the following steps:

1. Use the application generated with npm `init vue@3` as a starting point, or within the root folder of the code repository, navigate to the `Chapter02/Exercise2.02` folder, by using the following commands in order:

    ```
    > cd Chapter02/Exercise2.02/
    > yarn
    ```

2. Open the exercise project in your VS Code (by using the `code .` command within the project directory), or your preferred IDE.

3. Let's create a new Vue component called `Exercise2-02` by adding the `Exercise2-02.vue` file to the `./src/components/` folder:

Figure 2.6 – The components directory hierarchy

4. Open `Exercise2-02.vue` and let's create the code block structure for the Vue component, as follows:

    ```
    <template>
    </template>
    <script>
    export default {
    }
    </script>
    ```

5. Create an `input` field with a `v-model` value bound to a computed data value called `incrementOne`, return the value of a Vue data variable called `count` in the getter, and set the `count` variable in the setter:

    ```
    <template>
      <div class="container">
        <input type="number" v-model="incrementOne" />
        <h3>Get input: {{ incrementOne }}</h3>
    ```

```
      </div>
    </template>

    <script>
    export default {
      data() {
        return {
          count: -1,
        }
      },
      computed: {
        incrementOne: {
          // getter
          get() {
            return this.count + 1
          },
          // setter
          set(val) {
            this.count = val - 1
          },
        },
      },
    }
    </script>
```

The output of the preceding code will be as follows:

Get input: 123

Figure 2.7 – The first steps of a computed setter and getter

6. Next, let's utilize the setter again. We will divide whatever the new `val` argument is by 2, and save that to a new data variable called `divideByTwo`:

```
<template>
  <div class="container">
    <input type="number" v-model="incrementOne" />
    <h3>Get input: {{ incrementOne }}</h3>
    <h5>Set division: {{ divideByTwo }}</h5>
  </div>
</template>

<script>
export default {
  data() {
    return {
      count: -1,
      divideByTwo: 0,
    }
  },
//...
</script>
//...
```

7. Update the setter to divide `val` by 2, and bind this new value to the `divideByTwo` variable:

```
set(val) {
    this.count = val - 1
    this.divideByTwo = val / 2
},
```

8. Finally, run the application using the following command:

```
yarn dev
```

9. Upon visiting `http://localhost:3000` in the browser, and keying the input as `1000`, the output of the `divideByTwo` value should generate an outcome from the value entered in the `input` field, as follows:

Get input: 1000

Set division: 500

Figure 2.8 – The outcome of the divideByTwo value

This exercise demonstrates how we can use computed data to both get and set data reactively in our template by binding computed variables to the `v-model`. In the next section, we will explore how we can use watchers to actively listen to changes in component data or its property.

Exploring watchers

Vue **watchers** programmatically observe component data and run whenever a particular property changes. Watched data can contain two arguments: `oldVal` and `newVal`. This can help you when writing expressions to compare data before writing or binding new values. Watchers can observe objects as well as other types, such as `string`, `number`, and `array` types.

In *Chapter 1, Starting Your First Vue Project*, we introduced life cycle hooks that run at specific times during a component's lifespan. If the `immediate` key is set to `true` on a watcher, then when this component initializes, it will run this watcher on creation. You can watch all keys inside any given object by including the key and value `deep: true` (the default is `false`).

To clean up your watcher code, you can assign a `handler` argument to a defined component's method, which is considered best practice for large projects.

Watchers complement the usage of computed data since they passively observe values and cannot be used as normal Vue data variables, while computed data must always return a value and can be looked up. Remember *not* to use arrow functions if you need the Vue context of `this`.

The following example demonstrates the `immediate` and `deep` optional keys; if any key inside the `myDataProperty` object were to change, it would trigger a console log:

```
watch: {
    myDataProperty: {
```

```
        handler: function(newVal, oldVal) {
          console.log('myDataProperty changed:', newVal,
                    oldVal)
        },
        immediate: true,
        deep: true
    },
}
```

Now, let's set some new values with the help of watchers.

Exercise 2.03 – using watchers to set new values

In this exercise, you will use watcher arguments to watch data properties for changes, then use this watcher to set variables via a method.

You can find the complete code for this exercise at `https://github.com/PacktPublishing/Frontend-Development-Projects-with-Vue.js-3/tree/v2-edition/Chapter02/Exercise2.03`.

We create a Vue component that displays the shop watcher's price before and after the discount, with an option to update the discount price, by following these instructions:

1. Use the application generated with `npm init vue@3` as a starting point, or within the root folder of the code repository, navigate to the `Chapter02/Exercise 2.03` folder, by using the following commands in order:

   > **cd Chapter02/Exercise 2.03./**
   > **yarn**

2. Open the exercise project in your VS Code (by using the `code .` command within the project directory), or your preferred IDE.

3. Let's create a new Vue component called `Exercise2-03` by adding the `Exercise2-03.vue` file to the `./src/components/` folder:

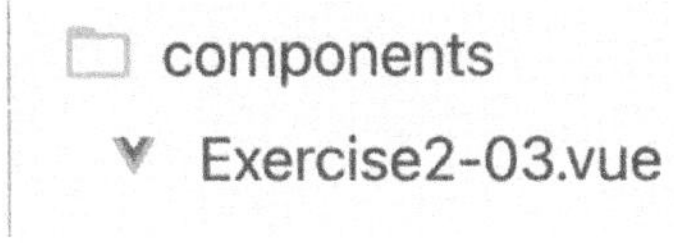

    📁 components
       ▾ Exercise2-03.vue

Figure 2.9 – The components directory hierarchy

4. Open `Exercise2-03.vue` and let's create the code block structure for the Vue component, as follows:

```
<template>
</template>
<script>
export default {
}
</script>
```

5. Set up the document by adding a `discount` and an `oldDiscount` data:

```
<template>
  <div class="container">
    <h1>Shop Watcher</h1>

    <div>
      Black Friday sale
      <strike>Was {{ oldDiscount }}%</strike>
      <strong> Now {{ discount }}% OFF</strong>
    </div>

  </div>
</template>

<script>
export default {
  data() {
    return {
      oldDiscount: 0,
      discount: 5,
    }
  },
}
</script>
```

6. We want to listen to the changes in the discount property. This can be achieved by adding it to the watch object and manually updating the oldDiscount value to oldValue received as follows:

```
watch: {
    discount(newValue, oldValue) {
      this.oldDiscount = oldValue
    },
  },
```

7. Now let's add a component method called updateDiscount. Inside the method, set the oldDiscount data prop to this.discount + 5:

```
methods: {
    updateDiscount() {
      this.discount = this.discount + 5
    },
  },
```

8. Then bind this method to button using the @click directive to trigger this method whenever the user clicks on the button and respectively trigger the watcher:

```
<button @click="updateDiscount">Increase Discount!</
button>
```

9. Add some CSS stylings to make our component look pretty:

```
<style scoped>
.container {
  margin: 0 auto;
  padding: 30px;
  max-width: 600px;
  font-family: 'Avenir', Helvetica, Arial, sans-serif;
  margin: 0;
}
button {
  display: inline-block;
  background: rgb(235, 50, 50);
  border-radius: 10px;
  font-size: 14px;
  color: white;
```

```
    padding: 10px 20px;
    text-decoration: none;
  }
  </style>
```

10. Finally, run the application using the following command:

    yarn dev

11. Upon visiting `http://localhost:3000` in the browser, the output of the preceding command will be as follows:

Shop Watcher

Black Friday sale ~~Was 145%~~ **Now 150% OFF**

Figure 2.10 – An example output of the shop watcher page

In this exercise, we explored how we can use watchers to observe and dynamically manipulate data when it is changed by triggering other methods in the Vue component.

Next, we will learn how to actively watch a specific nested property within a data object through deep watching.

Watching nested properties

When using Vue.js to watch a data property, you can observe changes belonging to nested keys of an object, rather than observing the changes to the object itself.

This is done by setting the optional `deep` property to `true`:

```
data() {
  return {
    organization: {
      name: 'ABC',
      employees: [
          'Jack', 'Jill'
      ]
    }
```

```
      }
   },
   watch: {
      organization: {
         handler(v) {
            this.sendIntercomData()
         },
         deep: true,
         immediate: true,
      },
   },
```

This code example demonstrates how we watch all available keys inside the organization data object for changes. If the name property inside organization changes, the organization watcher will trigger.

If you do not need to observe every key inside an object, it is more performant to assign a watcher to a specific key by specifying it following the syntax <object>.<key> string. For example, you may allow a user to edit their company name and trigger an API call when that specific key's value has been modified.

In the following example, the watcher is explicitly observing the name key of the organization object:

```
   data() {
      return {
         organization: {
            name: 'ABC',
            employees: [
               'Jack', 'Jill'
            ]
         }
      }
   },
   watch: {
      'organization.name': {
         handler: function(v) {
            this.sendIntercomData()
         },
```

```
        immediate: true,
      },
    },
```

We have seen how deep watching works. Now, let's try the next exercise and watch the nested properties of a data object.

Exercise 2.04 – watching nested properties of a data object

In this exercise, you will use watchers to observe keys within an object, which will update when a user triggers a method within the UI.

The complete code for the exercise can be found at https://github.com/PacktPublishing/Frontend-Development-Projects-with-Vue.js-3/tree/v2-edition/Chapter02/Exercise2.04.

Follow the instructions to create a component that displays a product's label and price, and dynamically modifies the discount price:

1. Use the application generated with npm init vue@3 as a starting point, or within the root folder of the code repository, navigate to the Chapter02/Exercise2.04 folder, by using the following commands in order:

    > **cd Chapter02/Exercise2.04/**

    > **yarn**

2. Open the exercise project in your VS Code (by using the code . command within the project directory), or your preferred IDE.

3. Let's create a new Vue component called Exercise2-04 by adding the Exercise2-04.vue file to the ./src/components/ folder:

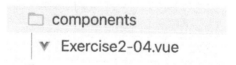

Figure 2.11 – The components directory hierarchy

4. In Exercise2-04.vue, let's start by defining a product object that contains price and label, and a discount key. Output these values into the template:

```
<template>
  <div class="container">
    <h1>Deep Watcher</h1>
```

```
    <div>
        <h4>{{ product.label }}</h4>
        <h5>${{ product.price }} (${{ discount }}
           Off)</h5>
    </div>
  </div>
</template>

<script>
export default {
  data() {
    return {
      discount: 0,
      product: {
        price: 25,
        label: 'Blue juice',
      },
    }
  },
}
</script>
```

5. Add CSS styling to our component:

```
<style scoped>
.container {
  margin: 0 auto;
  padding: 30px;
  max-width: 600px;
  font-family: 'Avenir', Helvetica, sans-serif;
  margin: 0;
}
button {
  display: inline-block;
  background: rgb(235, 50, 50);
  border-radius: 10px;
```

```
    font-size: 14px;
    color: white;
    padding: 10px 20px;
    text-decoration: none;
  }
</style>
```

6. Run the application using the following command and visit `http://localhost:3000` in the browser to view the component rendered.

    yarn dev

7. Now let's set up a button that will modify the price of the product. We achieve this by adding a `button` element with a `click` event bound to an `updatePrice` method that decrements the value of the price:

```
<template>
//...
    <button @click="updatePrice">Reduce Price!</button>
//...
</template>
<script>
//...
  methods: {
    updatePrice() {
      if (this.product.price < 1) return
      this.product.price--
    },
  },
//...
</script>
```

When you click the button, it should reduce the price, as seen in the following screenshot:

Deep Watcher

Blue juice

$15 ($0 Off)

Reduce Price!

Figure 2.12 – Screen displaying the reduced price of Blue juice

8. Time for the nested watcher. We will watch the `product` object's `price`, and increment the `discount` data prop:

```
watch: {
  'product.price'() {
    this.discount++
  },
},
```

Now, as you reduce `price`, the `discount` value will go up because of the watcher:

Deep Watcher

Blue juice

$20 ($5 Off)

Reduce Price!

Figure 2.13 – Output displaying an increased discount value

In this exercise, we used watchers to observe a key inside an object and then set new data with or without using the optional arguments parsed by the watcher.

In the next section, we will explore how to fetch and handle data using the Vue component's async methods.

Exploring async methods and data fetching

Asynchronous functions in JavaScript are defined by the `async` syntax and return a Promise. These functions operate asynchronously via the Event loop, using an implicit promise, which is an object that may return a result in the future.

As part of the JavaScript language, you can declare asynchronous blocks of code inside a Vue component's method by including the `async` keyword in front of a method.

You can use Promise chaining methods, such as the `then()` and `catch()` functions or try the `await` syntax of ES6 inside these Vue methods and return the results accordingly.

Here is an example using the built-in `fetch` API to fetch data inside a component method as an asynchronous function with `async/await` keywords:

```
export default {
  methods: {
    async getAdvice() {
      const response =
        await fetch('https://api.adviceslip.com/advice')
      return response;
    },
  },
}
```

Axios is a popular JavaScript library that allows you to make external requests for data using Node.js. It has wide browser support making it a versatile library when making HTTP or API requests. We will be using this library in the next exercise.

Exercise 2.05 – using asynchronous methods to retrieve data from an API

In this exercise, you will asynchronously fetch data from an external API source and display it on the frontend using computed props.

You can find the complete code for this exercise at `https://github.com/PacktPublishing/Frontend-Development-Projects-with-Vue.js-3/tree/v2-edition/Chapter02/Exercise2.05`.

We will create a component that will fetch quotes from an external data source and display a quote on the UI by following these instructions:

1. Use the application generated with `npm init vue@3` as a starting point, or within the root folder of the code repository, navigate to the `Chapter02/Exercise2.05` folder, by using the following commands in order:

    ```
    > cd Chapter02/Exercise2.05/
    > yarn
    ```

2. Open the exercise project in your VS Code (by using the `code .` command within the project directory), or your preferred IDE.

3. Let's create a new Vue component called `Exercise2-05` by adding the `Exercise2-05.vue` file to the `./src/components/` folder:

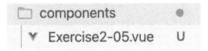

Figure 2.14 – The components directory hierarchy

4. In `Exercise2-05.vue`, let's start by importing `axios` into our component and creating a method called `fetchAdvice()`. We use `axios` to call a response from `https://api.adviceslip.com/advice` and then `console.log` the result. Also, let's include a button that has a `click` event bound to the `fetchAdvice()` call:

    ```
    <template>
      <div class="container">
        <h1>Async fetch</h1>
        <button @click="fetchAdvice()">Learn something
          profound</button>
      </div>
    </template>

    <script>
    import axios from 'axios'

    export default {
      methods: {
        async fetchAdvice() {
    ```

```
        return   axios.get
          ('https://api.adviceslip.com/advice').
          then((response) => {
          console.log(response)
        })
      },
    },
}
</script>

<style scoped>
.container {
  margin: 0 auto;
  padding: 30px;
  max-width: 600px;
  font-family: 'Avenir', Helvetica, Arial, sans-serif;
}
blockquote {
  position: relative;
  width: 100%;
  margin: 50px auto;
  padding: 1.2em 30px 1.2em 30px;
  background: #ededed;
  border-left: 8px solid #78c0a8;
  font-size: 24px;
  color: #555555;
  line-height: 1.6;
}
</style>
```

5. Finally, run the application using the following command:

```
yarn dev
```

Upon visiting `http://localhost:3000` in the browser, the output of the preceding command will be as follows:

Async fetch

Learn something profound

Figure 2.15 – Screen displaying a very large object in the console

6. We are only interested in the data object inside the `response` object. Assign this data object to a Vue data prop called `response`, which we can reuse:

```
export default {
  data() {
    return {
      axiosResponse: {},
    }
  },
  methods: {
    async fetchAdvice() {
      return axios.get
        ('https://api.adviceslip.com/advice').
        then(response => {
        this.axiosResponse = response.data
      })
    },
  },
}
```

7. Output quote from inside the response prop object using a computed prop that will update every time the response prop changes. Use a ternary operator to perform a conditional statement to check whether the response prop contains the slip object to avoid errors:

```
<template>
  <div class="container">
    <h1>Async fetch</h1>
    <button @click="fetchAdvice()">Learn something
      profound</button>

    <blockquote v-if="quote">{{ quote }}</blockquote>
  </div>
</template>

<script>
import axios from 'axios'

export default {
  data() {
    return {
      axiosResponse: {},
    }
  },
  computed: {
    quote() {
      return this.axiosResponse &&
        this.axiosResponse.slip
        ? this.axiosResponse.slip.advice
        : null
    },
  },
  methods: {
    async fetchAdvice() {
      return axios.get
        ('https://api.adviceslip.com/advice').
        then(response => {
        this.axiosResponse = response.data
      })
    },
```

```
    },
  }
</script>
```

Figure 2.16 displays the output generated by the preceding code:

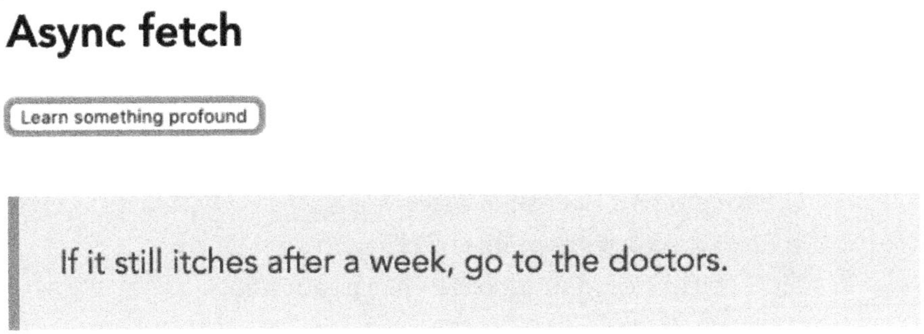

Async fetch

Learn something profound

If it still itches after a week, go to the doctors.

Figure 2.16 – Screen displaying the quote output in your template

8. As a final touch, include a `loading` data prop so the user can see when the UI is loading. Set `loading` to `false` by default. Inside the `fetchAdvice` method, set `loading` to `true`. When the GET request completes (resolve/reject), within the `finally()` chain, set it back to `false` after 4 seconds using the `setTimeout` function. You can use a ternary operator to change the button text between the loading state and its default state:

```
<template>
  <div class="container">
    <h1>Async fetch</h1>

    <button @click="fetchAdvice()">{{
      loading ? 'Loading...' : 'Learn something
      profound'
    }}</button>

    <blockquote v-if="quote">{{ quote }}</blockquote>
  </div>
</template>

<script>
import axios from 'axios'
```

```
export default {
  data() {
    return {
      loading: false,
      axiosResponse: {},
    }
  },
  computed: {
    quote() {
      return this.axiosResponse &&
        this.axiosResponse.slip
        ? this.axiosResponse.slip.advice
        : null
    },
  },
  methods: {
    async fetchAdvice() {
      this.loading = true
try {
        const response = await axios.get
          (https://api.adviceslip.com/advice);
        this.axiosResponse = response.data;
      } catch (error) {
        console.log(error);
      } finally {
        setTimeout(() => {
          this.loading = false;
        }, 4000);
      }
    },
  },
}
</script>
```

The output of the preceding code will be as follows:

Figure 2.17 – Screen displaying the loading button state output in your template

In this exercise, we saw how we can fetch data from an external source, assign it to a computed prop, display it in our template, and apply a loading state to our content.

At this point, we have explored the different approaches to working with the local data of a Vue component. In the next section, we will examine the pros and cons of each approach.

Comparing methods, watchers, and computed properties

Methods are best used as a handler to an event occurring in the DOM, and in situations where you need to call a function or perform an API call, for example, `Date.now()`. All values returned by methods are not cached.

For example, you can compose an action denoted by `@click`, and reference a method:

```
<template>
    <button @click="getDate">Click me</button>
</template>
<script>
export default {
    methods: {
        getDate() {
            alert(Date.now())
        }
    }
}
</script>
```

This code block will display an alert bar with the current Unix epoch time whenever a user clicks on the **Click me** button. Methods should not be used to display computed data, since the return value of the method, unlike computed props, is not cached, potentially generating a performance impact on your application if misused.

As mentioned, computed props are best used when reacting to data updates or for composing complicated expressions in your template. In the following instance, if the `animalList` data changes, the `animals` computed prop will also update by slicing the second item from the array and returning the new value:

```
<template>
      <div>{{ animals }}</div>
</template>
<script>
export default {
    data() {
        return {
            animalList: ['dog', 'cat']
        }
    },
    computed: {
        animals() {
            return this.animalList.slice(1)
        }
    }
}
</script>
```

Their reactive nature makes computed properties perfect for composing new data variables from existing data, such as when you are referencing specific keys of a larger, more complicated object.

Computed properties also help increase the readability of your Vue component's template and logic. In the following example, we output the authors in two different ways, but with the `authorName` computed prop, you can compose conditional logic cleanly without bloating the HTML template:

```
<template>
    <div>
        <p id="not-optimal">{{ authors[0].bio.name }}</p>
        <p id="optimal">{{ authorName }}</p>
    </div>
```

```
</template>
<script>
export default {
    data() {
        return {
            authors: [
                {
                    bio: {
                        name: 'John',
                        title: 'Dr.',
                    }
                }
            ]
        }
    },
    computed: {
        authorName () {
                return this.authors ?
                    this.authors[0].bio.name :
                    'No Name'
        }
    }
}
</script>
```

However, in many cases, using computed props can be overkill, such as when you only want to watch a specific data's nested property rather than the whole data object. Or when you need to listen and perform an action upon any changes of a data property or a specific property key nested inside a data property object, and then perform an action. In this case, data watchers should be used.

Because of the unique `newVal` and `oldVal` arguments of a watcher, you can watch a variable's changes and perform an action only when a certain value is reached:

```
<template>
  <div>
    <button @click="getNewName()">
      Click to generate name
    </button>
```

```
        <p v-if="author">{{ author }}</p>
    </div>
</template>
<script>
    export default {
        data() {
            return {
                data: {},
                author: '',
            }
        },
        watch: {
            data: function(newVal, oldVal) {
                this.author = newVal.first
                alert('Name changed from ${oldVal.first} to
                    ${newVal.first}')
            }
        },
        methods: {
            async getNewName() {
                await fetch('https://randomuser.me/api/').
                    then(response =>
                    response.json()).then(data => {
                        this.data = data.results[0].name
                })
            },
        },
    }
</script>
```

Based on these examples, we will build a simple search functionality using a method, computed props, and a watcher to achieve a similar outcome and demonstrate the ability of each method.

Exercise 2.06 – handling the search functionality using a Vue method, a watcher, and computed props

In this exercise, you will create a component that allows users to search data arrays using three different methods in Vue. By the end of the exercise, you will be able to see how each different method works.

You can find the complete exercise at `https://github.com/PacktPublishing/Frontend-Development-Projects-with-Vue.js-3/tree/v2-edition/Chapter02/Exercise2.06`.

We will create a component that displays three different filtered lists according to three `input` fields, each using a different approach discussed in this topic, by following these instructions:

1. Use the application generated with `npm init vue@3` as a starting point, or within the root folder of the code repository, navigate to the `Chapter02/Exercise 2.06` folder, by using the following commands in order:

    ```
    > cd Chapter02/Exercise 2.06/
    > yarn
    ```

2. Open the exercise project in your VS Code (by using the `code .` command within the project directory), or your preferred IDE.

3. Let's create a new Vue component called `Exercise2-06` by adding the `Exercise2-06.vue` file to the `./src/components/` folder:

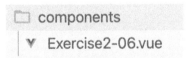

Figure 2.18 – The components directory hierarchy

4. In `Exercise2-06.vue`, within the `data` object, add a list of frameworks in an array, and assign it to the `frameworkList` property. Also, declare an `input` property with an empty string and `methodFilterList` with an initial value of an empty array:

    ```
    <script>
    export default {
      data() {
        return {
          // Shared
          frameworkList: [
            'Vue',
    ```

```
            'React',
            'Backbone',
            'Ember',
            'Knockout',
            'jQuery',
            'Angular',
          ],

          // Method
          input: '',
          methodFilterList: [],
        }
      },
    }
  </script>
```

5. In the template, include a `div` container, `title`, and a `column` container. Inside this `column` container, create an input that is bound to the `v-model` input, and bind the `keyup` event to the input to the `searchMethod` method:

```
<template>
  <div class="container">
    <h1>Methods vs watchers vs computed props</h1>

    <div class="col">
      <input
        type="text"
        placeholder="Search with method"
        v-model="input"
        @keyup="searchMethod"
      />

      <ul>
        <li v-for="(item, i) in methodFilterList"
          :key="i">
          {{ item }}</li>
      </ul>
```

```
      </div>
    </div>
</template>

<script>
export default {
  data() {
    return {
      // Shared
      frameworkList: [
        'Vue',
        'React',
        'Backbone',
        'Ember',
        'Knockout',
        'jQuery',
        'Angular',
      ],

      // Method
      input: '',
      methodFilterList: [],
    }
  },
  methods: {
    searchMethod(e) {
    console.log(e)
    },
  },
}
</script>
```

6. Then add some CSS stylings to make the output look pretty:

```
<style scoped>
.container {
  margin: 0 auto;
  padding: 30px;
  max-width: 600px;
  font-family: 'Avenir', Helvetica, Arial, sans-serif;
}
.col {
  width: 33%;
  height: 100%;
  float: left;
}
input {
  padding: 10px 6px;
  margin: 20px 10px 10px 0;
}
</style>
```

7. In the terminal, run the application using the following command:

yarn dev

8. Upon visiting http://localhost:3000 in the browser, the output of the preceding command will be as follows:

Figure 2.19 – Console output for the key input

9. Inside our searchMethod method, write a filter expression that binds the methodFilterList data prop to a filtered frameworkList array based on the input value. Trigger searchMethod on the created() life cycle hook so that when the component loads, a list is present:

```
<script>
export default {
  ...
  created() {
    this.searchMethod()
  },
  methods: {
    searchMethod() {
      this.methodFilterList =
        this.frameworkList.filter(item =>
          item.toLowerCase().includes(this.input.
            toLowerCase())
        )
    },
  },
}
</script>
```

On running the preceding code, you will be able to filter the list, as shown in *Figure 2:20*:

Methods vs watchers vs computed props

- Backbone
- Ember

Figure 2.20 – You should be able to filter the list using a Vue method

10. Let's make a filter using computed props. Include a new data prop called `input2` and create a `computed` prop called `computedList` that returns the same filter as `searchMethod` but does not need to bind to another data prop:

```
<template>
  <div class="container">

    ...

      <div class="col">
        <input type="text" placeholder=
          "Search with computed"
          v-model="input2" />

        <ul>
          <li v-for="(item, i) in computedList"
            :key="i">
            {{ item }}</li>
        </ul>
      </div>

    ...

  </div>
</template>

<script>
export default {
  data() {
    return {
      ...
      // Computed
      input2: '',
      ...

    }
  },
...
  computed: {
```

```
    computedList() {
      return this.frameworkList.filter(item => {
        return item.toLowerCase()
          .includes(this.input2.toLowerCase())
      })
    },
  },
  ...


}
</script>
```

You should now be able to filter the second column of frameworks with the help of computed props, as shown in the following screenshot:

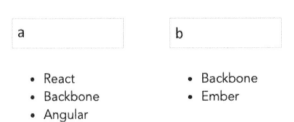

Methods vs watchers vs computed props

a	b

- React
- Backbone
- Angular

- Backbone
- Ember

Figure 2.21 – Filtering the second column of frameworks using computed props

11. Finally, let's filter the same list using a watcher. Include an `input3` prop with an empty string and a `watchFilterList` prop with an empty array. Also create a third `div` column, which contains an input bound to `input3` `v-model`, and a list outputting the `watchFilterList` array:

```
<template>
  <div class="container">


    ...
```

```
      <div class="col">
        <input type="text" placeholder="Search with
          watcher"
          v-model="input3" />

        <ul>
          <li v-for="(item, i) in watchFilterList"
            :key="i">
            {{ item }}</li>
        </ul>
      </div>
    </div>
  </template>

  <script>
  export default {
    data() {
      return {
        ...
        // Watcher
        input3: '',
        watchFilterList: [],
      }
    },
    ...
  </script>
```

12. Create a watcher that watches the input3 prop for changes and binds the result of the frameworkList filter to the watchFilterList array. Set the immediate key of input3 to true so it will run when the component is created:

```
  <script>
  export default {
  ...
    watch: {
      input3: {
        handler() {
```

```
        this.watchFilterList =
          this.frameworkList.filter(item =>
            item.toLowerCase()
              .includes(this.input3.toLowerCase())
          )
        },
        immediate: true,
      },
    },
    ...
  }
</script>
```

With the help of a watcher, you should now be able to filter the third column, as shown in the following screenshot:

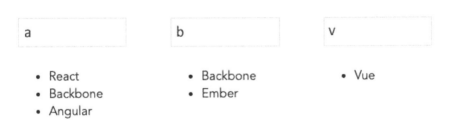

Methods vs watchers vs computed props

a	b	v
• React • Backbone • Angular	• Backbone • Ember	• Vue

Figure 2.22 – Filtering the list using a watcher in the third column

In this exercise, we have seen how we can achieve a filtered list using a method, computed props, and a watcher.

This section briefly demonstrated the three approaches. Each approach has its own pros and cons, and choosing the most suitable approach to apply or to combine requires practice and further understanding of each use case or project goal.

In the next section, we will apply what we have learned so far in this chapter to create a blog list application with computed properties, methods, and watchers with an external data API query.

Activity 2.01 – creating a blog list using the Contentful API

To access the code file for this activity, refer to `https://github.com/PacktPublishing/Frontend-Development-Projects-with-Vue.js-3/tree/v2-edition/Chapter02/Activity2.01`

This activity aims to leverage your knowledge regarding applying different approaches to working with an external data API source by building a blog that lists articles. This application activity will test your knowledge of Vue by using all the basic functions of a **Single-File Component** (**SFC**) and `async` methods to fetch remote data from an API and use computed properties to organize deeply nested object structures.

`Contentful` is a headless **content management system** (**CMS**) that allows you to manage content separately from your code repository. You can consume this content using the API inside as many code repositories as you need. For example, you may have a blog website that acts as a primary source of information, but your clients want a standalone page on a different domain that only pulls in the most recently featured articles. Using a headless CMS inherently allows you to develop these two separate code bases and use the same updated data source.

This activity will use the `Contentful` headless CMS. The access keys and endpoints will be listed in the solution.

The following steps will help you complete the activity:

1.   Create a Vue project using the scaffolding tool with Vite as a bundle management tool.

2.   Install the `Contentful` dependency (`https://www.npmjs.com/package/contentful`) into your project using the `yarn add contentful` command.

3.   Use computed properties to output the deeply nested data from the API response.

4.   Use data props to output the user's name, job title, and description.

5.   Use SCSS to style the page.

The expected outcome is as follows:

John Doe
Web Developer

Research and recommendations for modern stack websites.

Articles

MON DEC 30 2019

Hello world

Your very first content with Contentful, pulled in JSON format using the Content Delivery API.

SUN DEC 01 2019

Automate with webhooks

Webhooks notify you, another person or system when resources have changed by calling a given HTTP endpoint.

THU AUG 01 2019

Static sites are great

Worry less about security, caching, and talking to the server. Static sites are the new thing.

Figure 2.23 – The expected outcome with Contentful blog posts

After the activity has been completed, you should be able to use the `async` methods to pull remote data from an API source into your Vue components. You will find that computed props are a sophisticated way of breaking down the information into smaller chunks of reusable data.

Summary

In this chapter, you were introduced to Vue.js computed and watch properties, which allow you to observe and control reactive data. You also explored how to use methods to asynchronously fetch data from an API using the `axios` library. Then, you learned how to dynamically compose the received data into different outputs within the Vue template using computed props. The differences between using methods and computed and watch properties were demonstrated by building search functionality using each method.

The next chapter will cover Vite and show you how to use Vue DevTools to manage and debug your Vue.js applications that use these computed properties and events.

3
Vite and Vue Devtools

In the previous chapter, you learned how to utilize the Vue component's data reactivity and query the external data into the component's data system using methods, computed properties, and watch properties. This chapter introduces **Vite** and shows you how to debug these computed properties and events using Vue Devtools.

We will cover the following topics in the chapter:

- Using Vite
- Using Vue Devtools

Technical requirements

It would be best to have your Node.js version at least 14.18+ or 16+ and above. To check your Node version, run the following command in Command Prompt (or PowerShell):

```
node -v
```

You should have your npm version to 7.x and above since all our commands in the chapter are compatible with npm 7.x, and there is a slight difference with 6.x. And finally, you should install Yarn as our primary package management tool throughout the chapter.

The Node version has to be below v20 (preferable Yarn 1.22 and Node version above 16 and up to 19.x, and npm up to version 9.x.

The complete code for this chapter is available on GitHub at: https://github.com/PacktPublishing/Frontend-Development-Projects-with-Vue.js-3/tree/v2-edition/Chapter03

Using Vite

Vite.js is the build management tool aiming to do the following:

- Help you develop faster (locally develop your project with a more time-saving approach)
- Build with optimization (bundle files for production with better performance)
- Manage other aspects of your web project effectively (testing, linting, and so on)

It uses a Rollup bundler under the hood to perform chunk bundling and packaging of JavaScript projects.

Starting from Vue 3, Vite has replaced Vue CLI and become the default build tool for managing your Vue applications. Vite also supports TypeScript and provides a leaner developer experience when working on current web projects.

To initialize a new Vue project with Vite, you can use the following specific command:

```
npm init vue@latest
```

In this case, you will need to provide additional configurations for Vite to proceed, as shown in *Figure 3.1*:

```
Vue.js - The Progressive JavaScript Framework

  Project name:  chapter-3-vue-app
  Add TypeScript?      No    Yes
  Add JSX Support?     No    Yes
  Add Vue Router for Single Page Application development?   No   Yes
  Add Pinia for state management?   No   Yes
  Add Vitest for Unit Testing?   No   Yes
  Add Cypress for End-to-End testing?   No   Yes
  Add ESLint for code quality?   No   Yes
  Add Prettier for code formatting?   No   Yes
```

Figure 3.1 – Configuration prompt for a new Vue project

Figure 3.1 demonstrates configurations for a new Vue project with the name chapter-3-vue-app, including the following:

- Vue Router for routing management (which we will discuss further in *Chapter 7, Routing*), and Pinia for state management (which we will discuss further in *Chapter 9, The State of Vue State Management*)
- Vitest for enabling unit testing coverage for the project
- ESLint for linting and Prettier for organizing the project code

Based on these configurations, Vite will scaffold the desired project with the following file structure:

Figure 3.2 – File structure for a new Vue project created by Vite

Once done, the Vite package is also part of the dependency packages for the project. You now can run the following commands:

- npm run dev or yarn dev: Runs your project locally on localhost:3000 with **hot reloading mode (HRM)**. Port number 3000 is arbitrarily assigned, as it is above the well-known port numbers 1-1023 used in other areas of computing. If multiple Vue projects run simultaneously, the port number will differ between projects.

- npm run build or yarn build: Runs a production build that bundles your code into a single small file or several minimized small files, ready for deploying to production.

- npm run lint or yarn lint: Runs the process of linting, which will highlight code errors or warnings, making your code more consistent.

- npm run preview or yarn preview: Runs a preview version of the project in a specific port, simulating the production mode.

- npm run test:unit or yarn test:unit: Runs the project's unit tests using Vitest.

Now that you understand what Vite is and how to set up and manage Vue.js projects from scratch with it, we will next practice creating a Vue.js project using Vite.

Exercise 3.01 – setting up a Vue project

In this exercise, you will create your first Vue.js project using Vite commands.

To access the code file for this exercise, refer to https://github.com/PacktPublishing/Frontend-Development-Projects-with-Vue.js-3/tree/v2-edition/Chapter03/Exercise3.01.

You can create a Vue.js project by performing the following steps:

1. Open Command Prompt (Terminal) or PowerShell for Windows:

Figure 3.3 – A blank Command Prompt window

2. Run the npm init vue@3 command.
3. Upon running the preceding command, you will be asked to install the latest version of Vite. After confirming the action, the Terminal will install Vite and prompt a set of questions to configure the Vue.js app.

4. Provide the configurations as shown in the following screenshot using the navigation keyboard:

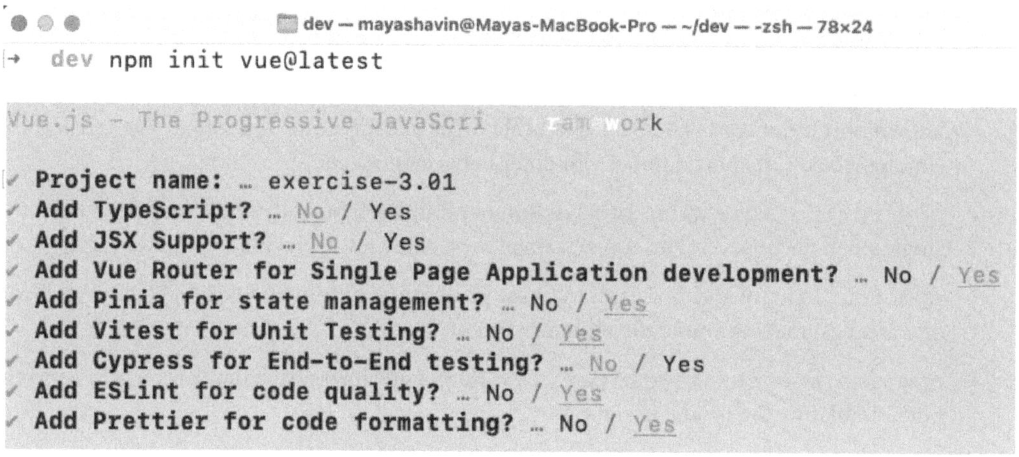

Figure 3.4 – Displaying a list of saved presets

For now, we will use Vue Router, Pinia, and Vitest for our application, with ESLint and Prettier to keep our code clean and organized.

5. Once finished, Vite will display a list of instructions for running the project, as seen in *Figure 3.5*:

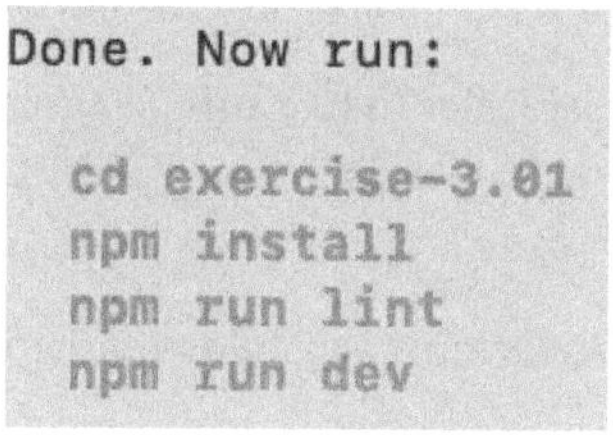

Figure 3.5 – Instructions generated by Vite

6. Navigate to your created project directory.

7. Run the `yarn` command. The output should look like this:

```
yarn install v1.22.10
info No lockfile found.
[1/4] Resolving packages...
```

8. Once the package installer has completed, run your project locally using the following command:

```
yarn dev
```

9. Running the preceding command, you can see the local server in the Terminal, as shown in *Figure 3.6*:

```
$ vite

VITE v3.0.6   ready in 591 ms

 →  Local:    http://127.0.0.1:5173/
 →  Network: use ––host to expose
```

Figure 3.6 – Local dev server is up and running

10. Click on the URL displayed in the Local: section, and you'll see a default Vue project screen in the browser, as follows:

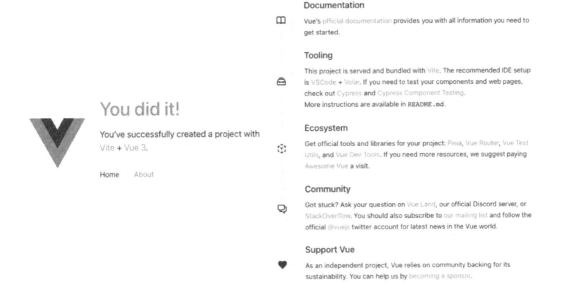

Figure 3.7 – The default Vue project screen will appear on your browser

We have now learned to set up a Vue.js project using Vite and Yarn via command prompts. Next, we will explore using Vue Devtools to debug your application.

Using Vue Devtools

Vue Devtools is a browser extension for Chrome and Firefox and an Electron desktop app. You can install and run it from your browser to debug your Vue.js projects during development. This extension does not work in production or remotely run projects. You can download the Vue Devtools extension from the Chrome extension page, as seen in the following screenshot:

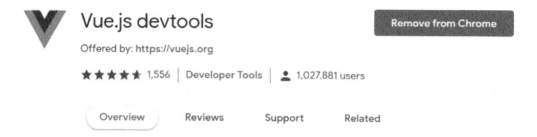

Figure 3.8 – Vue.js Devtools Chrome extension page

You can also download the Vue Devtools extension from Firefox (`https://addons.mozilla.org/en-US/firefox/addon/vue-js-Devtools/`):

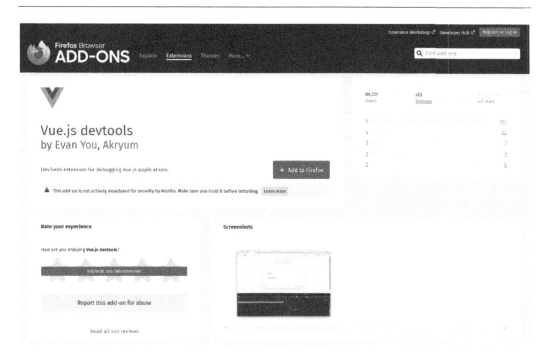

Figure 3.9 – Vue.js Devtools Firefox extension page

The Devtools extension reveals useful information within the browser's developer, including performance and event tracking for any Vue component in your application during running. Once enabled, the extension will add a **Vue** tab to the developer's console. The **Vue** tab displays a view with several tabs, which we will look at next.

There are two main tabs within the **Vue Devtools** view: **Components** and **Timeline**.

Components tab

The **Components** tab (previously Inspector) will by default be visible once you open the **Vue Devtools** tab. Once active, additional tabs appear, as detailed next.

Side actions (top-right corner)

You can select the Vue element from the browser UI using the **Select** component in a page icon (top-right corner), highlighted in *Figure 3.10*.

Figure 3.10 – Select component action icon

The second shortcut action is **Refresh**, which allows you to refresh the Devtools instance in the browser:

Figure 3.11 – Refresh action icon

Lastly, you can customize how the tab should look and feel by clicking on the three-dot icon representing **Settings**:

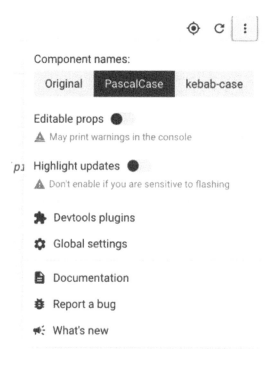

Figure 3.12 – Settings tab in Vue.js Devtools

When the **Components** tab is active, a tree of components within the app will be available on the left-side panel. The right-side panel will display the local state and details of any selected component from the tree.

There are small shortcut actions such as **Inspect DOM**, which takes you directly to the location of the highlighted component in the browser's DOM tree, and **Scroll to component**, which will auto-scroll to the component on the UI with highlights:

Figure 3.13 – Shortcut actions for a component

Next, let's look at the other tab of Vue.js Devtools—the **Timeline** tab.

Timeline tab

This tab records all events that happened in the app, divided into four main sections: **Mouse** events, **Keyboard** events, **Component**-specific events, and **Performance** events, as shown in *Figure 3.16*. You can use this tab to navigate and monitor the custom events emitted from your components:

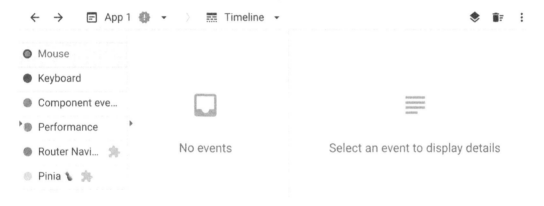

Figure 3.14 – Timeline tab in Vue.js Devtools

Other plugins (Pinia, Vue Router)

If you install additional Vue plugins such as Pinia or Vue Router and they support Vue Devtools, additional tabs will appear next to the **Component** tab, containing the relevant information for each plugin. *Figure 3.15* demonstrates an example of what the **Vue Router** tab looks like when it is enabled:

Figure 3.15 – Routes tab for Vue Router if selected

Vue Devtools helps you debug and monitor your Vue application during development. Next, we will build a Vue component and use the Vue Devtools extension to inspect the code and manipulate the local data state inside the component.

Exercise 3.02 – debugging a Vue application using Devtools

In this exercise, you will build a Vue component based on the knowledge gained in previous chapters and then debug it using Devtools. You will need to have Chrome, Firefox, or Edge installed with the Vue Devtools extension enabled.

You will use the **Vue** tab in the browser's developer console to inspect the code and manipulate the local data state of the component.

You can find the complete code for this exercise at https://github.com/PacktPublishing/ Frontend-Development-Projects-with-Vue.js-3/tree/v2-edition/Chapter03/ Exercise3.02.

Use the application generated with npm init vue@3 as a starting point, or within the root folder of the code repository, navigate into the Chapter03/Exercise3.02 folder by using the following commands in order:

```
> cd Chapter03/Exercise3.02/
> yarn
```

Open the exercise project in your VS Code editor (by using the code . command within the project directory) or your preferred IDE.

Create a new Exercise3-02.vue component in the src/components directory, and then proceed as follows:

1. Name the component Exercise and create a local data state using the data() field within the <script> section. The local data state has an array list of strings—frameworks—each representing a framework, and an empty input data prop:

    ```
    <script>
    export default {
      name: 'Exercise',
      data() {
        return {
          frameworks: [
            'Vue',
            'React',
            'Backbone',
    ```

```
            'Ember',
            'Knockout',
            'jQuery',
            'Angular',
          ],
        input: '',
      }
    },
  }
</script>
```

2. Next, create a `computed` property called `computedList` to filter the `frameworks` list based on the `input` prop value:

```
<script>
export default {
  //...
  computed: {
    computedList() {
      return this.frameworks.filter(item => {
        return item.toLowerCase().includes(this.input.
          toLowerCase())
      })
    },
  },
}
//...
</script>
```

3. In the Vue `template` block, add an `input` element and bound the `input` data prop to it using `v-model`. Then, add an `<ul>` element and display the values of `computedList` using the `v-for` loop attribute and `<li>` element:

```
<template>
  <div id="app" class="container">
    <h1>Vue Devtools debugging</h1>

    <input type="text" placeholder="Filter list"
      v-model=
```

```
      "input" />

    <ul>
      <li v-for="(item, i) in computedList"
        :key="i">{{ item }}
      </li>
    </ul>
  </div>
</template>
```

The full working code is shown here:

```
<template>
  <div id="app" class="container">
    <h1>Vue Devtools Debugging</h1>
    <input type="text" placeholder="Filter list"
      v-model="input" />
    <ul>
      <li v-for="(item, i) in computedList" :key="i">
        {{ item }}
      </li>
    </ul>
  </div>
</template>
<script>
export default {
  name: 'Exercise',
  data() {
    return {
      frameworks: [
        'Vue',
        'React',
        'Backbone',
        'Ember',
        'Knockout',
        'jQuery',
        'Angular',
```

```
        ],
          input: '',
      }
    },
    computed: {
      computedList() {
        return this.frameworks.filter(item => {
          return item.toLowerCase().includes(this.input.
            toLowerCase())
        })
      },
    },
  }
</script>
```

4. In App.vue, replace the default code with the following code to have our component rendered in the app:

```
<template>
  <Exercise />
</template>
<script>
import Exercise from "./components/Exercise3-02.vue";
export default {
  components: {
    Exercise,
  },
};
</script>
```

5. Run the application using the following command:

yarn dev

6. Upon visiting `http://localhost:3000` in the browser, the preceding code will generate a component that will display a filter input field and a list of filtered frameworks, as shown in *Figure 3.17*:

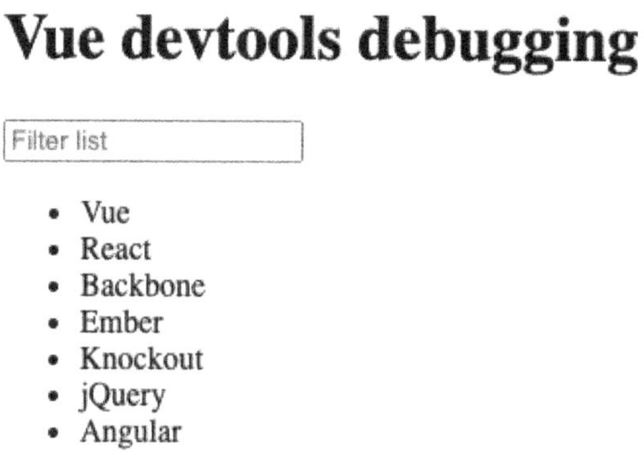
Vue devtools debugging
Filter list
Vue
React
Backbone
Ember
Knockout
jQuery
Angular

Figure 3.16 – The app should display a list and filter input

7. On the displayed page, right-click and choose **Inspect** to open the developer console or use the *Ctrl* + *Shift* + *J* shortcut (macOS users: *Cmd* + *Shift* + *J*). Then, navigate to the **Vue** tab. You should see the tab opened, as in the following screenshot:

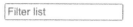

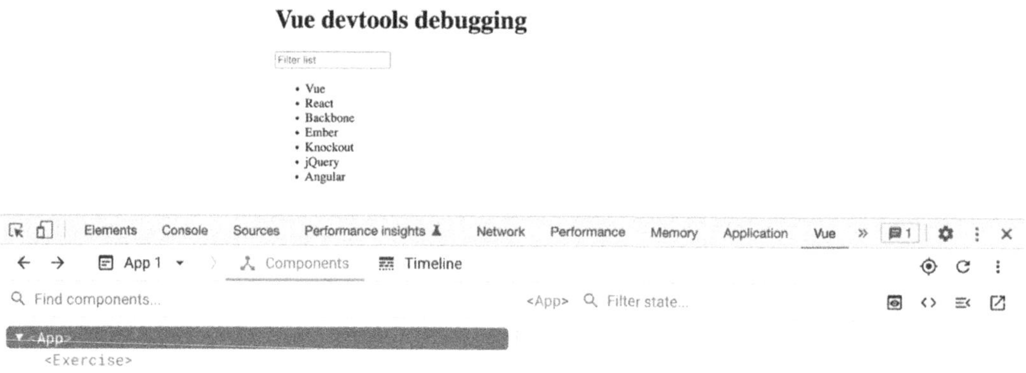
Vue devtools debugging
Filter list
Vue
React
Backbone
Ember
Knockout
jQuery
Angular
Elements
Console
Sources
Performance insights
Network
Performance
Memory
Application
Vue
App 1
Components
Timeline
Find components...
<App>
Filter state...
<App>
<Exercise>

Figure 3.17 – Vue tab in the developer console

8. By default, you will be in the **Components** tab. Select **Exercise** to inspect the data associated with that component. Click into the **Filter list** input field and type `V`. Two things will occur: in the right-hand panel, the `input` data prop now has the value of `v` and the computed list. `computedList` now only contains one element with the value `Vue`.

In the browser, this data will be reflected in the UI, as seen in *Figure 3.19*:

Figure 3.18 – How the app's options look in the Vue tab

9. Edit the data directly in the right-hand panel by clicking on the pencil icon next to the `input` prop:

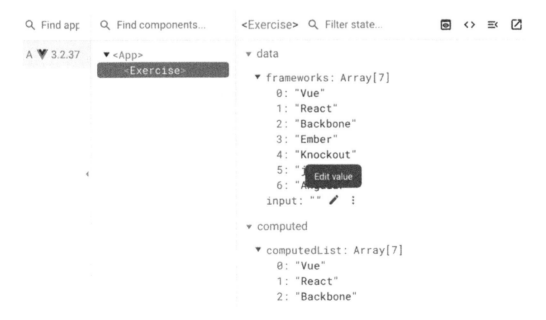

Figure 3.19 – Edit button appears on hover

10. Type R as the new value of the input prop and hit *Enter*. The DOM will reactively update for the direct change made to the input prop from the Devtools extension, as shown in the following screenshot:

Figure 3.20 – Live editing your local data value

After changing the value in Vue.js Devtools, the value will reactively change in the UI, where the input value in this example is now R, which then triggers the reactive computedList array to only show values containing the letter *R*, as displayed in *Figure 3.21*.

11. Switch to the **Timeline** tab and select **Performance** on the left-side panel. In the UI, search for several items by writing in the input box A, then B, then V. As you type text into the input box, you will see the performance metrics as blue bars, as seen in the following screenshot:

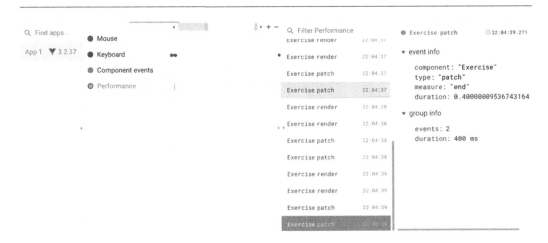

Figure 3.21 – The render performance metrics on each input change

12. Select one of the rows representing the recorded events for `Exercise` listed in the middle pane. You can observe the information, including the duration in seconds of that specific event in the right-side panel. This number reflects how long it took your component to render/update, as shown in the following screenshot:

Figure 3.22 – Selecting a performance record and seeing the details

> **Note**
> Repeating the test will allow you to compare benchmarks. However, if you refresh the page, you will lose them.

At the end of this exercise, you know how to use Vue Devtools to debug a component with the **Components** tab. You also experienced how to observe and edit data with the available functionalities of the Vue Devtools extension. Finally, you know how to use the **Performance** tab to monitor the performance of your component over lifecycle hooks during the life of the application.

Activity 3.01 – creating a Vue application with Pinia and Router using Vite

To access the code file for this activity, refer to `https://github.com/PacktPublishing/ Frontend-Development-Projects-with-Vue.js-3/tree/v2-edition/Chapter03/ Activity3.01`

In this activity, you will build a Vue project using the command line with Vite, with Vue Router and Pinia installed. This activity will test your ability to control the various Vue tools for your development.

The following steps will help you complete the activity:

1. Use Vite to create a new Vue project with Pinia and Vue Router enabled.
2. Create a component to render two string input fields that receive the first and last names and display the full name received.
3. Open the Devtools extension and observe that Pinia and Vue Router are available for debugging.
4. Add some text and observe how the component renders in **Performance**.

The expected outcome is as follows:

Activity 3.01

| First name | | Last name |

Full name:

Figure 3.23 – The final output

This activity also has the **Pinia** and **Routes** tabs available, as displayed in *Figure 3.25*:

Figure 3.24 – Devtools tab displays Pinia, Routes, and other info

After the activity has been completed, you should be able to use Vite and Vue Devtools to manage your future Vue projects. You will find that there are situations where you use both tools to enhance your development experience and make your applications more optimized.

Summary

In this chapter, you learned about Vite and how to create a Vue project managed by Vite through the command-line Terminal. You also learned about Vue Devtools and how to use its features, which will assist you on this book's journey to more advanced topics.

The next chapter focuses more on advanced Vue component features, such as passing data from one component to its nested components, validating data received from outside of the element, customizing the layout of a component with slots, and keeping the references of components for external control.

Part 2:
Building Your First Vue App

In this part, we will learn how to pass data from parent to children components using props and custom events, and how to create reusable component logic with the Composition API. We will also learn how to build a complex app structure with routing and animations. We will go through every essential topic and get to know how Vue handles it and how to use it effectively with hands-on exercises.

We will cover the following chapters in this section:

- *Chapter 4, Nesting Components (Modularity)*
- *Chapter 5, The Composition API*
- *Chapter 6, Global Component Composition*
- *Chapter 7, Routing*
- *Chapter 8, Animations and Transitions*

4

Nesting Components (Modularity)

In the previous chapter, we learned how to initialize, build, and debug a simple Vue application. In this chapter, you will discover how to modularize a Vue application using component hierarchies and nesting. This chapter introduces concepts such as props, events, prop validation, and slots. It also covers how to use refs to access DOM elements during runtime.

By the end of this chapter, you will be able to define communication interfaces between components using props, events, and validators, and be ready to build components for your Vue component library or a Vue application.

This chapter covers the following topics:

- Passing props
- Understanding prop types and validation
- Understanding slots, named slots, and scoped slots
- Understanding Vue refs
- Using events for child-parent communication

Technical requirements

In this chapter, you need to set up a basic Vue project following the instructions in *Chapter 1, Starting Your First Vue Project*. It's recommended to create a Vue component in a single file to practice the examples and concepts covered here with ease.

The Node version has to be below v20 (preferable Yarn 1.22 and Node version above 16 and up to 19.x, and npm up to version 9.x.

The complete code for this chapter is available on GitHub at: `https://github.com/PacktPublishing/Frontend-Development-Projects-with-Vue.js-3/tree/v2-edition/Chapter04`.

Passing props

Props in the context of Vue are fields defined in a child component accessible on that component's instance (`this`) and in the component's `template`.

The value of a prop depends on what the parent passes in its `template` to the child component at render time.

Defining a simple component that accepts props

Let's look at a simple `HelloWorld` single-file component. You can find this at `./src/components/HelloWorld.vue`, generated automatically when you create a Vue project with Vite.

Note how the `msg` value is set in the `props` array and that it is interpolated as a value using `{{ msg }}`.

The `props` property of a Vue component can be an array of strings or an object literal, each property field of which is a component's prop definition.

When a value is defined in `props`, it is then accessible as an instance variable in the `template` section of the Vue component:

```
<template>
  <div class="hello">
    <h1>{{ msg }}</h1>
    <!-- … -->
  </div>
</template>
<script>
export default {
  name: 'HelloWorld',
  props: ['msg']
}
</script>
```

We will now learn how to render a component using props.

Passing props to a component

What follows is a demonstration of how to use the `HelloWorld` component in our Vue application.

First, we need to import `HelloWorld` in our `App.vue` file using `<script setup>`:

```
<script setup>
import HelloWorld from "./components/HelloWorld.vue";
</script>
```

Then, in the `template` section, we need to render `<HelloWorld>` with the `msg` attribute set to `"Vue.js"`, as follows:

```
<template>
  <div id="app">
    <HelloWorld msg="Vue.js"/>
  </div>
</template>
```

This will render the following on the page:

```
Hello Vue.js
```

We have seen how to use a component with props from its parent. This is useful for code reuse and for abstracting application behavior into component-sized chunks.

Next, we will look at a practical example of a `Greeting` component.

Exercise 4.01 – Implementing a Greeting component

In this exercise, we will create a component that lets you customize both the `greeting` (for example, `Hello`, `Hey`, or `Hola`) and who to greet (for example, `World`, `Vue.js`, or `JavaScript developers`) using what we've just learned about passing props from parent to child.

To access the code file for this exercise, refer to `https://github.com/PacktPublishing/Frontend-Development-Projects-with-Vue.js-3/tree/v2-edition/Chapter04/Exercise4.01`.

Work through the following steps to complete this exercise:

1. Use the application generated with `npm init vue@3` as a starting point, or within the root folder of the code repository, navigate to the `Chapter04/Exercise4.01` folder using the following commands in order:

```
> cd Chapter04/Exercise4.01/
> yarn
```

2. Open the exercise project in VS Code (by using the `code` `.` command within the project directory), or alternatively in your preferred IDE.

3. Create a new file named `Greeting.vue` in the `./src/components` directory. This will be our single-file component.

4. Start by scaffolding the component with empty `template` and `script` tags:

    ```
    <template>
      <div>Empty</div>
    </template>
    <script>
    export default {}
    </script>
    ```

5. Next, we need to tell Vue that our component expects props. For this, we will add a `props` property to our component options object as an array with two fields, `greeting` and `who`, as shown in the following code block:

    ```
    export default {
      props: ['greeting', 'who']
    }
    ```

6. Now, we want to render `greeting` and `who` in the template as follows:

    ```
    <template>
      <div>{{ greeting }} {{ who }}</div>
    </template>
    ```

    The `Greeting` component is now ready to be used from `App.vue`.

7. Open the `src/App.vue` file and import the `Greeting` component from `./src/components/Greeting.vue` into the `script` section:

    ```
    <script setup>
    import Greeting from './components/Greeting.vue'
    </script>
    ```

8. Now we can use `Greeting` in `template`:

    ```
    <template>
      <div id="app">
        <Greeting greeting="Hey" who="JavaScript"/>
    ```

```
      </div>
    </template>
```

9. Run the application using the following command:

    yarn dev

10. You will see the following when visiting your app in the browser:

    ```
    Hey JavaScript
    ```

11. Modify the greeting and who props using the attribute values in template:

    ```
    <template>
      <div id="app">
        <Greeting greeting="Hi" who="everyone"/>
      </div>
    </template>
    ```

12. Open a Vue tab in the browser DevTools and you will see the values of the two greeting and who props have been updated:

Figure 4.1 – Output in a Vue tab for the Greeting component

And the browser now displays the following:

```
Hi Everyone
```

In this exercise, we have learned how we can use props to enable communication between parent and child while keeping the component reusable. Instead of the component rendering static data, its parent passes it the data to render.

In the next section, we will learn how to set prop values dynamically.

Binding reactive data to props

In the previous section, we saw how to pass static data as props to a component. What if we want to pass reactive data from the parent to the child?

This is where **binding** comes in. You can use v-bind: (or : for short) to enable **one-way binding** of a parent's reactive data to the child component's props.

In the following code example, we bind the appWho data to the msg prop of the HelloWorld component:

```
<template>
  <div id="app">
    <HelloWorld :msg="appWho"/>
  </div>
</template>
<script setup>
import HelloWorld from './components/HelloWorld.vue'
const appWho = 'Vue.js'
</script>
```

The output will be as follows:

```
Hello Vue.js
```

Let's add two buttons that change the value of appWho, one to JavaScript and the other to Everyone, by triggering a setWho method with the appropriate value as follows:

```
<template>
  <div id="app">
    <HelloWorld :msg="appWho"/>
    <button @click="setWho('JavaScript')">JavaScript
      </button>
    <button @click="setWho('Everyone')">Everyone</button>
  </div>
</template>
<script>
import HelloWorld from './components/HelloWorld.vue'

export default {
  components: {
    HelloWorld
```

```
  },
  data () {
    return {
      appWho: 'Vue.js'
    }
  },
  methods: {
    setWho(newWho) {
      this.appWho = newWho
    }
  }
}
</script>
```

The browser now displays the following output:

Hello Vue.js

JavaScript   Everyone

Figure 4.2 – Browser displays the component with two buttons

When you click the **JavaScript** button, Vue updates the `appWho` value and then re-renders the `HelloWorld` child component with the new value passed to the `msg` prop. Thus, `Hello JavaScript` is displayed, as follows:

Hello JavaScript

JavaScript   Everyone

Figure 4.3 – Hello JavaScript displayed after clicking the JavaScript button

Similarly, when you click the **Everyone** button, the browser now displays Hello Everyone, as follows:

Hello Everyone

JavaScript [Everyone]

Figure 4.4 – Hello Everyone displayed after clicking the Everyone button

As we have seen, we are able to bind reactive data to props so that any data updated in the parent will be reflected in the child component's data accordingly.

Exercise 4.02 – Passing reactive data that changes frequently to props

In this exercise, we will implement a component that allows users to change the name of the person to greet and pass it to the Greeting component we built in *Exercise 4.01*.

To access the code file for this exercise, refer to https://github.com/PacktPublishing/ Frontend-Development-Projects-with-Vue.js-3/tree/v2-edition/Chapter04/ Exercise4.02.

Work through the following steps to complete this exercise:

1. Use the application built in *Exercise 4.01* or navigate to the Chapter04/Exercise4.02 folder using the following commands in order:

    ```
    > cd Chapter04/Exercise4.02/
    > yarn
    ```

2. Open the exercise project in VS Code (by using the code . command within the project directory) or in your preferred IDE.

3. In the script section of App.vue, let's remove the setup attribute from the script tag, and register Greeting as a child component in the components field as follows:

    ```
    <script>
    import Greeting from './components/Greeting.vue'
    export default {
    ```

```
components: {
        Greeting
    },
}
</script>
```

4. Then create a `data` top-level method that returns an initial `greeting` and `who`:

```
<script>
export default {
  /*...*/
  data() {
    return {
      greeting: 'Hello',
      who: 'Vue.js'
    }
  }
}
</script>
```

The browser should display the same output as in *Exercise 4.01*.

5. We will now create an `input` field that accepts a string value for `who` from users and binds the `who` data to the `who` prop of `Greeting`:

```
<template>
<div id="app">
  <input placeholder="What is your name" v-model="who"
     >
  <Greeting greeting="Hi" :who="who"/>
</div>
</template>
```

6. Now when you type any name in the input field, the greeting message will change accordingly, as shown in the following screenshot:

Figure 4.5 – Output of greeting value updated according to users' inputs

Next, we will learn how to add type hints and validation to our component's props to ensure they are used correctly.

Understanding prop types and validation

We use props to define the interfaces of Vue components and ensure other developers use our components correctly. We need to define their interfaces with types and validation. Vue offers that capability out of the box by changing how we pass the props as string elements to the `props` property in an object form.

Primitive prop validation

Assume we want a `Repeat.vue` component that takes a `times` prop and a `content` prop and then calculates the array of `repetitions` using `computed` based on the `times` value. We can define the following:

```
<template>
  <div>
    <span v-for="r in repetitions" :key="r">
      {{ content }}
    </span>
  </div>
</template>
<script>
export default {
  props: ['times', 'content'],
  computed: {
    repetitions() {
```

```
            return Array.from({ length: this.times });
        }
    }
}
</script>
```

In App.vue, we can consume our Repeat component as follows:

```
<template>
  <div id="app">
    <Repeat :times="count" content="Repeat" />
    <button @click="increment()">Repeat</button>
  </div>
</template>
<script>
import Repeat from './components/Repeat.vue'
export default {
  components: {
    Repeat
  },
  data() {
    return { count: 1 }
  },
  methods: {
    increment() {
      this.count += 1
    }
  }
}
</script>
```

The preceding code will lead to the following output in the browser:

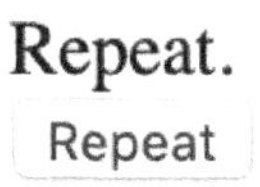

Repeat.

Repeat

Figure 4.6 – Output of the repeat example in action (no clicks)

Whenever clicking the Repeat button, the Repeat component will display the content one more time, as follows:

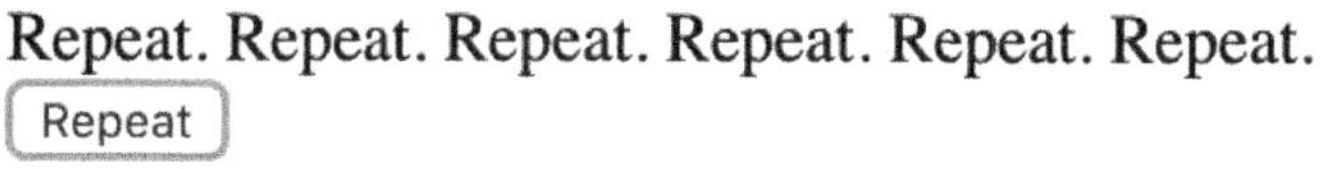

Repeat. Repeat. Repeat. Repeat. Repeat. Repeat.

Repeat

Figure 4.7 – Output of the repeat example after five clicks

Now, for this component to work properly, we need times to be a Number type and, ideally, content to be a String type.

> **Note**
>
> Props type in Vue can be any type including String, Number, Boolean, Array, Object, Date, Function, and Symbol.

Let's define the times prop as a Number and the content props as a String:

```
<script>
export default {
  props: {
    times: {
      type: Number
    },
    content: {
      type: String
    }
  },
  // rest of component definition
}
</script>
```

Let's see what happens if we update App to pass the wrong prop type to Repeat – for example, let's say times is a String and content is a Number:

```
<template>
  <div id="app">
    <Repeat :times="count" :content="55" />
  </div>
```

```
</template>

<script>
// no changes to imports
export default {
  data() {
    return { count: 'no-number-here' }
  },
  // other properties
}
</script>
```

In this case, the `Repeat` component will fail to render, and the following errors will be logged to the console:

```
⚠ ▸ [Vue warn]: Invalid prop: type check failed for prop "times". Expected
    Number with value NaN, got String with value "no-number-here".
      at <Repeat times="no-number-here" content=55 >
      at <App>
⚠ ▸ [Vue warn]: Invalid prop: type check failed for prop "content". Expected
    String with value "55", got Number with value 55.
      at <Repeat times="no-number-here" content=55 >
      at <App>
```

Figure 4.8 – Mistyping prop errors

The `times` prop check fails with a message that explains that we passed a `String` to a prop that expects to receive a `Number`:

```
Invalid prop: type check failed for prop "times". Expected
Number with value NaN, got String with value "no-number-here"
```

The same occurs with the `content` prop check, with a message that explains that we passed a `Number` as a prop that was supposed to be a `String`:

```
Invalid prop: type check failed for prop "content". Expected
String with value "55", got Number with value 55
```

Next, let's explore custom prop types and union types.

Understanding union and custom prop types

Vue supports union types. A **union** type is a type that is one of many other types, and is represented by an array of types, such as [String, Number]. We declare a prop to accept a union type by using the type field of that data prop object. For example, we set content to accept a union type that will be either a number or a string:

```
<script>
export default {
  props: {
    // other prop definitions
    content: {
      type: [String, Number]
    }
  }
  // rest of component definition
}
</script>
```

In this case, we can consume the Repeat component as follows without errors:

```
<template>
  <div id="app">
    <Repeat :times="3" :content="55" />
  </div>
</template>
```

We can also use any valid JavaScript constructor as a prop's type, such as a Promise or a custom User class constructor, as in the following example with the TodoList component:

```
<script>
import User from './user.js'
export default {
  props: {
    todoListPromise: {
      type: Promise
    },
    currentUser: {
      type: User
```

```
    }
  }
}
</script>
```

Note here we import the `User` custom type from another file. We can use this `TodoList` component as follows:

```
<template>
  <div>
    <div v-if="todosPromise && !error">
      <TodoList
        :todoListPromise="todosPromise"
        :currentUser="currentUser"
      />
    </div>
    {{ error }}
  </div>
</template>
<script>
import TodoList from './components/TodoList.vue'
import User from './components/user.js'

const currentUser = new User()

export default {
  components: {
    TodoList
  },
  mounted() {
    this.todosPromise = fetch('/api/todos').then(res => {
      if (res.ok) {
        return res.json()
      }
      throw new Error('Could not fetch todos')
    }).catch(error => {
      this.error = error
```

```
      })
    },
    data() {
      return { currentUser, error: null }
    }
  }
</script>
```

In the preceding code, we only fetch `todosPromise` once Vue mounts the component instance, and create a new instance of `User` using `new User()`.

We have now seen how to use the union and custom types to validate Vue props.

> **Note**
>
> Vue uses `instanceof` validation internally, so make sure any custom types are instantiated using the relevant constructor.
>
> Passing `null` or `undefined` will fail the check for `Array` and `Object`.
>
> Passing an array will pass the check for `Object` since an array is also an instance of `Object` in JavaScript.

Next, we will explore how to enable validation for props on certain types.

Custom validation of arrays and objects

Vue allows custom validators to be used as props using the `validator` property. This allows us to implement deep checks regarding object and collection types.

Let's look at a `CustomSelect` component.

On a basic level, the prop interface for `select` comprises an array of `options` and a `selected` option.

Each option should have a `label` that represents what is displayed in `select`, and a `value` representing its actual value. The `selected` option's value can be empty or be equal to the `value` field for one of our `options`.

We can implement `CustomSelect` in a naive way (no validation of the inputs) as follows:

```
<template>
  <select>
    <option
      :selected="selected === o.value"
      v-for="o in options"
```

```
          :key="o.value"
      >
         {{ o.label }}
      </option>
   </select>
</template>
<script>
export default {
  props: {
    selected: {
      type: String
    },
    options: {
      type: Array
    }
  }
}
</script>
```

Then use `CustomSelect` to display a list of British crisp flavors (in `src/App.vue`):

```
<template>
  <div id="app">
    <CustomSelect :selected="selected" :options="options"
      />
  </div>
</template>

<script>
import CustomSelect from './components/CustomSelect.vue'

export default {
  components: {
    CustomSelect
  },
  data() {
    return {
```

```
        selected: 'salt-vinegar',
        options: [
          {
            value: 'ready-salted',
            label: 'Ready Salted'
          },
          {
            value: 'cheese-onion',
            label: 'Cheese & Onion'
          },
          {
            value: 'salt-vinegar',
            label: 'Salt & Vinegar'
          },
        ]
      }
    }
  }
</script>
```

The preceding example outputs a `select` element where `Salt & Vinegar` is the default selected option, as shown in the following screenshot:

Figure 4.9 – Collapsed CustomSelect with Salt & Vinegar selected

The following screenshot shows the three flavor options displayed when the dropdown is opened:

Figure 4.10 – Open CustomSelect with flavor options and Salt & Vinegar selected

Now we can implement a prop `validator` method to enable further validation for our component's logic, as follows:

```
<script>
export default {
  // other component properties
  props: {
    // other prop definitions
    options: {
      type: Array,
      validator(options) {
        return options.every(o => Boolean(o.value
          && o.label))
      }
    }
  }
}
</script>
```

If we pass an option with a missing `value` or `label`, we will get the following message in the console:

```
⚠ ▶ [Vue warn]: Invalid prop: custom validator check failed      runtime-core.esm-bundler.js:40
    for prop "options".
    at <CustomSelect selected="salt-vinegar" options=
  ▼ (3) [{…}, {…}, {…}] 🛈                                 >
    ▶ 0: {value: 'ready-salted'}
    ▶ 1: {value: 'cheese-onion', label: 'Cheese & Onion'}
    ▶ 2: {value: 'salt-vinegar', label: 'Salt & Vinegar'}
      length: 3
    ▶ [[Prototype]]: Array(0)
    at <App>
```

Figure 4.11 – Console warning when a custom validator fails

With that, we have learned how to use a custom validator to do in-depth validation for complex props. Next, we will learn how the `required` property of a prop works.

Understanding required props

To mark a prop as required, we can use the `required` prop type property.

In the `CustomSelect` example, we can make `selected` a required prop by adding `required: true` to its prop definition, as follows:

```
<script>
export default {
```

```
    // other component properties
    props: {
      selected: {
        type: String,
        required: true
      }
      // other prop definitions
    }
  }
</script>
```

Now, if we don't pass a value to the `selected` prop of `CustomSelect` on the parent component, we will see the following error:

```
⚠ ▶ [Vue warn]: Missing required prop: "selected"
    at <CustomSelect options= ▶ (3) [{…}, {…}, {…}] >
    at <App>
```

Figure 4.12 – Console warning when the selected required prop is missing

With that, we have learned how to mark props as required and saw what happens when we don't pass a value to a required prop. Next, we will learn how to set the default value for a prop and see why it is a good practice to do so.

Setting the default props value

There are situations where setting the default value for a prop is good practice to follow.

Take a `PaginatedList` component, for instance. This component takes a list of `items`, a `limit` number of items to display, and an `offset` number. Then it will display a subset of items – `currentWindow` – based on the `limit` and `offset` values:

```
<template>
  <ul>
    <li
      v-for="el in currentWindow"
      :key="el.id"
    >
      {{ el.content }}
```

```
    </li>
  </ul>
</template>
<script>
export default {
  props: {
    items: {
      type: Array,
      required: true,
    },
    limit: {
      type: Number
    },
    offset: {
      type: Number
    }
  },
  computed: {
    currentWindow() {
      return this.items.slice(this.offset, this.limit)
    }
  }
}
</script>
```

Instead of passing the values of limit and offset every time, it might be better to set limit to a default value (like 2) and offset to 0 (this means that by default, we show the first page, which contains 2 results).

We can implement this change using the default property for each prop definition object as follows:

```
<script>
export default {
  props: {
    // other props
    limit: {
      type: Number,
```

```
        default: 2,
      },
      offset: {
        type: Number,
        default: 0,
      }
    },
    // other component properties
  }
</script>
```

Then in App.vue, we can use PaginatedList without passing limit and offset. Vue automatically falls back to the default values in case no value is passed:

```
<template>
  <main>
    <PaginatedList :items="snacks" />
  </main>
</template>
<script>
import PaginatedList from './components/PaginatedList.vue'

export default {
  components: {
    PaginatedList
  },
  data() {
    return {
      snacks: [
        {
          id: 'ready-salted',
          content: 'Ready Salted'
        },
        {
```

```
          id: 'cheese-onion',
          content: 'Cheese & Onion'
        },
        {
          id: 'salt-vinegar',
          content: 'Salt & Vinegar'
        },
      ]
    }
  }
}
</script>
```

The browser will display only the first two items, as shown in the following screenshot:

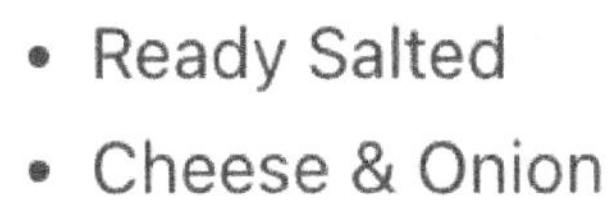

- Ready Salted
- Cheese & Onion

Figure 4.13 – Output of a snack list with first two items only by default

When you pass values for offset or limit, Vue will use these values instead of the defaults and render the component accordingly.

In cases where a prop is an array or an object, we can't assign its default value with a static array or object. Instead, we need to assign it a function that returns the desired default value. We can set the default value of items from the PaginatedList component to an empty array, as follows:

```
<script>
export default {
  props: {
    items: {
      type: Array,
      default() {
        return []
      }
    }
    // other props
  },
```

```
    // other component properties
}
</script>
```

At this point, we have learned how to set default values for component props. Note here that once you set a `default` value, you don't need to set `required` field anymore. We can use a `default` value to ensure our props are always with values, regardless of whether this is required or optional.

Registering props in <script setup> (setup hook)

If you use `<script setup>`, since there is no options object, we can't define the component's props using the `props` field. Instead, we use the `defineProps()` function from the `vue` package and pass all the relevant props' definitions to it, just as we did with the `props` field. For example, in the `MessageEditor` component, we can rewrite the event registering with `defineEmits()` as follows:

```
<script setup>
import { defineProps, computed } from 'vue'

const props = defineProps({
    items: {
       type: Array,
       required: true,
    },
    limit: {
       type: Number
    },
    offset: {
       type: Number
    }
});

const currentWindow = computed(() => {
  return props.items.slice(props.offset, props.limit)
})
</script>
```

`defineProps()` returns an object containing all the props' values. We can then access a prop such as `items` using `props.items` instead within the `script` section, and `items` as usual in the `template` section. In the previous example, we also use `computed()` to declare a reactive data `currentWindow` for this component, the usage of which we will discuss further in *Chapter 5, The Composition API*.

Let's practice writing component props with defaults, types, and validators in the next exercise.

Exercise 4.03 – Validating an Object property

In this exercise, we will write a `Repeat` component that accepts a `config` data prop for passing `times`, which is a `Number`, and `content`, which is a `String`.

We will write a custom validator to make sure `times` and `content` exist and are of the correct type.

To access the code file for this exercise, refer to `https://github.com/PacktPublishing/Frontend-Development-Projects-with-Vue.js-3/tree/v2-edition/Chapter04/Exercise4.03`.

Work through the following steps to complete this exercise:

1. Use the application generated with npm `init vue@3` as a starting point. Otherwise, within the root folder of the code repository, navigate to the `Chapter04/Exercise4.03` folder using the following commands in order:

    ```
    > cd Chapter04/Exercise4.03/
    > yarn
    ```

2. Open the exercise project in VS Code (using the `code .` command within the project directory) or in your preferred IDE.

3. Create a new file named `Repeat.vue` in the `./src/components` directory.

4. Define a prop `config` for `Repeat.vue`. This prop will be of the `Object` type, as follows:

    ```
    <script>
    export default {
      props: {
        config: {
          type: Object,
          required: true,
        }
      }
    }
    </script>
    ```

5. Config contains two fields – times and content. We compute a reactive data array called repetitions for the Repeat component with its length based on config.times:

```
<script>
export default {
  // other component properties
  computed: {
    repetitions() {
      return Array.from({ length: this.config.times })
    }
  }
}
</script>
```

6. Set up <template> so that it renders config.content for each of the repetitions items:

```
<template>
  <div>
    <span v-for="r in repetitions" :key="r">
      {{ config.content }}
    </span>
  </div>
</template>
```

7. We need to ensure that content and times will receive the correct value by implementing a validator for config. The validator will check whether the received value's times and content typeof are of number and string, respectively:

```
<script>
export default {
  props: {
    config: {
      type: Object,
      required: true,
      validator(value) {
        return typeof value.times === 'number' &&
          typeof value.content === 'string'
      }
    }
```

```
    },
    // other component properties
  }
</script>
```

8. Next, we import and use `Repeat` in `src/App.vue`:

```
<template>
  <main>
    <Repeat :config="{}" />
  </main>
</template>

<script>
import Repeat from './components/Repeat.vue'

export default {
  components: {
    Repeat
  }
}
</script>
```

Unfortunately, this will not render anything since `config` is an empty object. You will observe a warning in the console, as follows:

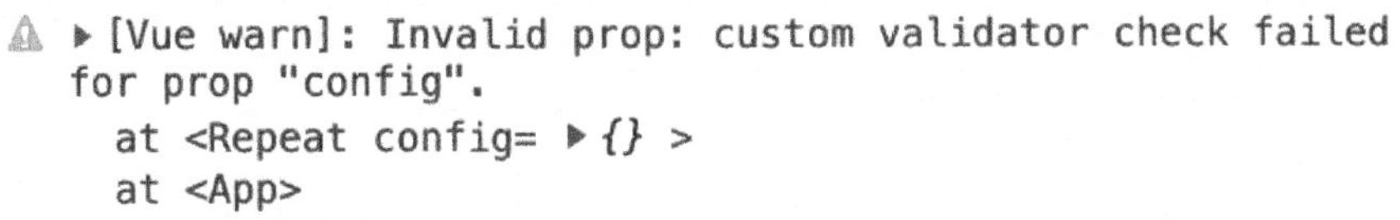

```
⚠ ▶ [Vue warn]: Invalid prop: custom validator check failed
   for prop "config".
    at <Repeat config= ▶ {} >
    at <App>
```

Figure 4.14 – Console warning due to the config prop's custom validator check failing

9. We will see this same error in the following cases:

- We only add a `times` property, that is, `<Repeat :config="{ times: 3 }" />`

- We only add a `content` property, that is, `<Repeat :config="{ content: 'Repeat me.' }" />`

- `times` is of the wrong type, that is, `<Repeat :config="{ times: '3', content: 'Repeat me.' }" />`

- content is of the wrong type property, that is, `<Repeat :config="{ times: 3, content: 42 }" />`

10. For Repeat to work correctly, we can amend the line consuming it in `template` to the following:

    ```
    <Repeat :config="{ times: 3, content: 'Repeat me.' }" />
    ```

    This shows no errors in the console and renders Repeat me. three times, as follows:

    ```
    Repeat me.Repeat me.Repeat me.
    ```

We have demonstrated how we use a validator to better define components with props.

In the next section, we will have a deep dive into slots, a mechanism we use to compose our components by deferring template logic.

Understanding slots, named slots, and scoped slots

Slots are sections of a component where the template/rendering is delegated back to the parent of the component. We can consider slots as templates or markup that are passed from a parent to a child for rendering in its main template.

Passing markup to a component for rendering

The simplest type of slot is the default child slot.

We can define a Box component with a slot as follows:

```
<template>
  <div>
    <slot>Slot's placeholder</slot>
  </div>
</template>
```

The following markup is for the parent component (`src/App.vue`):

```
<template>
  <div>
    <Box>
      <h3>This whole h3 is rendered in the slot</h3>
    </Box>
  </div>
</template>
<script>
```

```
import Box from './components/Box.vue'
export default {
  components: {
    Box
  }
}
</script>
```

The preceding code will render the following text in the browser:

```
This whole h3 is rendered in the slot
```

If there is no template content passed to Box, Vue will fall back to the default template defined in the Box component, which is the following text:

```
Slot's placeholder
```

Behind the scenes, Vue compiles the `template` section of Box and replaces `<slot />` with the content wrapped inside `<Box />` from the parent (App). The scope of the replaced content, however, stays within the parent's scope.

Consider the following example:

```
<template>
  <div>
    <Box>
      <h3>This whole h3 is rendered in the slot with parent
        count {{ count }}</h3>
    </Box>
    <button @click="count++">Increment</button>
  </div>
</template>
<script>
import Box from './components/Box.vue'
export default {
  components: {
    Box
  },
  data() {
    return { count: 0 }
```

```
    }
  }
</script>
```

The preceding code will render `count` per its value in the parent component. It does not have access to the `Box` instance data or props and will generate the following output:

This whole h3 is rendered in the slot with parent count 0

Increment

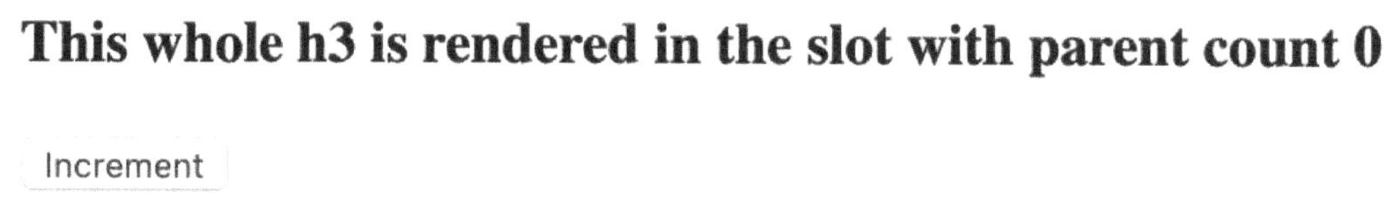

Figure 4.15 – Initial h3 with a count of 0, per the initial data in the parent component

Incrementing the `count` from the parent updates the template content, since the `count` variable in the template passed to `Box` was bound to data on the parent. This will generate the following output:

This whole h3 is rendered in the slot with parent count 5

Increment

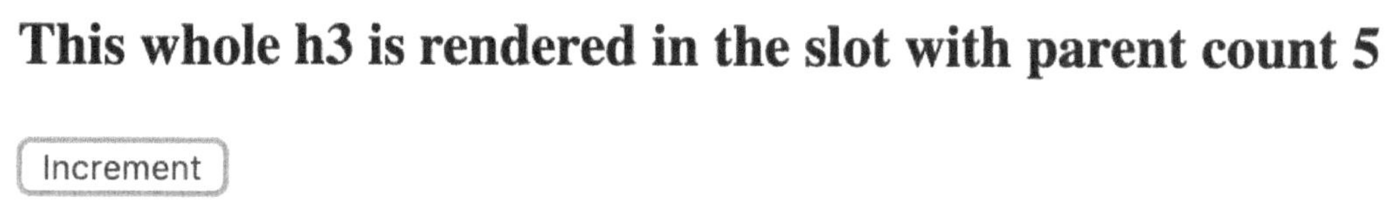

Figure 4.16 – h3 with a count of 5 after five increments of the count in the parent component's scope

Slots are a way to let the parent have control over rendering a section of a child's template. Any references to instance properties, data, or methods will use the parent component instance. This type of slot does not have access to the child component's properties, props, or data.

In the next section, we will look at how to use named slots to render multiple sections.

Using named slots to delegate rendering of multiple sections

We use named slots when a child component wants to allow its parent to customize the multiple sections in its template.

For example, an `Article` component might delegate rendering of `title` and `excerpt` to its parent.

In this case, we will use multiple `slot` and assign each with an appropriate `name` attribute value, shown as follows:

```
<template>
  <article>
```

```
      <div>Title: <slot name="title" /></div>
      <div>Excerpt: <slot name="excerpt" /></div>
    </article>
  </template>
```

By doing so, we allow the parent of `article` to override the slots named `title` and `excerpt` with its desired UI templates.

To pass content to the desired slot, we use `template` with the `v-slot:name` directive (where name should be replaced with the slot's name).

For example, for the slot named `title`, we will use `v-slot:title`, while for the `excerpt` slot, we will use `v-slot:excerpt`:

```
<template>
  <div>
    <Article>
      <template v-slot:title>
        <h3>My Article Title</h3>
      </template>
      <template v-slot:excerpt>
        <p>First paragraph of content</p>
        <p>Second paragraph of content</p>
      </template>
    </Article>
  </div>
</template>
<script>
import Article from './components/Article.vue'
export default {
  components: {
    Article
  }
}
</script>
```

When the preceding application is seen in the browser, it will look as follows:

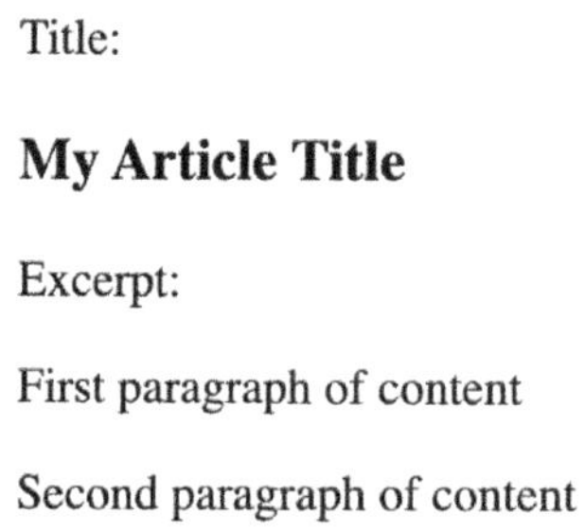

Title:

My Article Title

Excerpt:

First paragraph of content

Second paragraph of content

Figure 4.17 – Article using named slots to render templates defined by the parent

As you can see, the named slots do indeed render the expected content.

The shorthand syntax for `v-slot:slot-name` is `#slot-name`. We can refactor our template that consumes `Article` as follows:

```
<template>
  <div>
    <Article>
      <template #title>
        <h3>My Article Title</h3>
      </template>
      <template #excerpt>
        <p>First paragraph of content</p>
        <p>Second paragraph of content</p>
      </template>
    </Article>
  </div>
</template>
```

Note here that `v-slot` cannot be used with native elements. You can only use it with `template` and /or with the component itself. For example, the following `<template>` section attempts to set a `v-slot` on a h3 element:

```
<template>
  <div>
    <Article>
      <h3 v-slot:title>My Article Title</h3>
    </Article>
```

```
    </div>
  </template>
```

This template will fail with a compilation error of `v-slot can only be used on components or <template>`, as shown in the following screenshot:

```
 error  in ./src/App.vue?vue&type=template&id=7ba5bd90&

Module Error (from ../node_modules/vue-loader/lib/loaders/templateLoader.js):
(Emitted value instead of an instance of Error)

  Errors compiling template:

  v-slot can only be used on components or <template>.

  2 |   <div>
  3 |     <Article>
  4 |       <h3 v-slot:title>My Article Title</h3>
    |           ^^^^^^^^^^^^
  5 |     </Article>
  6 |   </div>
```

Figure 4.18 – v-slot on a native element – compilation error

> **Note**
> Everything that applies to the default slot applies to named slots. In fact, the default slot is a named slot called `default`. This means that named slots also have access to the parent instance but not the child instance.

The default slot is just a slot named `default` and we can define it with no name. The `default` slot is implicitly inferred as follows:

```
<template>
  <div>
    <template>Default template</template>
  </div>
</template>
```

We can also denote the default slot with shorthand slot notation:

```
<template>
  <MyComponent>
    <template #default>Default template</template>
  </MyComponent>
</template>
```

Or we can denote the default slot with longhand slot notation as follows:

```
<template>
  <MyComponent>
    <template v-slot:default>Default template</template>
  </MyComponent>
</template>
```

We have now seen how named slots allow components to delegate templating of certain sections to a consumer, as well as how these named slots can have a default template to cater for cases where a named slot is optional.

In the next section, we will learn how scoped slots are used to wrap prop-passing logic.

Using scoped slots to wrap prop-passing logic

The types of slots we have explored so far only have access to the component instance where slot template content is passed – the parent component.

In many scenarios, it is handier to let the parent component decide how to render the UI while letting the child component handle the data and pass it to the slot. We use scoped slots for this purpose.

A **scoped slot** starts with the child component's slots, where the slot element receives props and passes them to the related template content by using v-bind or the shorthand, :.

In the following code example, we bind the slot's item prop to el, which is an element of the currentWindow data in the PaginatedList component:

```
<template>
  <ul>
    <li
      v-for="el in currentWindow"
      :key="el.id"
    >
```

```
      <slot :item="el" />
    </li>
  </ul>
</template>
<script>
export default {
  props: ['items', 'limit', 'offset'],
  computed: {
    currentWindow() {
      return this.items.slice(this.offset, this.limit)
    }
  }
}
</script>
```

On the consumer side (the parent component), Vue renders the template for that slot with a props object containing all the data props passed to the slot from the child component. We need to let Vue know what data prop we want to access within a template content by specifying it with the following syntax:

```
<template #slot-name="{ propName }">
```

Or, we can specify the name of the props object to be used within the template content as follows:

```
<template #slot-name="slotProps">
```

Then within the template content, we can access a data prop by using `propName` or `slotProps. propName`, depending on which approach you use. Note here that you can change the `propName` value to any prop's name, and the same goes for `slotProps`. If the slot doesn't have a name, we will use `default` to denote `slot-name` instead.

For example, to access the `item` data prop passed to the slot in `PaginatedList`, we add the following to its parent:

```
<template #default="{ item }">
  {{ item.content }}
</template>
```

Our `template` section in `App.vue` with the parent of `PaginatedList` will now look as follows:

```
<template>
  <div>
```

```
      <PaginatedList :items="snacks">
        <template #default="{ item }">
          {{ item.content }}
        </template>
      </PaginatedList>
    </div>
  </template>
```

The `script` section (with snacks to render) will be as follows:

```
<script>
import PaginatedList from './components/PaginatedList.vue'
export default {
  components: {
    PaginatedList
  },
  data() {
    return {
      snacks: [
        {
          id: 'ready-salted',
          content: 'Ready Salted'
        },
        {
          id: 'cheese-onion',
          content: 'Cheese & Onion'
        },
        {
          id: 'salt-vinegar',
          content: 'Salt & Vinegar'
        },
      ]
    }
  }
}
</script>
```

We get the following output in the browser:

- Ready Salted
- Cheese & Onion
- Salt & Vinegar

Figure 4.19 – Snacks displayed using a scoped slot

And we have learned how scoped slots give components increased flexibility to delegate templating logic to consumers.

Now, let's learn how to implement a card component with the help of these named slots.

Exercise 4.04 – Implementing a card component using named slots

In this exercise, we will implement a card component using named slots. The card will have a title, image, and description sections. We will use slots to allow `title`, `image`, and `description` to be defined by a parent component.

To access the code file for this exercise, refer to `https://github.com/PacktPublishing/Frontend-Development-Projects-with-Vue.js-3/tree/v2-edition/Chapter04/Exercise4.04`.

Follow these steps to complete this exercise:

1. Use the application generated with `npm init vue@3` as a starting point, or within the root folder of the code repository, navigate to the `Chapter04/Exercise4.04` folder using the following commands in order:

    ```
    > cd Chapter04/Exercise4.04/
    > yarn
    ```

2. Open the exercise project in your VS Code (by using the `code .` command within the project directory), or in your preferred IDE.

3. We will start by creating a new `src/components/Card.vue` component that has a template that supports three named slots – `title`, `image`, and `description`:

    ```
    <template>
      <div>
        <slot name="image" />
        <slot name="title" />
        <slot name="description" />
    ```

```
    </div>
  </template>
```

4. We will then import our `Card.vue` component into the `script` section of a new `src/App.vue` file:

```
<script>
import Card from './components/Card.vue'
export default {
  components: {
    Card
  }
}
</script>
```

5. We can now use `Card` in our `template`:

```
<template>
  <div id="app">
    <Card>
      <template #image>
        <img src="https://picsum.photos/id/1015/300"
          />
      </template>
      <template #title>
        <h2>My Holiday picture</h2>
      </template>
      <template #description>
        <p>
          Here I can describe the contents of the
            picture.
        </p>
        <p>
          For example what we can see in the photo is
            a nice landscape.
        </p>
      </template>
    </Card>
```

```
    </div>
  </template>
```

6. Run the app, and the output will be as follows:

My Holiday picture

Here I can describe the contents of the picture.

For example what we can see in the photo is a nice landscape.

Figure 4.20 – Card component with an image, title, and description

With that, we have learned how different types of slots can help to create more generic components. Slots allow child components to defer the rendering of certain parts of themselves to their parent component (consumer).

As we learned, Vue provides an abstraction layer over the actual DOM. When it's crucial to access the DOM's elements directly, such as to integrate a DOM library, Vue provides a first-class way to do so with refs. We will learn about Vue references in the next section.

Understanding Vue refs

In Vue, **refs** are references to DOM elements or other component instances that have been mounted to the DOM.

One of the major use cases for refs is direct DOM manipulation and integration with DOM-based libraries (that usually take a DOM node they should mount to), such as an animation library.

We define refs by using the syntax `ref="name"` on a native element or child component in the template. In the following example, we will add a reference to the input element under the name `theInput`:

```
<template>
  <div id="app">
    <input ref="theInput" />
  </div>
</template>
```

Refs can be accessed from the Vue component instance through `this.$refs[refName]`. So, in the preceding example, where we had a ref defined as `ref="theInput"`, it can be accessed through `this.$refs.theInput`.

Now let's programmatically focus on the `input` field when clicking the **Focus Input** button, as follows:

```
<template>
  <div id="app">
    <input ref="theInput" />
    <button @click="focus()">Focus Input</button>
  </div>
</template>
<script>
export default {
  methods: {
    focus() {
      this.$refs.theInput.focus()
    }
  }
}
</script>
```

When clicking the **Focus Input** button, the input field will be focused, as shown in the following screenshot:

Figure 4.21 – Input focused on a button click

Note here that we can only access $refs once the component is mounted to the DOM. Hence this.$refs.theInput in our example is only available in the mounted() life cycle hook. Also, if you use <script setup>, there is no $refs available since there is no this and setup runs before the component instance is created. Hence to use DOM references with <script setup> or the setup hook, we use the ref() function from the Composition API instead, which we will discuss further in *Chapter 5, The Composition API*.

We have learned how to use $refs to access the DOM elements from the component. When you need select a DOM node directly, we recommend you use a ref instead of using the DOM API (querySelector/querySelectorAll).

In the following exercise, we will learn how the Countable library helps increase interactivity in a project.

Exercise 4.05 – Wrapping Countable.js in Vue application

Countable is a library that, given an element (usually an HTML textarea or input), will add live counts of paragraphs, words, and characters. Live metrics on the text being captured can be quite useful to increase interactivity in a project where editing text is a core concern.

One of the large use cases of refs in Vue is to be able to integrate with libraries that act directly on the DOM.

In this exercise, we will create a component with paragraph/word/character-counting functionality for content in a textarea by using Countable.js and Vue refs.

To access the code file for this exercise, refer to https://github.com/PacktPublishing/Frontend-Development-Projects-with-Vue.js-3/tree/v2-edition/Chapter04/Exercise4.05.

Work through the following steps to complete this exercise:

1. Use the application generated with npm init vue@3 as a starting point, or within the root folder of the code repository, navigate to the Chapter04/Exercise4.05 folder using the following commands in order:

    ```
    > cd Chapter04/Exercise4.05/
    > yarn
    ```

2. Open the exercise project in VS Code (using the code . command within the project directory), or in your preferred IDE.

3. Create a new `src/components/TextEditorWithCount.vue` component with a `textarea` that we will have a `ref` to:

```
<template>
  <div>
    <textarea
      ref="textArea"
      cols="50"
      rows="7"
    >
    </textarea>
  </div>
</template>
```

4. Next, we will import and render the component in `src/App.vue`:

```
<template>
  <div id="app">
    <TextEditorWithCount />
  </div>
</template>
<script>
import TextEditorWithCount from './components/
  TextEditorWithCount.vue'

export default {
  components: {
    TextEditorWithCount
  }
}
</script>
```

The application renders a `textarea` field, as follows:

Figure 4.22 – A bare textarea field, as rendered by the application

5. We now need to integrate `Countable`. We will import it and initialize it with `this.$refs.textArea`. We will also store the counts on the instance as `this.count`:

```
<script>
import * as Countable from 'countable'
export default {
  mounted() {
    Countable.on(this.$refs.textArea, (count) => {
      this.count = count
    })
  },
  data() {
    return {
      count: null
    }
  }
}
</script>
```

6. With a small update to `template`, we can display the counts we care about:

```
<template>
  <div id="app">
    <!-- textarea -->
    <ul v-if="count">
      <li>Paragraphs: {{ count.paragraphs }}</li>
      <li>Sentences: {{ count.sentences }}</li>
      <li>Words: {{ count.words }}</li>
```

```
          </ul>
        </div>
     </template>
```

Now, we can see the counts set to 0 when `textarea` is empty, as follows:

- Paragraphs: 0
- Sentences: 0
- Words: 0

Figure 4.23 – textarea with counts set to 0 when empty

If we drop some *Lorem ipsum* filler text into our `textarea`, the counts will update accordingly, as follows:

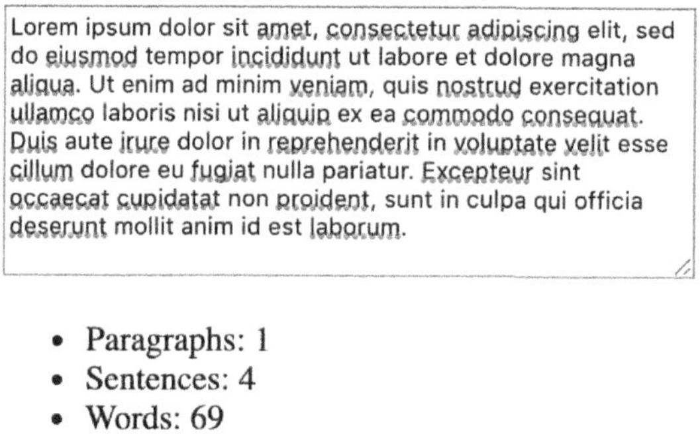

Lorem ipsum dolor sit amet, consectetur adipiscing elit, sed
do eiusmod tempor incididunt ut labore et dolore magna
aliqua. Ut enim ad minim veniam, quis nostrud exercitation
ullamco laboris nisi ut aliquip ex ea commodo consequat.
Duis aute irure dolor in reprehenderit in voluptate velit esse
cillum dolore eu fugiat nulla pariatur. Excepteur sint
occaecat cupidatat non proident, sunt in culpa qui officia
deserunt mollit anim id est laborum.

- Paragraphs: 1
- Sentences: 4
- Words: 69

Figure 4.24 – textarea with counts updated when filled

7. One last thing we need to do is remove the `Countable` event listener when the component is unmounted:

```
<script>
// imports
export default {
  mounted() {
```

```
      Countable.on(this.$refs.textArea, (count) => {
        this.count = count
      })
    },
    beforeUnmount() {
      Countable.off(this.$refs.textArea)


    },
    // other component properties
  }
</script>
```

This integration of a JavaScript/DOM library inside a Vue app is a key application of Vue refs. Refs allow us to pick from the existing ecosystem of libraries and wrap or integrate them into a component.

Vue refs are useful for integrating DOM libraries or for accessing DOM APIs directly.

To round off our examination of component composition, we need to know how to pass data from child components back to their parents, which we will explore next.

Using events for child-parent communication

We have already seen that props are used to pass data from a parent component to a child component. To pass data from a child component back to a parent component, Vue offers custom events.

In a component, we can emit an event using the $emit method; with this.$emit('eventName', payload) within <script>; or just with $emit within the template section.

Assuming we have got a reactive instance property, this.message, we could emit a send event with the message value in the script section using this.$emit. This could be the basis for a MessageEditor component:

```
<script>
export default {
  data () {
        return {
            message: null
        }
    },
  methods: {
    send() {
```

```
        this.$emit('send', this.message);
      }
    }
  }
</script>
```

In the same scenario, we could trigger a send event from the template section as follows:

```
<template>
  <div>
    <input v-model="message" />
    <button @click="$emit('send', message)">Emit inline
      </button>
  </div>
</template>
```

From a parent component, we can use v-on:event-name or the shorthand @event-name. event-name must match the name passed to $emit. Note eventName and event-name are not equivalent.

For instance, in the parent component we want to listen to the send event and modify some data accordingly. We bind @send with some event handler logic, which can be a JavaScript expression or a method declared using methods.

Vue will trigger this event handler and pass the event's payload object to it when applicable. You can use $event in the JavaScript expression of the template as the payload, as shown in the following example of the template section in App:

```
<template>
  <div id="app">
    <p>Message: {{ parentMessage }}</p>
    <MessageEditor @send="parentMessage = $event" />
    <button @click="parentMessage = null">Reset</button>
  </div>
</template>
```

We can also extract the JavaScript expression to a component's updateParentMessage method and bind it as follows:

```
<template>
  <div id="app">
```

```
    <p>Message: {{ parentMessage }}</p>
    <MessageEditor @send="updateParentMessage" />
    <button @click="parentMessage = null">Reset</button>
  </div>
</template>
<script>
import MessageEditor from './components/MessageEditor.vue'
export default {
  components: {
    MessageEditor
  },
  data() {
      return {
          parentMessage: null
      }
    },
  methods: {
    updateParentMessage(newMessage) {
      this.parentMessage = newMessage
    }
  }
}
</script>
```

Using either approach yields the same result. The full app should look as follows in the browser:

Message: Hello World!

Emit in Send Method   Emit inline
Reset

Figure 4.25 – Hello World! message being emitted from child-parent

Custom events support passing any JavaScript type as the payload. The event name, however, must be a String.

Registering events with <script setup> (or setup hook)

If you use <script setup>, since there is no component's options object, we can't define custom events using the emits field. Instead, we use the defineEmits() function from the vue package and pass all the relevant events' definitions to it.

For example, in the MessageEditor component, we can rewrite the event-registering functionality with defineEmits() as follows:

```
<script setup>
import { defineEmits, ref } from  'vue'

const message = ref(null)
const emits = defineEmits(['send'])

emits('send', message.value);
</script>
```

defineEmits() returns a function that we can trigger in the same concept with this.$emits. We will certainly need to use ref() to declare a reactive data message for this component, the usage of which we will discuss further in *Chapter 5, The Composition API*.

Now, let's complete an activity based on everything we've learned so far.

Activity 4.01 – A local message view with reusable components

To access the code file for this activity, refer to https://github.com/PacktPublishing/Frontend-Development-Projects-with-Vue.js-3/tree/v2-edition/Chapter04/Activity4.01

This activity aims to leverage components, props, events, and refs to render a chat interface where the user can add messages and have them displayed.

Follow these steps to complete this activity:

1. Create a MessageEditor component (in src/components/MessageEditor.vue) that displays a textarea field to the user.

2. Add a message reactive instance variable to MessageEditor, defaulted to ''.

3. Listen to change events for textarea and set the value of message to the value of the content of textarea (it is exposed as the value of the event).

4. Add a Send button that, on click, emits a send event with message as the payload.

5. Add a main component to src/App.vue that renders MessageEditor.

6. In App, listen to send events from MessageEditor and store each message in a messages reactive data variable (messages is an array).

7. Create a MessageFeed (in src/components/MessageFeed.vue) that has a required messages prop, which is an array.

8. In MessageFeed, render each passed message from the messages prop in a paragraph (the p element).

9. Import and render MessageFeed into App, binding the messages app instance variable as the messages prop of MessageFeed.

10. Improve MessageEditor so that the message is reset and focused after the message is sent. To do this, we will need to set textarea.value using a ref, reset the message instance variable accordingly, and use textarea.focus() to focus on textarea programmatically.

> **Note**
>
> The easier way to reset textarea would have been to use v-model="message" in the first place instead of binding @change and manually syncing textarea.value to message.

The expected output is as follows:

Hello World!

Hello JavaScript!

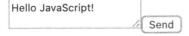

Figure 4.26 – Message app with Hello World! and Hello JavaScript! sent

Summary

Throughout this chapter, we have explored how to enable data communication between components using props and custom events. We explored slots and saw how we enable UI template customization for a component from its parent. We also learned how to use refs to unlock integration opportunities with third-party JavaScript or DOM libraries by allowing us to access DOM elements directly.

We're now able to create and compose components that clearly define their interfaces with inputs (props and slots) and outputs (rendered templates and events), while also visiting commonly faced use cases (such as wrapping a DOM library).

In the next chapter, we'll look at advanced component composition patterns and techniques that enable better code reuse.

5

The Composition API

In the previous chapter, we learned how to establish data communication between nesting components using props, refs, and slots.

This chapter will introduce us to a new and scalable approach to writing components with the `setup()` lifecycle hook – the Composition API. By the end of the chapter, you will be able to write isolated composables (or custom hooks) to reuse in multiple components by using the Composition API with the `setup()` method, and build a scalable component system for your Vue project beyond the classic Options API.

This chapter covers the following topics:

- Creating components with the `setup()` lifecycle method
- Working with data
- Understanding composable lifecycle functions
- Creating your composable (custom hook)

Technical requirements

In this chapter, you need to set up a basic Vue project following the instructions in *Chapter 1*, *Starting Your First Vue Project*. Creating a single file Vue component is recommended to practice the examples and concepts mentioned easily.

The Node version has to be below v20 (preferable Yarn 1.22 and Node version above 16 and up to 19.x, and npm up to version 9.x.

You can find this chapter's source code here: `https://github.com/PacktPublishing/Frontend-Development-Projects-with-Vue.js-3/tree/v2-edition/Chapter05`.

Creating components with the setup() lifecycle method

Starting from Vue 3.x, the Vue team has introduced the Composition API as a new way to compose Vue components within the `setup()` lifecycle method. As mentioned in *Chapter 1*, *Starting Your First Vue Project*, `setup()` is the first hook the Vue engine will run in a component's lifecycle before the `beforeCreate()` hook. At this point, Vue hasn't defined a component instance or any component data.

This lifecycle method runs once before the initialization and creation of a component and is part of the Options API. The Vue team has dedicated `setup()` to working with Composition API and any custom hooks (composables) written with the Composition API as an alternative approach to creating reactive components besides the Options API.

You can start using the `setup()` method with the following syntax:

```
setup(props, context) {
  // ...
  return {
  //...
  }
}
```

`Setup()` accepts two arguments, which are as follows:

- `props`: All the reactive props data is passed to the component from its parent. You need to declare the props using the `props` field in the Options API as usual. Note that you shouldn't de-structure the `props` object to avoid losing the reactivity for the de-structured field.

- `context`: These are all the non-reactive fields for the component, such as `attrs`, `slots`, `emit`, and `expose`.

`setup()` returns an object containing the component's internal reactive/static data state, its methods, or a render function.

The equivalent version of `setup()` without the Options API is `<script setup>`. The Vue engine will compile the code defined within the `<script setup>` section into the appropriate code block inside `setup()`, as seen in the following example:

```
<script setup>
const message = 'Hello World'
</script>
```

The preceding code is equal to the following using `setup()`:

```
<script>
export default {
  setup() {
    const message = 'Hello World'
    return {
```

```
      message
    }
  }
}
</script>
```

In both preceding examples, we define an internal data state – message – for our component. We then can display message in the <template> section as required.

With <script setup>, if you need to use the props parameter, you need to import defineProps() from the vue package and define the props within the <script setup> section, as shown in the following example:

```
<script setup>
import { defineProps } from 'vue'
const { userName } = defineProps({ userName: string }
</script>
```

In the preceding example, userName is now available in the template section as the component's data props. You can also do something similar with defineEmits() for all the custom events of a component, useSlots() and useAttrs() for the component's slots, and attrs when using <script setup> instead of the setup() method.

Next, let's create our first component with the setup() method.

Exercise 5.01 – creating a greeting component with setup()

In this exercise, we will create a component that renders a pre-defined greeting message using setup(), and then rewrite it using <script setup>.

To access the code file for this exercise, refer to https://github.com/PacktPublishing/Frontend-Development-Projects-with-Vue.js-3/tree/v2-edition/Chapter05/Exercise5.01.

Follow the given steps to complete this exercise:

1. Use the application generated by npm init vue@3 as a starting point, or within the root folder of the code repository, navigate into the Chapter05/Exercise5.01 folder by using the following commands in order:

    ```
    > cd Chapter05/Exercise5.01/
    > yarn
    ```

2. Open the exercise project in VS Code (by using the `code .` command within the project directory) or your preferred IDE.

3. Create a new file named `Greeting.vue` in the `./src/components` directory.

4. Start by scaffolding the component with empty `template` and `script` tags:

```
<template>
  <div>Empty</div>
</template>
<script>
export default {}
</script>
```

5. Next, we will implement the logic of our `setup()` method, which will return an internal data state, `greeting`, with a static value of `"Hello"`, and another internal data state, `who`, with a static value of `"John"`:

```
<script>
export default {
  setup() {
    const greeting = "Hello";
    const who = "John";
    return { greeting, who }
  }
}
</script>
```

6. In the `template` section, let's display the values of `greeting` and `who` as shown in the following code block:

```
<template>
  <div>{{ greeting }} {{ who }}</div>
</template>
```

7. Run the application using the following command:

    yarn dev

8. You will see the following when visiting your app in the browser:

```
Hello John
```

9. Add the `setup` attribute to your `<script>` tag:

    ```
    <script setup>
    //...
    </script>
    ```

10. Then, change the content within the `script` tag to the following:

    ```
    <script setup>
      const greeting = "Hello";
      const who = "John";
    </script>
    ```

11. The output of the browser should stay the same:

    ```
    Hello John
    ```

Next, we will explore how we can combine `setup()` and the render function, `h()`, from the Composition API to create a component.

Creating a component with setup() and h()

In many scenarios where you need to render a static functional component or a static component structure based on the context and props received, using `h()` and `setup()` can be helpful. The `h()` function syntax is as follows:

```
h(Element, props, children)
```

`h()` receives the following parameters:

- A string representing a DOM element (`'div'`, for instance) or a Vue component.
- The props to pass to the created component node, including native properties and attributes, such as `class`, `style`, and so on, and event listeners. This parameter is optional.
- The array of children for the component or object of the slot functions. This parameter is also optional.

Instead of returning the object containing a static internal data state and using the `template` section, `setup()` will return a function that returns the component node created by the `h()` function based on the parameters received. In the following example, we render a `div` element containing a `"Hello World"` message in blue:

```
<script>
import { h } from 'vue';
```

```
export default {
  setup() {
    const message = 'Hello World'
    return () => h('div', { style: { color: 'blue' } },
      message)
  }
}
</script>
```

And the browser will output as follows:

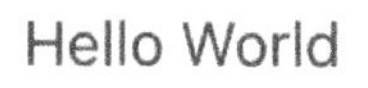

Hello World

Figure 5.1 – Hello World text in blue color

In the next exercise, we will practice creating a static component with setup() and h() based on the props received.

Exercise 5.02 – creating a dynamic greeting component with the setup() and h() functions

This exercise will create a component that renders a pre-defined greeting message depending on the props received, using setup() and h().

To access the code file for this exercise, refer to https://github.com/PacktPublishing/ Frontend-Development-Projects-with-Vue.js-3/tree/v2-edition/Chapter05/ Exercise5.02.

Follow the given steps to complete this exercise:

1. Use the application generated by npm init vue@3 as a starting point, or within the root folder of the code repository, navigate into the Chapter05/Exercise5.02 folder by using the following commands in order:

   ```
   > cd Chapter05/Exercise5.02/
   > yarn
   ```

2. Open the exercise project in VS Code (by using the code . command within the project directory) or your preferred IDE.

3. Create a new file named Greeting.vue in the ./src/components directory.

4. Start by scaffolding the component with empty `template` and `script` tags:

```
<template>
  <div>Empty</div>
</template>
<script>
export default {}
</script>
```

5. Next, define the acceptable props for `Greeting` using the `props` field, with two string props – `greeting` and `who` – as shown in the following code block:

```
export default {
  props: ['greeting', 'who']
}
```

6. We import the `h()` function from the `vue` package and implement `setup()` to return a render function that renders a `div` element that displays `greeting` and `who`, as follows:

```
import { h } from "vue";
export default {
  props: ["greeting", "who"],
  setup(props) {
    return () => h("div", `${props.greeting} ${props.
who}`);
  },
};
```

7. Open the `src/App.vue` file and import the `Greeting` component from `./src/components/Greeting.vue` into the `script` section:

```
<script setup>
import Greeting from './components/Greeting.vue'
</script>
```

8. We can use `Greeting` in the template:

```
<template>
  <div id="app">
    <Greeting greeting="Hey" who="JavaScript"/>
  </div>
</template>
```

9.   Run the application using the following command:

```
yarn dev
```

10. You will see the following when visiting your app in the browser:

```
Hey JavaScript
```

11. Within setup(), we want to check whether the parent passes the values for greeting or who or not:

```
const hasValue = props.greeting && props.who;
```

12. Based on the result, we will render a div element that displays the full message if there are values for both greeting and who, or a div element displaying an error message – "There is not enough information to display" – in red otherwise:

```
return () =>
  hasValue
    ? h("div", `${props.greeting} ${props.who}`)
    : h(
        "div",
        { style: { color: "red" } },
        "There is not enough information to
          display"
      );
```

13. In the parent component (App.vue), let's remove greeting value:

```
<template>
<div id="app">
  <Greeting who= "JavaScript"/>
</div>
</template>
```

14. The browser will now display the following message:

There is not enough information to display

Figure 5.2 – Error message when one of the props does not have value

That's it. You have now learned how to combine `setup()` and `h()` to compose a dynamic component based on its props. Next, we will explore how we can use different Composition APIs, such as `ref()`, `reactive()`, and `computed()`, to create a reactive data state for our component.

> **Note**
>
> We will use `<script setup>` from now on for readability and code convenience.

Working with data

In the Options API, we use the `data()` method to initialize a component's local state. By default, all the data properties received from `data()` are reactive, which can be overkill in many scenarios. Vue has introduced the `ref()` and `reactive()` functions, which allow us to decide which local states should be reactive and which shouldn't be.

Setting a reactive local state with ref()

`ref()` is a function that accepts a single input parameter as the reactive data's initial value and returns a reference object for the created reactive data state. We call this reference object a `ref` object. To start using `ref()`, you first need to import it from the `vue` package.

For example, we can create a reactive data called `isLightOn`, which accepts `false` as its initial value as follows:

```
import { ref } from 'vue';
const isLightOn = ref(false);
```

In the `template` section, you can access the value of `isLightOn` in the same way as before, as shown in the following code block:

```
<template>
  <div>Light status: {{ isLightOn }}</div>
</template>
```

However, within the `<script setup>` section of the `setup()` method, if you want to access the value of `isLightOn`, you need to use `isLightOn.value` instead of direct access, like in `template`. In the following example, we will create a component's method, `toggle`, that will output the value of `isLightOn` to the console:

```
const toggle = () => {
console.log(isLightOn.value)
};
```

In the `template` section, let's add a `button` element that triggers this method upon the user's click:

```
<button @click="toggle">Toggle</button>
```

Upon the button being clicked, the console outputs the value of `isLightOn`, which has the initial value of `false`, as seen in the following screenshot:

Figure 5.3 – Console output of the light status

Note that here if you output `isLightOn` and not `isLightOn.value`, the console outputs the `ref` object created by Vue as follows:

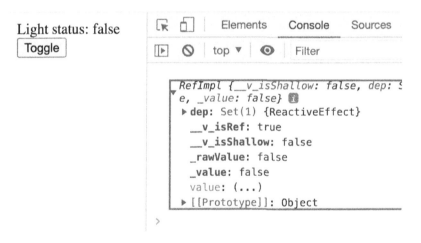

Figure 5.4 – Console output of the ref object for isLightOn

`isLightOn` is reactive and mutable, which means you can set its value directly using the `.value` field. We will modify the `toggle()` method to toggle the value of `isLightOn` instead. The code will become the following:

```
const toggle = () => {
  isLightOn.value = !isLightOn.value;
};
```

Now, whenever the user clicks on the **Toggle** button, isLightOn will update its value, and Vue will update the component accordingly, as seen in the following screenshot:

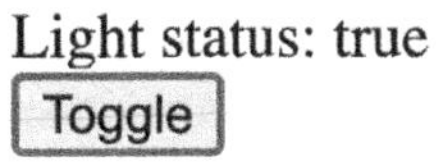

Light status: true

Toggle

Figure 5.5 – Light status updates to true upon Toggle being clicked

ref() is generally sufficient to create a reactive state for any data types, including primitive (boolean, number, string, and so on) and object types. However, for an object type, using ref() means that Vue will make the desired data object and its nested properties reactive and mutable. For example, we declare a reactive object, livingRoomLight, with ref() as shown in the following code block:

```
const livingRoomLight = ref({
    status: false,
    name: 'Living Room'
})
```

Then, we add two methods, one to modify its single property – status – and the second to replace the whole object with a new one, as shown in the following code block:

```
const toggleLight = () => {
    livingRoomLight.value.status =
        !livingRoomLight.value.status
}

const replaceLight = () => {
    livingRoomLight.value = {
        status: false,
        name: 'Kitchen'
    }
}
```

In the template section, let's display the details of livingRoomLight, as follows:

```
<div>
    <div>Light status: {{ livingRoomLight.status }}</div>
    <div>Light name: {{ livingRoomLight.name }}</div>
    <button @click="toggleLight">Toggle</button>
```

```
    <button @click="replaceLight">Replace</button>
  </div>
```

When a user clicks on **Toggle**, only the status changes its value, but if a user clicks on the **Replace** button, lightRoomLight now becomes the Kitchen light with different details, as shown in the following figure:

Figure 5.6 – Light name changed to Kitchen after clicking on Replace

Unfortunately, this mechanism of making the object and its nested properties reactive can lead to unwanted bugs and potential performance issues, especially for reactive objects with a complex hierarchy of nested properties.

In a scenario in which you only want to modify the whole object's value (replacing it with a new object) but not its nested properties, we suggest you use shallowRef(). In a scenario in which you only need to modify the object's nested properties (such as elements of an array object and each element's fields), you should use reactive() instead. We will take a look at the reactive() function next.

Setting a reactive local state with reactive()

Like ref(), the reactive() function returns a reference to a reactive object based on the initial value passed to it. Unlike ref(), reactive() only accepts object-type input parameters and returns a reference object whose value can be accessed directly without needing a .value field.

The following example shows how we define a reactive array of books, and a reactive book object, newBook, for the BookList component:

```
<script setup>
import { reactive } from "vue";

const newBook = reactive({
  title: "",
  price: 0,
  currency: "USD",
```

```
    description: "",
});


const books = reactive([]);
</script>
```

In template, we define a fieldset element that contains several input fields, each bound to an area of the newBook data using v-model, and a button element, Add, as follows:

```
<fieldset :style="{ display: 'flex', flexDirection: 'column'}">
        <label>
            Title:
            <input v-model="newBook.title" />
        </label>
        <label>
            Price:
            <input v-model.number="newBook.price" />
        </label>
        <label>
            Currency:
            <input v-model="newBook.currency" />
        </label>
        <label>
            Description:
            <input v-model="newBook.description" />
        </label>
        <button @click="addBook">Add</button>
    </fieldset>
```

The browser will display the following layout:

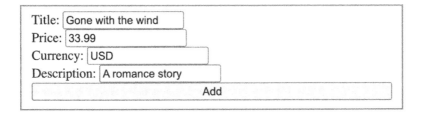

Figure 5.7 – Filling in the details of the new book before adding

We need to implement the `addBook` method, which will add a new book to the `books` list based on the information from `newBook` and clear up the properties of `newBook`, as in the following code:

```
const addBook = () => {
  books.push({
    ...newBook,
  });

  newBook.title = "";
  newBook.price = 0;
  newBook.currency = "USD";
  newBook.description = "";
};
```

Note that here, we don't push `newBook` directly to `books` but rather clone its properties to the new object using the spread literal, ..., instead. `reactive()` only creates a proxy version of the original object passed to it. Hence, if you don't clone `newBook` before adding it to `books`, any changes made to its properties later will also be reflected in the element added to the `books` list.

Now, after filling in a new book's details, open your browser's developer tools, and in the **Vue** tab, you should see the component's local data and methods nested in the `setup` section, as shown in the following figure:

```
▼ setup
  ▼ books: Reactive
  ▼ newBook: Reactive
      currency: "USD"
      description: "A romance story"
      price: 33.99
      title: "Gone with the wind"
  ▼ setup (other)
      addBook: function addBook()
```

Figure 5.8 – The component's setup section in Vue Devtools

All the reactive data created with `reactive()` will have the `Reactive` text indicator (for `ref()`, it will be the `Ref` indicator). Once you click on the **Add** button, you will see the `books` array updated with the new values, while `newBook` is reset to its original value in Devtools, as shown in *Figure 5.8*:

```
▼ books: Reactive
  ▼ 0: Object
      currency: "USD"
      description: "A romance story"
      price: 33.99
      title: "Gone with the wind"
  ▼ newBook: Reactive
      currency: "USD"
      description: ""
      price: 0
      title: ""
```

Figure 5.9 – How the array of books looks after adding a new book

You can also use shallowReactive() to limit the reactivity mechanism to apply only to the root's properties and not their descendants. By doing so, you can avoid performance issues caused by too many reactive fields within a complex data object.

At this point, we have learned how to use ref() and reactive() to define reactive data depending on its type and use cases. Next, we are going to apply what we learned to write a reactive component using these two functions.

Exercise 5.03 – binding a component with ref() and reactive()

In this exercise, you will use ref() to define a search box for blogs, and reactive() to define different reactive blog lists, in which you can favorite a blog.

To access the code for this exercise, refer to https://github.com/PacktPublishing/Frontend-Development-Projects-with-Vue.js-3/tree/v2-edition/Chapter05/Exercise5.03.

We are going to implement a component that receives the user's first name and last name and accepts multi-lingual input, and displays the user's full name and the number of languages received accordingly by performing the following steps:

1. Use the application generated by npm init vue@3 as a starting point, or within the root folder of the code repository, navigate into the Chapter05/Exercise5.03 folder by using the following commands in order:

    ```
    > cd Chapter05/Exercise5.03/
    > yarn
    ```

2. Open the exercise project in VS Code (by using the code . command within the project directory), or your preferred IDE.

3. Let's create a new Vue component called `BlogGallery` by adding the `BlogGallery.vue` file to the `./src/components/` folder.

4. Open `BlogGallery.vue` and let's create the code block structure for the Vue component as follows:

```
<template>
</template>
<script setup>
</script>
```

5. Within the `<script setup>` section, we define our reactive data – `searchTerm` – for the search input with an empty string as its initial value using `ref()`:

```
import { ref, reactive } from 'vue';
const searchTerm = ref('');
```

6. We will define our reactive blog list – `blogs` – with each item containing `title`, `description`, `author`, and `isFavorite` fields as follows:

```
const blogs = reactive([{
    title: 'Vue 3',
    description: 'Vue 3 is awesome',
    author: 'John Doe',
    isFavorite: false
}, {
    title: 'Vue 2',
    description: 'Vue 2 is awesome',
    author: 'John Doe',
    isFavorite: false
}, {
    title: 'Pinia state management',
    description: 'Pinia is awesome',
    author: 'Jane Smith',
    isFavorite: false
}, {
    title: 'Vue Router',
    description: 'Vue Router is awesome',
    author: 'Jane Smith',
    isFavorite: false
}, {
```

```
            title: 'Testing with Playwright',
            description: 'Playwright is awesome',
            author: 'Minnie Mouse',
            isFavorite: false
        }, {
            title: 'Testing with Cypress',
            description: 'Cypress is awesome',
            author: 'Mickey Mouse',
            isFavorite: false
        }]);
```

7. In the `<template>` section, we will bind `searchTerm` to an input field with a `placeholder` element of `"Search by blog's title"`, and a `label` element of `What are you searching for?`, as shown in the following code block:

```
<label>
    What are you searching for?
    <input
        type="text"
        v-model="searchTerm"
        placeholder="Search by blog's title"
    />
</label>
```

8. Then, we add a `<ul>` element, use `v-for` to iterate through `blogs`, and render a list of `<li>` elements. Each `<li>` element contains `<article>`, in which there is `<h3>` for the title, `<h4>` for the author's name, `<p>` for description, and a `<button>` element for adding the blog to your favorites:

```
<ul>
    <li v-for="(blog, index) in blogs" :key="index">
        <article>
            <h3>{{ blog.title }}</h3>
            <h4>{{ blog.author }}</h4>
              <p>{{ blog.description }}</p>
              <button>Add to favorite</button>
        </article>
    </li>
</ul>
```

9. Navigate back to the `<script setup>` section, where we will add the implementation for a `toggleFavorite()` method, which receives index and toggles the `blogs[index].isFavorite` value:

```
const toggleFavorite = (index) => {
  blogs[index].isFavorite = !blogs[index].isFavorite;
}
```

10. Go back to the `<template>` section. We will bind the `toggleFavorite()` method to the `button` element created and change its name according to the status of `isFavorite`:

```
<button @click="toggleFavorite(index)">
  {{
    blog.isFavorite ? 'Remove from favorites' : 'Add
      to favorites'
  }}
</button>
```

11. We need to filter the blogs according to `searchTerm`, so let's add another method to return a sorted list – `getFilteredBlogs()` – which will produce a filtered array of blogs according to the blog titles, as follows:

```
const getFilteredBlogs = () => {
    return blogs.filter(
      blog => blog.title.toLowerCase().includes(
        searchTerm.value.toLowerCase()
        )
      );
};
```

12. Then, in the `template` section, replace `blogs` in the `v-for` iteration with `getFilteredBlogs()`, as seen in the following code block:

```
<li v-for="(blog, index) in getFilteredBlogs()"
:key="index">
```

13. We need to add some basic CSS styling to make our component prettier, as follows:

```
<style scoped>
label {
    display: flex;
    flex-direction: column;
}

li {
    list-style: none;
    gap: 10px;
    width: 200px;
}

ul {
    display: flex;
    flex-wrap: wrap;
    gap: 10px;
    padding-inline-start: 0px;
}
</style>
```

14. Now, in App.vue, import the BlogGallery component into <script setup>:

```
<script setup>
import BlogGallery from "./components/BlogGallery.vue";
</script>
```

15. Render BlogGallery in the template section:

```
<template>
  <BlogGallery />
</template>
```

16. Finally, run the application using the following command:

```
yarn dev
```

17. Go to the browser. You will see the list displayed and a search box with an empty value, as in the following screenshot:

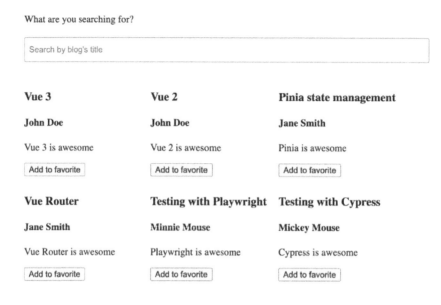

Figure 5.10 – How BlogGallery looks in the browser

18. When typing in a search term, the application will display the filtered list accordingly, as shown in the following screenshot:

Figure 5.11 – Only filtered blogs are displayed according to the user's input

With the preceding exercise, you have learned how to define reactive data for a component using `ref()` and `reactive()`.

In theory, you can use `ref()` and `reactive()` together to create new reactive data from other reactive data. However, we strongly recommend not doing so due to the performance complications of the wrapping/unwrapping reactivity mechanism in Vue. For this kind of scenario, you should use the `computed()` function, which we will explore next.

Computing a reactive state from another local state with computed()

Like `computed()` in the Options API, `computed()` is for creating new reactive data based on other reactive data for a component. It accepts a function that returns the reactive data value as its first parameter. It will return a read-only and cached reference object:

```
<script setup>
import { computed } from 'vue'
const computedData = computed(() => { //... })
</script>
```

Unlike reference objects returned from `reactive()` and `ref()`, we can't directly reassign their value. In the following example, we will compute a filtered version of a given `books` array using `computed()`, according to the matching term, `vue`:

```
import { computed, reactive, ref } from 'vue';

const books = reactive([{
    title: 'Vue 3',
    description: 'Vue 3 is awesome',
}, {
    title: 'Vue 2',
    description: 'Vue 2 is awesome',
}, {
    title: 'Pinia state management',
    description: 'Pinia is awesome',
}, {
    title: 'Vue Router',
    description: 'Vue Router is awesome',
}, {
    title: 'Testing with Playwright',
    description: 'Playwright is awesome',
}, {
```

```
        title: 'Testing with Cypress',
        description: 'Cypress is awesome',
    }]);


const searchTerm = ref('vue')


const filteredBooks = computed(
    () => books.filter(book => book.title.toLowerCase()
      .includes(searchTerm.value))
);
```

And in `template`, we will display `filteredBooks` using the following code:

```
<ul>
        <li v-for="(book, index) in filteredBooks"
          :key="index">
            <article>
                <h3>{{ book.title }}</h3>
                <p>{{ book.description }}</p>
            </article>
        </li>
    </ul>
```

In the browser, you will see only three books displayed as shown in the following figure:

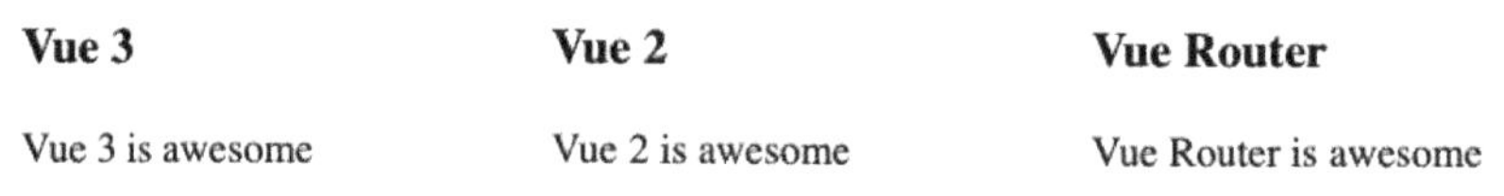

Vue 3   **Vue 2**   **Vue Router**

Vue 3 is awesome   Vue 2 is awesome   Vue Router is awesome

Figure 5.12 – List of books filtered by the vue term

Whenever there is any change to the `books` list or the search term used for filtering, Vue automatically updates and caches the value calculated for `filteredBooks` for display accordingly. In the **Vue** tab of the browser's Devtools, you can see `filteredBooks` displayed as part of the `setup` section, with the `Computed` text indicator as shown in *Figure 5.12*:

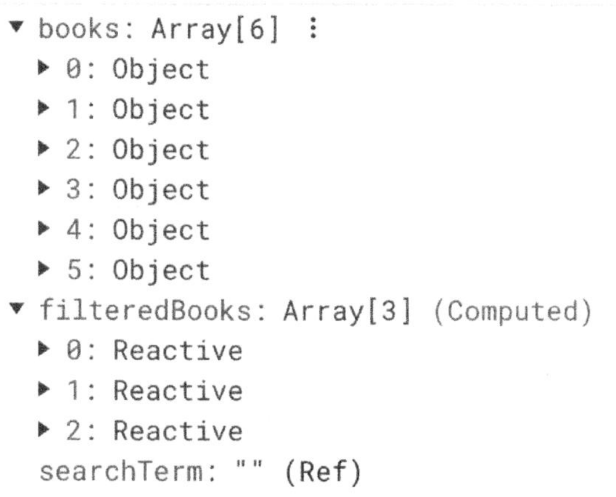

```
▼ books: Array[6]  ⋮
  ▶ 0: Object
  ▶ 1: Object
  ▶ 2: Object
  ▶ 3: Object
  ▶ 4: Object
  ▶ 5: Object
▼ filteredBooks: Array[3] (Computed)
  ▶ 0: Reactive
  ▶ 1: Reactive
  ▶ 2: Reactive
  searchTerm: "" (Ref)
```

Figure 5.13 – How filteredBooks looks in the Vue tab

Generally, computed() works in the same way as the compute properties in the Options API (*Chapter 2, Working with Data*). Computed data is a valuable Vue feature that allows developers to create reusable and readable code. You can also make the computed data writable by passing an object with a setter and getter to computed() instead of a function. However, we do not recommend doing so as general good Vue practice.

Next, we will practice implementing complex computed data for a Vue component using computed().

Exercise 5.04 – implementing computed data with computed()

In this exercise, you will use computed() to define the complex reactive data based on the existing one.

To access the code for this exercise, refer to https://github.com/PacktPublishing/ Frontend-Development-Projects-with-Vue.js-3/tree/v2-edition/Chapter05/ Exercise5.04.

We are going to implement a component that receives the user's first name and last name and accepts multi-lingual input and displays the user's full name and the number of languages received accordingly by performing the following steps:

1. Use the application generated by npm init vue@3 as a starting point, or within the root folder of the code repository, navigate into the Chapter05/Exercise5.04 folder by using the following commands in order:

    ```
    > cd Chapter05/Exercise5.04/
    > yarn
    ```

2. Open the exercise project in VS Code (by using the code . command within the project directory) or your preferred IDE.

3. Let's create a new Vue component called UserInput by adding the UserInput.vue file to the ./src/components/ folder.

4. Open UserInput.vue and let create the code block structure for the Vue component, as follows:

```
<template>
</template>
<script>
export default {
}
</script>
```

5. In <template>, create an input field for the first name, and use v-model to bind firstName to this field:

```
<input v-model="firstName" placeholder="First name" />
```

6. Create a second input field for the last name, and use v-model to bind the lastName data prop to this field:

```
<input v-model="lastName" placeholder="Last name" />
```

7. Create another input field for languages, only we will bind the *Enter keyup* event to a method called addToLanguageList this time, as shown in the following code block:

```
<input
  placeholder="Add a language"
  @keyup.enter="addToLanguageList" />
```

8. In <script setup>, define lastName, firstName, and languages as reactive using ref() and reactive(), as follows:

```
<script setup>
import { ref, reactive } from 'vue';

const firstName = ref('');
const lastName = ref('');
const languages = reactive([]);
</script>
```

9. Then, declare the `addToLanguageList` method, which receives an event and adds the event target's value to the language list if it is not empty:

```
const addToLanguageList = (event) => {
    if (!event.target.value) return;

    languages.push(event.target.value);
    event.target.value = '';
};
```

10. Import `computed()` from the `vue` package:

```
import { ref, reactive, computed } from 'vue';
```

11. Create a computed data variable called `fullName`:

```
const fullName = computed(
    ()=> '${firstName.value} ${lastName.value}'
);
```

12. Then, create another computed variable called `numberOfLanguages`, as follows:

```
const numberOfLanguages = computed(() => languages.
length);
```

13. Underneath your `input` fields, output the computed data using the h3 tag:

```
<h3 class="output">{{ fullName }}</h3>
```

14. Add another `<p>` element, which will display the number of languages next to the list of languages received, as shown in the following code block:

```
<p>
    Languages({{ numberOfLanguages }}):
        {{languages.toString()}}
</p>
```

15. We also add some basic scoped CSS styles to make the component prettier:

```
<style>
.container {
    margin: 0 auto;
    padding: 30px;
    max-width: 600px;
```

```
  }
  input {
    padding: 10px 6px;
    margin: 20px 10px 10px 0;
  }
  .output {
    font-size: 16px;
  }
</style>
```

16. Finally, run the application using the following command:

    yarn dev

17. Upon visiting http://localhost:3000 in the browser and keying in Maya for the first name, Shavin for the last name, and adding several languages (JavaScript, C++, and so on), the page will generate the following output:

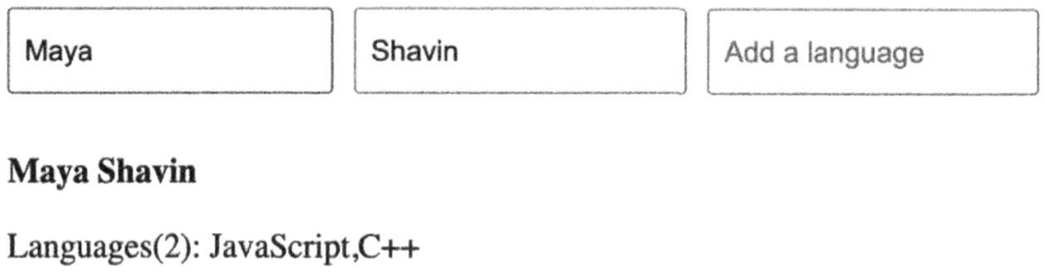

Maya	Shavin	Add a language

Maya Shavin

Languages(2): JavaScript,C++

Figure 5.14 – Output of the computed data will show the full name and list of languages

This exercise demonstrates how we can use computed() to define combined reactive data properties such as the first name and last name into a single output variable with fullName and calculate the number of languages reactively, which can be reused within the component.

Next, we will learn about using the watch() function from the Composition API to define our watchers.

Using watchers with watch()

In *Chapter 2, Working with Data*, we learned about watchers and how to enable watchers on data properties with the watch property from the Options API. The Composition API introduces the watch() function with the same context and slightly different syntax, as shown in the following code block:

```
const watcher = watch(source, handler, options)
```

`watch()` accepts three parameters, including the following:

- `source` as a single target data object or getter function (which returns the data's value) to watch, or an array of targets.

- `handler` is the function that Vue executes whenever `source` changes. The handler function receives `newValue` and `oldValue` as its source's next value and previous value respectively. It also accepts the third argument as its side-effect cleanup method. Vue will trigger this clean-up function before the next handler is invoked – if any are.

- `options` are the additional configurations for the watcher, including the following:

  - Two `boolean` flags: `deep` (whether Vue should watch over the nested properties of the source) and `immediate` (whether to invoke the handler immediately after the component is mounted).

  - `flush` as the execution order for the handler (`pre`, `post`, or `sync`). By default, Vue executes the handler in the `pre` order (before updating).

  - Two debugging callbacks, `onTrack` and `onTrigger`, for development mode.

The following example demonstrates how we can add a watcher manually to `searchTerm`:

```
import { ref, watch } from 'vue';

const searchTerm = ref('');

const searchTermWatcher = watch(
  searchTerm,
  (newValue, oldValue) => console.log(
    `Search term changed from ${oldValue} to ${newValue}`
  )
);
```

Vue will passively observe the changes in `searchTerm` and invoke the handler of `searchTermWatcher` accordingly. In the browser's console log, you will see the following records when changing the value of `searchTerm` in the input field:

```
Search term changed from  to p
Search term changed from p to pi
Search term changed from pi to pin
Search term changed from pin to pini
Search term changed from pini to
pinia
```

Figure 5.15 – The output logs whenever searchTerm changes in value

Unlike the watch property from the Options API, the watch() method returns a stopper function to stop the watcher whenever you no longer need to observe the target data. Also, in a scenario in which you explicitly wish to watch a nested data property, you can define the target source as a getter function that returns that specific data property. For example, if you wanted to watch the description property of a book data object, you would need the following code using the watch property from the Options API:

```
data() {
 return {
  book:{
    title: 'Vue 3',
    description: 'Vue 3 is awesome',
  }
 }
},
watch: {
  'book.description': (newValue, oldValue) => { /*…*/ }
}
```

With watch(), you only need to set a getter that returns book.description instead, as shown in the following code block:

```
const book = reactive({
    title: 'Vue 3',
    description: 'Vue 3 is awesome',
})
const bookWatcher = watch(
    () => book.description,
    (newValue, oldValue) => console.log(
      `Book's description changed from ${oldValue} to
```

```
        ${newValue}`
    )
);
```

By specifying the exact target data that you want to observe, Vue will not trigger the watcher's handler on the whole data object, avoiding undesired performance overhead.

Now, let's practice using a watcher in the next exercise.

Exercise 5.05 – using watchers to set new values

In this exercise, you will use watcher arguments to watch for changes to data properties, and then use this watcher to set variables via a method.

You can find the complete code for this exercise at `https://github.com/PacktPublishing/Frontend-Development-Projects-with-Vue.js-3/tree/v2-edition/Chapter05/Exercise5.05`.

We create a Vue component that displays the shop watcher's price before and after the discount, with an option to update the discount price, by following the given instructions:

1. Use the application generated by `npm init vue@3` as a starting point, or within the root folder of the code repository, navigate into the `Chapter05/Exercise5.05` folder by using the following commands in order:

    > **cd Chapter05/Exercise5.05/**

    > **yarn**

2. Open the exercise project in VS Code (by using the `code .` command within the project directory), or your preferred IDE.

3. Let's create a new Vue component called `PizzaItem` by adding the `PizzaItem.vue` file to the `./src/components/` folder.

4. Open `PizzaItem.vue` and let's create the code block structure for the Vue component, as follows:

    ```
    <template>
    </template>
    <script>
    export default {
    }
    </script>
    ```

5. Set up the document by adding discount, pizza, and newPrice objects:

```
import { ref, reactive, watch } from "vue";

const discount = ref(5);
const pizza = reactive({
  name: "Pepperoni Pizza",
  price: 10,
});
```

6. We want to listen for changes to the discount property by using the watch() function imported from the vue package. Upon discount changing, we manually recalculate the value for newPrice as follows:

```
watch(
  discount,
    (newValue) => {
      newPrice.value = pizza.price - (pizza.price *
        newValue)/ 100;
    },
    {
      immediate: true
    }
);
```

Notice that here, we set immediate to true so that Vue triggers this handler immediately after mounting the component and updates newPrice with the correct value.

7. Now let's add a component method called updateDiscount. Inside the method, set the oldDiscount data prop to this.discount + 5:

```
const updateDiscount = () => {
  discount.value = discount.value + 5;
};
```

8. In the template section, we will display pizza.name, discount, the old price, and the new price for the pizza after discount has been applied, as follows:

```
<template>
  <div class="container">
    <h1>{{ pizza.name }}</h1>
    <div class="campaign-wrapper">
```

```
        Monday Special: {{ discount }}% off!
        <strike>Was ${{ pizza.price }}</strike>
        <strong> Now at ${{ newPrice }} ONLY</strong>
      </div>
    </div>
  </template>
```

9. Then, bind the `updateDiscount` method to a `button` element using `@click`:

```
<button @click="updateDiscount" class="decrease-btn">
    Get a discount!
</button>
```

Whenever a user clicks on the preceding button, Vue will trigger `updateDiscount()` to increase the `discount` value, hence invoking the handler to update the `newPrice` value accordingly.

10. Now, let's add some CSS styling to make it pretty:

```
<style scoped>
.container {
  margin: 0 auto;
  padding: 30px;
  max-width: 600px;
  font-family: "Avenir", Helvetica, Arial, sans-serif;
  margin: 0;
}
.campaign-wrapper {
  margin: 20px 0;
  display: flex;
  flex-direction: column;
}

button {
  display: inline-block;
  border-radius: 10px;
  font-size: 14px;
  color: white;
  padding: 10px 20px;
  text-decoration: none;
  margin-inline-end: 10px;
```

```
}
.decrease-btn {
  background: rgb(241, 34, 34);
}
</style>
```

11. In App.vue, import the component into <setup script> and render it in template as follows:

```
<template>
  <PizzaItem />
</template>

<script setup>
import PizzaItem from "./components/PizzaItem.vue";
</script>
```

12. Finally, run the application using the following command:

    yarn dev

13. Upon visiting http://localhost:3000 in the browser, the output of the preceding command will be as follows:

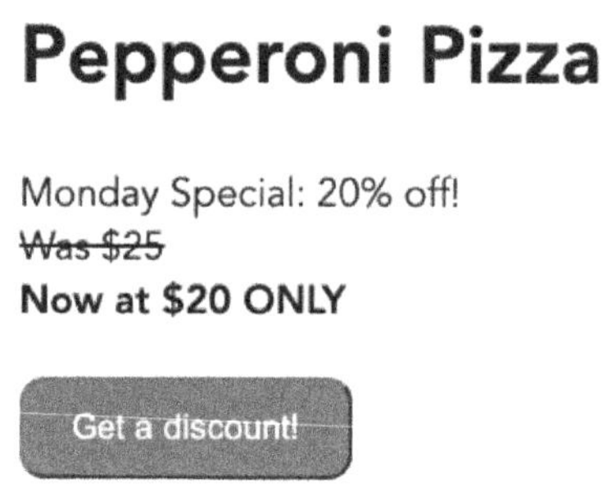

Pepperoni Pizza

Monday Special: 20% off!

~~Was $25~~

Now at $20 ONLY

Get a discount!

Figure 5.16 – An example output of the pizza sales

14. Now, let's add a watcher explicitly for the pizza.price field, and perform the same recalculation of newPrice, as shown in the following code block:

```
watch(
  () => pizza.price,
```

```
    (newValue) => {
      newPrice.value = newValue - (newValue *
        discount.value) / 100;
    }
);
```

15. We also add another method called `increasePrice()` to increase the pizza's price whenever triggered:

```
const increasePrice = () => {
  pizza.price = pizza.price + 5;
};
```

16. In the `template` section, we add another button to allow users to click to increase the pizza's price, hence updating the new discounted price accordingly:

```
<button @click="increasePrice" class="increase-btn">
  Increase the price!
</button>
```

17. In the `style` section, we also add a different `background` color for the preceding button:

```
.increase-btn {
  background: rgb(34, 100, 241);
}
```

18. Navigate back to the main browser's screen, and now you will see the updated layout with an additional button, as shown in the following screenshot:

Pepperoni Pizza

Monday Special: 20% off!
~~Was $25~~
Now at $20 ONLY

Figure 5.17 – Pizza sales with the option to modify the price

19. Upon clicking on the **Increase the price!** button, you will see the price and the discounted price change, as in the following screenshot:

Pepperoni Pizza

Monday Special: 20% off!
~~Was $30~~
Now at $24 ONLY

Get a discount!   Increase the price!

Figure 5.18 – The prices changed after clicking on the Increase the price! button

In this exercise, we explored how we can use watch() within <script setup> to dynamically observe and manipulate data when changes are applied.

The next section will explore how we can use the lifecycle functions from the Composition API to set up the lifecycle hooks.

Understanding composable lifecycle functions

In *Chapter 1*, *Starting Your First Vue Project*, we learned about the component's lifecycle and its available hooks in Vue's Options API. In the Composition API, these lifecycle hooks are now available as standalone functions and need to be imported from the vue package before use.

Generally, the lifecycle functions in the Composition API are similar to the ones from the Options API, with a prefix of on. For example, beforeMount() in the Options API is onBeforeMount() in the Composition API, and so on.

The following is the list of available lifecycle functions from the Composition API, ready to use within the setup() method or <script setup>:

- onBeforeMount(): Before the first render of the component

- onMounted(): After rendering and mounting the component to the DOM

- onBeforeUpdate(): After starting the component's update process, but before the actual rendering of the updated component

- onUpdated(): After rendering the updated component

- onBeforeMount(): Before the process of unmounting the component starts

- onUnmounted(): After the component's instance has been destroyed

Since we use `setup()` or `<script setup>` to define the component's data and internal logic in combination with other Composition API, there is no need for equivalent versions of `created()` and `beforeCreate()` from the Options API.

All the lifecycle methods from the Composition API receive a callback function as their arguments. Vue will invoke this callback function whenever applied.

Let's do an exercise to learn how to use these lifecycle methods in your Vue component.

Exercise 5.06 – using the lifecycle functions to control the data flow

In this exercise, we will learn how and when to use Vue's lifecycle hooks, and when they are triggered by using JavaScript alerts. By the end of the exercise, we will understand and be able to use multiple lifecycle functions from the Composition API.

To access the code file for this exercise, refer to `https://github.com/PacktPublishing/Frontend-Development-Projects-with-Vue.js-3/tree/v2-edition/Chapter05/Exercise5.06`.

We will build a list of different elements, demonstrating how to add different quantities to a cart. Then, we will display the updated cart's total value in a currency format by performing the following:

1. Use the application generated by `npm init vue@3` as a starting point, or within the root folder of the code repository, navigate into the `Chapter05/Exercise5.06` folder by using the following commands in order:

    ```
    > cd Chapter05/Exercise5.06/
    > yarn
    ```

2. Run the application using the following command:

    ```
    yarn dev
    ```

3. Open the exercise project in VS Code (by using the `code .` command within the project directory) or your preferred IDE.

4. Create a new Vue component file named `Exercise5-06.vue` under the `src/components` directory.

5. Inside `Exercise5-06.vue`, we will start by creating an array of data to iterate through in a `list` element, set the key to n, and output the value, `{{item}}`, inside of the `<li>` element using curly braces:

    ```
    <template>
      <div>
    ```

```
      <h1>Vue Lifecycle hooks</h1>
      <ul>
        <li v-for="(item, n) in list" :key="n">
          {{ item }}
        </li>
      </ul>
    </div>
  </template>
  <script setup>
  import { ref } from "vue";
  const list = ref([
    "Apex Legends",
    "A Plague Tale: Innocence",
    "ART SQOOL",
    "Baba Is You",
    "Devil May Cry 5",
    "The Division 2",
    "Hypnospace Outlaw",
    "Katana ZERO",
  ]);
```

6. Import all the lifecycle functions from the vue package, as shown in the following code block:

```
import {
  ref,
  onMounted,
  onBeforeMount,
  onUpdated,
  onBeforeUpdate,
  onUnmounted,
  onBeforeUnmount,
} from "vue";
```

7. Define the callbacks for onBeforeMount() and onMounted() to trigger an alert displaying the relevant message:

```
onMounted(() => {
  alert("mounted: DOM ready to use");
```

```
  });

  onBeforeMount(() => {
    alert("beforeMount: DOM not ready to use");
  });
```

8. When you refresh your browser, you should also see these alerts before you see your list load on the page:

Figure 5.19 – Observing the onBeforeMount() hook alert

9. The following screenshot displays the onMounted() hook alert after the onBeforeMount() hook:

Figure 5.20 – Observing the onMounted() hook alert after the onBeforeMount() hook

10. Add a new button element inside your <li> element that renders the item output. Use a @click directive to bind this button to a method called deleteItem and pass the item value as an argument:

```
<template>
  <div>
    <h1>Vue Lifecycle hooks</h1>
    <ul>
      <li v-for="(item, n) in list" :key="n">
        {{ item }}
        <button @click="deleteItem(item)">
          Delete</button>
      </li>
```

```
        </ul>
      </div>
    </template>
```

11. Add a method called `deleteItem` into a `methods` object above your hooks to pass `value` as an argument and filter out items from the `list` array based on this value. Then, replace the existing list with the new list:

```
const deleteItem = (value) => {
  list.value = list.value.filter((item) => item !==
    value);
};
```

12. Add `onBeforeUpdate()` and `onUpdated()` and set an alert inside them:

```
onUpdated(() => {
  alert("updated: virtual DOM will update after you
    click OK");
});

onBeforeUpdate(() => {
  alert(
    "beforeUpdate: we know an update is about to
      happen, and have the data"
  );
});
```

When you delete a list item by clicking on the **Delete** button in your browser, you should see these alerts. For example, when deleting the first item in the list, `onBeforeUpdated()` will trigger the handler:

Figure 5.21 – onBeforeCreated is called first after clicking on any Delete button

Then, onUpdated is triggered as shown in the following screenshot:

Figure 5.22 – onUpdated is called when the Vue engine finishes updating the component

13. Continue adding onBeforeUnmount() and onUnmounted() to the component options as function properties. Set an alert inside these hooks so that you can see when they are triggered:

```
onUnmounted(() => {
  alert("unmounted: this component has been
    destroyed");
});

onBeforeUnmount(() => {
  alert("beforeUnmount: about to blow up this
    component");
});
```

14. Add a new string to your list array – for example, testing unmounted hooks:

```
const list = ref([
  "Apex Legends",
  "A Plague Tale: Innocence",
  "ART SQOOL",
  "Baba Is You",
  "Devil May Cry 5",
  "The Division 2",
  "Hypnospace Outlaw",
  "Katana ZERO",
  'testing unmounted hooks',
]);
```

15. You should see the unmount alerts according to this order: `onBeforeUnmount` – `onBeforeMount` – `onUnmounted` – `onMounted`. An example output screen displaying an alert for `onBeforeUnmount` is shown in the following figure:

Figure 5.23 – Alert displaying when a component is about to be unmounted

Next, we will discuss how we can use the available methods from the Composition API and create our custom composable (or custom hook) to control the state of the component dynamically.

Creating your composable (custom hook)

In many scenarios, we want to group some components' logic into reusable code blocks for other components that share similar functionalities. In Vue 2.x, we use mixins to achieve this goal. However, mixins are not the best practical solution, and they can create code complexity due to the order of merging and invoking overlapping data and lifecycle hooks.

Starting from Vue 3.0, you can use the Composition API to divide the common data logic into small and isolated composables, using them to create a scoped data control in different components and return the created data if there is any. A composable is a regular JavaScript function that uses Composition API methods and performs data state management internally.

To get started, we create a new JavaScript (`.js`) file, which exports a function acting as the composable. In the following example, we create a `useMessages` composable, which returns a list of `messages` and some methods to modify the messages accordingly:

```
// src/composables/useMessages.ts
import { ref } from 'vue'

export const useMessages = () => {
  const messages = ref([
    "Apex Legends",
    "A Plague Tale: Innocence",
    "ART SQOOL",
    "Baba Is You",
```

```
    "Devil May Cry 5",
    "The Division 2",
    "Hypnospace Outlaw",
    "Katana ZERO",
  ]);

  const deleteMessage = (value) => {
   messages.value = messages.value.filter((item) => item
     !== value);
  };

  const addMessage = (value) => {
   messages.value.push(value)
  }
  return { messages, deleteMessage, addMessage }
 }
```

To use useMessages() in your component, you can import it into the component's <script setup> section, and retrieve the relevant data, as follows:

```
<script setup>
 import { useMessages } from '@/composables/useMyComposable'

 const { messages, deleteMessage, addMessage } = useMessages ()
</script>
```

Then, we can use messages, deleteMessage and addMessage returned from the composable in the component as its local data and methods, as shown in the following code block:

```
<template>
  <button @click="addMessage('test message')">
    Add new message
  </button>
  <ul>
    <li v-for="(message, n) in messages" :key="n">
      {{ message }}
      <button @click="deleteMessage(message)">
        Delete</button>
    </li>
```

```
    </ul>
  </template>
```

Since `messages`, `deleteMessage`, and `addMessage` are declared within the `useMessages()` function, every execution of `useMessages` returns different data instances, keeping the reactive data defined by the composable isolated and relevant only to the component that consumes it. With composables, components share logic, not data. You can also compose a new composable based on another composable, not only the Composition API.

That's it – you have learned how to create a simple composable with the Composition API. Next, let's apply what we learned so far about the Composition API and create our first composable.

Exercise 5.07 – creating your first composable

In this exercise, you will create a composable that will retrieve data from an external API, and return the data, the loading/error status of the request, and a search composable that we can reuse for different components.

You can find the complete code for this exercise on `https://github.com/PacktPublishing/Frontend-Development-Projects-with-Vue.js-3/tree/v2-edition/Chapter05/Exercise5.07`.

We will create a composable that fetches movies from an external source and another one that allows you to search through the list of movies by following the given instructions:

1. Use the application generated by `npm init vue@3` as a starting point, or within the root folder of the code repository, navigate into the `Chapter05/Exercise5.07` folder by using the following commands in order:

    ```
    > cd Chapter05/Exercise5.07/
    > yarn
    ```

2. Open the exercise project in VS Code (by using the `code .` command within the project directory), or your preferred IDE.

    Let's create a new composable called `useMovies` by adding `useMovies.js` to the `./src/composables` folder.

3. Within `useMovies.js`, we will add the following code to export the composable as a module for use in other files:

    ```
    import { } from 'vue';

    export const useMovies = () => {
      return {};
    };
    ```

4. We define the reactive data for the composable, such as `movies`, `isLoading`, and `error`, using `ref()` with the appropriate initial values:

```
import { ref } from 'vue';
export const useMovies = () => {
  const movies = ref([]);
  const isLoading = ref(false);
  const error = ref(null);
  return {};
};
```

5. Then, we will import the `onBeforeMount()` method and start fetching the movies from `https://swapi/dev/api/films` using the `fetch()` method, as shown in the following code block:

```
import { ref, onBeforeMount } from 'vue';
export const useMovies = () => {

//...
const getMovies = async () => {
    try {
      const response = await fetch(
        "https://swapi.dev/api/films");

      if (!response.ok) {
        throw new Error("Failed to fetch movies");
      }

      const data = await response.json();
      movies.value = data.results;
    } catch (err) {
    } finally {}
  };

  onBeforeMount(getMovies);
  //...
};
```

6. We also need to reset the `isLoading` value to indicate the fetching status and assign the value to `error` if any error has occurred:

```
const getMovies = async () => {
    isLoading.value = true;
    error.value = null;

    try {
        //...
    } catch (err) {
        error.value = err;
    } finally {
        isLoading.value = false;
    }
};
```

7. We return the reactive data so that other Vue components can use it:

```
import { ref, onBeforeMount } from 'vue';
export const useMovies = () => {
return {
    movies,
    isLoading,
    error,
    };
};
```

8. Next, create a new Vue component called `Movies` by adding the `Movies.vue` file to the `./src/components/` folder with the following code:

```
<template>
</template>
<script setup>
</script>
```

9. In the `script` section, we will import `useMovies` and use its return data – `movies`, `isLoading`, and `error`:

```
<script setup>
import { useMovies } from '../composables/useMovies.js'
```

```
const { movies, error, isLoading } = useMovies();
</script>
```

10. In the `template` section, we will display the loading state, error state, and the list of movies according to the statuses of `isLoading` and `error` using `v-if`:

```
<template>
  <h1>Movies</h1>
  <div v-if="isLoading">
    <p>Loading...</p>
  </div>
  <div v-else-if="error">
  <p>{{ error }}</p>
  </div>
  <div v-else>
    <ul>
      <li v-for="movie in movies" :key="movie.id">
        <article>
          <h3>{{ movie.title }}</h3>
          <h4>Released on: {{ movie.release_date }}
          </h4>
          <h5>Directed by: {{ movie.director }}</h5>
          <p>{{ movie.opening_crawl }}</p>
        </article>
      </li>
    </ul>
  </div>
</template>
```

11. Navigate to the browser and you will see the following output when the component loads the movies:

Loading...

Figure 5.24 – The loading state when fetching movies

12. After the component finishes fetching them, Vue automatically updates the view to display the list of movies, as shown in the following figure:

Movies

- **A New Hope**

  Released on: 1977-05-25

  Directed by: George Lucas

  It is a period of civil war. Rebel spaceships, striking from a hidden base, have won their first victory against the evil Galactic Empire. During the battle, Rebel spies managed to steal secret plans to the Empire's ultimate weapon, the DEATH STAR, an armored space station with enough power to destroy an entire planet. Pursued by the Empire's sinister agents, Princess Leia races home aboard her starship, custodian of the stolen plans that can save her people and restore freedom to the galaxy....

- **The Empire Strikes Back**

  Released on: 1980-05-17

  Directed by: Irvin Kershner

  It is a dark time for the Rebellion. Although the Death Star has been destroyed, Imperial troops have driven the Rebel forces from their hidden base and pursued them across the galaxy. Evading the dreaded Imperial Starfleet, a group of freedom fighters led by Luke Skywalker has established a new secret base on the remote ice world of Hoth. The evil lord Darth Vader, obsessed with finding young Skywalker, has dispatched thousands of remote probes into the far reaches of space....

- **Return of the Jedi**

Figure 5.25 – The list of movies after fetching happens successfully

13. If an error is encountered, the component displays an error state, as shown in the following example output:

← → C ⌂   ⓘ localhost:3000

TypeError: Failed to fetch

Figure 5.26 – Error state during fetching

14. Next, we will add another composable that gives the component the ability to search – `useSearch()` in `./src/composables/useSearch.js`.

15. This `useSearch()` composable receives a list of `items`, and a list of filters available for filtering with the default filter, `title`. The composable returns `searchTerm` for storing the input for searching, and the filtered array of items:

```
import { ref, computed } from 'vue';

export const useSearch = (items, filters = ['title']) =>
```

```
{
  const searchTerm = ref('');
  const filteredItems = computed(() => {
    return items.value.filter(item => {
      return filters.some(
        filter => item[filter].toLowerCase().includes(
          searchTerm.value.toLowerCase()
        );
      });
    });
  });

  return {
    searchTerm,
    filteredItems,
  }
}
```

16. Go back to `Movies.vue`. In the `script` section, we import `useSearch` and execute it to get `searchTerm` and filtered array of `filteredMovies` to use in our component:

```
<script setup>
import { useMovies } from '../composables/useMovies.js'
import { useSearch } from '../composables/useSearch.js'

const { movies, error, isLoading } = useMovies();
const {
  searchTerm,
  filteredItems: filteredMovies } = useSearch(movies);
</script>
```

17. In the `template` section, we add an input field that binds to `searchTerm` using `v-model` and replaces `movies` in the `v-for` iteration with `filteredMovies`:

```
<div v-else>
  <div>
    <label for="search">Search:</label>
```

```
      <input type="text" id="search"
        v-model="searchTerm" />
    </div>
    <ul>
      <li v-for="movie in filteredMovies"
        :key="movie.id">
        <!-- … -->
      </li>
    </ul>
  </div>
```

18. Navigate back to the browser. Now, you can load the movie list and start searching for the movie by title, as shown in the following screenshot:

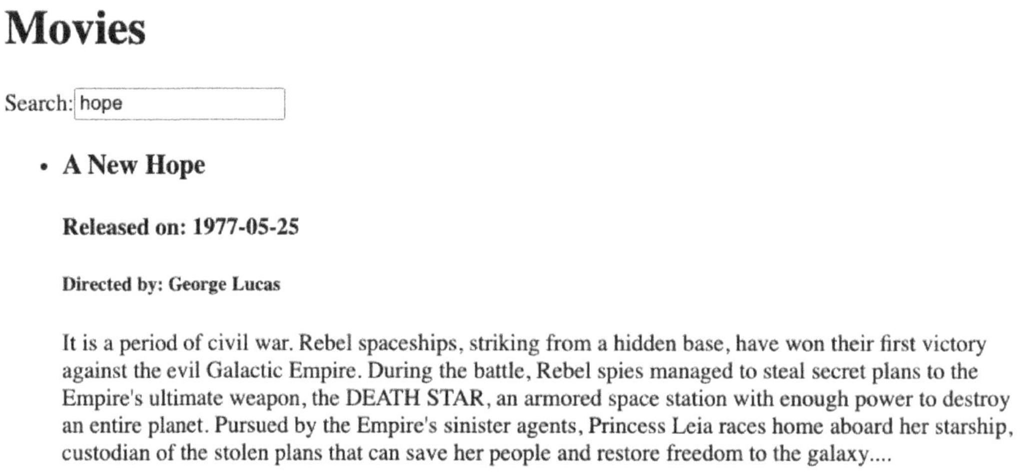

Movies

Search: hope

- **A New Hope**

   Released on: 1977-05-25

   Directed by: George Lucas

   It is a period of civil war. Rebel spaceships, striking from a hidden base, have won their first victory against the evil Galactic Empire. During the battle, Rebel spies managed to steal secret plans to the Empire's ultimate weapon, the DEATH STAR, an armored space station with enough power to destroy an entire planet. Pursued by the Empire's sinister agents, Princess Leia races home aboard her starship, custodian of the stolen plans that can save her people and restore freedom to the galaxy....

Figure 5.27 – Filtered movies by titles containing the word hope

Additionally, you can extend the search composable created to support a list of filters as input selection from the users, or re-format the fields of received movies to be friendlier for your application. In this exercise, we observed how we can create standalone and reusable logic for different use cases in a component with the Composition API, such as the ability to search. We also see how composables make our code cleaner and more organized.

Activity 5.01 – creating a BlogView component with the Composition API

To access the code file for this activity, refer to `https://github.com/PacktPublishing/Frontend-Development-Projects-with-Vue.js-3/tree/v2-edition/Chapter05/Activity5.01`

This activity aims to leverage your knowledge in combining different Composition APIs with components' props and events to create a view in which the user can see a list of blogs and add or remove any blog item.

This activity will require the use of a headless CMS, Contentful. The access keys and endpoints are listed in the solution.

Follow these steps to complete this activity:

1. Create a new Vue project with Vite.

2. Install the `contentful` dependency into your project.

3. Create another composable, `useListAction`, which receives a list of `items`, and returns the following:

    -   `addItem`: Adds a new item to the given list

    -   `deleteItem`: Deletes an item based on its ID

4. Create a `useBlogs` composable, which will fetch `blogs` from Contentful and use `useListActions()` to get the actions for the fetched `blogs`.

5. Define `useBlogs` to return the `blogs` list, a `loading` status, an `error` for the fetch status, and the `addItem` and `deleteItem` actions received from `useListActions`. The returned `blogs` should be an array of blog items with the following fields: `title`, `description`, `heroImage`, `publishDate`, and `id` (a slug).

6. Create a `useSearch` composable, which receives a list of `items`, and returns the following:

    -   `searchTerm`: The search value.

    -   `filters`: A list of fields to filter based on the user's choice. By default, it's `title`.

    -   `filteredItems`: The filtered list of the given items.

7. Create a `BlogEditor` component that displays several `input` fields for the `title` field, the author's name, the blog's `id` field, `textarea` for the blog's content, and a `button` element for saving the blog. When this button is clicked, `BlogEditor` emits an `addNewItem` event with the new blog's details as the payload and resets the fields.

8. Create a `Blogs` component that receives a list of `blogs`, an `isLoading` flag, and an `error` object as its props and then renders the state of the component according to `isLoading` and `error` and the details of each blog item on the UI when applicable.

9. In `Blogs`, use `useSearch()` on the list of `blogs` received as props and display a search `input` field to allow users to filter the blogs according to `title`.

10. Replace the original list iterations with the filtered list of blogs.

11. We then add `fieldset` containing two `input` fields of the `checkbox` type, each binding to the array of `filters`. The two `input` fields will also have corresponding labels of **By title** or **By content**, with values of `title` and `description` respectively.

12. Add a `button` element to each row of the blog rendered in the blog list, with a **Remove** label.

13. Also, define an `emit` event, `deleteBlog`, for `Blogs`.

14. On clicking on the **Remove** button, the component should emit a `deleteBlog` event with the `id` value of the blog item as its payload.

15. Create a `BlogView` component that renders `BlogEditor` and `Blogs`.

16. In `BlogView`, create a toggle flag, `showEditor`, which will display `BlogEditor` if true. Otherwise, the component will display an **Add new blog** button that toggles the `showEditor` value when clicked on.

17. `BlogView` will use `useBlogs()` and pass the data received from this composable (`blogs`, `isLoading`, `error`, and `deleteItem`) as props and events to `Blogs`. You should bind `deleteItem` to the `deleteBlog` custom event of `Blogs`.

18. `BlogView` also binds the `addItem` method returned from `useBlogs()` to the `addNewItem` event of `BlogEditor`.

19. Add some CSS styling to the components accordingly.

The expected outcome is as follows:

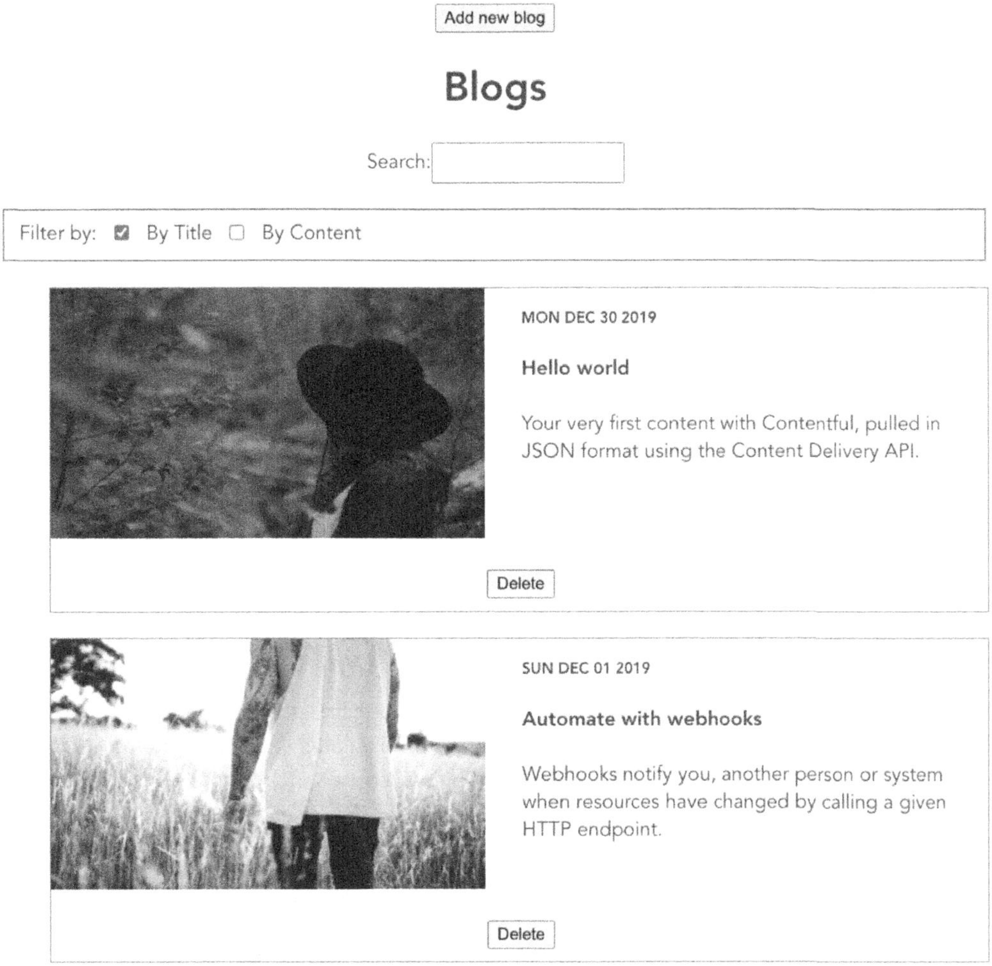

Figure 5.28 – Output when there aren't blogs to display and the user hasn't clicked on Add new blog

When a user clicks on **Add new blog**, the editor will appear as follows:

Figure 5.29 – Blog editor in action

Summary

Throughout this chapter, we learned about composing components using the Composition API and the setup() lifecycle hooks (or <script setup>) as an alternative to the Options API. We also learned how to use different Composition functions to create watchers and lifecycle callbacks to control our components' local states.

Finally, we learned how to create our custom composable function based on the Composition API and other composables, making our components more organized and readable in groups of similar logic.

In the next chapter, we will explore how we can create global components using plugins and mixins and compose dynamic components.

6

Global Component Composition

In the previous chapter, we learned how to use Composition API to create component logic and how to write custom reusable composables in a Vue application. There are many approaches to sharing similar logic between other components besides composables. In this chapter, we will learn how to use mixins, plugins, and how to render dynamic components.

By the end of this chapter, you will be ready to organize your code using mixins and plugins, achieve global composition, and keep code **DRY (Don't Repeat Yourself)** in any project. You will also understand the advantages and drawbacks of global composition, thus deciding the right approach to maximize a component's flexibility.

This chapter covers the following topics:

- Understanding mixins
- Understanding plugins
- Registering components globally
- Understanding component tags
- Writing functional components

Technical requirements

In this chapter, you need to set up a basic Vue project following the instructions in *Chapter 1, Starting Your First Vue Project*. It's recommended to create a single-file Vue component to practice the examples and concepts mentioned easily.

The Node version has to be below v20 (preferable Yarn 1.22 and Node version above 16 and up to 19.x, and npm up to version 9.x.

You can find this chapter's source code here: `https://github.com/PacktPublishing/Frontend-Development-Projects-with-Vue.js-3/tree/v2-edition/Chapter06`.

Understanding mixins

With mixins, we can add additional methods, data properties, and life cycle methods to a component's `option` object.

In the following example, we first define a mixin that contains a `greet` method and a `greeting` data field:

```
/** greeter.js */
export default {
  methods: {
    greet(name) {
        return `${this.greeting}, ${name}!`;
    }
  },
  data() {
    return {
      greeting: 'Hello'
    }
  }
}
```

Then we can use the `greeter` mixin by importing and assigning it as part of the `mixins` field in the component's `option` object, as follows:

```
<script>
import greeter from './mixins/greeter.js'
export default {
  mixins: [greeter]
}
</script>
```

`mixins` is an array that accepts any mixin as its element, while a `mixin` is in fact a component's `option` object. Mixins allow multiple components to share common data and logic definitions independently.

Once we add a mixin to a component, Vue will merge all the data and methods into the existing data and methods (mix in). A `mixin`'s properties and methods are then available in the component for use as its own data and methods, like how we use the `greet` method from the `greeter` mixin in the following template:

```
<template>
  <div>{{ greet('World') }}</div>
</template>
```

And in the browser, we will see the following message:

Hello World

Figure 6.1 – Display Hello World using a greeter mixin

When there is an overlapping of naming data properties or methods, Vue will prioritize the component's own options. We can explain this mechanism as the component adopting the mixin as its default options unless a similar declaration already exists. In this case, the instance will ignore the mixin's definition and take the component's definition instead.

For example, let's add a `data()` initializer, which returns `greeting` data with the value `Hi` to the component that uses the `greeter` mixin:

```
<script>
import greeter from './mixins/greeter.js'
export default {
  mixins: [greeter],
  data() {
    return {
      greeting: 'Hi'
    }
  }
}
</script>
```

greeter also defines greeting, but so does the component. In this case, the component *wins*, and we will see Hi displayed instead of Hello (as defined in the mixin), as in the following screenshot:

Hi World

Figure 6.2 – Component displays Hi World with overridden greeting data value

However, this mechanism doesn't apply to life cycle hooks. The hooks defined in the mixins will take priority in execution, and Vue always triggers the component's hooks last. If there is more than one mixin added to the component, the execution order follows their order of appearance in the mixins field.

We can observe this execution order in the following example. Let's create two mixins that implement the mounted life cycle hook – firstMixin and secondMixin, as follows:

```
const firstMixin = {
  mounted() {
    console.log('First mixin mounted hook')
  }
}
const secondMixin = {
  mounted() {
    console.log('Second mixin mounted hook')
  }
}
```

Then we also implement the same hook in the component, as shown in the following code block:

```
export default {
  mixins: [firstMixin, secondMixin],
  mounted() {
    console.log('Component mounted hook')
  }
}
```

The full code will look like the following:

```
<template>
  <div>Mixin lifecycle hooks demo</div>
</template>
```

```
<script>
const firstMixin = {
  mounted() {
    console.log('First mixin mounted hook')
  }
}
const secondMixin = {
  mounted() {
    console.log('Second mixin mounted hook')
  }
}
export default {
  mixins: [firstMixin, secondMixin],
  mounted() {
    console.log('Component mounted hook')
  }
}
</script>
```

The browser's console output for this component will be as follows:

```
First mixin mounted hook
Second mixin mounted hook
Component mounted hook
```

Figure 6.3 – Console log outputs demonstrate the order of
execution for the hooks of mixins and components

Now let's practice what we have learned so far by implementing your first mixin in the next exercise.

Exercise 6.01 – creating your mixin

In this exercise, we will create a mixin called `debugger`. It contains a `debug` method that receives `Object` as its argument and returns a string representing its structure using the `JSON.stringify()` function. This method is handy for printing data in a readable format when debugging Vue.js on the browser instead of the console.

To access the code file for this exercise, refer to `https://github.com/PacktPublishing/Frontend-Development-Projects-with-Vue.js-3/tree/v2-edition/Chapter06/Exercise6.01`.

Execute the following steps to complete this exercise:

1. Use the application generated with npm init vue@3 as a starting point, or within the root folder of the code repository, navigate to the Chapter06/Exercise6.01 folder, by using the following commands in order:

```
> cd Chapter06/Exercise6.01/
> yarn
```

2. Open the exercise project in your VS Code (by using the code . command within the project directory), or your preferred IDE.

3. Create a new src/mixins folder and a src/mixins/debugger.js file where we will define the skeleton of our mixin:

```
export default {}
```

4. We add a debug method under methods. The debug method will take an obj parameter and return the output of JSON.stringify for that input parameter. We will use JSON.stringify(obj, null, 2) to output two-space pretty-printed JSON:

```
export default {
  methods: {
    debug(obj) {
      return JSON.stringify(obj, null, 2)
    }
  }
}
```

5. We are now able to import the debugger mixin in src/App.vue and register it under the mixins property:

```
<script>
import debug from './mixins/debugger.js'
export default {
  mixins: [debugger],
}
</script>
```

6. To see the `debug` method in action, we will add a `data` method that returns a `myObj` data property and a `created` hook where we will compute the output of debug for `myObj`:

```
<script>
// imports
export default {
  // other component properties
  data() {
    return {
      myObj: {
        some: 'data',
        other: 'values'
      }
    }
  },
  created() {
    console.log(this.debug(this.myObj))
  }
}
</script>
```

You should get the following output:

```
{
  "some": "data",
  "other": "values"
}
```

Figure 6.4 – Browser console output due to the created hook

7. `debug` is also available in the template. We can display its output wrapped with a `pre` tag so that whitespace is respected:

```
<template>
  <div id="app">
    <pre>{{ debug(myObj) }}</pre>
  </div>
</template>
```

The application, as well as this template, will look as follows:

```
{
  "some": "data",
  "other": "values"
}
```

Figure 6.5 – Browser printing myObj using the debug method from the mixin

We have learned how we can use mixins to inject shared logic and data into multiple components in a manner that is quite explicit (a `mixins` property). However, due to the mechanism of data overriding and executing for hooks, mixins can lead to potential bugs and unwanted behaviors in a large code base. *Thus, we recommend considering creating shared logic and data as composable with Composition API whenever possible instead.*

We will now look at how to inject instance and global functionality and distribute it through plugins.

Understanding plugins

Vue plugins are a way to add custom functionality to Vue.js globally. Classic examples of plugin candidates are translation/internationalization libraries (such as `i18n-next`) and HTTP clients (such as the `axios`, `fetch`, and `GraphQL` clients). The plugin initializer has access to the `Vue` instance, so it can be a good way to wrap global directives and components and inject resources across the application.

A Vue plugin is an object that exposes an `install` method. The `install` function is called with an `app` instance and `options`:

```
const plugin = {
  install(app, options) {}
}
```

Within the `install` method, we can register directives and components and add global and instance properties and methods:

```
const plugin = {
  install(app, options) {
    app.directive('fade', { bind() {} })
    app.component(/*Register component globally*/)
    app.provide(/*Provide a resource to be injectable*/)
    app.config.globalProperties.$globalValue = 'very-
      global-value'
```

```
      }
  }
```

We can register a plugin using the `use` instance method, as follows:

```
import plugin from './plugin'
const app = createApp(/*…*/)
app.use(plugin)
```

We can pass an options as the second argument to the `use()` method. These options are passed to the plugin:

```
app.use(plugin, { optionProperty: true })
```

`use()` does not allow you to register the same plugin twice, avoiding edge case behavior when attempting to instantiate or install the same plugin multiple times.

A popular HTTP client to use in combination with Vue is Axios. It is common to configure Axios with interceptors or Axios options to achieve things such as retries, passing cookies, or following redirects.

Axios can be installed using `npm install –save axios`. In the next exercise, we will create a plugin wrapping Axios inside our application.

Exercise 6.02 – creating a custom Axios plugin

In order to avoid having to add `import axios from 'axios'` or having to wrap our custom Axios instance under an `http` or `transport` internal module, we'll inject our custom Axios instance into the Vue object and Vue component instances under `Vue.axios` and `this.axios`. This will make it easier and more ergonomic to use in our application, which needs to call out to an API using Axios as the HTTP client.

To access the code file for this exercise, refer to `https://github.com/PacktPublishing/ Frontend-Development-Projects-with-Vue.js-3/tree/v2-edition/Chapter06/ Exercise6.02`.

Execute the following steps to complete this exercise:

1. Use the application generated with `npm init vue@3` as a starting point, or within the root folder of the code repository, navigate into the `Chapter06/Exercise6.02` folder, by using the following commands in order:

    ```
    > cd Chapter06/Exercise6.02/
    > yarn
    ```

2. Open the exercise project in VS Code (by using the `code` . command within the project directory) or your preferred IDE.

3. To organize our code properly, we will create a new folder in `src/plugins` and a new file for our `axios` plugin at `src/plugins/axios.js`. In the new file, we will scaffold the `axios` plugin:

```
import axios from 'axios'
export default {
  install(app, options) {}
}
```

4. We will now register our `axios` plugin on the Vue.js instance in `src/main.js`:

```
// other imports
import axiosPlugin from './plugins/axios.js'
// Vue instantiation code
const app = createApp(App)
app.use(axiosPlugin)
app.mount('#app')
```

5. We will now install Axios through npm using the following command. This will allow us to import Axios and expose it on Vue through a plugin:

npm install --save axios

6. We will now add Axios to Vue as a global property in `src/plugins/axios.js`:

```
import axios from 'axios'
export default {
  install(app) {
    app.config.globalProperties.$axios = axios
  }
}
```

7. Axios is now available on Vue. In `src/App.vue`, we can make a request to an API that will populate a list of `todo`s:

```
<template>
  <div id="app">
    <div v-for="todo in todos" :key="todo.id">
      <ul>
```

```
        <li>Title: {{ todo.title }}</li>
        <li>Status: {{ todo.completed ? "Completed" :
          "Not Completed" }}</li>
      </ul>
    </div>
  </div>
</template>
<script>
import Vue from 'vue'
export default {
  async mounted() {
    const { data: todos } = await
      this.$axios(
        'https://jsonplaceholder.typicode.com/todos'
      )
    this.todos = todos
  },
  data() {
    return { todos: [] }
  }
}
</script>
```

The following is the expected output:

- Title: delectus aut autem
- Status: Not Completed

- Title: quis ut nam facilis et officia qui
- Status: Not Completed

- Title: fugiat veniam minus
- Status: Not Completed

- Title: et porro tempora
- Status: Completed

Figure 6.6 – Global this.$axios todo display sample

8. We can also provide Axios as an injectable when necessary, instead of making it available in every component, by using `app.provide()` as follows:

```
// imports
export default {
  install(app, options) {
    // other plugin code
    app.provide('axios', axios)
  }
}
```

9. Now we can access Axios through `this.axios` in `src/App.vue` if we inject `'axios'` into this component by using the `inject` property:

```
<script>
export default {
  inject: ['axios'],
  async mounted() {
    const { data: todos } = await this.axios(
        'https://jsonplaceholder.typicode.com/todos'
      )
    this.todos = todos
  },
  data() {
    return { todos: [] }
  }
}
</script>
```

The output of the above code stays the same as in *Figure 6.6*.

With that, we have used a plugin to inject both global and instance-level properties and methods.

We will now look at how globally registering components can help reduce boilerplate for high-usage components in a code base.

Globally registering components

A reason for using plugins is to reduce boilerplate in all Vue application files by removing `imports` and replacing it with access to `this`.

Vue.js components are usually defined in a single-file component and imported explicitly. Much for the same reasons as we define global methods and properties, we might want to register components globally. This will allow us to use these components in all our other component templates without having to import them and register them under the `components` property.

A situation where this can be very useful is when using a design system or when a component is used across the code base.

Globally registering a component helps with some types of updates, such as if the filename is not exposed to the consumer so that when changing the filename, there is only one path to update as opposed to one per user.

Let's assume we have a `CustomButton` component in the `CustomButton.vue` file that looks as follows:

```
<template>
  <button @click="$emit('click', $event)">
    <slot />
  </button>
</template>
```

We can register `CustomButton` globally as follows (this is usually done in the `main.js` file):

```
// other imports
import CustomButton from './components/CustomButton.vue'


app.component('CustomButton', CustomButton)
```

We can now use it in the `App.vue` file without locally registering it or importing it:

```
<template>
  <div>
    <CustomButton>Click Me</CustomButton>
  </div>
</template>
```

This renders as expected, with a button called **Click Me**:

Figure 6.7 – CustomButton rendering with a Click Me button

With that, we have explored how globally registering components can cut down on boilerplate when components are used often across a code base.

The next section is dedicated to deepening our understanding of Vue.js components by learning how to use them without .vue files.

Using non-SFC Vue components

Most of the examples we have seen of Vue.js components have leveraged .vue single-file components. This is not the only way to define a Vue.js component. In this section, we will look at four different ways to define Vue.js components without using a .vue file.

Evaluating these options will help us understand what a Vue.js component is at its core.

Runtime definition with a string template

A component can use a template property that accepts a string value. This is commonly called a **string template**. This template is evaluated at runtime (in the browser).

We can define a component in the StringTemplate.js file by defining an object with a template property:

```
export default {
  template: '<div>String Template Component</div>'
}
```

This can then be consumed from the App.vue file, as follows:

```
<template>
  <div id="app">
    <StringTemplate />
  </div>
</template>
<script setup>
```

```
import StringTemplate from './components/StringTemplate.js'
</script>
```

Unfortunately, the browser won't display the content of StringTemplate, and in the console log, you will find the following Vue warning:

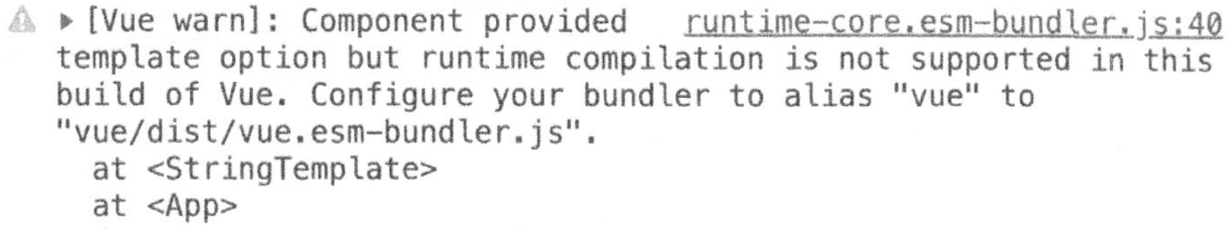

⚠ ▸ [Vue warn]: Component provided   runtime-core.esm-bundler.js:40
    template option but runtime compilation is not supported in this
    build of Vue. Configure your bundler to alias "vue" to
    "vue/dist/vue.esm-bundler.js".
      at <StringTemplate>
      at <App>

Figure 6.8 – Vue runtime compiler missing warning

For this component to work, we need to include the Vue runtime compiler. We can do so by manually adding 'vue/dist/vue.esm-bundler.js' as a vue alias for the Vite engine to resolve.

Your vite.config.js file should look like the following:

```
export default defineConfig({
  plugins: [vue()],
  resolve: {
    alias: {
      "@": fileURLToPath(new URL("./src",
        import.meta.url)),
      vue: "vue/dist/vue.esm-bundler.js",
    },
  },
});
```

After re-starting the development server, a message from the StringTemplate component appears in the browser:

```
String Template Component
```

Next, let's explore how to create components using the render function.

Understanding the render function

Behind the scenes, the template section gets compiled into a render function at build time.

Starting from Vue 3, a render method in a component's options no longer takes a createElement argument and then returns a virtual DOM node received from the execution of createElement. Instead, Vue provides an h function, which performs the same thing.

We can define a component in a JavaScript file (`RenderFunction.js`) with a `render` property like so:

```
import { h } from 'vue'
export default {
  render() {
    return h(
      'h2',
      'Render Function Component'
    )
  }
}
```

This can be rendered in the `App.vue` file as follows:

```
<template>
  <div id="app">
    <RenderFunction />
  </div>
</template>
<script setup>
import RenderFunction from './components/RenderFunction.js'
</script>
```

This component displays an h2 with the text `Render Function Component` in the browser:

```
Render Function Component
```

Beyond writing components in non `.vue` files, `render` functions can be useful for highly dynamic components.

JSX

JSX is a superset of JavaScript that allows HTML-style tags and interpolation using braces in React, like SFC to Vue.

React, like Vue, does not render the raw JSX to the DOM. React also use `render` to render a component's content to the Virtual DOM. The Virtual DOM is then *reconciled* (synced) with the real DOM.

Vite and Vue CLI both support the JSX compiler out of the box for the Vue application. You just need to turn on JSX support during the installation configuration when using `create-vue`. This means we can write the following `JSXRender.js` file, which is the equivalent of the `RenderFunction` component:

```
export default {
  render() {
    return <h2>JSX Render Function Component</h2>
  }
}
```

The equivalent `render` function without JSX looks as follows:

```
import { h } from 'vue'
export default {
  render() {
    return h(
      'h2',
      'JSX Render Function Component'
    )
  }
}
```

The following `App.vue` file renders `JSXRender` to the browser:

```
<template>
  <div id="app">
    <JSXRender />
  </div>
</template>
<script setup>
import JSXRender from './components/JSXRender.js'
</script>
```

Now, we can see h2 from `JSXRender` on the screen with the expected content:

```
JSX Render Function Component
```

We will now look at how components can be rendered dynamically from runtime data using the Vue.js component tag.

Understanding components

JSX and `render` functions are great for situations where the component being rendered needs to be very dynamic. We can also achieve this capability using the Vue `component`.

To render a dynamic component, we use a `component` tag with a bound `is` property (here, we are using the shorthand `:is`, which is equivalent to `v-bind:is`):

```
<component :is="componentName" />
```

We will now learn how to render dynamic components using a name or component reference.

Rendering dynamic components by name or component reference

Let's say we have a grid that contains items whose display can be toggled between a card display (a design element with an image and text) or an image-only view.

First, we need to import the relevant components and register them as components. We will also set some fixture data to loop through for the grid:

```
<template>
  <div id="app">
    <div class="grid">
      <component
        class="grid-item"
        v-for="item in items"
        :key="item.id"
      />
    </div>
  </div>
</template>
<script>
import Card from './components/Card.vue';
import ImageEntry from './components/ImageEntry.vue';
export default {
  components: {
    Card,
    ImageEntry
  },
```

```
  data() {
    return {
      items: [
        {
          id: '10',
          title: 'Forest Shot',
          url: 'https://picsum.photos/id/10/1000/750.jpg',
        },
        {
          id: '1000',
          title: 'Cold cross',
          url:
            'https://picsum.photos/id/1000/1000/750.jpg',
        },
        {
          id: '1002',
          title: 'NASA shot',
          url:
            'https://picsum.photos/id/1002/1000/750.jpg',
        },
        {
          id: '866',
          title: 'Peak',
          url: 'https://picsum.photos/id/866/1000/750.jpg'
        },
      ]
    }
  }
}
</script>
```

We can then reference the components by name – that is, Card and ImageEntry – and set itemComponent as the value for is:

```
<template>
    <!-- rest of template -->
    <component
```

```
          :is="itemComponent"

          class="grid-item"
          v-for="item in items"
          :key="item.id"
        />
        <!-- rest of template -->
      </template>
      <script>
      // rest of script
      export default {
        // other component properties
        data() {
          return {
            itemComponent: 'Card',
            // other data properties eg. 'items'
          }
        }
      }
      </script>
```

In the preceding code, Vue will render the `Card` component since we set the `itemComponent` value as `card`.

If we set `itemComponent` to `image-entry`, Vue renders the `ImageEntry` component. This switch can be made as follows using `v-model`:

```
<template>
  <!-- rest of template -->
  Display mode:
  <input
    type="radio"
    name="style"
    value="Card"
    v-model="itemComponent"
    id="card-radio"
  />
```

```
  <label for="card-radio">Card</label>

  <input
    type="radio"
    name="style"
    value="ImageEntry"
    v-model="itemComponent"
    id="image-radio"
  />
  <label for="image-radio">Image</label>

  <!-- rest of template -->
</template>
```

We can also pass components to is using the component reference itself (instead of using the name). For example, we could set itemComponent to Card:

```
<script>
// rest of script
export default {
  // other component properties
  data() {
    return {
      itemComponent: 'Card',
      // other data properties eg. 'items'
    }
  }
}
</script>
```

In this case, switching between card and image views would be more difficult since we would need to use component references instead of using names.

We can pass props to components that have been dynamically rendered with component like we would pass regular props either with v-bind:prop-name or the :prop-name shorthand:

```
<template>
    <!-- rest of template -->
    <component
```

```
        class="grid-item"
        v-for="item in items"
        :key="item.id"
        :is="itemComponent"

        :url="item.url"
        :title="item.title"
      />
      <!-- rest of template -->
  </template>
```

Given the following Card and ImageEntry components, we get an application that has toggleable views for grid items.

Card.vue renders the image and the title and has a 150px maximum width:

```
<template>
  <div class="card">
    <img :src="url" width="100" />
    <h3>{{ title }}</h3>
  </div>
</template>

<script>
export default {
  props: {
    url: String,
    title: String
  }
}
</script>

<style scoped>
.card {
  margin: 10px;
  max-width: 150px;
}
h3 {
```

```
    font-weight: normal;
  }
</style>
```

Your output will display the entries in the card view, as follows:

Display mode: ● Card ○ Image

Forest Shot   Cold cross   NASA shot   Peak

Figure 6.9 – Grid rendering entries in the card view

Use `ImageEntry.vue` to render only the image at double the width of the card view:

```
<template>
  <img class="image" :src="url" />
</template>

<script>
export default {
  props: {
    url: String
  }
}
</script>

<style scoped>
.image {
  margin: 20px;
  max-width: 300px;
}
</style>
```

You will now see the entries in the image view, as shown in the following screenshot:

Figure 6.10 – Grid rendering entries in the image view

A caveat of the component tag is that the rendered dynamic component gets completely torn down when it is not displayed anymore. In this example, the dynamic components being rendered do not have any state, so this teardown does not create any issues.

We will now learn how a dynamic component state is cached.

Caching a dynamic component state with keep-alive

Components that are dynamically rendered through the component tag can have state, such as in a multipart form, with a name field and an address field on the next page.

Let's implement this with a component tag, as follows:

```
<template>
  <div id="app">
    <component
      :is="activeStep"
      @next="activeStep = 'second-step'"
      @back="activeStep = 'first-step'"
```

```
      />
    </div>
  </template>
  <script>
  import FirstStep from './components/FirstStep.vue'
  import SecondStep from './components/SecondStep.vue'

  export default {
    components: {
      FirstStep,
      SecondStep
    },
    data() {
      return {
        activeStep: 'first-step',
      }
    }
  }
  </script>
```

And in the FirstStep component, we will implement an input field that requires the user's name, as follows:

```
<template>
  <label> Name: <input v-model="name" /> </label>
  <button @click="next">Next</button>
</template>
<script setup>
import { ref } from "vue";

const name = ref("");
const emits = defineEmits(["next"]);

const next = () => {
  emits('next', name.value);
};
</script>
```

And for `SecondStep.vue`, we will implement another input field with two buttons to navigate back and forward, as shown in the following code block:

```
<template>
  <label> Address: <input v-model="address" /> </label>
    <button @click="next">Next</button>
    <button @click="back">Back</button>
</template>
<script setup>
import { ref } from "vue";

const emits = defineEmits(["next", "back"]);

const next = () => {
  emits("next", name.value);
};

const back = () => {
  emits("back");
};

const address = ref("");
</script>
```

By doing this, we can enter data in the **Name** field:

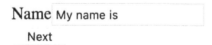

Figure 6.11 – "My name is" is entered in the name field

If we navigate, using **Next**, to the address part of the form and then use **Back**, the name will disappear, as shown in the following screenshot:

Name
Next

Figure 6.12 – Empty Name field upon clicking Next and then Back in the address step

This is due to the component being unmounted when it is not the currently rendered dynamic component.

To fix this, we can use the `keep-alive` element around the `component` tag:

```
<template>
  <!-- rest of template -->
  <keep-alive>
    <component
      :is="activeStep"
      @next="activeStep = 'second-step'"
      @back="activeStep = 'first-step'"
    />
  </keep-alive>
  <!-- rest of template -->
</template>
```

In this manner, filling out the name and going back from the address section of the form shows the following:

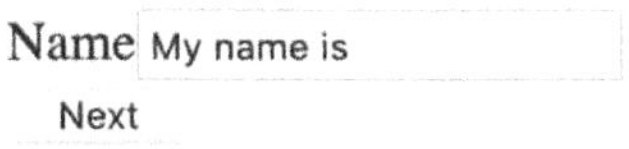

Name My name is

Next

Figure 6.12 – "My name is" is still the value in the Name field after navigation

We have learned how to use the `component` tag to denote an area within which we can dynamically display a component based on a string or the component itself (as imported). We have also explored how to work around the main gotcha of `component`; namely, how to use `keep-alive` to maintain the component state when it is not the component being actively used in the `component` tag.

Now let's practice what we learned in the next exercise.

Exercise 6.03 – creating a dynamic card layout with the component tag

A modern application layout is a grid with cards. Card layouts have the benefit of being well suited to mobile, desktop, and tablet displays. In this exercise, we will create a dynamic card layout with three different modes and a way to select between the three of them. This layout will allow the user to select how much information is displayed on the screen to suit their preference:

- The `Rich` view will display all the details for an item, including the image, the title, and the description

- The Compressed view will display all the details but not the image preview

- The List view will only display the title and should be a vertical layout

Each of the card views will be implemented as a separate component that will then be dynamically rendered using the component tag.

To access the code file for this exercise, refer to https://github.com/PacktPublishing/ Frontend-Development-Projects-with-Vue.js-3/tree/v2-edition/Chapter06/ Exercise6.03.

Execute the following steps to complete this exercise:

1. Use the application generated with npm init vue@3 as a starting point, or within the root folder of the code repository, navigate into the Chapter06/Exercise6.03 folder, by using the following commands in order:

```
> cd Chapter06/Exercise6.03/
> yarn
```

2. Open the exercise project in your VS Code (by using the code . command within the project directory) or your preferred IDE.

3. Create the rich layout at src/components/Rich.vue. It contains three props called url (the image URL), title, and description and renders the image, the title, and the description, respectively:

```
<template>
  <div class="card">
    <img :src="url" width="200" />
    <h3>{{ title }}</h3>
    <p>{{ description }}</p>
  </div>
</template>

<script setup>
import { defineProps } from 'vue'
const { url, title, description } = defineProps(
    ['url', 'title', 'description']
)
</script>

<style scoped>
```

```css
.card {
  display: flex;
  flex-direction: column;
  max-width: 200px;
}
h3 {
  font-weight: normal;
  margin-bottom: 0;
  padding-bottom: 0;
}
</style>
```

4. Set up src/App.vue with some fixture data:

```vue
<template>
  <div id="app">
  </div>
</template>
<script setup>
const items = [
      {
        id: '10',
        title: 'Forest Shot',
        description: 'Recent shot of a forest
          overlooking a lake',
        url:
        'https://picsum.photos/id/10/1000/750.jpg',
      },
      {
        id: '1000',
        title: 'Cold cross',
        description: 'Mountaintop cross with
          snowfall from Jan 2018',
        url:
        'https://picsum.photos/id/1000/1000/750.jpg',
      },
    ]
</script>
```

5. Import the `Rich` view component into `src/App.vue` and register it locally:

```
<script setup>
import Rich from './components/Rich.vue'
// other component properties, eg. "data"
</script>
```

6. Once we have got the `Rich` view component, wire it into the application in `src/App.vue`, render it with `component`, and pass the relevant props through:

```
<template>
  <!-- rest of template -->
      <component
        v-for="item in items"
        :key="item.id"
        :is="layout"
        :title="item.title"
        :description="item.description"
        :url="item.url"
      />
  <!-- rest of template -->
</template>
<script setup>
  import { shallowRef } from 'vue'

  const layout = shallowRef(Rich)
  // other data definitions eg. 'items'
</script>
```

7. This is a good point to add a bit of styling to make the grid look like a grid:

```
<template>
  <!-- rest of template -->
    <div class="grid">
      <component
        v-for="item in items"
        :key="item.id"
        :is="layout"
        :title="item.title"
```

```
            :description="item.description"
            :url="item.url"
        />
    </div>
    <!-- rest of template -->
</template>

<style scoped>
.grid {
    display: flex;
}
</style>
```

This displays the following output:

Figure 6.14 – Rich component rendering dynamically

8. Now, implement the Compressed view, which is just the Rich view without the image in the Compressed.vue file:

```
<template>
    <div class="card">
        <h3>{{ title }}</h3>
        <p>{{ description }}</p>
    </div>
</template>
<script setup>
import { defineProps } from 'vue'
```

```
const { title, description } = defineProps(
    ['title', 'description']
)
</script>

<style scoped>
.card {
  display: flex;
  flex-direction: column;
  min-width: 200px;
}
h3 {
  font-weight: normal;
  padding-bottom: 0;
}
p {
 margin: 0;
}
</style>
```

9. Import and register the Compressed component in src/App.vue. Then create our layoutOptions array with two elements. Each has two fields: name of the layout and the component instance for the two components – Rich and Compressed respectively, as shown in the following code block:

```
<script setup>
// other imports
import Compressed from './components/Compressed.vue'
const layoutOptions = [ {
  name: 'Rich',
  component: Rich
}, {
  name: 'Compressed',
  component: Compressed
}]

  // other component properties
</script>
```

10. Add `select` to switch between views. It will take options from the `layoutOptions` array using `v-for`, and bind its selected value to `layout` using `v-model`:

```
<template>
  <!-- rest of template -->
  Layout: <select v-model="layout">
    <option
      v-for="(option, index) in layoutOptions"
      :key="index"
      :value="option.component"
      >{{option.name}}</option>
    </select>
  <!-- rest of template -->
</template>
```

Using `select`, we can switch to the **Compressed** layout, which looks as follows:

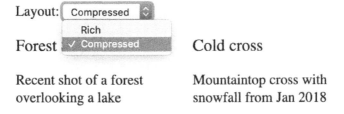

Figure 6.15 – Compressed layout with options dropdown for selection

11. Add the `List` layout to `src/components/List.vue`. The `List` view is the compressed view but without the description:

```
<template>
  <h3>{{ title }}</h3>
</template>

<script setup>
import { defineProps } from 'vue'
const { title } = defineProps(['title'])
</script>

<style scoped>
h3 {
```

```css
  width: 100%;
  font-weight: normal;
}
</style>
```

12. Import the `List` component into `src/App.vue` and register it locally:

```html
<script setup>
// other imports
import List from './components/List.vue'
const layoutOptions = [ {
  name: 'Rich',
  component: Rich
}, {
  name: 'Compressed',
  component: Compressed
}, {
  name: 'List',
  component: List
}]
  // other component properties
</script>
```

When switching to the **List** layout, the items are displayed in a horizontal row, as follows:

Forest Shot   Cold cross

Figure 6.16 – List view with incorrect horizontal stacking

13. To fix this horizontal stacking, create a new `grid-column` class that sets `flex-direction: column` (as opposed to `row`, which is the default) and conditionally applies it when the layout is `List`:

```html
<template>
  <!-- rest of template -->
    <div class="grid" :class="{ 'grid-column': layout
      === List }">
      <!-- grid using component tag -->
```

```
      </div>
    <!-- rest of template -->
  </template>

  <style scoped>
  /* existing rules */
  .grid-column {
    flex-direction: column;
  }
  </style>
```

Our **List** layout now looks as follows:

Figure 6.17 – List view with vertical stacking

With that, we have learned how to use the component tag to dynamically render different components both by name and by using the component object itself. We have also explored the pitfalls of stateful dynamic components, namely the teardown of components when they are not displayed anymore and how to circumvent them using the keep-alive element.

We will now look at how simple components can be implemented using only a render function or template tag using functional components.

Writing functional components

In Vue 2.0, you can declare a component as a functional one by setting the functional field to true in the component's options:

```
export default {
  functional: true,
}
```

This can also be done by setting `functional` directly on the `template` tag:

```
<template functional>
  <!— template code -->
</template>
```

And you can set how to render the component using the `render()` method of the component or the `template` section. However, if both fields exist, Vue takes the `render()` method.

In Vue 3.0 onward, however, Vue removed the `functional` attribute and you can only declare a functional component using a JavaScript function, which is the `render` function Vue will trigger to create the component:

```
const functionComp = (props, context) => {
  return h(/*…*/)
}
```

Once declared as functional, the component does not have any reactive state, and you can't access `this` instance since it is not available. Instead, Vue triggers the `render` function and passes to it the component's props and necessary context including `attrs`, `slots`, and the passed event handler's `emit`:

```
const functionComp = (props, { attrs, slots, emit }) => {
  return h(/*…*/)
}
```

You can also define the accepted props and events by directly setting its field `props` and `emits`:

```
functionComp.props = [/* props */]
functionComp.emits = [/* emits */]
```

To start using JSX code, you will need to create the Vue project with JSX support enabled using Vite. Otherwise, in `vite.config.js`, you will need to manually import `vueJsx` from the `'@vitejs/plugin-vue-jsx'` package, as follows:

```
import vueJsx from '@vitejs/plugin-vue-jsx'
```

And then add the imported `vueJsx` plugin to the `plugins` array, as seen in the following code:

```
plugins: [vue(), vueJsx()],
```

With the preceding configuration, your Vue project created by Vite now supports functional components with JSX, which we will demonstrate in the following example.

The following code block is an example of how we define a functional component, GreetComponent.jsx:

```
import { h } from 'vue';
export function GreetComponent(props, context) {
  return h(
    <div>
      <h2>{ props.greeting} {props.audience} </h2>
      <button
        onClick={() => context.emit('acknowledge', true) }
      >
        Acknowledge
      </button>
    </div>
  )
}
```

We also declare props and emits explicitly for GreetComponent:

```
GreetComponent.props = {
    greeting: String,
    audience: String,
}


GreetComponent.emits = ['acknowledge']
```

Note that here, since we use JSX syntax to define the component, we need to make sure the file extension of GreetComponent is .jsx and not .js (GreetComponent.jsx). Also, we need to make sure we turn on JSX support when creating the project with the create-vue command (Vite).

Now we can import and use GreetComponent in App.vue as a regular component:

```
<script setup>
import { GreetComponent } from './components/GreetComponent.
jsx'
const acknowledge = () => {
  console.log('Acknowledged')
}
</script>
<template>
```

```
  <GreetComponent
    greeting="Hi"
    audience="World"
    @acknowledge="acknowledge"
  />
</template>
```

This renders the following to the browser:

Figure 6.18 – Functional component rendering

You can also combine with Composition API to create functional components with states. In the following example, we create a Message component with a reactive message:

```
import { ref } from 'vue'
export function Message(props, context) {
  const message = ref('Hello World')

  return (
    <div>
      <span>{ message.value }</span>
    </div>
  )
}
```

Note that here, we display the message value by using message.value, not message directly.

At this point, we have learned how to write functional components – stateless or stateful – using Composition API. We will now build a to-do application that uses all the patterns we have looked at throughout this chapter.

Activity 6.01 – building a Vue.js application with plugins and reusable components

To access the code file for this activity, refer to https://github.com/PacktPublishing/Frontend-Development-Projects-with-Vue.js-3/tree/v2-edition/Chapter06/Activity6.01

In this activity, we will build a to-do app that integrates `jsonplaceholder` as a data source.

Our to-do app will load todos and display them as a list. It will display a checkbox based on whether the to-do has been completed, as well as the name of the to-do.

When checking off a to-do, the application will sync it to the API.

We will inject Axios as a plugin to query against `https://jsonplaceholder.typicode.com`.

Follow these steps to complete this activity:

1. Install `axios` in the project.

2. To inject `axios` as a property into `this` component instances, create a `src/plugins/axios.js` plugin file that, on install, will mean component instances have an injectable `axios` property.

3. For the plugin to work, import and register it in `src/main.js`.

4. We also want to inject our API's `$baseUrl` into all our components as a global scope. We will create a plugin inline with the `src/main.js` file to do this.

5. We now want to fetch all the to-dos from `src/App.vue`. A good place to do this is in the `mounted` life cycle method.

6. To display the to-do list, we will create a `TodoList` component in `src/components/TodoList.vue` that takes a `todos` prop, loops through the items, and defers rendering of the to-do under a `todo` scoped slot that binds the to-do.

7. We can now use the `TodoList` component to render out the *todos* we have already fetched in `src/App.vue`.

8. We now need to create a `TodoEntry` component where we will implement most of the to-do-specific logic. A good practice for components is to have the props be very specific to the component's role. In this case, the properties of the `todo` object we will tackle are `id`, `title`, and `completed`, so those should be the props that our `TodoEntry` component receives. We will not make `TodoEntry` a functional component since we will need a component instance to create HTTP requests.

9. We will then update `src/App.vue` so that it consumes `TodoEntry` (making sure to bind `id`, `title`, and `completed`).

10. Add the ability to toggle the **Complete** status of a `todo`. We will implement the majority of this in `src/components/TodoEntry.vue`. We will listen to the `input` change event. On changing, we will want to read the new value and send a `PATCH` request to `/todos/{todoId}` with an object containing `completed` set to the new value. We will also want to emit a `completedChange` event in Vue.js so that the `App` component can update the data that's in memory.

11. In `App.vue`, we will want to update the relevant `todo` when `completeChange` is triggered. Since `completeChange` does not include the ID of the `todo`, we will need to read that from the context when setting the `handleCompleteChange` function to listen to `completeChange`.

The expected output is as follows:

- delectus aut autem
- quis ut nam facilis et officia qui
- fugiat veniam minus
- et porro tempora ☑
- laboriosam mollitia et enim quasi adipisci quia provident illum
- qui ullam ratione quibusdam voluptatem quia omnis
- illo expedita consequatur quia in
- quo adipisci enim quam ut ab ☑
- molestiae perspiciatis ipsa
- illo est ratione doloremque quia maiores aut ☑
- vero rerum temporibus dolor ☑
- ipsa repellendus fugit nisi ☑
- et doloremque nulla
- repellendus sunt dolores architecto voluptatum ☑
- ab voluptatum amet voluptas ☑
- accusamus eos facilis sint et aut voluptatem ☑
- quo laboriosam deleniti aut qui ☑
- dolorum est consequatur ea mollitia in culpa
- molestiae ipsa aut voluptatibus pariatur dolor nihil ☑
- ullam nobis libero sapiente ad optio sint ☑
- suscipit repellat esse quibusdam voluptatem incidunt
- distinctio vitae autem nihil ut molestias quo ☑
- et itaque necessitatibus maxime molestiae qui quas velit
- adipisci non ad dicta qui amet quaerat doloribus ea
- voluptas quo tenetur perspiciatis explicabo natus ☑
- aliquam aut quasi ☑
- veritatis pariatur delectus ☑
- nesciunt totam sit blanditiis sit
- laborum aut in quam
- nemo perspiciatis repellat ut dolor libero commodi blanditiis omnis ☑
- repudiandae totam in est sint facere fuga
- earum doloribus ea doloremque quis
- sint sit aut vero

Figure 6.19 – Our to-do app using jsonplaceholder data

Summary

Throughout this chapter, we have looked at global composition patterns and advanced component setups that we can take advantage of to create a reusable code base for a Vue.js application. We learned about mixins, plugins, how to use component tags for dynamic component rendering, and functional components, both stateful and stateless.

So far, we have learned how to build applications in terms of components, mixins, and plugins. To build applications that span multiple pages, we need to implement routing. This is what we will tackle in the next chapter.

7
Routing

In the previous chapter, you learned about sharing common logic between components using mixins, creating app plugins, and other approaches to creating components, such as dynamic and functional components.

This chapter will guide you through how routing and Vue Router work. You will learn how to set up, implement, and manage the routing system in your app with Vue Router. You will look at dynamic routing for passing parameter values and nested routes for better reusability in complex applications. In addition, we will also look at JavaScript Hooks, which are helpful for authentication and error handling.

By the end of this chapter, you will be ready to handle static and dynamic routing in any Vue application.

This chapter covers the following topics:

- Understanding routing
- Understanding Vue Router
- Exploring the `RouterView` element
- Defining the routes
- Setting up a default layout for your app
- Setting up navigation links with `RouterLink`
- Passing route parameters
- Understanding Router Hooks
- Decoupling params with props
- Dynamic routing
- Catching error paths
- Nested routes
- Using layouts

Technical requirements

In this chapter, you need to set up a basic Vue project following the instructions in *Chapter 1, Starting Your First Vue Project*. It's recommended to create a single file Vue component to practice working with the examples and concepts mentioned easily.

The Node version has to be below v20 (preferable Yarn 1.22 and Node version above 16 and up to 19.x, and npm up to version 9.x.

You can find this chapter's source code here: `https://github.com/PacktPublishing/Frontend-Development-Projects-with-Vue.js-3/tree/v2-edition/Chapter07`.

Understanding routing

Routing is one of the most essential and primary parts of building dynamic web applications. You may be familiar with the word in its everyday context. It is the process of getting a user to their desired location. Users who enter `website.com/about` into their URL bar will be redirected to the **About** page.

In web development, routing is the matching mechanism by which we decide how to connect HTTP requests to the code that handles them. We use routing whenever there is a need for URL navigation in our application. Most modern web applications contain a lot of different URLs, even single-page ones.

Thus, routing creates a navigation system and helps users quickly move around our application and the web. With **Single-Page Applications** (**SPAs**), routing allows you to smoothly navigate within an application without the need for page refreshing.

In short, routing is a way for an application to interpret what resource users want based on the URL provided. It is a system for web-based resource navigation with URLs, such as paths to assets (images and videos), scripts, and stylesheets.

Understanding Vue Router

As stated in the Vue.js documentation, **Vue Router** is the official router service for any Vue.js application. It provides a single-entry point for communication between components with routes and therefore effectively controls the application's flow, regardless of the user's behavior.

Installing Vue Router

Vue Router is not installed by default; however, it can easily be enabled when creating an application with Vite. Create a new application by running the following command:

```
npm init vue@3
```

Select the Yes option for adding Vue Router to the project as shown in *Figure 7.1*:

```
Vue.js - The Progressive JavaScript Framework

  Project name:    chapter-3-vue-app
  Add TypeScript?        No    Yes
  Add JSX Support?       No    Yes
  Add Vue Router for Single Page Application development?   No    Yes
  Add Pinia for state management?    No    Yes
  Add Vitest for Unit Testing?   No    Yes
  Add Cypress for End-to-End testing?    No    Yes
  Add ESLint for code quality?   No    Yes
  Add Prettier for code formatting?    No    Yes
```

Figure 7.1 – Adding Vue Router during creating a project

> **Note**
>
> If you would like to add Vue Router to an existing Vue.js application, you can install it as an
> application's dependency with the following command:

```
npm install vue-router
```

The next step is understanding how Vue Router synchronizes the browser URL and the application's view.

First, let's look at the RouterView element.

Exploring the RouterView element

RouterView is a Vue component whose job is to do the following:

- Render different child components

- Mount and unmount itself automatically at any nesting level, depending on the route's given path

Without RouterView, it is almost impossible to render dynamic content correctly for users at runtime. For example, when a user navigates to the **Home** page, RouterView knows and only generates the content related to that page.

Let's see how we can pass props to the view through RouterView.

Passing props to view

Since RouterView is a component, it can also receive props. The only prop it receives is name, which is the same name registered in the corresponding route's record defined in the router object at the initialization phase.

The Vue engine automatically passes any other additional HTML attributes to any view component that `RouterView` renders.

Take the following `RouterView` component with a `"main-app-view"` class, for instance:

```
<RouterView class="main-app-view"/>
```

Let's say we have a view component's template with the following code:

```
<template>
  <div>Hello World</div>
</template>
```

In this case, the child component will receive the `"main-app-view"` attribute class when it's the active view. The actual output after rendering will be as follows:

```
<div class="main-app-view">Hello World</div>
```

Next, let's look at how `RouterView` works.

Working with RouterView

In your newly created application, let's navigate to `App.vue` and replace the default code of `<template>` with the following:

```
<template>
  <div id="app">
    <RouterView/>
  </div>
</template>
```

Then, go to `src/router/index.js` and comment out the generated code within the `routes` array, as shown in the following code block:

```
const router = createRouter({
  history: createWebHistory(import.meta.env.BASE_URL),
  routes: [
    // {
    //   path: '/',
    //   name: 'home',
    //   component: HomeView
    // },
```

```
  // {
  //    path: '/about',
  //    name: 'about',
  //    component: () => import('../views/AboutView.vue')
  // }
  ]
})
```

When you run the app locally and open the local server URL in the browser, the output will be as seen in *Figure 7.2*:

Figure 7.2 – Output of the app when there is no route defined

The output is an empty page because we have not set up any router configurations in our file, including mapping the paths with the related view. Without this step, the routing system cannot dynamically pick the suitable view component and render it into our RouterView element.

In the next section, we will see how to set up Vue Router.

Setting up Vue Router

When we add Vue Router to our project, Vite creates and adds a router folder to the /src directory with a single auto-generated index.js file. This file contains the necessary configurations for our router system, which we will explore in the next section.

In the src/main.js file, we import the defined configuration object and uses the Vue instance method use() to install the router system into the application, as seen in the following code:

```
import { createApp } from 'vue'
import App from './App.vue'
import router from './router'

const app = createApp(App)
app.use(router)
```

app.use is an instance method with a built-in mechanism to prevent you from installing a plugin more than once.

After executing `app.use(router)`, the following objects are available for access in any component:

- `this.$router`: The global router object
- `this.$route`: The current route object points to the element in context

If you are using `setup()` and Composition API (or `<script setup>`), you can import `useRoute()` and `useRouter()` functions from `vue-router` package and get the current route object (instead of `this.$route`), and global router object (instead of `this.$router`) respectively.

```
<script setup>
import { useRoute, useRouter } from 'vue-router'

const route = useRoute();
const router = useRouter();

// component's logic…
</script>
```

Now that we have registered the use of Vue Router in our application, let's move on to the next step – defining the routes for the configuration object of the router instance.

Defining the routes

In a web application, a route is a URL path pattern. Vue Router will map it to a specific handler. This handler is a Vue component, defined and located in a physical file. For example, when the user enters the `localhost:3000/home` route, if you map the `HomeView` component to this specific route, the routing system knows how to render `HomeView` content accordingly.

As seen in *Figure 7.2*, it is crucial to set up `routes` (or paths) for navigation within the application; otherwise, your application will display as empty.

Each route is an object literal that uses the `RouteRecordRaw` interface with the following properties:

```
interface RouteRecordRaw = {
  path: string,
  component?: Component,
  name?: string, // for named routes
  components?: { [name: string]: Component }, // for named
    views
  redirect?: string | Location | Function,
  props?: boolean | Object | Function,
```

```
  alias?: string | Array<string>,
  children?: Array<RouteConfig>, // for nested routes
  beforeEnter?: (to: Route, from: Route, next: Function) =>
    void,
  meta?: any,
  sensitive?: Boolean,
  strict?: Boolean
}
```

We define all the routes needed for an application as a list of `routes`:

```
const routes = [
  //Route1,
  //Route2,
  //...
]
```

We return to the `src/router/index.js` file and uncomment the code inside `routes`. For convenience, there will be two predefined routes called `home` and `about`, each being an object located in the `routes` array.

Let's take a closer look at the first route as an example:

```
{
  path: '/',
  name: 'home',
  component: HomeView
}
```

The `path` property is a required string that indicates the path of the targeted route. Vue Router resolves this property to an absolute URL path for the browser's navigation. For instance, the `/about` path will be translated into `<app domain>/about` (`localhost:8080/about` or `example.com/about`).

In this case, Vue Router understands `/` – the empty path – as the default path for loading the application when there is no other indicator after the forward slash (`/`) – for example, when the user navigates to `<app-domain>` or `<app-domain>/` (without setting `strict: true`).

The next property is `name`, a string indicating the name given to the targeted route. Even though it is optional, we recommend defining every path with a name for better code maintenance and route tracking purposes, which we will discuss later in this chapter in the *Passing route parameters* section.

The last property is component, which is a Vue component instance. RouterView uses this property to reference the view component to render the page content when the path is active.

Here, the route is defined as the home route, mapped as the default path to the application, and tied to the HomeView component for content.

Vite also auto-generates two simple components for these two sample routes – HomeView and AboutView, located in the src/views folder.

In the next section, we'll go over some tips that can be helpful when you use loading components with routes.

Tips on loading components for route configuration

Indeed, we need to import the component to tie it to the targeted route in the same index.js file. The classic and most popular way is to import it at the top of the file as follows:

```
import Home from '../views/HomeView.vue'
```

Often, we add this code line under the main imports as shown in *Figure 7.3*:

```
1    import { createRouter, createWebHistory } from 'vue-router'
2    import HomeView from '../views/HomeView.vue'
3
```

Figure 7.3 – Importing the HomeView component on line 2 – src/router/index.js

However, a more efficient way is to lazy-load the component.

Lazy loading, also known as on-demand loading, is a technique that aims to optimize the content of a website or web application at runtime. It helps to reduce the time consumption and number of resources required to download an application on the first load.

This optimization is critical to ensure the best user experience possible, where every millisecond of waiting matters. Besides this, lazy loading also enables better code-splitting at the route level and performance optimization in large or complex applications.

We can lazy-load the component by using Vite (and Rollup). Instead of importing the AboutView component into the top of the file, as we did with HomeView (see *Figure 7.3*), we can dynamically add the following right after defining the name of the about route instead:

```
component: () => import('../views/AboutView.vue')
```

Here, we dynamically lazy-load the AboutView view component for the about route. During compilation, Vite generates a separate chunk with the designated name (about) for the target route and only loads it when the user visits this route.

In most cases, since the user will likely land on the default path on the first go, it is better not to lazy-load the default component (`HomeView` in our app) but to import it in the usual way. Hence, the tip here is to determine which elements should be lazily loaded when designing your routing and combine the two methods for the most benefit.

We will now see how to set up the router instance.

Setting up the router instance

After defining the routes, the final step is to create the `router` instance based on the given configuration options by using the `createRouter` method, as shown here:

```
import { createRouter, createWebHistory } from 'vue-router'

const router = createRouter({
  history: createWebHistory(import.meta.env.BASE_URL),
  routes
})
```

A configuration is an object consisting of different properties that help to form the app's router. We will now examine these properties in the following subsections.

routes

`routes` is a required option. Without this, the router won't be able to recognize the paths and direct users to the suitable view content accordingly.

history

`history` determines the router's mode. There are two modes in Vue Router for URLs:

- **HTML History mode**: You can use the `createWebHistory()` method to leverage the default `history.pushState()` API, as well as the HTML5 History API. It allows us to achieve URL navigation without a page reload and makes the URL path human-readable – for example, `yourapplication.com/about`.

- **Hash mode**: You can use the `createWebHashHistory()` method to create a hash mode, which allows you to use a hash symbol (#) to simulate a URL – for example, `yourapplication.com/#about` for an **About** page or `youapplication.com/#/` for the **Home** URL of your application.

base

base determines the base URL for the app. For example, when we set it to process.env.BASE_ URL, it allows developers to control the base URL from outside the application code, specifically from a .env file. Hence, developers can set the directory from which the hosting platform serves the code at runtime.

With base finally out of the way, we have created the router instance. All that is left is to export it:

```
export default router
```

In main.js, we import the router instance and use it in the router plugin right after the creation of the main app instance received from createApp, as shown here:

```
import { createApp } from 'vue'
import App from './App.vue'
import router from './router'


const app = createApp(App)
app.use(router)
app.mount('#app')
```

In App.vue, replace <template> with the following code:

```
<template>
  <header>
    <img alt="Vue logo" class="logo"
      src="@/assets/logo.svg" width="125" height="125" />
    <div class="wrapper">
      <HelloWorld msg="You did it!" />
    </div>
  </header>
  <RouterView />
</template>
```

Our application will now render as follows:

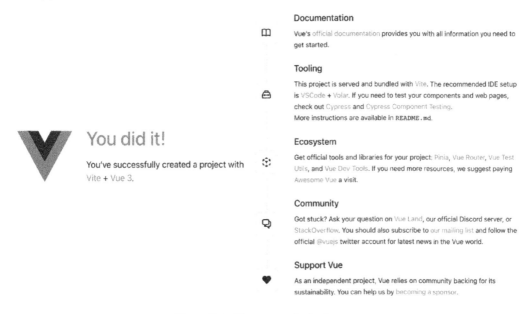

Figure 7.4 – Home page in the browser

If we navigate to /about, let's assume the content of the about component from the auto-generated code is as shown in the following code block:

```
<template>
  <div class="about">
    <h1>This is an about page</h1>
  </div>
</template>
```

The website should look like that shown in *Figure 7.5*:

Figure 7.5 – The About page of the application in the browser

In this section, we looked at how we can lazy-load components to speed up large and complex SPAs. We also looked at some options for setting up your router systems, such as `routes`, `history`, and `base`.

You also saw the Vue engine renders both pages, `/about` and `/home`, with the same header content, as shown in *Figure 7.6*:

Figure 7.6 – The Home page with the same header displayed in the About page in Figure 7.5

The reason is that Vue only replaces the placeholder component, `RouterView`, with the target view's content, and whatever template is defined outside this scope will remain. In this way, we can create a default layout for all our views in the app.

Setting up a default layout for your app

For our template to be functional, it should also contain the `<RouterView/>` element. One standard setup is to have a navigation menu, `<nav>`, within the template and `RouterView` underneath. That way, the content changes between pages while the `header` menu stays the same.

Navigate to App.vue and ensure that your template has the following code:

```
<template>
  <header>
    <nav>
      <RouterLink to="/">Home</RouterLink>
      <RouterLink to="/about">About</RouterLink>
    </nav>
  </header>

  <RouterView />
</template>
```

Your output should now contain a static header with two navigation links – **Home** and **About** – while the content changes depending on the route:

Home   About

📖 **Documentation**

Vue's official documentation provides you with all information you need to get started.

📦 **Tooling**

This project is served and bundled with Vite. The recommended IDE setup is VSCode + Volar. If you need to test your components and web pages, check out Cypress and Cypress Component Testing.
More instructions are available in README.md.

⠿ **Ecosystem**

Get official tools and libraries for your project: Pinia, Vue Router, Vue Test Utils, and Vue Dev Tools. If you need more resources, we suggest paying Awesome Vue a visit.

💬 **Community**

Got stuck? Ask your question on Vue Land, our official Discord server, or StackOverflow. You should also subscribe to our mailing list and follow the official @vuejs twitter account for latest news in the Vue world.

♥ **Support Vue**

As an independent project, Vue relies on community backing for its sustainability. You can help us by becoming a sponsor.

Figure 7.7 – The Home page's content

Once you navigate to the /about page, the header links will not change, while the content now become the following:

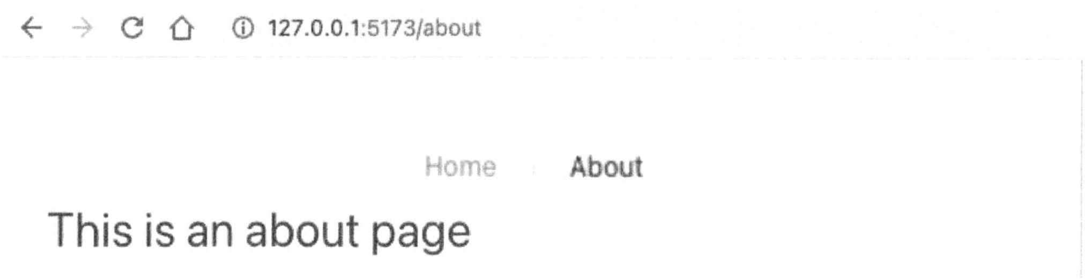

← → C ⌂   ⓘ 127.0.0.1:5173/about

Home   **About**

This is an about page

Figure 7.8 – The About page's content

By this point, you have learned how to create a default layout and render the target content view using RouterView dynamically. In the next section, we will learn how to implement and add a **Message Feed** page with the help of Vue Router.

Exercise 7.01 – implementing a Message Feed page using Vue Router

In this exercise, you will use RouterView to render a new view component that displays a message feed.

To access the code file for this exercise, refer to https://github.com/PacktPublishing/Frontend-Development-Projects-with-Vue.js-3/tree/v2-edition/Chapter07/Exercise7.01.

We are going to create a new page that displays a list of messages to the user. Users will be able to visit this page whenever they enter the localhost:3000/messages path in the browser. Perform the following steps:

1. Use the application generated by npm init vue@3 as a starting point, or within the root folder of the code repository, navigate into the Chapter07/Exercise7.01 folder by using the following commands in order:

    ```
    > cd Chapter07/Exercise7.01/
    > yarn
    ```

2. Open the exercise project in VS Code (by using the code . command within the project directory) or your preferred IDE.

3. Let's create a new view component called MessageFeed by adding a MessageFeed.vue file to the ./src/views/ folder:

Figure 7.9 – The views directory hierarchy

This component will render a list of messages. We define messages – an array of strings – as our local data using <script setup> as follows:

```
<template>
  <div>
    <h2> Message Feed </h2>
    <p v-for="(m, i) in messages" :key="i">
    {{ m }}
    </p>
  </div>
</template>
<script setup>
const messages = [
        'Hello, how are you?',
        'The weather is nice',
        'This is the message feed',
        'And I am the fourth message'
    ]
</script>
```

4. Create a router file at src/router/index.js if it doesn't exist. Make sure you import createRoute and createWebHistory from 'vue-router' and the HomeView component, as shown in the following code:

```
import { createRouter, createWebHistory } from
'vue-router'
import HomeView from '../views/HomeView.vue'
```

5. We declare a route designated to MessageFeed, named messageFeed with its path set to
    /messages. We will also lazy-load the component. This step will be completed by appending
    an object with the required information to the routes array:

```
export const routes = [
  {
    path: '/',
    name: 'home',
    component: HomeView
  },
  {
    path: '/about',
    name: 'about',
    component: () => import('../views/AboutView.vue')
  },
  {
    path: '/messages',
    name: 'messageFeed',
    component: () =>
      import('../views/MessageFeed.vue')
  }
]
```

6. Finally, within the same file, create a router instance using the routes array we defined
    and with the createRouter and createWebHistory functions we imported:

```
const router = createRouter({
  history: createWebHistory(import.meta.env.BASE_URL),
  routes
})
export default router
```

7. Make sure that in src/main.js. we import the created router instance and attach it to
    the app instance as a plugin by using app.use(router):

```
import router from './router'
const app = createApp(App)
app.use(router)
app.mount('#app')
```

8. In `App.vue`, make sure `<template>` only contains the following code:

    ```
    <template>
      <RouterView />
    </template>
    ```

9. Run the application using the following command:

    ```
    yarn dev
    ```

10. Upon visiting `localhost:3000/messages` in the browser (or any local server Vite has created), the page should appear with the correct content – the **Message Feed** page as shown in the following screenshot:

Message Feed

Hello, how are you?
The weather is nice
This is the message feed
And I am the fourth message

Figure 7.10 – The Message Feed Page

This exercise demonstrates how simple it is to add a new page route to a Vue.js application using Vue Router, while keeping your code organized and easy to read. Now that we have our routes ready to use, we can allow users to navigate between pages without typing the full path.

Setting up navigation links with RouterLink

As we know, `RouterView` oversees rendering the correct active view content relative to the URL path; `RouterLink`, on the other hand, oversees mapping the routes to navigable links. `RouterLink` is a Vue component that helps users navigate within an app with routing enabled. `RouterLink` by default renders an anchor tag, `<a>`, with a valid `href` link generated by its `to` prop.

In our example app generated by Vite, since there are two routes pre-populated, there are also two RouterLink instances added to the `<template>` section of App.vue as the header navigation menu:

```
<nav>
  <RouterLink to="/">Home</RouterLink>
  <RouterLink to="/about">About</RouterLink>
</nav>
```

Since we are using the web history mode with `createWebHistory()`, the `to` prop of each RouterLink should receive an identical value with the `path` property declared in the targeted route object (as in the list of routes defined in `src/router/index.js`).

Since we name our routes, an alternative way of using the `to` prop is to bind it with an object containing the route name instead of the path. Using the name is highly recommended to avoid complex link refactoring when we need to adjust the paths given to certain routes in our app. Hence, we can rewrite our links as follows:

```
<nav>
  <RouterLink :to="{ name: 'home' }">Home</RouterLink>
  <RouterLink :to="{ name: 'about' }">About</RouterLink>
</nav>
```

Also, Vue Router adds an extra CSS class, `router-link-active`, to the `<a>` tag when the route in question is active. We can customize this class selector through the `active-class` prop of the RouterLink component.

In the **Element** tab of the browser dev tools, we can see the RouterLink component rendered as follows:

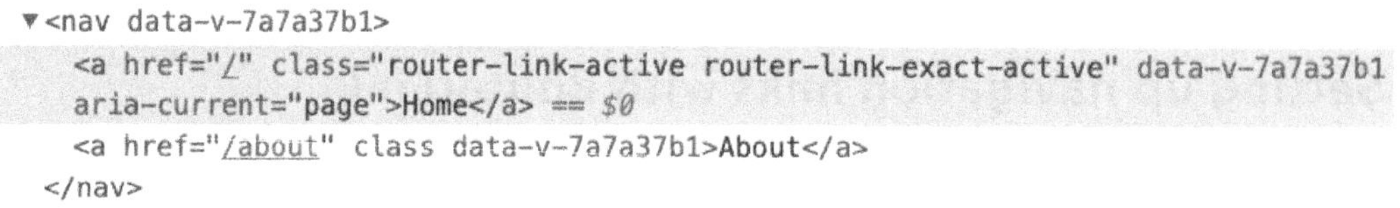

```
▼ <nav data-v-7a7a37b1>
    <a href="/" class="router-link-active router-link-exact-active" data-v-7a7a37b1
    aria-current="page">Home</a> == $0
    <a href="/about" class data-v-7a7a37b1>About</a>
  </nav>
```

Figure 7.11 – RouterLink in the browser's Element tab

The view in the browser will be as follows:

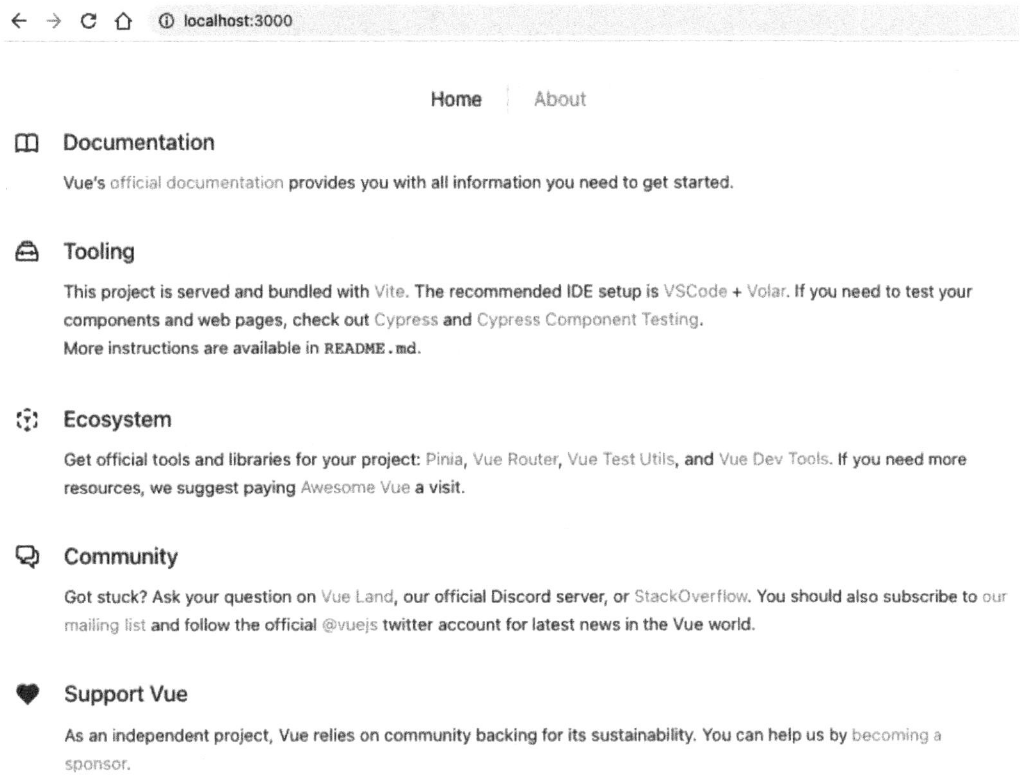

Figure 7.12 – The Home page with navigation links

Note that since we have access to this.$router within a component, we can trigger a navigation route programmatically by using this.$router.push() and pass a path or a router object in a similar way to using to:

```
this.$router.push('/home')
```

Or within the <script setup>, we can perform the following alternative code:

```
import { useRouter } from 'vue-router'

const router = useRouter();
router.push('/home');
```

In this section, we looked at how you can use the `<RouterLink/>` element to navigate between our views as with traditional HTML `<a>` tags.

Next, we will see how you can programmatically send a user to their last viewed route in a manner similar to the web browser's **Back** button.

Tip for implementing the Back button

Sometimes, we want to navigate back to the previous page. Using `this.$router.push()` can achieve this, but it adds more routes in the history stack instead of going back. The correct technique is to use `this.$router.go(steps)`, in which `steps` is an integer that indicates the number of steps to go back or forward in the history stack. This functionality works similarly to `window.history.go(steps)`.

Consider the following example:

```
this.$router.go(-1) // similar to window.history.back()  -
    go back one page
```

Besides this, you can also navigate forward to a page that was loaded before and still exists in the history stack by using the same method as follows:

```
this.$router.go(1) // similar to window.history.forward() -
    go forward one page
```

Alternatively, we can rewrite the above code using useRouter() and <script setup>, as follows:

```
import { useRouter } from 'vue-router'

const router = useRouter();
router.go(1); //forward one page
router.go(-1); //back one page
```

Next, we'll make use of navigation links to add our new message feed page to our application's nav menu.

Exercise 7.02 – adding the navigation link to the MessageFeed route

We will add a quick link to the `MessageFeed` route we created in *Exercise 7.01*, using the `to` prop and `RouterLink` as explained in the preceding topic.

To access the code file for this exercise, refer to `https://github.com/PacktPublishing/Frontend-Development-Projects-with-Vue.js-3/tree/v2-edition/Chapter07/Exercise7.02`.

Let's go through the following steps:

1. Use the application generated with `npm init vue@3` as a starting point, or within the root folder of the code repository, navigate into the `Chapter07/Exercise7.02` folder by using the following commands in order:

   ```
   > cd Chapter07/Exercise7.02/
   > yarn
   ```

2. Open the exercise project in VS Code (by using the `code .` command within the project directory) or your preferred IDE.

3. Follow the instructions in *Exercise 7.01* to create the `MessageFeed` component, register it to `/messages` path, and make sure your router is enabled in the application.

4. In the `./src/App.vue` file, besides the auto-generated `RouterLink` components for home and about, add another `RouterLink` component that points to `/messages`:

   ```
   <template>
     <header>
       <nav>
         <RouterLink to="/">Home</RouterLink>
         <RouterLink to="/about">About</RouterLink>
         <RouterLink to="/messages">Message Feed
           </RouterLink>
       </nav>
     </header>
     <RouterView />
   </template>
   ```

5. Run the application using the following command:

   ```
   yarn dev
   ```

We will see the navigation links available in any view – they will not disappear when users navigate away since they are not a part of the RouterView component. Our screen should look as follows:

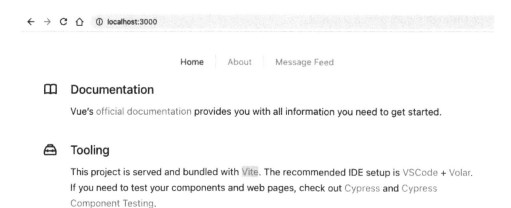

Figure 7.13 – The Home page with updated navigation links

6. Within App.vue, let's change the to value to point to the object named messageFeed. This is the name value given to this route defined in ./src/router/index.js:

```
<RouterLink :to="{ name: 'messageFeed' }">Message Feed
    </RouterLink>
```

7. The navigation should work as before; clicking on the **Message Feed** button should direct you to /messages, as shown in the following screenshot:

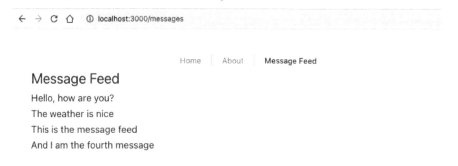

Figure 7.14 – Active page changes to Message Feed after clicking on the Message Feed link

8. Now, open the `index.js` file located in the `./src/router/` folder and change the path defined for the `messageFeed` route from `/messages/` to `/messagesFeed`:

```
export const routes = [
  {
    path: '/',
    name: 'home',
    component: HomeView
  },
  {
    path: '/about',
    name: 'about',
    component: () => import('../views/AboutView.vue')
  },
  {
    path: '/messagesFeed',
    name: 'messageFeed',
    component: () =>
      import('../views/MessageFeed.vue')
  }
]
```

9. Navigate to the app's Home page and click on **Message Feed** again. It should display the same **Message Feed** page as before but note that the URL path has changed to `/messagesFeed`:

Home | About | **Message Feed**

Message Feed

Hello, how are you?

The weather is nice

This is the message feed

And I am the fourth message

Figure 7.15 – The Message Feed page with a new URL path

Note how straightforward it is to set up the link to the `/messages` path with just one line of code and update the related path accordingly.

So far, we have defined some simple routes without additional parameters for the targeted route – this will be our next challenge.

Passing route parameters

Previously we learnt each route was a standalone view and did not need to pass or connect any data to the other routes. But Vue Router doesn't limit the power of routing to only this. With named routes, we can also easily enable data communication between routes.

In our example app, we want our about page to be able to receive a data string called user as the user's name from the link triggered. Prior to Vue Router 4.1.4, we can achieve this feature by changing the to prop from a string literal to an object literal with a name and params properties, as shown below:

```
<RouterLink :to="{ name: 'about', params: { user: 'Adam' }}">
  About
</RouterLink>
```

This change informs the router to pass the desired parameters to the About page when users click on the targeted link. These additional parameters are not visible on the rendered href link, as shown in the following screenshot:

```
▼ <nav>
    <a href="/" class="router-link-exact-active router-link-
    active">Home</a>
    " | "
    <a href="/about" class>About</a>
  </nav>
```

Figure 7.16 - Generated href link is without parameters

The output will be as follows:

Home   About

About Adam

Figure 7.17 – The About page renders the user passed through route params

However, there is one significant downside to this approach.

Let's refresh the page while you are still on the `./about` path. The output will be an page without user's name, as seen below:

Figure 7.18 – About page on refresh loses user's details

Upon refresh, the Vue engine triggers route without any `user` passed to the route's `params` field, unlike when the user clicked on a specific predefined link. And parameters passed using this approach was not saved or cached. We consider this an anti-pattern for Vue practice.

Starting from Vue Router 4.1.4, passing params directly on the `to` object is deprecated. for passing params to a route, we should use alternative approach such as using Pinia as the global's data store, or to use the query params of the URL.

Query params for a URL route starts after the question mask - ?, as seen in the syntax below:

```
<your-app-url>?<param1>=<value1>&<param2>=<value2>
```

In the above syntax, each parameter field is separated by & symbol. For example, to pass the user parameter to our `/about` page, we will construct our URL as follows:

```
localhost:3000/about?user=Adam
```

And in the About component, we will retrieve the `query` field from the `route`

object, and get the relevant field's value, as shown in the following code:

```
<script setup>
import { useRoute} from 'vue-router'

const route = useRoute();
const { user } = route.query;
</script>
```

In the `template` section, we can replace `$route.params.user` to `user`, and the output stays the same, even on refreshing the page.

```
<template>
  <div class="about">
```

```
    <h1>About {{ user }}</h1>
  </div>
</template>
```

In the following section, we will learn how to intercept the navigation flow and dynamically assigning params between routes with **Router Hooks**.

Understanding Router Hooks

To understand Vue Router Hooks, first, we need to understand the general flow of route navigation as described in the following diagram:

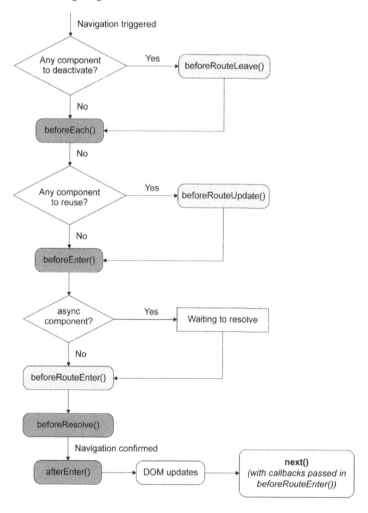

Figure 7.19 – Navigation resolution flow diagram

Once navigation is triggered for a certain route, Vue Router provides several primary navigation guards, or Hooks, for developers to guard or intercept that navigation process. These guards can be hooked either globally or in the component, depending on the type.

Some examples are as follows:

- **Globally**: `beforeEach`, `beforeResolve`, and `afterEach`
- **Per component**: `beforeEnter`
- **In-component**: `beforeRouteUpdate`, `beforeRouteEnter`, and `beforeRouteLeave`

For Composition API, those in-component Hooks are available as `onBeforeRouteUpdate`, and `onBeforeRouteLeave`. There is no `onBeforeRouteEnter` since this is equivalent to using the `setup()` (or `script setup`) itself.

As seen in *Figure 7.19*, the Vue engine considers navigation only after all the Hooks or guards have been resolved, including any asynchronous guard.

Now, let's see how to set up `beforeEach` Hooks.

Setting up beforeEach Hooks

`beforeEach` is a global Hook and is called at the very beginning of navigation, *before* the other global and in-component Hooks are triggered (except for `beforeRouteLeave` in the previous view component). It should be defined as a global method of the `router` instance during initialization in the `index.js` file and takes the following syntax:

```
const router = createRouter({
  //...
})


router.beforeEach(beforeEachCallback)
```

In the preceding snippet, `beforeEachCallback` is a hook function that receives three arguments:

```
const beforeEachCallback = (
  to, // The destination route
  from, //The source route
  next //The function to trigger to resolve the hook
) => { ... })
```

We could write this directly as follows:

```
router.beforeEach((to, from, next) => { … })
```

For example, if we want to display a different page to display a generic message whenever a user navigates to About without a value for the user passed to query params, we can hook beforeEach as follows:

```
router.beforeEach((
    to, // The destination route
    from, //The source route
    next //The function to trigger to resolve the hook
) => {
    if (to.name === 'about' && (!to.query?.user)) {
        next({ name: 'error' })
    }
    else {
        next();
    }
})
```

Here, we check whether the destination route is about, and if it doesn't pass any additional parameters nor any value for the user parameter, we will navigate to an error route instead. Otherwise, we will just proceed as normal with next().

> **Note**
>
> next() is required to be called *exactly once in any given non-overlapped flow logic* (once for if and once for else); otherwise, there will be errors.

We still need to create an error page with an Error.vue view component that displays a simple message:

```
<template>
    <div>
        <h2>No param passed.</h2>
    </div>
</template>
```

Also, make sure to register the path accordingly:

```
{
    path: '/error',
    name: 'error',
    component: () => import('../views/Error.vue'),
}
```

Now, in the default view, after clicking on the **About** link, the app will render the **Error** page instead of the **About** page, as seen in the following screenshot:

← → C ⌂ ⓘ 127.0.0.1:3000/error

Home | About

No param passed.

Figure 7.20 – The Error page displayed when About is clicked without param being passed

Now, let's go to the App.vue file and assign the to prop to the path "/about?user=Adam":

```
<RouterLink to="/about?user=Adam">About</RouterLink>
```

And in the About.vue file, we use the following template code:

```
<div class="about">
    <h1>About {{ $route.query.user }}</h1>
</div>
```

Let's navigate back to our app's **Home** page and click on the **About** link. Since we have a proper user passed, the output will be as follows:

← → C ⌂ ⓘ 127.0.0.1:3000/about?user=Adam

Home | About

About Adam

Figure 7.21 – The About page displayed when there is a user passed in query params

We shall now look at a few key points that differentiate the beforeEach and beforeResolve Hooks.

Distinguishing between the beforeEach and beforeResolve Hooks

We can also register a global Hook with beforeResolve with the same syntax. Unlike beforeEach, which is triggered when navigation is set up, beforeResolve will be triggered just before the navigation is carried out and confirmed *after all the Hooks (both global and in-component) are resolved*:

```
router.beforeResolve((
  to, // The destination route
  from, //The source route
  next //The function to trigger to resolve the hook
) => {
  if (to.name === 'about' && (!to.query?.user)) {
    next({ name: 'error' })
  }
  else {
    next();
  }
})
```

The output results will remain the same as in *Figure 7.20* and *Figure 7.21*.

Let's now look at the afterEach Hook in detail.

The afterEach Hook

The afterEach() Hook is the last global navigation guard to be triggered after the navigation is confirmed (which means after beforeResolve()). Unlike the other global guards, the hook function to pass to afterEach() does not receive a next function – hence, it won't affect the navigation.

In addition, the to and from parameters are read-only Route objects. Hence, the best use case for afterEach is to save data such as the last visited Route object for a **Back** button, the passed parameters of the route destination, or page view tracking.

For example, we can have a default value of `user`, assign it, and save it whenever needed:

```
let user = 'Adam';

router.beforeEach((to, from, next) => {
  if (to.name === 'about' && (!to.query?.user)) {
    next({ name: 'about', query: { user }})
  }
  else {
    user = to.query.user;
    next()
  }
});

router.afterEach((to, from) => {
  if (to.name === 'about' && to.query && to.query.user) {
    user = to.query.user;
  }
})
```

Now, in the App.vue file, let's change the value of `user` to `Alex`:

```
<RouterLink to="/about?user=Alex"> About </RouterLink>
```

The output when clicking on the **About** link now is as follows:

←   →   C   ⌂   ⓘ 127.0.0.1:3000/about?user=Alex

Home | About

About Alex

Figure 7.22 – The About page displaying the new user's name (Alex)

However, on navigating to "/about" only, the **About** page renders with the default user – **Adam** – instead, as follows:

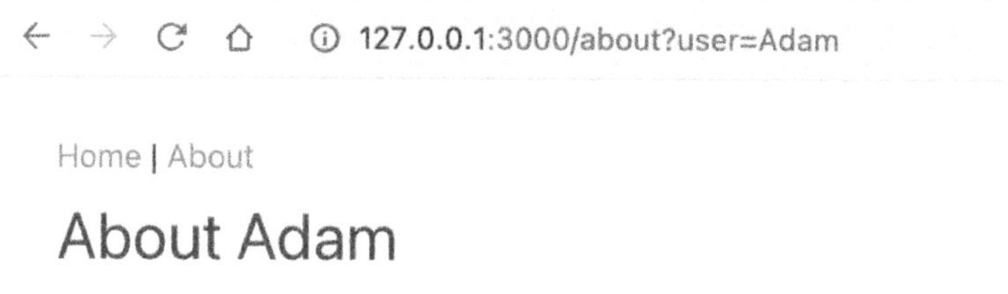

Home | About

About Adam

Figure 7.23 – The About page displaying the default user value on reloading (Adam)

In this section, we looked at the afterEach Hook. We used the afterEach Hook to pass data through to the **About** page without having to contain that data in the URL. This same technique can be used for updating other behavior such as the desired target page when pressing the Back button.

Personalizing Hooks per route

Instead of defining a global Hook, which can cause unseen bugs and requires a route check, we can define a beforeEnter guard directly in the targeted route's configuration object – for example, our about route:

```
beforeEnter: (to, from, next) => {
    if (!to.query?.user) {
      to.query = { user : 'Adam' }
    }
    next()
}
```

With this approach, whether reloading the page or clicking on the link to navigate to the **About** page, the output is now consistent, but the URL doesn't show the default params (*Figure 7.24*)

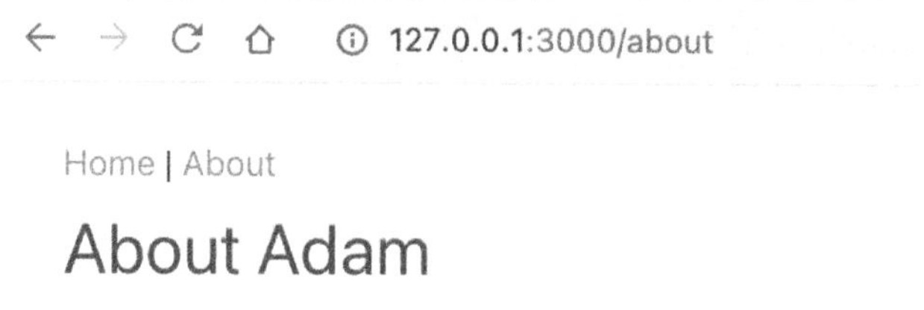

Home | About

About Adam

Figure 7.24 – The About page displaying the default user (Adam) without URL updated

> **Note**
>
> With `beforeEnter()`, `to` is writeable and you will have access to `this` (which points to the specific route – `About`). It will only be triggered when users trigger navigation to the About page.

In this section, we looked at the different Router Hooks available in Vue, including `beforeEach`, `beforeResolve`, and `afterEach`. We saw how each of these Hooks is called at a different point in the routing process. As a practical example, we looked at a route that, if not provided a parameter, instead directs the user to an **Error** page. These Hooks can be very useful, especially when setting up an authenticated route.

In the next section, we'll look at setting up in-component Hooks.

Setting up in-component Hooks

Finally, we can also use in-component Hooks as component lifecycle Hooks when we want to scope those Hooks at the component level for better code maintenance or enhance the workflow when the same component needs to behave differently in a certain use case.

We can have the `about` component now with the `beforeRouteEnter()` Hook defined as follows:

```
<script>
export default {
  data() {
    return {
      user: ''
    }
  },
  beforeRouteEnter(to, from, next) {
    if (!to.params || !to.params.user) {
      next(comp => {
        comp.user = 'Alex'
      })
    }
    else {
      next();
    }
  }
}
</script>
```

As you can see, we don't have access to the this scope of the component during beforeRouteEnter because the view component is still being created. Luckily, we can access the instance through a callback passed to next(). Whenever the navigation is confirmed, which means the component is created, the callback will be triggered, and the component instance will be available as the sole argument (comp) of the callback.

Alternatively, we can rewrite the above code using Composition API and the hook useRoute imported from 'vue-router' package, as follows:

```
import { useRoute } from 'vue-router';
import { ref } from 'vue';

const user = ref('');
const route = useRoute();

if (!route.params || !route.params.user) {
  user.value = 'Alex'
}
```

> **Note**
> For beforeRouteUpdate and beforeRouteLeave, the component has been created – hence, this instance is available and there is no need for a callback for next(). In fact, a callback function is only supported in next() within the use of beforeRouteEnter().

beforeRouteUpdate (or onBeforeRouteUpdate) is called when the same component is reused for a different route. This applies when we use dynamic routing, which will be discussed in the next section.

beforeRouteLeave (or onBeforeRouteLeave) is triggered when the component is deactivated or before the user navigates away from the current view. This is called right before the beforeEach guard of the new navigation and is usually used in editor components to prevent users from navigating away without saving.

In this guard, we can cancel the new navigation by passing false to the next() function.

For example, imagine that we add the following Hook to the component's option in the AboutView.vue file:

```
import { onBeforeRouteLeave } from 'vue-router';
onBeforeRouteLeave((to, from, next) => {
  const ans = window.confirm(
```

```
        'You are about to leave the About page. Are you sure?'
    );
    next(!!ans);
})
```

When we navigate away from the **About** page, a pop-up dialog will appear asking for confirmation, as shown in the following screenshot, and then continue navigating accordingly:

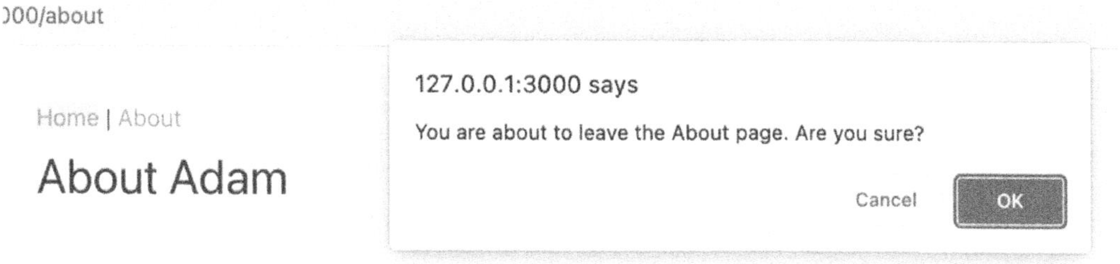

)00/about

Home | About

About Adam

127.0.0.1:3000 says

You are about to leave the About page. Are you sure?

Cancel   OK

Figure 7.25 – Dialog asking to confirm before navigating away from the About page

In this section, we looked at setting up in-component Hooks – that is, Hooks that are scoped to specific components. We set up an in-component Hook for the about component that asks a user to confirm before leaving the page.

We will now see how to decouple passed parameters into props.

Decoupling Params with Props

In the index.js file, let's adjust the configuration of the about route with an additional property called props.

By setting this property's value as a function which accepts a route and returns an object containing an user field of value based on route.query.user, the router will automatically understand and map any route.query parameters into the props of the view component accordingly:

```
{
    path: '/about',
    name: 'about',
    component: () => import('../views/AboutView.vue'),
     props: route => ({ user: route.query.user || 'Adam' })
}
```

In the `AboutView.vue` file, we will define a prop type `user` as follows:

```
<script setup>
import { defineProps } from 'vue'
const props = defineProps({
    user: String
})
</script>
```

And in the `<template>` section, we will replace `$route.query.user` with `user`:

```
<template>
  <div class="about">
    <h1>About {{user}}</h1>
  </div>
</template>
```

The output will still be the same, as shown in the following screenshot:

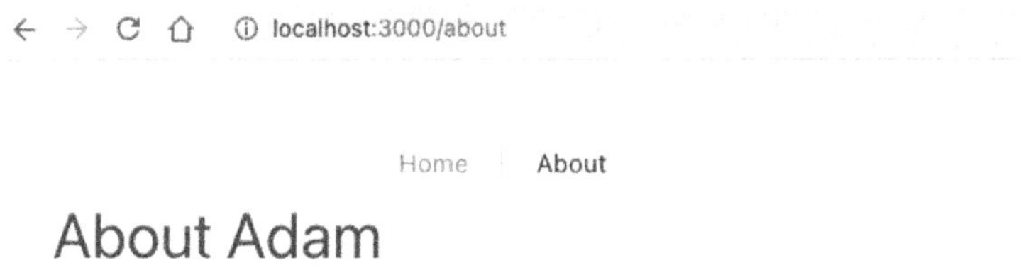

Figure 7.26 – The user is passed through route params and mapped to props

Also, you can define a static data that you want to pass within the `props` property of the `route` configuration. Instead of a `Function` value, `props` can now be declared as an object with the required data, as in the following example:

```
{
    //...
    props: { age: 32 },
}
```

With a similar step, we will declare `age` as a `props` component in `AboutView.vue`, and print it out to the screen as text:

```
<template>
  <div class="about">
```

```
    <h2>Age: {{age}}</h2>
  </div>
</template>
<script setup>
import { defineProps } from 'vue'
const props = defineProps({
    age: Number
})
</script>
```

Now when the About page is clicked, the page will render as follows:

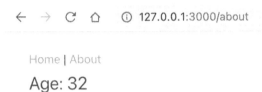

Figure 7.27 – With the props preset in the router configuration

Exercise 7.03: Passing the content of the selected message to a new message page and having it printed out

We shall continue from *Exercise 7.02, Adding the Navigation Link to the MessageFeed Route*, where we defined the MessageFeed route with a URL path to messages. This view will render a list of predefined messages in the data property of the view component's options.

To access the code file for this exercise, refer to https://github.com/PacktPublishing/ Frontend-Development-Projects-with-Vue.js-3/tree/v2-edition/Chapter07/ Exercise7.03.

In this exercise, we will create a new /message page, designated to render the content of a message selected by the user. It should be reusable.

Do the following:

1. In the ./src/views/ folder, we create a new single-file component called Message.vue. This component receives a content prop of type string and renders it under a <p> tag:

```
<template>
    <div>
        <p>{{content}}</p>
```

```
        </div>
    </template>
    <script setup>
    import { defineProps } from 'vue'
    const props = defineProps({
        content: {
            default: '',
            type: String
        }
    })
    </script>
```

2. Let's register a new route with the Message component to the existing routes in ./src/router/index.js. We will define the new route as a message with the path to /message:

```
export const routes = [
  //…,
  {
    path: '/message',
    name: 'message',
    component: () => import('../views/Message.vue'),
  }
]
```

3. Since the route is registered and ready to be used, we need to make changes to the <template> section of ./src/views/MessageFeed.vue to ensure each message line is now clickable and will redirect the user to the new route when clicked.

    Let's replace the <p> tag with router-click. And because we have named our new route as message, we will set to of each RouterLink to bind to /message.

```
<template>
  <div>
  <h2> Message Feed </h2>
  <div v-for="(m, i) in messages" :key="i" >
    <RouterLink :to="`/message`">
```

```
        {{ m }}
      </RouterLink>
    </div>
  </div>
</template>
```

4. Under `template`, we'll add a `<script setup>` tag containing some sample data for our messages:

```
<script setup>
const messages = [
    'Hello, how are you?',
    'The weather is nice',
    'This is the message feed',
    'And I am the fourth message'
]
</script>
```

5. Within the message route definition (`router/index.js`), we add `props: route => ({ content: route.query.content })` to map all `content` query passed to the route to the related prop.

```
export const routes = [
  //...,
  {
    path: '/message',
    name: 'message',
    component: () => import('../views/Message.vue'),
    props: route => ({ content: route.query.content })
  }
]
```

6. When you open the `./messages` page, all the messages are now clickable as shown in the following screenshot:

Figure 7.28 – Each message now is a navigable link

7. Now when the user clicks on a message, it will open a new page. However, the page content will be empty, as we have not passed any content parameter to the `<RouteLink>` component, as shown in the following screenshot:

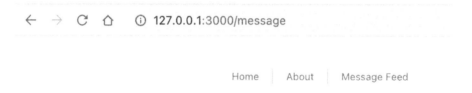

Figure 7.29 – Empty message page

8. Let's go back to `./src/views/MessageFeed.vue` and add `?content=${m}` to the route link of message, in which m is the `message` at index `i` in the `messages` list, in the `<template>` section:

```
<div>
<h2> Message Feed </h2>
<div v-for="(m, i) in messages" :key="i" >
  <RouterLink :to="`/message?content=${m}`">
    {{ m }}
  </RouterLink>
</div>
</div>
</template>
```

9. Now when you click on the first message, `Hello, how are you?`, the output will be the following:

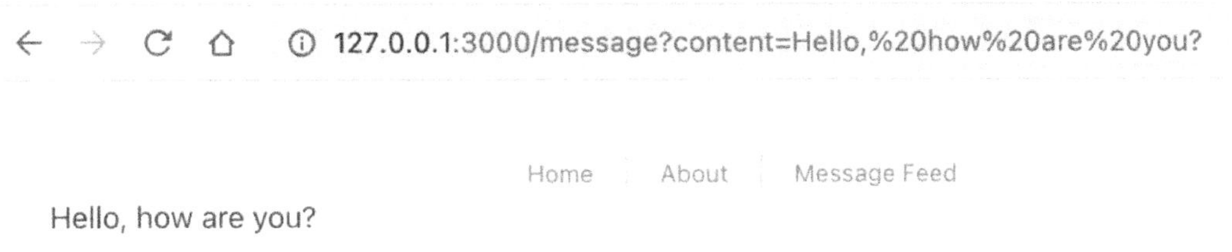

← → C ⌂   ⓘ **127.0.0.1:3000/message?content=Hello,%20how%20are%20you?**

Home   About   Message Feed

Hello, how are you?

Figure 7.30 – Message page with the passed content

10. Next, let's extract the `messages` static data from `./src/views/MessageFeed.vue` and save it in `./src/assets/messages.js`:

```
const messages = [
    'Hello, how are you?',
    'The weather is nice',
    'This is the message feed',
    'And I am the fourth message'
];


export default messages;
```

11. In `./src/views/MessageFeed.vue`, we will replace the local data property with `props` which has a `messages` array type, as follows:

```
<script setup>
import { defineProps } from 'vue'
const props = defineProps({
    messages: {
        default: [],
        type: Array
    }
})
</script>
```

12. Now, we need to load the list of `messages` and assign it the `props` upon navigating to the `/messages` route. We will do this by using the Function `props` of the route definition, and the hook `beforeEnter()` to normalize the data into related `props` for rendering. You can do that by modifying your `messageFeed` route defined in `src/router/index.js` as follows:

```
{
    path: '/messages',
    name: 'messageFeed',
    component: () =>
      import('../views/MessageFeed.vue'),
    props: route => ({
    messages: route.query.messages?.length > 0
             ? route.query.messages : []
    }),
    async beforeEnter(to, from, next) {
      next()
    }
  },
```

13. Within `beforeEnter`, we will lazy-load the list of messages with `import`:

```
const module = await import ('../assets/messages.js');
```

14. Then, we can retrieve the needed information as follows:

```
const messages = module.default;
if (messages && messages.length > 0) {
  to.query.messages = messages;
}
```

15. The full code for the route in `src/router/index.js` should be the following:

```
{
    path: '/messages',
    name: 'messageFeed',
    component: () =>
      import('../views/MessageFeed.vue'),

    props: route => ({
```

```
              messages: route.query.messages?.length > 0
                ? route.query.messages : []
          }),
          async beforeEnter(to, from, next) {
              if (!to.query || !to.query.messages) {
                const module = await import
                  ('../assets/messages.js');
                const messages = module.default;
                if (messages && messages.length > 0) {
                  to.query.messages = messages;
                }
              }

              next()
          }
      },
```

When viewing the website, we should see a message feed like in *Figure 7.28*.

At this point, we have learned and practiced how to configure routers, pass parameters, and intercept navigation between pages in the application using different routing Hooks. In the next section, we are going to look at a more advanced topic – **dynamic routing**.

Dynamic routing

If there is a lot of data that follows the same format, such as a list of users or a list of messages, and it's required to create a page for each of them, so we need to use a routing pattern. With a routing pattern, we can create a new route dynamically from the same component based on some additional information.

For example, we want to render the User view component for every user but with different id values. Vue Router provides us with the ability to use dynamic segments denoted by a colon (:) to achieve dynamic routing.

Instead of using params, which doesn't persist its value when you refresh the page or appear in the URL, we define the required params directly in the path as follows:

```
{
    path: '/user/:id',
    name: 'user',
    component: () => import('../views/User.vue'),
```

```
    props: true,
}
```

In the preceding code, `:id` means `params` here is not static. When the route matches the given pattern, Vue Router will render the corresponding component with the appropriate content while keeping the URL as it should be. The value of `:id` will be exposed as `$route.params.id` in that view component's instance:

```
<template>
  <div>
    <h1>About a user: {{$route.params.id}}</h1>
  </div>
</template>
```

When users select URLs such as `/user/1` or `/user/2` (`./src/App.vue`), Vue will automatically generate sub-pages using our template.

Navigation paths will be mapped to the same route pattern and component but with different information, as shown in the following screenshot:

Figure 7.31 – Navigating to /user/2

When you click on **User 1**, you will see the following:

Figure 7.32 – Navigating to /user/1

We can also normalize `id` to `props` of the `User` component with `props: true` and load the data of the selected user before the instance is created and rendered:

```
<script setup>
import users from '../assets/users.js';
import { ref } from 'vue'

const name = ref('');
const age = ref(0);

const props = defineProps(['id'])
name.value = users[props.id - 1].name;
age.value = users[props.id - 1].age;
</script>
```

Now, we can adjust `<template>` to print out the details of the user:

```
<template>
  <div>
    <h1>About a user: {{id}}</h1>
    <h2>Name: {{name}}</h2>
    <p>Age: {{age}}</p>
  </div>
</template>
```

The output when selecting `/user/1` will now be as follows:

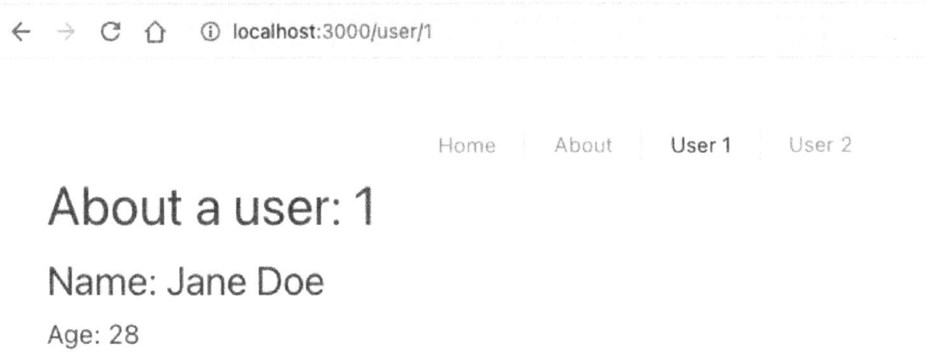

Figure 7.33 – Navigating to /user/1 with an updated UI

In this section, we looked at dynamic routing by setting up a route that extracts a parameter from a given URL. This technique allows you to create user-friendly URLs and pass information to routes dynamically. In the next section, we will look at catching error paths.

Catching error paths

Other important routes that we always need to remember to handle besides the **Home** page (`'/'`) include error routes, such as `404 Not found` when the URL path doesn't match any registered path, among others.

For `404 Not found`, we can use the Regex pattern, `/:pathMatch(.*)*`, which stands for *matching every other URLs,* to collect all the cases that don't match the definted routes. The router's configuration should be located at the end of the array routes to avoid matching the wrong path:

```
{
    path: '/:pathMatch(.*)*',
    name: '404',
    component: () => import('../views/404.vue'),
}
```

When we type the wrong path for `/users`, the output will be as follows:

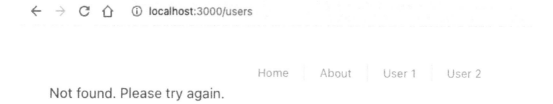

Figure 7.34 – Redirecting to 404 when the /users path is not found

In this section, we looked at how to use the Regex pattern to create a catch-all `404` page displayed to anyone that navigates to a non-existent route. Next, we will be implementing a message route that passes relevant data to the URL itself using the dynamic routing pattern.

Exercise 7.04 – implementing a message route for each message with the dynamic routing pattern

This exercise will get you familiar with creating and maintaining dynamic routes in combination with other navigation Hooks.

To access the code file for this exercise, refer to `https://github.com/PacktPublishing/Frontend-Development-Projects-with-Vue.js-3/tree/v2-edition/Chapter07/Exercise7.04`.

Let's go back to our message feed in *Exercise 7.03*, we will refactor our `Message` path to use routing patterns to dynamically navigate to a specific `message` path upon the user's selection and perform the following steps:

1. Let's open `./src/router/index.js` and change the path configuration of the message route to `/message/:id`, where `id` will be the index of a given `message` in the list of messages:

```
{
    path: '/message/:id',
    name: 'message',
    component: () => import('../views/Message.vue'),
    //...
}
```

2. Now, navigate to `./src/views/MessageFeed.vue`, and change the `to` prop of `RouterLink` for each message to the following:

```
<RouterLink :to="'/message/${i}'">
```

3. Let's go back to `./src/router/index.js`. Here, define `beforeEnter` as an asynchronous Hook for the `/message` route and lazy-load the content of the message into the `content` field of the route's `query`:

```
async beforeEnter(to, from, next) {
  if (to.params && to.params.id) {
    const id = to.params.id;
    const module = await import
      ('../assets/messages.js');
    const messages = module.default;
    if (messages && messages.length > 0 && id <
      messages.length) {
      to.query.content = messages[id];
    }
  }
  next()
},
```

4. Then we will define the props field as a function that returns an object containing the original params.id, and the query.content as id and content fields, respectively.

```
props: route => ({
  id: route.params.id,
  content: route.query.content
}),
```

The full routes should look like this:

```
const routes = [
  //...
  {
    path: '/message/:id',
    name: 'message',
    component: () => import('../views/Message.vue'),
    props: route => ({
      id: route.params.id,
      content: route.query.content
    }),
    async beforeEnter(to, from, next) {
      if (to.params && to.params.id) {
        const id = to.params.id;
        const module = await import ('../assets/messages.
js');
        const messages = module.default;
        if (messages && messages.length > 0 && id <
          messages.length) {
          to.query.content = messages[id];
        }
      }
      next()
    },
  }
]
```

5. Run the application using the following command:

    yarn dev

    When clicking on the first message in **Message Feed**, the next page will be as follows:

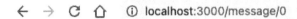

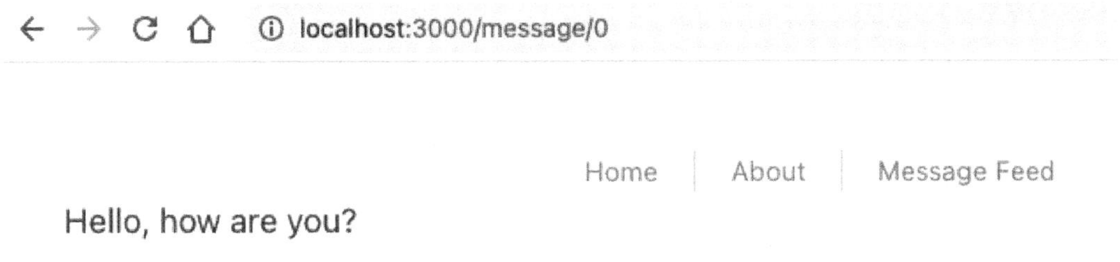

Home | About | Message Feed

Hello, how are you?

Figure 7.35 – The page displayed when visiting the /message/0 path

6. Alternatively, you can also set props: true, and instead of mapping the content to query.content in beforeEnter hook, you can also map it to the route.params directly, as seen below:

```
{
  path: '/message/:id',
    name: 'message',
    component: () => import('../views/Message.vue'),
    props: true,
    async beforeEnter(to, from, next) {
      if (to.params && to.params.id) {
        const id = to.params.id;
        const module = await import
          ('../assets/messages.js');
        const messages = module.default;
        if (messages && messages.length > 0 && id <
          messages.length) {
          to.params.content = messages[id];
        }
      }
      next()
    },
}
```

The output should stay the same.

Now that you have learned how to use dynamic routing, you can play around even further with more layers of routing patterns, such as message/:id/author/:aid. For these scenarios, we normally use a better approach – **nested routes**.

Nested routes

Many applications are composed of components that consist of several multiple-level nested components. For example, /user/settings/general indicates that a general view is nested in the settings view and this settings view is nested within the user view. It represents the **General information** section of a user's settings page.

Most of the time, we want the URL to correspond to such a structure, as demonstrated in the following screenshot:

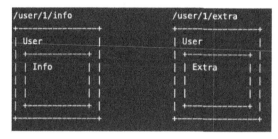

Figure 7.36 – User with two nested views – Info and Extra

Vue Router makes it easy to achieve this structure using nested route configurations and the RouterView component.

Let's go back to the User.vue view in our previous example (located in ./src/views/) and add a nested RouterView component in the <template> section:

```
<div>
  <h1>About a user: {{$route.params.id}}</h1>
  <RouterLink :to="`/user/${$route.params.id}/info`">
    Info
  </RouterLink> |
  <RouterLink :to="`/user/${$route.params.id}/extra`">
    Extra
  </RouterLink>

  <RouterView />
</div>
```

To start rendering components to this RouterView, we will configure the user route to have the children option, which accepts an array of route configurations for the child routes. For our example, we'll be adding an info and extra page for each user.

These child routes will be accessed as /user/:id/info and /user/:id/extra giving each user a unique info and extra page:

```
{
    path: '/user/:id',
    name: 'user',
    component: () => import('../views/User.vue'),
    props: true,
    children: [{
        path: 'info',
        name: 'userinfo',
        component: () => import('../views/UserInfo.vue'),
        props: true,
    }, {
        path: 'extra',
        component: () => import('../views/UserExtra.vue')
    }]
}
```

Certainly, we must create two new views. The first one is UserInfo, which will render all the information about a user based on the id value received:

```
<template>
  <div>
    <h2>Name: {{name}}</h2>
    <p>Age: {{age}}</p>
  </div>
</template>
<script setup>
import users from '../assets/users.js';
import { ref } from 'vue';
import { onBeforeRouteUpdate } from 'vue-router';

const props = defineProps(['id'])
```

```
const name = ref('')
const age = ref(0)

const user = users[props.id - 1];

name.value = user.name;
age.value = user.age;

onBeforeRouteUpdate((to, from, next) => {
  const user = users[props.id - 1];
  name.value = user.name;
  age.value = user.age;
  next();
})
</script>
```

We also create UserExtra.vue, which will render any extra information (if there is any). In this example, it will only render simple text:

```
<template>
  <div>
    <h2>I'm an extra section</h2>
  </div>
</template>
```

The nested views are ready! Whenever the user clicks on the **Info** link, it will load the UserInfo view and update the URL as follows:

Figure 7.37 – The User page with the nested UserInfo view

When the user clicks on **Extra**, they will see the same, as is shown in the following screenshot:

Home   About   User 1   User 2

About a user: 1

Info | Extra

I'm an extra section

Figure 7.38 – The User page with the nested UserExtra view

In this section, we looked at nested routes – routes that have multiple children. In our example, the child routes were /user/:id/info and /user/:id/extra. This pattern allows us to create pages that extend their parent pages.

In the preceding example, we can now make edits to the **About a user** header and apply them to all child routes. As projects grow, making use of this pattern will allow you to avoid duplicating code across multiple views.

In the next section, we will use what we've learned so far to create navigation tabs for our message view component.

Exercise 7.05 – building navigation tabs within the message view

We will adapt the knowledge learned in the *Nested routes* section to build a **Navigation** tab section within the Message view from *Exercise 7.04*.

To access the code file for this exercise, refer to https://github.com/PacktPublishing/Frontend-Development-Projects-with-Vue.js-3/tree/v2-edition/Chapter07/Exercise7.05.

Perform the following steps:

1. Firstly, let's make some changes to our messages database in src/assets/messages.js by adding the following author and sent fields:

    ```
    const messages = [
      {
        content: 'Hello, how are you?',
        author: 'John',
        sent: '12 May 2019'
    ```

```
    },  {
      content:  'The  weather  is  nice',
      author:  'Lily',
      sent:  '12  Jun  2019'
    },
    {
      content:  'This  is  message  feed',
      author:  'Smith',
      sent:  '10  Jan  2020'
    },
    {
      content:  'And  I  am  the  fourth  message',
      author:  'Chuck',
      sent:  '1  Apr  2021'
    },
  ];
```

2. In `MessageFeed.vue`, we update the field to render as `message.content`, and not message since `message` is no longer a string:

```
<RouterLink  :to="`/message/${i}`">
  {{  m.content  }}
</RouterLink>
```

3. Next, we will create a `MessageAuthor.vue` view that only renders the name of the creator of the message:

```
<template>
  <h3>Author:</h3>
  <p>{{message.author}}</p>
</template>
<script setup>
import  {  defineProps  }  from  'vue'
const  {  message  }  =  defineProps({
  id:  {
    default:  '',
    type:  String
  },
```

```
    message: {
      default: () => ({ author: '' }),
      type: Object
    }
  })
</script>
```

4. Then, we will create a `MessageInfo.vue` view that renders the `message.sent` value:

```
<template>
  <div>
    <h3>Message info: </h3>
    <p>{{message.sent}}</p>
  </div>
</template>
<script setup>
import { defineProps } from 'vue'
const { message } = defineProps({
  id: {
    default: '',
    type: String
  },
  message: {
    default: () => ({ sent: '' }),
    type: Object
  }
})
</script>
```

5. Once we are done with the components, we need to register the new nested route under the children of the `message` route inside our router at `src/router/index.js`:

```
{
    path: '/message/:id',
    name: 'message',
    component: () => import('../views/Message.vue'),
    async beforeEnter(to, from, next) { ... },
    props: true,
```

```
      children: [{
        path: 'author',
        name: 'messageAuthor',
        props: true,
        component: () =>
          import('../views/MessageAuthor.vue'),
      }, {
        path: 'info',
        props: true,
        name: 'messageInfo',
        component: () =>
          import('../views/MessageInfo.vue'),
      }]
    }
```

6. We need to move the logic of `beforeEnter` for the `message` route to a separate function
    – `beforeEnterMessage`:

```
    async function beforeEnterMessage(to, from, next) {
      const id = to.params.id;
      const module = await import
        ('../assets/messages.js');
      const messages = module.default;
      if (messages && messages.length > 0 && id <
        messages.length) {
        to.params.message = messages[id];
      }


      next()
    }
```

7. Then, bind it to the `message` route's `beforeEnter`, and also to each of its child route's
    `beforeEnter` Hook, as shown in the following code block:

```
    {
        path: '/message/:id',
        name: 'message',
        component: () => import('../views/Message.vue'),
```

```
      beforeEnter: beforeEnterMessage,
      props: true,
      children: [{
        path: 'author',
        name: 'messageAuthor',
        props: true,
        component: () =>
          import('../views/MessageAuthor.vue'),
          beforeEnter: beforeEnterMessage,
      }, {
        path: 'info',
        props: true,
        name: 'messageInfo',
        component: () =>
          import('../views/MessageInfo.vue'),
          beforeEnter: beforeEnterMessage,
      }]
    }
```

8. Finally, in `Message.vue`, we will refactor the code to the following:

```
<template>
  <div>
    <p>Message content: {{message.content}}</p>
    <RouterLink :to="{ name: 'messageAuthor'}">
Author
</RouterLink> |
    <RouterLink :to="{ name: 'messageInfo'}">
      Info
    </RouterLink>
    <RouterView/>
  </div>
</template>
<script setup>
import { defineProps } from 'vue'
const { message } = defineProps({
    message: {
```

```
            default: () => ({ content: '' }),
            type: Object
        },
        id: {
            default: '',
            type: String
        }
    })
    </script>
```

9. Run the application using the following command:

    yarn dev

    You will see the following when you select the **Author** option:

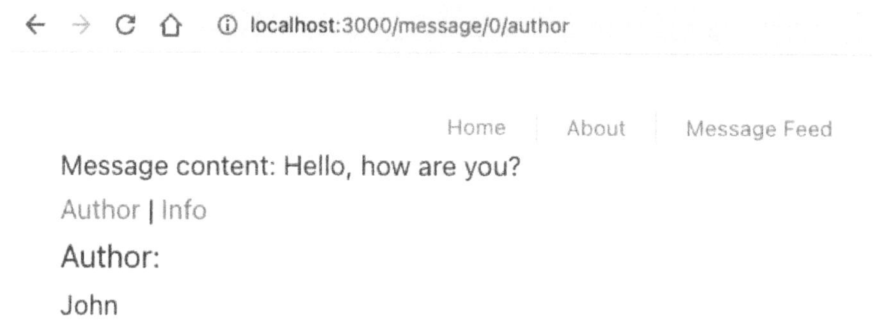

    ← → C ⌂   ⓘ localhost:3000/message/0/author

    Home | About | Message Feed

    Message content: Hello, how are you?
    Author | Info
    ## Author:
    John

    Figure 7.39 – Message page with Author selected

    When we navigate to the **Info** tab, the output becomes:

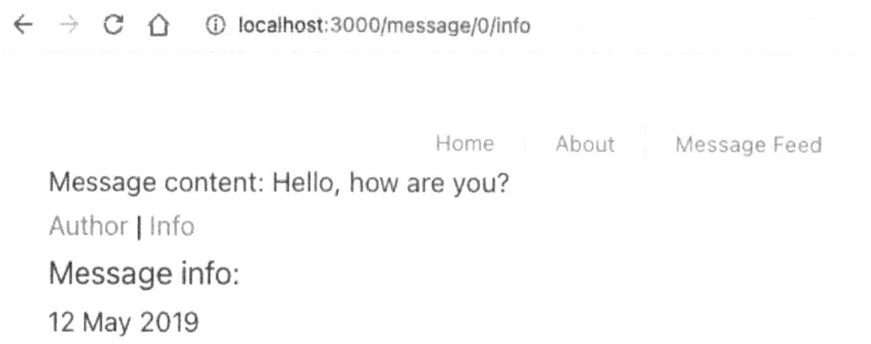

    ← → C ⌂   ⓘ localhost:3000/message/0/info

    Home | About | Message Feed

    Message content: Hello, how are you?
    Author | Info
    ## Message info:
    12 May 2019

    Figure 7.40 – The Message page with Info selected

With this exercise, we have covered almost all the basic functionalities of Vue Router, especially in terms of handling dynamic and nested routing. In the final section, we will go through how to create a reusable layout for the view by templating our application.

Using layouts

There are many ways to implement layouts in a Vue application. One of them is using a slot and creating a static wrapper `layout` component on top of `RouterView`. Despite its flexibility, this approach results in a heavy performance cost, both in terms of the unnecessary recreation of the component and in the extra data fetching required for every route change.

In this section, we will discuss a better approach, which is to take advantage of the power of the dynamic component. The components are as follows:

```
<component :is="layout"/>
```

Let's create an `src/layouts` folder with a `default` layout component. This component has a simple header navigation, a `main` slot to render the actual content (which is whatever `<RouterView>` renders), and a footer:

```
<template>
  <div class="default">
    <nav>
      <RouterLink to="/">Home</RouterLink> |
      <RouterLink to="/about">About</RouterLink>
    </nav>
    <main class="main">
      <slot/>
    </main>
    <footer>
      <div>Vue Workshop Chapter 07</div>
    </footer>
  </div>
</template>
```

In the App.vue file, we will change the default view generated by Vite to only `<RouterView>` and a wrapper around it. This wrapper is a dynamic component that will render whatever in the `layout` variable:

```
<template>
  <component :is="layout">
```

```
        <RouterView/>
    </component>
</template>
```

We will also initialize layout to be the default.vue component:

```
<script setup>
import Default from './layouts/default.vue'
const layout = Default
</script>
```

Now, to render the layout component in response to corresponding route changes, RouterView should control which layout to render. In other words, layout should be updatable and decided by the view component rendered inside RouterView.

To achieve this, we will pass layout to the currentLayout prop and update layout with the @update event in <RouterView>:

```
<component :is="layout">
    <RouterView
        :currentLayout="layout"
        @update:currentLayout="newLayout => layout = newLayout"
    />
</component>
```

In the <script setup> section, we change layout into a reactive variable using shallowRef as follows:

```
import Default from './layouts/default.vue'
import { shallowRef } from 'vue'


const layout = shallowRef(Default)
```

Upon creating an instance of the HomeView.vue component, we will emit an update:currentLayout event to update and render the desired layout accordingly:

```
<script setup>
import TheWelcome from '@/components/TheWelcome.vue'
import DefaultLayout from '../layouts/default.vue';
const props = defineProps(['currentLayout']);
```

```
const emits = defineEmits(["update:currentLayout"]);
emits('update:currentLayout', DefaultLayout);
</script>
```

The output will be as follows:

Figure 7.41 – The Home page rendered with a layout

Since the `layout` component is not part of the `RouterView` component, it will only re-render whenever the layout changes from within the view. This will maintain the performance of the app during user navigation.

In this section, we looked at how a dynamic component can be used to provide different layouts for different routes. This gives us the ability to have different common layouts – for example, one global menu for user-facing pages and another for admin pages, rendered based on the routes used.

In the next section, we'll build on what we learned here by creating a message application with dynamic nested routing and layouts.

Activity 7.01 – creating a message SPA with dynamic, nested routing, and layouts

To access the code file for this activity, refer to `https://github.com/PacktPublishing/ Frontend-Development-Projects-with-Vue.js-3/tree/v2-edition/Chapter07/ Activity7.01`

This activity aims to leverage your knowledge about Vue Router regarding registering routes and handling dynamic routes, nested routes, and route Hooks to create a **Message SPA**. This application will allow users to compose new messages, view a message feed, and navigate between messages to see their details:

1. Create a `MessageEditor` view (at `src/views/MessageEditor.vue`), which will render a view with `textarea` to the user, and a `submit` button to save the message.

2. Register the `editor` route with `MessageEditor` as its view in `src/router/index.js`.

3. Create a `MessageList` view (at `src/views/MessageList.vue`) that will render a list of `message id` values wrapped by an `a` tag, which will direct to the single message page with the given `id` upon selection.

4. Register the `list` route with `MessageList` as its view in `src/router/index.js`.

5. Add the `Messages` view (at `src/views/Messages.vue`), which will render links to either `editor` or `list` as its nested routes and render the nested view accordingly.

6. When the user navigates away from `editor`, should some content not yet have been submitted, display a message asking whether they want to save before navigating away. `Yes` will continue and `No` will abort the navigation.

7. Add a `Message` view (at `src/views/Message.vue`), which will render message content from `props`, and a `back` button to go back to the previous view. By default, it should go to `messages`.

8. Register the `Message` view with the dynamic route of `message/:id` in `src/router/index.js`.

9. Improve the UI by creating two different simple layouts, one for `messages` (with the title only) and one for `message` (with both the title and the `back` button).

The expected output is as follows:

- After adding messages via the editor route, the `/list` view that displays a feed of messages should look as follows:

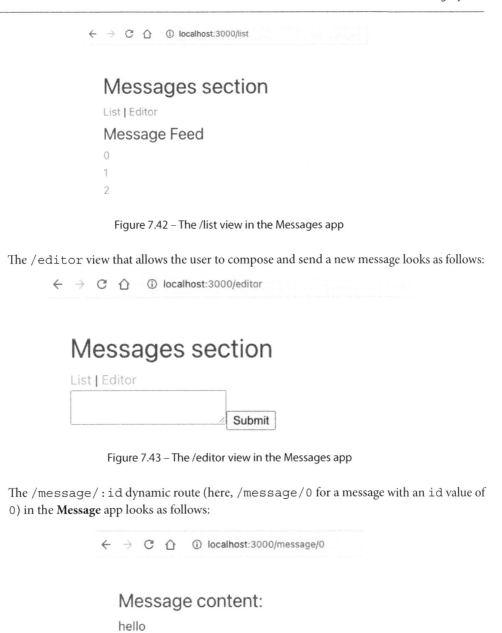

Figure 7.42 – The /list view in the Messages app

- The /editor view that allows the user to compose and send a new message looks as follows:

Figure 7.43 – The /editor view in the Messages app

- The /message/:id dynamic route (here, /message/0 for a message with an id value of 0) in the **Message** app looks as follows:

Figure 7.44 – The /message/0 view in the Message app

An alert will be displayed when the user tries to navigate away with an unsaved message as shown in the following screenshot:

Figure 7.45 – The /editor view when the user tries to leave the page with an unsaved message

Summary

Throughout this chapter, we have learned about the most basic and useful functionalities offered by Vue Router for building routing for any Vue.js application in an effective and organized way.

`RouterView` and `RouterLink` allow app developers to easily set up the navigation paths to their related views and maintain the SPA concept. The fact that they are Vue components themselves provides us as developers with the benefits of the Vue architecture, giving us flexibility in implementing nested views or layouts.

Defining the route as an object with different properties simplifies the architecture process, including refactoring existing paths and adding a new route to the system. Using router parameters and patterns provides dynamic routing with reusable views and enables communication and data preservation between pages.

Finally, with Hooks, we saw how we can intercept the navigation flow, set up authentication where needed, redirect to the desired path, or even load and keep certain important data before the user lands on the targeted page. There is an unlimited number of use cases in which these Hooks can be extremely useful, such as when implementing a back button, for instance. With Vue Router, we are now capable of composing a Vue.js application with a proper navigation system for users to explore.

In the next chapter, we will explore how we can enhance the UI experience for users by adding transitions and animations to our application.

8

Animations and Transitions

In the previous chapter, you learned about routes and how to set up an essential routing navigation system using Vue Router. Empowering a smooth transition between different routes or providing your application with the proper animation effects when users interact with it is the next level to achieve.

Throughout this chapter, you will explore the essentials of Vue transitions—how to create your transitions, including single-element animations and animations that use a group of elements, and how to combine them with external libraries for further custom animations. You will also learn how to create full-page animations with transition routes.

By the end of the chapter, you will be ready to implement and handle the fundamental transition and animation effects for any Vue application.

This chapter covers the following topics:

- Understanding Vue transitions
- Exploring JavaScript Hooks for transitions
- Transitioning groups of elements
- Examining transition routes
- Using the GSAP library for animation

Technical requirements

In this chapter, you need to set up a basic Vue project following the instructions in *Chapter 1*, *Starting Your First Vue Project*. You also need to add Vue Router, as learned about in *Chapter 7*, *Routing*, in some of its examples and exercises. It's recommended to create a single file Vue component to practice the examples and concepts mentioned easily.

The Node version has to be below v20 (preferable Yarn 1.22 and Node version above 16 and up to 19.x, and npm up to version 9.x.

You can find this chapter's source code here: `https://github.com/PacktPublishing/Frontend-Development-Projects-with-Vue.js-3/tree/v2-edition/Chapter08`.

Understanding Vue transitions

Unlike other frameworks, Vue.js provides developers with built-in support for animating Vue.js applications, including transitions and animations. Transitioning is implemented in such a simple manner that developers can easily configure and add it to their applications. The Vue.js transition mechanism supports CSS transitions, programmatic manipulation with JavaScript, and even integration with third-party animation libraries such as **GreenSock Animation API** (**GSAP**) or `Animate.css`.

Before diving into this topic, let's discuss the difference between transitions and animations. A **transition** happens when a component (or element) moves from one state to another, such as hovering on a button, navigating from one page to another, displaying a pop-up modal, and so on. Meanwhile, **animations** are like transitions but are not limited to just two states.

Understanding the basics of transitions will allow you to get started with animations.

Using the transition element

To access the code file for this example, refer to `https://github.com/PacktPublishing/Frontend-Development-Projects-with-Vue.js-3/tree/v2-edition/Chapter08/Example8.01`

In this example, to enable transitions for a single component or element, Vue.js provides the built-in `transition` component, which will wrap around the targeted element, as seen in `./Example8.01/src/components/Example8-01.vue`:

```
<transition name="fade-in">
  <h1 v-show="show">{{ msg }}</h1>
</transition>
```

The `transition` component adds two transition states—`enter` and `leave`—for any targeted element or component, including components with conditional rendering (`v-if`) and conditional display (`v-show`):

- `enter`: This transition state happens when the component *enters* the DOM
- `leave`: This transition state happens when the component *leaves* the DOM

The `transition` component receives a prop called `name` that represents the name of the transition—in this case, it's `fade-in`—and is also the prefix for the transition class names, which will be discussed next.

Exploring transition classes

Vue.js implements a CSS-based and class-based transition effect for `leave` and `enter`—hence, the transition will be applied to the target component using a set of class selectors.

Each of these class selectors has the `v-` prefix in case there is no `name` prop given for the `transition` component. The standard classes are grouped into two main groups.

The first group of transition classes is for the `enter` transition when the component is first displayed. Here is a list of the `enter` transition classes:

- `v-enter-from` (or `<name>-enter-from`): This is the starting state and is added to the component before the component is added or updated. This class will be removed after the component is inserted into the DOM and the transition finishes. In the `<style>` section of `./Example8.01/src/components/Example8-01.vue`, we will set the `.fade-in-enter-from` starting state as completely hidden with `opacity: 0`:

  ```
  <style>
  .fade-in-enter-from {
    opacity: 0;
  }
  </style>
  ```

- `v-enter-active` (or `<name>-enter-active`): This class defines the delay, duration, and easing curve when the component is actively entering the transition. It will be added to the component before the component is inserted, applied to the component during the entire entering phase, and removed once the effect completes. Using `Example 8-01` from the previous section, let's add `.fade-in-enter-active`, which will transition into an adjusted `opacity` state within 3 seconds:

  ```
  .fade-in-enter-active {
    transition: opacity 3s ease-in;
  }
  ```

- `v-enter-to` (or `<name>-enter-to`): This is the last sub-state of entering, where the effect frame is added after the component is inserted and removed when the effect finishes. In our example, we do not need to define anything since the `opacity` value for this state should be 1.

The second group of classes consists of the `leave` transitions, which trigger when the component is disabled or removed from view:

- `v-leave-from` (or `<name>-leave-from`): This is the starting state for the leaving transition. As with `v-enter-to`, we don't need to define styling effects for this state.

- `v-leave-active` (or `<name>-leave-active`): This is applied during the leaving phase and acts similarly to `v-enter-active`. Since we want to have a fade-out effect, we will use the same styling as with `fade-in-enter-active`:

  ```
  .fade-in-enter-active, .fade-in-leave-active {
    transition: opacity 3s ease-in;
  }
  ```

- v-leave-to (or <name>-leave-to): This is the ending state, with similar behavior to v-enter-to. Since the component is going to disappear from view, we will reuse the styling defined for the starting phase of fade-in-enter-from for fade-in-leave-to:

```
.fade-in-enter-from, .fade-in-leave-to {
  opacity: 0;
}
```

The following screenshot is a recap of all the states of transition described so far:

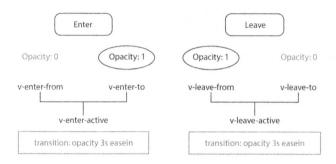

Figure 8.1 – Diagram of transition phases

In this section, we looked at three different enter transition states and three leave transition states. We also walked through using a transition state to slowly fade in some text when the text component enters a user's view, and this also applies when the text disappears from the user's view.

In the next section, we will explore adding animation effects to a component using these transition states that we have learned about.

An animation for a component

To access the code file for this example, refer to https://github.com/PacktPublishing/Frontend-Development-Projects-with-Vue.js-3/tree/v2-edition/Chapter08/Example8.02

Since an animation is basically an extended form of a transition (with more than two states), it is applied in the same way as a transition, with the exception that v-enter will only be removed for an animationend event triggered by Vue.js.

> **Note**
>
> animationend is a DOM event that is fired once the CSS animation finishes execution, with the condition that the target element still exists within the DOM and the animation is still attached to that element.

For example, in the `<template>` section in *Exercise 8.02*, we can define a new transition called `slide` using an animation CSS effect as a wrapper for the `h1` element that displays `msg`. This transition provides the animation effect of sliding from the left-hand side of the screen to the middle on entering and vice versa on leaving.

To get started, generate a `vue` starter project using the CLI with the following command:

```
npm init vue@3
```

Next, open up the project, go into `Example8.02/src/components/Example8-02.vue`, and then modify the existing `<h1>{{msg}}</h1>` code:

```
<transition name="slide">
  <h1 v-if="show">{{ msg }}</h1>
</transition>
```

In `<style>`, we need to define keyframes for the `slide` animation effect:

```
@keyframes slide {
  0% { transform: translateX(-100px) }
  100% { transform: translateX(0px) }
}
```

The related transition classes will be assigned the following styling:

```
.slide-enter-from, .slide-leave-to {
  transform: translateX(-100px);
}

.slide-enter-active {
  animation: slide 5s;
}

.slide-leave-active {
  animation: slide 5s reverse;
}
```

This means at the starting phase of `enter` and the ending phase of `leave`, the text position will be `-100px` from the designated position on the page. The browser will animate the element using the `slide` keyframe for a duration of 5 seconds, and in the `active` state of leaving, the animation will be exactly the opposite of the one in the active state of entering.

You'll also want to add `show` as a local data variable. You can do this by modifying the `<script setup>` section, as shown in the following code block:

```
import { ref } from 'vue'

const show = ref(true);
const msg = "Welcome to your Vue.js App";
const toggle = () => show.value = !show.value;
```

With that, we have implemented our animation. Now, comes the next challenge: what if we want to combine different animation or transition effects with `leave` and `enter` states, or use an external CSS library for these states? Let's look at custom transition classes.

Exploring custom transition classes

In this section, again, we'll be starting from the default starter project created with `npm init vue@3`. Instead of setting the transition name and letting the Vue.js mechanism populate the required class names, there is an option to provide custom classes through the following attributes and replace the conventional defaults.

For entering a state, use the following:

- `enter-from-class`
- `enter-active-class`
- `enter-to-leave`

For leaving a state, use the following:

- `leave-from-class`
- `leave-active-class`
- `leave-to-class`

We will start by creating a file based on the previous example (*Exercise 8.02*), but now we will use a `swing` animation effect for the active state of entering, and the `tada` effect for the active state of leaving. We will define the `enter-active-class` and `leave-active-class` attributes in our `transition` component as follows:

```
<transition
    name="slide"
    enter-active-class="swing"
    leave-active-class="tada"
```

```
    >
        <h1 v-if="show">{{ msg }}</h1>
</transition>
```

After that, in the `<style>` section, we just need to define `.tada` and `.swing` without any suffix pattern:

```
.tada {
  animation-fill-mode: both;
  animation-name: tada;
  animation-duration: 3s;
}

.swing {
  animation-fill-mode: both;
  transform-origin: top center;
  animation-duration: 2s;
  animation-name: swing;
}
```

The preceding code demonstrates the following animation classes:

- `tada`, which applies CSS animation styles defined by `tada` to its target element *both before and after* the execution, with a duration of 2 seconds

- `swing`, which applies CSS animation styles defined by `swing` to its target element both *before and after the execution,* with the origin point of transformation set to the top-center edge (`transform-origin`) and with a duration of 2 seconds

To set up the animation CSS styles, we add the dedicated keyframes:

```
@keyframes tada {
  0% {
    transform: scale3d(1, 1, 1);
  }

  10%, 20% {
    transform: scale3d(.8, .9, .8) rotate3d(0, 0, 1, -
                                            5deg);
  }
```

```
  30%, 50%, 70%, 90% {
    transform: scale3d(1.1, 1.1, 1.1) rotate3d(0, 0, 1,
                                          5deg);
  }

  40%, 60%, 80% {
    transform: scale3d(1.1, 1.1, 1.1) rotate3d(0, 0, 1, -
                                          5deg);
  }

  100% {
    transform: scale3d(1, 1, 1);
  }
}
@keyframes swing {
  20% { transform: rotate(5deg); }
  40% { transform: rotate(-10deg); }
  60% { transform: rotate(5deg); }
  80% { transform: rotate(-10deg); }
  100% { transform: rotate(0deg); }
}
```

For the tada animation, we set different CSS styles for each target keyframe (a time percentage of the animation sequence), such as resizing (scale3d()) and rotating (rotate3d()) the element in a 3D space. For the swing animation, we set different rotation effects for keyframes of 20%, 40%, 60%, 80%, and 100%.

You'll also want to add a show data variable. You can do this by modifying the existing export, as shown in the following code block:

```
export default {
  data() {
    return {
      msg: "Welcome to your Vue.js App",
      show: true,
    };
  },
  methods: {
```

```
    toggle() {
      this.show = !this.show;
    },
  },
}
```

When we run the application using the yarn dev command, we will have our animations for entering and leaving set separately. The following screenshot displays how the screen will now appear:

Figure 8.2 – The swing animation effect in action

You should see the welcome text shrink while rotating, transitioning from what was shown in *Figure 8.2* to what is shown in *Figure 8.3*:

Figure 8.3 – The tada animation effect in action

In this section, we looked at creating custom transition effects. As an example, we made `swing` and `tada`. We did this by defining the transition classes in our stylesheet and then adding keyframes for each of the effects. This technique can be used to create all kinds of custom transition effects. In the next section, we'll look at JavaScript Hooks and how they can be used for more complex animations.

Exploring JavaScript Hooks for transitions

To access the code file for this example, refer to `https://github.com/PacktPublishing/Frontend-Development-Projects-with-Vue.js-3/tree/v2-edition/Chapter08/Example8.03`

As we learned in the previous section, we can use custom transition classes to integrate external third-party CSS animation libraries for styling effects. However, there are external libraries that are JavaScript-based rather than CSS-based, such as Velocity.js or GSAP, which require Hooks to be set using JavaScript events and external animation handlers.

To use the Velocity.js or GSAP libraries in the Vue app, you need to install them separately by using the `npm install` or `yarn add` command, as follows:

- To install Velocity.js, use these commands:

```
npm install velocity-animate
#Or
yarn add velocity-animate
```

- To install GSAP, use these commands:

```
npm install gsap
#or
yarn add gsap
```

Being a Vue.js component means the `transition` component supports binding custom handlers to a list of events as props. Let's take a look at the following example:

```
<transition
  @before-enter="beforeEnter"
  @enter="enter"
  @leave="leave"
>
  <h1 v-if="show">{{ msg }}</h1>
</transition>
```

We bind the animation methods programmatically to the respective events on the transition element:

- beforeEnter is the animation state before the component is inserted—similar to the v-enter-from phase.

- enter is the animation state during the entire entering phase—similar to the v-enter-active phase.

- leave for the animation during the entire leaving phase. This is similar to the v-leave-active phase.

We need to define these event handlers in the methods section of the Example8.03/src/components/Example8-03.vue component's configuration:

```
<script setup>
export default {
  name: 'HelloWorld',
  props: {
    msg: String
  },
  data() {
    return {
      msg: '
      show: false
    }
  },
  methods: {
    beforeEnter() {
      //...
    },
    enter() {
      //...
    },
    leave() {
      //...
    }
  }
}
</script>
```

In this example, we will create our animation events using the `gsap.to()` and `gsap.timeline()` functionalities provided by the GSAP library, as follows:

```
beforeEnter(el) {
  el.style.opacity = 0;
},
enter(el, done) {
  gsap.to(el, {
    duration: 2,
    opacity: 1,
    fontSize: "20px",
    onComplete: done,
  });
},
leave(el, done) {
  const tl = gsap.timeline({
    onComplete: done,
  });

  tl.to(el, { rotation: -270, duration: 1,
       ease: "elastic" })
    .to(el, { rotation: -360 })
    .to(el, {
      rotation: -180,
      opacity: 0,
    });
}
```

For both `gsap.to` and the `return` variable of `gsap.timeline().to`, the syntax is pretty straightforward:

```
gsap.to(<element>, { <effect properties>, <time position> })
gsap.timeline().to(<element>, { <effect properties>, <time
position> })
```

Most of the effect properties have a similar syntax to CSS, so they're straightforward to learn how to use. In addition, we must pass a `done` callback received from the event emitter for events such as `enter` and `leave` to `onComplete` to make sure it is triggered and that the Hooks will not be called synchronously. Also, note that all the event emitters also pass `el`, which is a pointer to the current element in transition for use.

Other than these three events, there are other events we can bind, depending on the complexity of the animations and transitions, such as `afterEnter`, `enterCancelled`, `beforeLeave`, `afterLeave`, and `leaveCancelled`.

Please note that it's highly recommended to add `v-bind:css="false"` (or `:css="false"`) if you are using transitions with JavaScript only. This is to prevent Vue.js from detecting and applying any related CSS, therefore avoiding transition interference by accident:

```
<transition
    @before-enter="beforeEnter"
    @enter="enter"
    @leave="leave"
    :css="false"
  >
    <h1 v-if="show">{{ msg }}</h1>
</transition>
```

In this section, we looked at how external JavaScript libraries can be used for animations. We also implemented a simple tween using the GSAP library, making use of animation and timeline animation functions.

Let's now learn how to add a new message using an animation effect.

Exercise 8.01 – adding a new message with an animation effect

In this exercise, you will use the `transition` component and its CSS transition classes to add animation effect to a component.

To access the code file for this exercise, refer to `https://github.com/PacktPublishing/Frontend-Development-Projects-with-Vue.js-3/tree/v2-edition/Chapter08/Exercise8.01`.

We are going to create a message editor in which the user will compose and submit a new message. The new message will be displayed instantly with a sliding-from-the-right animation effect. To do this, see the following:

1. Use the application generated with `npm init vue@3` as a starting point, or within the root folder of the code repository, navigate into the `Chapter08/Exercise8.01` folder by using the following commands in order:

    ```
    > cd Chapter08/Exercise8.01/
    > yarn
    ```

2. Open the exercise project in your VS Code (by using the `code .` command within the project directory) or your preferred IDE.

3. Create a new component called `Exercise8-01.vue` located in the `/src/components/` folder. In this component, `<template>` will contain two element sections:

    *   `textarea`, for composing a new message with a button to submit it.

    *   `section`, where the newly composed message will be displayed:

```
<template>
  <div>
    <div class="editor--wrapper">
      <textarea ref="textArea" class="editor" />
      <button @click="onSendClick()"
        class="editor--submit">Submit</button>
    </div>
    <section v-if="message" class="message--display">
      <h4>Your saved message: </h4>
      <span>{{message}}</span>
    </section>
  </div>
</template>
```

4. Next, wrap the whole `message` section with the `transition` element, to prepare for our animation:

```
<transition name="slide-right">
    <section v-if="message" class="message--display">
        <h4>Your saved message: </h4>
        <span>{{message}}</span>
    </section>
</transition>
```

5. Let's define a method to update the message text called `onSendClick` by adding the following `script` code:

```
<script>
export default {
  data() {
    return {
      message: ''
```

```
        }
      },
    methods: {
      onSendClick() {
        const message = this.$refs.textArea.value;
        this.message = message;
        this.$refs.textArea.value = '';
      }
    }
  }
</script>
```

6. Next, we will define the `slide-right` animation effect using `@keyframes` in our `style` section by using the following command:

```
<style scoped>
@keyframes slide-right {
  100% {
    transform: translateX(0)
  }
}
</style>
```

This means it will re-position the element that has this effect horizontally (on the *x*-axis) to the original starting point, `(0,0)`.

7. Now, we will define the two classes, one for sliding in from left to right (`slide-right`) and one from right to left (`slide-left`):

```
.slide-right {
  animation: 1s slide-right 1s forwards;
  transform:translateX(-100%);
  transition: border-top 2s ease;
}

.slide-left {
  animation: 1s slide-right 1s reverse;
  transform:translateX(-100%);
}
```

8. Add `border-top:0` as the starting point for our `slide-right` transition to add a bit of an effect to `border-top` of this section:

    ```
    .slide-right-enter-from {
      border-top: 0;
    }
    ```

9. Next, using what we have learned about custom transition classes, let's bind `enter-active` to the `slide-right` class, and similarly bind `leave-active` to `slide-left`. We will then add these three properties to the `transition` element added in *step 4*:

    ```
    <transition
        name="slide-right"
        enter-active-class="slide-right"
        leave-active-class="slide-left"

    >
    ```

10. Add CSS stylings using CSS Flexbox to make the editor look nice:

    ```
    .editor--wrapper {
      display: flex;
      flex-direction: column;
    }

    .editor {
      align-self: center;
      width: 200px;
    }

    .editor--submit {
      margin: 0.5rem auto;
      align-self: center;
    }

    .message--display {
      margin-top: 1rem;
      border-top: 1px solid lightgray;
    }
    ```

11. Finally, run the application using the following command:

```
yarn dev
```

Upon visiting `http://localhost:3000` in the browser, the previous code will generate a component that will display the typed message with a sliding animation effect, as shown in *Figure 8.4*:

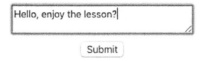

Figure 8.4 – Message editor text area

The following screenshot shows how the message component appears with a slide-from-left-to-right animation effect:

Figure 8.5 – The message in transition for display

After animating in from the left, the component should stop in the centered position, as shown in *Figure 8.6*:

Figure 8.6 – Message after the animation

This exercise helped you to get used to some of the `transform` effects in CSS, such as `translateX` and `transition`. It also demonstrates how easy it is to add animation to an element in a Vue application.

But what about transitioning with multiple elements in the same group, such as a list? We will find out in the next topic.

Transitioning groups of elements

To access the code file for this example, refer to `https://github.com/PacktPublishing/Frontend-Development-Projects-with-Vue.js-3/tree/v2-edition/Chapter08/Example8.04`

So far, we have gone through the fundamentals of Vue transition elements for simple components and elements, with both custom CSS-only and JavaScript-only support for animations. Next, we will explore how to apply a transition to a group of components – for instance, a list of items that will be rendered simultaneously by using `v-for`.

Vue.js provides another component for this specific purpose, the `transition-group` component.

We will now assume that we have a list of messages displayed on a feed, and we would like to add a transition to this list to provide some kind of effect when each item appears on the screen. Take the following component code, for instance (`./Example8.04/src/components/Example8-04.vue`):

```
<template>
  <div>
    <button @click="showList">Show list</button>
    <p v-for="message in messages" :key="message"
      v-show="show">
      {{ message }}
    </p>
  </div>
</template>
<script>
export default {
  data() {
    return {
      messages: [
        "Hello, how are you?",
        "The weather is nice",
        "This is the message feed",
        "And I am the fourth message",
        "Chapter 8 is fun",
        "Animation is super awesome",
```

```
              "Sorry, I didn't know you called",
              "Be patient, animation comes right up",
          ],
    show: false,
        };
      },
    methods: {
      showList () {
        this.show = true;
      },
    },
  };
</script>
```

The component contains a button element that binds to the showList method, and a conditional list element based on the show variable. This list element renders a list of messages whenever the **Show list** button is clicked.

Let's wrap the list elements with a transition-group component and pass the same props we used previously for our transition component—name="fade". Both transition-group and transition receive the same props:

```
<transition-group name="fade" >
  <p v-for="message in messages":key="message"
    v-show="show">
    {{message}}
  </p>
</transition-group>
```

We need to set the CSS styling effect for the transition effect passed as fade, following the same syntax rules for transition classes:

```
.fade-enter-active, .fade-leave-active {
  transition: all 2s;
}
.fade-enter-from, .fade-leave-active {
  opacity: 0;
  transform: translateX(30px);
}
```

Upon running the application using the `yarn dev` command, your list's item will have a fading effect when it appears. The following screenshot displays how your screen should appear:

Figure 8.7 – Fading of the list item

Note that unlike the `transition` component, which does not render any wrapper container element at all, `transition-group` will render an actual element if you define an element's tag name by using a `tag` prop, such as a `div` wrapper element, as in the following code:

```
<transition-group
  name="fade"
  tag="div"
>
  <p v-for="message in messages" :key="message"
    v-show="show">
    {{message}}
  </p>
</Transition-group>
```

In the browser, the actual HTML output will look as follows:

```
▼<div>
    <p style="display: none;">Hello, how are you?</p>
    <p style="display: none;">The weather is nice</p>
    <p style="display: none;">This is message feed</p>
    <p style="display: none;">And I am the forth message</p>
  </div>
```

Figure 8.8 – Transition container element rendered according to the tag attribute

Furthermore, all the `transition` classes will only be applied to the list item elements that have the `v-for` attribute and not to the wrapper.

Finally, you *must* have the `:key` attribute for every list item in order for Vue.js to index and know which item to apply the transition to.

We will now create a moving effect on the list.

Creating a moving effect while transitioning a list

In many cases, we want to add additional animation to each list item during its position transitioning, not only during its visibility transitioning. Position transitioning happens when shuffling, sorting, filtering, and so on are applied to the given list. The list items are already visible, and only change in their position — hence, using `enter` and `leave` won't work.

To achieve this animation goal, `transition-group` provides us another attribute, `v-move`; this attribute allows us to add additional animation effects to the list elements when each of the target elements changes its position:

```
<transition-group name= "fade"
  v-move="moveItemEffect">
    <!—list element --!>
</transition-group>
```

They can also be manually assigned using the `move-class` attribute:

```
<transition-group name= "fade"
  move-class="fade-move-in">
    <!—list element --!>
</transition-group>
<style>
.fade-move-in {
  transition: transform 2s ease-in;
}
</style>
```

Alternatively, we can simply define the CSS class with a prefix that matches the name attribute, as in the following:

```
<transition-group name= "fade">
    <!—list element --!>
</transition-group>
```

```
<style>
.fade-move {
  transition: transform 2s ease-in;
}
</style>
```

The Vue engine will automatically detect and attach the relevant class for a `transition` effect when it is applicable.

Next, we will look at making animations on the initial rendering of a page or component.

Configuring an animation on initially rendering

Usually, the list of items will be displayed on the first initial page load, and our animation won't work because the element is already in View. To trigger the animation, we need to use a different transition attribute, `appear`, to force the animation when the page initially renders, right after it has been loaded:

```
<transition-group
    appear="true"
    tag="div"
>
    <p v-for="message in messages" :key="message">
      {{message}}</p>
</transition-group>
```

We can also set Hooks with `v-on:after-appear`, `v-on:appear`, `v-on:after-appear`, and `v-on:appear-cancelled`, or we can create custom classes by using the following format:

```
<transition-group
  appear="true"
  appear-class="fade-enter"
  appear-active-class="fade-enter-active"
  tag="div"
>
  <p v-for="message in messages"
    :key="message">{{message}}</p>
</transition-group>
```

Note that in case you use the JavaScript Hooks related to `appear`, you need to set the `appear` prop to `true` along with binding the Hooks. Otherwise, it won't work.

Animating on render is a commonly used feature applicable to many situations, such as fading in components, as we did here. In the next section, we will look at sorting a list of messages with an animation.

Exercise 8.02 – sorting a list of messages with an animation

In this short exercise, we will implement an animation effect on a list of elements using the `transition-group` component.

To access the code file for this exercise, refer to `https://github.com/PacktPublishing/Frontend-Development-Projects-with-Vue.js-3/tree/v2-edition/Chapter08/Exercise8.02`.

Based on the code of *Exercise 8.01*, within the `Exercise8-01.vue` component, we will add additional functionality to the message list: **sorting**. Upon sorting (A-Z or Z-A), there will be a flipping animation effect applied to the list. To do this, see the following:

1. Use the application generated with `npm init vue@3` as a starting point, or within the root folder of the code repository, navigate into the `Chapter08/Exercise8.02` folder by using the following commands in order:

   ```
   > cd Chapter08/Exercise8.02/
   > yarn
   ```

2. Open the exercise project in your VS Code (by using the `code .` command within the project directory) or your preferred IDE.

3. Let's wrap the list of messages with a `transition-group` component. Do not forget to set the `tag` name to `div`, and add a `flip` animation by using the `name` attribute:

   ```
   <transition-group
     name="flip"
     tag="div"
   >
     <p
       v-for="message in messages"
       :key="message"
       class="message--item"
     >
       {{message}}
     </p>
   </transition-group>
   ```

4. Add `appear="true"`, or simply `appear` for short, to animate the element only after the page has finished loading:

```
<transition-group
    appear
    name="flip"
    tag="div"
>
  //...
</transition-group>
```

5. Run the application using the following command:

```
yarn dev
```

6. Upon visiting `http://localhost:3000` in the browser, the output will be as follows:

Figure 8.9 – Message list before the animation

7. At this point, there's no animation because we haven't defined the CSS animation styling for `flip` yet. In the `<style>` section of `src/components/Exercise8-02.vue`, we will add `opacity: 0` and then reposition each element in the list vertically (on the *y*-axis) by `20px` from its original position. This should be the initial state when the element enters `flip-enter-from` or is about to leave the transition with `flip-leave-to`:

```
<style scoped>
  .flip-enter-from, .flip-leave-to {
```

```
        opacity: 0;
        transform: translateY(20px);
    }
</style>
```

8. In the same `<style>` section, add custom CSS styling to each `message` element (the message–item class) with `transition: all 2s`. This is to make sure the transition effect for the element will be applied to all CSS properties within 2 seconds:

    ```
    .message--item {
      transition: all 2s;
    }
    ```

9. Once `flip-move` is in action, we need to add the transition effect just for `transform` (which was defined previously as vertically `20px` away). We can see the moving-up-and-down effect for each message flawlessly. In addition, we also need to add `position: absolute` for when the transition is in the middle of the leaving state:

    ```
    .flip-leave-active {
      position: absolute;
    }
    .flip-move {
      transition: transform 1s;
    }
    ```

10. We will next add three buttons—allowing you to sort from A to Z, sort from Z to A, and shuffle randomly:

    ```
    <button @click="sorting()">Sort A-Z</button>
    <button @click="sorting(true)">Sort Z-A</button>
    <button @click="shuffle()">Shuffle</button>
    ```

11. We also need to add our basic component `export` code, as well as our message feed data. Feel free to use any content you like for `messages`:

    ```
    export default {
      data() {
        return {
          messages: [
            "Hello, how are you?",
            "The weather is nice",
    ```

```
            "This is the message feed",
            "And I am the fourth message",
            "Chapter 8 is fun",
            "Animation is super awesome",
            "Sorry, I didn't know you called",
            "Be patient, animation comes right up",
        ],
        show: false,
      };
    },
  };
```

12. Next, we'll add the logic for sorting and shuffling. The methods section should be inside the export component from the last step:

```
methods: {
  sorting(isDescending) {
    this.messages.sort();

    if (isDescending) { this.messages.reverse(); }
  },
  shuffle() {
    this.messages.sort(() => Math.random() - 0.5);
  }
}
```

The output after clicking on one of the buttons will be like the following:

Figure 8.10 – Message list during sorting

In this exercise, we learned how to add a `flip` animation effect with `transition-group` to a list of components dynamically based on a change in the order of its element. Note that the algorithm used for shuffling the list of messages is naïve, and you should not use it in real-life scenarios due to the complexity of its performance.

Next, let's explore how to apply transition effects when navigating between pages.

Examining transition routes

With the combination of the `router-element` component from Vue Router and the `transition` component, we can easily set up the transition effects when a user navigates from one URL (route) to another.

To give you a more fundamental understanding, we demonstrate in the following section an underlying case where a user redirects from the `home` page to the `about` page on a website.

To enable a transition across routing, with Vue Router 4.x and above, we need to combine the `v-slot` API with a dynamic `component` element. We use the `v-slot` attribute to pass and bind view `Component` of the current route to the `is` props of the `component` element nested under `transition`, as seen here:

```
<router-view v-slot="{ Component }">
  <transition :name="zoom">
    <component :is="Component" />
  </transition>
</router-view>
```

Here, we add a `zoom` transition effect when navigating from one page to another. We can also use the `mode` attribute to indicate the transition mode. There are currently two modes to set:

- `in-out`: The new element comes in first, and only after that will the current element go out of view.

- `out-in`: The current element goes out first, and only then will the new element come in. We will use this for our example and it's more common than the previous one.

Then, we just need to set up the transition CSS effect with the `transition` classes as usual and it's done. Simple as that:

```
/**Zoom animation */
.zoom-enter-active,
.zoom-leave-active {
  animation-duration: 0.3s;
  animation-fill-mode: both;
```

```
    animation-name: zoom;
}


.zoom-leave-active {
  animation-direction: reverse;
}


@keyframes zoom {
  from {
    opacity: 0;
    transform: scale3d(0.4, 0.4, 0.4);
  }


  100% {
    opacity: 1;
  }
}
```

In this section, we looked at transition routes. Transition effects are animations that occur between the rendering of routes, such as navigating from one page to another. In the next exercise, we will look at creating a transition effect for each route navigated in our application.

Exercise 8.03 – creating a transition effect for each route navigated

In this exercise, we will adapt what we have learned about transitions with the `router` element from the *Examining transition routes* section to create different transition effects for different routes.

To access the code file for this exercise, refer to `https://github.com/PacktPublishing/ Frontend-Development-Projects-with-Vue.js-3/tree/v2-edition/Chapter08/ Exercise8.03`.

We will create a new route view for displaying the messages using the code from *Exercise 8.02* and add the transition effect when navigating to this view. The default effect will be `fade`:

1. Use the application generated with `npm init vue@3` as a starting point, with Vue Router added. Alternatively, within the root folder of the code repository, navigate into the `Chapter08/ Exercise8.03` folder by using the following commands in order:

    ```
    > cd Chapter08/Exercise8.03/
    > yarn
    ```

2. Open the exercise project in your VS Code (by using the `code` . command within the project directory) or your preferred IDE.

3. Create a new route view for the `Messages.vue` view, located in the `src/views/` folder. Reuse the code for `Exercise8-02.vue` from *Exercise 8.02* for this view component to render the /messages page route.

4. Register this /messages route by adding a new `route` object to `routes`, as seen in the following code:

```
const router = createRouter({
  history: createWebHistory(import.meta.env.BASE_URL),
  routes: [
    {
      path: "/",
      name: "home",
      component: HomeView,
    },
    {
      path: "/messages",
      name: "messages",
      meta: {
        transition: "zoom",
      },
      component: () =>
        import("../views/Messages.vue"),
    },
  ],
});
```

5. Add a link to this newly created route in `App.vue`:

```
<nav>
  <RouterLink to="/">Home</RouterLink>
  <RouterLink to="/messages">Messages</RouterLink>
</nav>
```

6. Next, in App.vue, we bind the global route instance (mentioned in *Chapter 7, Routing*) to slot, and dynamically assign the transition defined for the specific route using the meta property (or using the local transition data). We also bind the transition mode to the local mode data:

```
<router-view v-slot="{ Component, route }">
  <transition :name="route.meta.transition ||
    transition" :mode="mode">
    <component :is="Component" />
  </transition>
</router-view>
```

7. Inside the script section of App.vue, make sure we define the default value for transition and mode:

```
<script setup>
import { RouterLink, RouterView } from "vue-router";

let transition = "fade";
const mode = "out-in";
</script>
```

8. Add the CSS style for fading in and out using the following CSS in App.vue:

```
<style>
  .fade-enter-from, .fade-leave-to {
    opacity: 0;
  }

  .fade-enter-active, .fade-leave-active {
    transition: opacity 1s ease-in;
  }
</style>
```

9. At this point, all the pages are loaded with the fade effect, even /messages. But we want to make the messages page load with a different effect: the zoom effect. Next, add the relevant CSS code for the zoom animation inside the same style tag:

```
/**Zoom animation */
.zoom-enter-active,
.zoom-leave-active {
```

```
  animation-duration: 0.5s;
  animation-fill-mode: both;
  animation-name: zoom;
}


.zoom-leave-active {
  animation-direction: reverse;
}


@keyframes zoom {
 from {
    opacity: 0;
    transform: scale3d(0.4, 0.4, 0.4);
  }


  100% {
    opacity: 1;
  }
}
```

10. We will now add some standard CSS styling for the app's default layout with the help of the following code:

```
#app {
  font-family: 'Avenir', Helvetica, Arial, sans-serif;
  -webkit-font-smoothing: antialiased;
  -moz-osx-font-smoothing: grayscale;
  text-align: center;
  color: #2c3e50;
}

#nav {
  padding: 30px;
}

#nav a {
```

```
      font-weight: bold;
      color: #2c3e50;
   }


   #nav a.router-link-exact-active {
      color: #42b983;
   }
```

11. Now, we need to map the /messages route with this specific transition effect without affecting other routes. In order to do that, we need to add a field called transition to the meta property of this route configuration, in src/router/index.js:

```
{
   path: '/messages',
   name: 'messages',
   meta: {
      transition: 'zoom',
   },
   component: () => import '../views/Messages.vue')
}
```

12. Check the code for your routes object to confirm that it's the same as the following code. Here, we match each URL for our application with a view file:

```
const router = createRouter({
   history: createWebHistory(import.meta.env.BASE_URL),
   routes: [
      {
         path: "/",
         name: "home",
         component: HomeView,
      },
      {
         path: "/messages",
         name: "messages",
         meta: {
            transition: "zoom",
         },
         component: () =>
            import("../views/Messages.vue"),
```

```
      },
    ],
  });
```

13. Run the application using the following command:

    yarn dev

14. Now, if you open localhost:3000 in your browser and navigate to /messages, you should see something similar to *Figure 8.11*:

Home | Messages

Sort A-Z | Sort Z-A | Sort Z-A

Hello, how are you?

The weather is nice

This is the message feed

And I am the fourth message

Chapter 8 is fun

Animation is super awesome

Sorry, I didn't know you called

Be patient, animation comes right up

Figure 8.11 – Navigating to /messages with a zoom effect in progress

While navigating to other routes, we should see the default transition shown in *Figure 8.12*:

Home | Messages

This is homepage

Figure 8.12 – Navigating to /home with a message with a fade effect

This exercise demonstrates how we can easily set up different transitions for different pages with minimum effort by combining the right Hooks and methods. You can experiment a bit further with an external library to make your app animation smoother and livelier.

Using the GSAP library for animation

GSAP is an open source, scripted library that focuses solely on fast animation using JavaScript and provides cross-platform consistency support. It supports animation on a wide range of element types, such as **Scalar Vector Graphics (SVG)**, React components, canvas, and so on.

GSAP is flexible, easy to install, and will adjust to any configuration given, from CSS properties or SVG attributes to a numeric value for rendering an object into a canvas.

The core library is a suite of different tools, divided into core tools and others, such as plugins, easing tools, and utilities.

Installing GSAP

Installing GSAP is straightforward using `npm install` or `yarn add`:

```
yarn add gsap
#or
npm install gsap
```

After installation, you should see a successful output such as that shown in the following screenshot:

```
→  Example8.03 git:(master) ⨯ yarn add gasp
yarn add v1.22.10
warning package.json: No license field
warning example8-03@0.0.0: No license field
[1/4] 🔍  Resolving packages...
[2/4] 🚚  Fetching packages...
[3/4] 🔗  Linking dependencies...
[4/4] 🔨  Building fresh packages...
success Saved lockfile.
warning example8-03@0.0.0: No license field
success Saved 2 new dependencies.
info Direct dependencies
└─ gasp@0.0.2
info All dependencies
├─ gasp@0.0.2
└─ q@1.5.1
✨  Done in 4.80s.
→  Example8.03 git:(master) ⨯ ▊
```

Figure 8.13 – Results after successful installation

Now that we have GSAP installed, we'll look at basic tweens in GSAP.

Basic tweens

A tween is a concept defined by the creator of the GSAP library as a high-performance setter for performing all the desired animation work based on the user's configuration inputs. We can use the targeted objects, a period, or any specific CSS properties as input for animation. Upon performing the animation, the tween figures out what the values of CSS properties should be according to the given duration and applies them accordingly.

The following are the essential methods to create basic tweens.

gsap.to()

The most commonly used tween is `gsap.to()`, which is called to create an animation based on these two main parameters:

- **Targets**: These are the elements to which we want to apply the animation. Targets can be an array of elements, a raw object, a DOM element, or an element selector text, such as `#myId`.

- **Vars**: An object containing all the animation configuration properties – for example, CSS-like properties such as `opacity: 0`, `rotation: 90`, or `fontSize: '20px'`; animation properties such as `duration: 1`, `stagger: 0.2`, or `ease: "elastic"`; and event handler properties such as `onComplete` or `onUpdate`.

For example, if we want to animate the logo of Vue in `HelloWorld.vue`, we run the following:

```
gsap.to(el, {duration: 3, opacity: 1, onComplete: done});
```

Alternatively, use the following to move an object with x properties (the same as `transform: translateX()`):

```
gsap.to(".green", {duration: 3, x: 500, rotation: 360});
```

The preceding code locates an element with the `green` class and rotates it `360` degrees within a `500`-px distance horizontally when that element comes into view.

gsap.from() and gsap.fromTo

We don't always want to define the expected animation effect for the element in view. Instead, we define the default values from which the animation should start for the targeted element – that's when we use `gsap.from()`.

For example, assuming the current `opacity` value of a box is 1, the `scale` value is 1, and the x position is 0, we want to set up an animation to these current values *from* an x position of 300, with an `opacity` value of 0 and a `scale` value of 0.5. In other words, the animation will be from {x: 300, opacity: 0, scale: 0.5} to whatever values the element has currently:

```
gsap.from(".red", {duration: 3, x: 300, scale: 0.5, opacity: 0});
```

However, in many cases, we need to set up the start and end values for an animation since one side is not good enough. For that purpose, GSAP provides `gsap.fromTo()` with the following syntax:

```
gsap.fromTo(target, fromValues, toValues)
```

Let's define an animation for a gray box with original values of `{ opacity: 0, scale: 0.5, x: 300 }` to the values of `{ opacity: 1, scale: 1, x: 100, rotation: 360}`:

```
gsap.fromTo(".grey",
    { duration: 3, opacity: 0, scale: 0.5, x: 600 },
    { duration: 3, opacity: 1, scale: 1, x: 200, rotation:
      360}
)
```

In order to translate all the CSS-like values into the corresponding CSS values, one of the core plugins for GSAP is `CSSPlugin`. This plugin will detect whether the target is a DOM element automatically, intercept the values passed, translate them into proper CSS values, and then apply them to the element as inline styles accordingly.

In the next section, we'll walk through an exercise of creating a simple tween using GSAP.

Exercise 8.04 – tweening with GSAP

The goal of this exercise is to get you comfortable with working with external libraries such as GSAP.

To access the code file for this exercise, visit `https://github.com/PacktPublishing/Frontend-Development-Projects-with-Vue.js-3/tree/v2-edition/Chapter08/Exercise8.04`.

We'll set up a simple animation, but you can apply this same pattern anywhere in your Vue code. We'll be applying the animation during mount, but JavaScript animations can be triggered dynamically based on things such as timers, random integers, or inputs such as buttons:

1. Use the application generated with `npm init vue@3` as a starting point, with Vue Router added. Alternatively, within the root folder of the code repository, navigate into the `Chapter08/Exercise8.04` folder by using the following commands in order:

   ```
   > cd Chapter08/Exercise8.04/
   > yarn
   ```

2. Open the exercise project in your VS Code (by using the `code .` command within the project directory) or your preferred IDE.

3. Install GSAP with `yarn` or npm using one of the following commands:

    ```
    yarn add gsap
    # OR
    npm install gsap
    ```

4. Find the existing `img` tag in `src/App.vue` and add `ref="logo"` to it as follows:

    ```
    <img ref="logo" alt="Vue logo" src="./assets/logo.png">
    ```

5. In the `<script setup>` section of `src/App.vue`, import GSAP:

    ```
    import gsap from 'gsap'
    ```

6. We use the `ref()` Hook to define `logo` as a reactive variable, which contains the reference to the `img` element set in *step 4*:

    ```
    import { ref } from 'vue'
    const logo = ref();
    ```

7. Then, we use an `onMounted()` lifecycle Hook to add an animation, which is 10 rotations over 30 seconds:

    ```
    import { onMounted, ref } from 'vue'
    onMounted(() => {
      gsap.from(logo.value, { duration: 30, rotation: 3600
      });
    });
    ```

    The full component code for the `script` section will be like the following:

    ```
    <script setup>
    import HelloWorld from "./components/HelloWorld.vue";
    import gsap from "gsap";
    import { onMounted, ref } from 'vue'

    const logo = ref();

    onMounted(() => {
      gsap.from(logo.value, { duration: 30, rotation: 3600
      });
    });
    </script>
    ```

8.   Next, start the application by running `yarn dev` in the terminal.

9.   Open your browser to `localhost:3000` and you should see the default Vue starter page but with the logo spinning, as shown in the following screenshot:

Figure 8.14 – Simple animation with GSAP

In this exercise, we learned how to implement a simple spinning animation using GSAP in Vue. Next, we will see how we can modify the look and feel of an animation with easing.

Modifying the look and feel with easing

Easing is important because it determines the movement style between the original starting point and the destination point of an animation. It controls the rate of change during a tween; hence, a user has the time to see the effect, whether it be smooth, sudden, bouncy, or another kind of transition effect:

```
gsap.from(".bubble", {
    duration: 2,
    scale: 0.2,
    rotation: 16,
    ease: "bounce",
})
```

In the previous example code, `duration` is in milliseconds, representing the amount of time for the animation to be active.

Also, there are additional built-in plugins in GSAP that provide extra capabilities for configuring the easing effect, such as `power`, `back`, `elastic`, and so on.

To make the movement smooth to a certain degree, we use the following syntax:

```
ease: "<ease-name>.<ease-type>(<addition-inputs>)"
```

Take a bubble effect, for instance – we can enable the smooth elastic easing-out effect by using the following code:

```
gsap.to(".bubble", 4, {
    duration: 4,
    scale: 1.2,
    rotation: '-=16',
    ease: 'elastic(2.5, 0.5)',
})
```

Or, add elastic easing as follows:

```
gsap.to(".bubble", 4, {
    duration: 4,
    scale: 1.2,
    rotation: '-=16',
    ease: 'elastic.in(2.5, 0.5)',
})
```

With ease, we can make the same animation look completely different based on the style set. Next, we'll look at stagger, another option that affects the look and feel of an animation.

Modifying the look and feel with stagger

We have gone through how to animate a list of items using Vue transitions in the previous sections. Staggering is one of the animations we should take into consideration for a list of objects since it makes animation for this type of target easy and with an appropriate delay between each of the item's animations.

For example, by assigning a value to the stagger property, we can create and apply some configuration options besides just the delay duration number (in milliseconds):

```
gsap.to('.stagger-box', 2, {
    duration: 2,
    scale: 0.1,
    y: 60,
    yoyo: true,
    repeat: 1,
    ease: "power3.inOut",
    delay:1,
    stagger: {
```

```
    amount: 1.5,
    grid: "auto",
    from: "center"
  }
})
```

You can use `repeat` to define how many times the animation should repeat. A negative number will make it repeat infinitely.

Using Timeline

Timeline is a schedule of tweens under your total control to define overlaps or gaps between the tweens. It's useful when you need to control a group of animations according to an order, build a sequence of animations, chain the animations for a final callback, or modularize your animation code for reusability.

In order to use Timeline, you can create a `timeline` instance by using the built-in `gsap.timeline()` and set up the instance with a set of configurations, as follows:

```
import gsap from 'gsap';
const tl = gsap.timeline( { onComplete: done });
```

We will look briefly into the two main use cases of Timeline – sequencing and chaining.

Creating a chain of animation effects by sequencing

With similar core functionalities to GSAP, Timeline also provides `to()`, `from()`, and `fromTo()` methods. All animations by default can be sequenced one after another, with the option to force timing to control where or when things go using the `position` attribute, which is an optional argument, as seen in the following code:

```
const tl = gsap.timeline({ repeat: -1});
tl.to("#box-green", {duration: 2, x: 550})

//1 second after end of timeline (gap)
tl.to("#box-red", {duration: 2, x: 550, scale: 0.5}, "+=1")

//0.5 seconds before end of timeline (overlap)
tl.to("#box-purple", {duration: 2, rotation: 360, x:550,
      scale: 1.2, ease: "bounce"}, "-=1")
```

In this section, we looked at using the GSAP Timeline feature to schedule a series of animations all running one after the other, some with a gap and others with an overlap. In the next section, we'll look further at sequencing animations with the concept of chaining.

Chaining

As with sequencing, chaining arranges animation into an order. Instead of calling each animation separately with the instance method each time, it will be placed in a chain. All the special values that are used between the child tweens can be defined. In the instance created as `defaults`, or alternatively in the first call, get other timelines (list of animations) in the chain to inherit these values:

```
const tl = gsap.timeline({ defaults: { duration: 2 },
                                 repeat: -1});

tl.to("#box-green", { x: 550 })
  .to("#box-red", { scale: 0.5, x: 450 })
  .to("#box-purple", { scale: 1.2, ease: "bounce", x: 500
  })
```

We can also intercept the timing position of each chained timeline using `position`, as described earlier:

```
tl.to("#box-green", { x: 550 })
  .to("#box-red", { scale: 0.5, x: 450 }, "+=1")
  .to("#box-purple", { scale: 1.2, ease: "bounce", x: 500
        }, "-=1")
```

GSAP has very detailed documentation, so just visit `https://greensock.com/get-started` and start animating.

In the next section, we'll build on what we've learned about GSAP to make a message-viewing app with animated transitions.

Activity 8.01 – building a messages app with transitions and GSAP

To access the code file for this activity, refer to `https://github.com/PacktPublishing/Frontend-Development-Projects-with-Vue.js-3/tree/v2-edition/Chapter08/Activity8.01`

In this activity, you will use CSS to write custom transitions, use transition groups and routes to set up more complex transitions, and use a third-party transition library such as GSAP to create animations and transitions in the app.

You will be creating a simple messages app that makes use of transition effects.

The following steps will help you complete this activity:

1. Create a new Vue application with npm init vue@3 as a starting point, with Vue Router added.

2. Create a Messages route (at src/views/Messages.vue) that renders two nested views: Messages (src/views/MessageList.vue), for displaying a list of messages, and MessageEditor (src/views/MessageEditor.vue), with one textarea and a submit button for creating a new message.

3. Create a Message route (at src/views/Message.vue) that renders a view of a single message with a given ID.

4. Register all the routes.

5. Add a transition to the main router-view in the src/App.vue file with a simple transition name, fade, and the out-in mode.

6. Add the transition to the nested router-view in src/views/Messages.vue by using custom transition classes.

7. Create an animation effect for zooming in on entering the route and zooming out on leaving the route.

8. Create another animation effect for fading in on a leaving event.

9. Add a transition to the list of messages in MessageList.vue with a bounce-in effect.

10. Use GSAP to animate the bounce-in effect.

11. Add a moving effect for an item when it appears.

12. When navigating from the **List** page to the **Editor** page, you should see the feed slide away to the left as the **Editor** page appears, as shown in *Figure 8.15*:

Figure 8.15 – Fade out when navigating from the message list view to the editor view

When navigating from the message view to the editor view, you should see the text input slide out to the left, as shown in *Figure 8.16*:

Messages section

List I Editor

Message Feed

Figure 8.16 – Fade out when navigating from the editor view to the message list view

Next, the message list will appear with the numbers spinning with a bounce effect, as shown in *Figure 8.17*:

Messages section

List I Editor

Message Feed

0

1

Figure 8.17 – Bounce effect when displaying the message feed in the message list view

When clicking on a specific message, **0** or **1** in our example, our list will slide out to the left and you should see the message content, as shown in *Figure 8.18*:

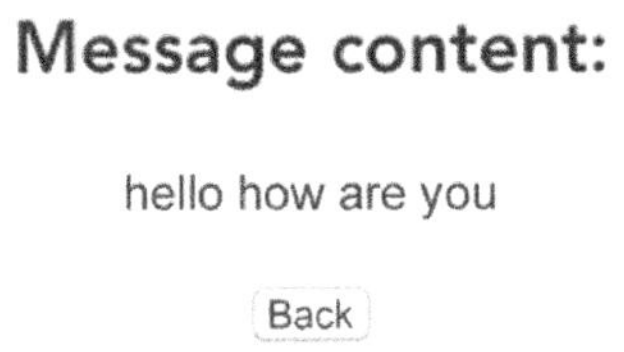

Message content:

hello how are you

Back

Figure 8.18 – A single message view

At this point, you have learned about the basics of GSAP, such as tweens and Timeline. You also experimented with creating easing and staggering animations by combining transition and GSAP functionalities in your Vue component.

Summary

In this chapter, we explored the built-in support Vue.js has for transitions and animations, both for single and multiple components, and we saw how easy it is to set it up. At this point, you have created transition and animation effects for routes and components and witnessed all the basic features of Vue.js transitions: the custom transition class, group transition, and transition modes. Moreover, you also learned about other leading animation third-party libraries such as GSAP, and saw how to integrate them with your Vue application in order to get better animation effects on the web.

The next chapter focuses on another crucial topic for building a production-ready Vue application – state management and how components within an application communicate with one another using Pinia, a state management library.

Part 3:
Global State Management

In this part, we will explore how data is managed and stored within a Vue application. We will start with examples of how to handle state in Vue natively, and then continue on to show how the Pinia library makes it easier.

We will cover the following chapters in this section:

- *Chapter 9, The State of Vue State Management*
- *Chapter 10, State Management with Pinia*

9

The State of Vue State Management

You've now seen how to build Vue.js applications and have begun to string together multiple different components into your first set of real applications. As the size of your application grows, so does the complexity. In this chapter, it's time to take a look at how you can begin managing that complexity by integrating **state management**.

Here, you'll begin by taking a look at how problems with states arise, how state management can help address it, and what features Vue.js 3 has to help you deal with it directly. You'll learn this while building a simple *profile card* application that uses multiple components between which the state needs to be synchronized. The next chapter will introduce a tool to further help with this, called **Pinia**.

So, in this chapter, we will cover the following topics:

- Understanding the component architecture and the problem of the state
- Holding the state in a common ancestor component
- Adding simple state management
- Deciding when to use a local state or global state

Technical requirements

There are no technical requirements for this chapter outside of the npm CLI you have previously used to scaffold applications with Vue.js.

The Node version has to be below v20 (preferable Yarn 1.22 and Node version above 16 and up to 19.x, and npm up to version 9.x.

You can find this chapter's source here: `https://github.com/PacktPublishing/Frontend-Development-Projects-with-Vue.js-3/tree/v2-edition/Chapter09`

Understanding the component architecture and the problem of the state

In previous chapters, we have seen how to use a local state and `props` to hold the state and share it in a parent-child component hierarchy.

Now, we will begin by showing how to leverage `state`, `props`, and `events` to share states between components that do not have a **parent-child** configuration. These types of components are called **siblings**.

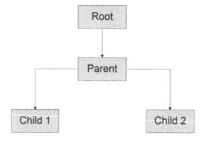

Figure 9.1 – Child 1 and Child 2 are "sibling" components

Throughout the chapter, we will be building a **profile card generator** app that demonstrates how the state flows down the component tree as props in an application, and how updates are propagated as backup using events, event buses, and store updates.

Given that we want to build a profile card generator, we can break the application down into three sections: a *header*, where we will have global controls and display the title of the page; a *profile form*, where we will capture data; and finally, a *profile display*, where we will display the profile card. In *Figure 9.2*, you can see our root component (**App (root)**), as well as three sibling child components.

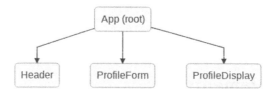

Figure 9.2 – Representation of a profile card application component tree

We have now seen how to think of our application as a component tree and how our application can be structured as a component tree. In the next section, we'll demonstrate putting all of the shared states in the root component.

Holding the state in a common ancestor component

To only hold the state with the `state` component and `props`, and update it with `events`, we will store it in the nearest common ancestor component.

`state` is only propagated through `props` and is only updated through `events`. In this case, all the `state` components will live in a shared ancestor of the components that require them. The `App` component, since it is the root component, is a good default for holding a shared state.

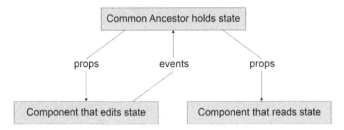

Figure 9.3 – Common ancestor component holds state with props and event propagation

To change `state`, a component needs to emit `events` up to the component holding our `state` (the shared ancestor). The shared ancestor needs to update `state` according to the data and type of `events`. This, in turn, causes a re-render, during which the ancestor component passes the updated `props` to the component reading `state`.

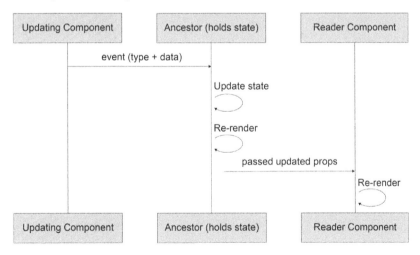

Figure 9.4 – Updating a sibling component when the ancestor holds state

Let's look at an example of this by working on a *profile card editor*. To build a header, we need to create an `AppHeader` component in the `AppHeader.vue` file, which will contain a template and an h2 heading with TailwindCSS classes.

> **Note**
> You can learn more about using Tailwind CSS with Vue3 here: `https://tailwindcss.com/docs/guides/vite`.

To do this, add the following code:

```
<template>
  <header class="w-full block p-4 border-b bg-blue-300
    border-gray-700">
    <h2 class="text-xl text-gray-800">Profile Card
      Generator</h2>
  </header>
</template>
```

We will then import the header, register it, and render it in the App.vue file:

```
<script setup>
import AppHeader from '@/components/AppHeader.vue'
</script>

<template>
  <div id="app">
    <AppHeader/>
  </div>
</template>
```

The output of the preceding code will be as follows:

Figure 9.5 – AppHeader displayed in the profile card generator

We will similarly create an `AppProfileForm` file; the purpose of this component is to lay out the labels and form fields for editing the profile:

```
<template>
  <section class="md:w-2/3 flex flex-col p-12 items-center
    bg-red-200">
  <!-- Inputs -->
  </section>
</template>
```

We will then create an `AppProfileDisplay` file; this component handles displaying the profile so the user can preview their edits:

```
<template>
  <section class="md:w-1/3 h-64 bg-blue-200 flex">
  <!-- Profile Card -->
  </section>
</template>
```

Both of our containers (`AppProfileForm` and `AppProfileDisplay`) can now be imported and rendered in App:

```
<script setup>
import AppHeader from '@/components/AppHeader.vue'
import AppProfileDisplay from '@/components/AppProfileDisplay.
vue'
import AppProfileForm from '@/components/AppProfileForm.vue'
</script>

<template>
  <div id="app">
    <AppHeader/>
    <div class="flex flex-col md:flex-row">
      <AppProfileForm />
      <AppProfileDisplay />
    </div>
  </div>
</template>
```

The output of the preceding code will be as follows:

Profile Card Generator

Figure 9.6 – App skeleton with AppHeader, AppProfileForm, and AppProfileDisplay

To add a form field, in this case, name, we will start by adding an input to AppProfileForm:

```
<template>
  <section class="md:w-2/3 h-64 bg-red-200 flex flex-col
    p-12 items-center">
    <!-- Inputs -->
    <div class="flex flex-col">
      <label class="flex text-gray-800 mb-2" for="name">
        Name
      </label>
      <input
        id="name"
        type="text"
        name="name"
        class="border-2 border-solid border-blue-200
          rounded px-2 py-1"
      />
    </div>
  </section>
</template>
```

The preceding code will display as follows:

Figure 9.7 – AppProfileForm with a name field and label

To keep track of the name input data, we will add a two-way binding to it using `v-model` and set a name property in the component's `data` initializer:

```
<template>
      <!-- rest of the template -->
      <input
        id="name"
        type="text"
        name="name"
        class="border-2 border-solid border-blue-200
          rounded px-2 py-1" v-model="name"
      />
      <!-- rest of the template -->
</template>
<script setup>
import { ref } from 'vue'
const emit = defineEmits(['submit'])

const name = ref('');
</script>
```

We will also need a `submit` button that, upon being clicked, sends the form data to the parent by emitting a `submit` event with the form's contents:

```
<template>
    <!-- rest of template -->
    <div class="flex flex-row mt-12">
```

```
        <button type="submit" @click="submitForm()">Submit
        </button>
    </div>
    <!-- rest of template -->
</template>
<script setup>
import { ref } from 'vue'
const emit = defineEmits(['submit'])

const name = ref('');

function submitForm() {
  emit('submit', {
    name: this.name
  });
}
</script>
```

This will display as follows:

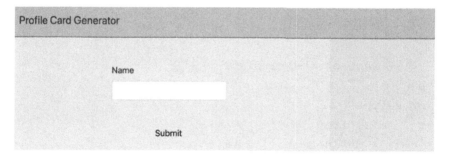

Figure 9.8 – AppProfileForm with a wired-up Submit button

The next step is to store the form's state in the App component. It is a good candidate for storing form state since it is a common ancestor to AppProfileForm and AppProfileDisplay.

To begin with, we will need a formData attribute returned from reactive(). We will also need a way to update formData. Hence, we will add an update(formData) method:

```
<script setup>
import AppHeader from '@/components/AppHeader.vue'
```

```
import AppProfileDisplay from '@/components/AppProfileDisplay.
vue'
import AppProfileForm from '@/components/AppProfileForm.vue'

import { reactive } from 'vue'

const formData = reactive({name:''});

function update€ {
  formData.name = e.name;
}
</script>
```

Next, we need to bind update() to the submit event emitted by AppProfileForm. We will do this using the @submit shorthand and with the magic event object notation as update($event):

```
<template>
    <!-- rest of template -->
      <AppProfileForm @submit="update($event)" />
    <!--rest of template -->
</template>
```

To display the name inside of AppProfileDisplay, we will need to add formData as a prop:

```
<script setup>
const props = defineProps({formData:Object});
</script>
```

We will also need to display the name using formData.name. We will add a p-12 class to the container to improve the appearance of the component:

```
<template>
  <section class="md:w-1/3 h-64 bg-blue-200 flex p-12">
   --- Profile Card -->
    <h3 class="font-bold font-lg">{{ formData.name }}</h3>
  </section>
</template>
```

Finally, `App` needs to pass `formData` to `AppProfileDisplay` as a prop:

```
<template>
    <!-- rest of template -->
        <AppProfileDisplay :form-data="formData" />
    <!-- rest of template -->
</template>
```

We are now able to update the name on the form. When you click on the **Submit** button, it will show the name in the profile card display as follows:

Figure 9.9 – App storing state, passing as props to AppProfileDisplay

We have now seen how to store a shared state in the `App` component and how to update it from `AppProfileForm` and display it in `AppProfileDisplay`.

In the next topic, we will see how to add an additional field to the profile card generator.

Exercise 9.01 – adding an occupation field to the profile card generator

Following on from the example of storing the `name` shared state, another field that would be interesting to capture in a profile card is the occupation of the individual. To this end, we will add an `occupation` field to `AppProfileForm` to capture this extra part of the state, and we'll display it in `AppProfileDisplay`.

The complete code for this exercise can be found at `https://github.com/PacktPublishing/Frontend-Development-Projects-with-Vue.js-3/tree/v2-edition/Chapter09/Exercise9.01`

Follow these steps in order to add the field:

1. The first place to start is by adding the new `occupation` field to `src/components/`
    `AppProfileForm`. We'll also take this opportunity to get rid of the `h-64` and `bg-red-200`
    classes from the `section` element (if they're present), which will mean the form is displayed
    without a background and a set height:

```
<template>
  <section class="md:w-2/3 flex flex-col p-12
    items-center">
   <!-- rest of template -->
   <div class="flex flex-col mt-2">
      <label class="flex text-gray-800 mb-2"
        for="occupation">Occupation</label>
      <input
        id="occupation"
        type="text"
        name="occupation"
        class="border-2 border-solid border-blue-200
          rounded px-2 py-1"
      />
   </div>
   <!-- rest of template -->
  </section>
</template>
```

The output of the preceding code will be as follows:

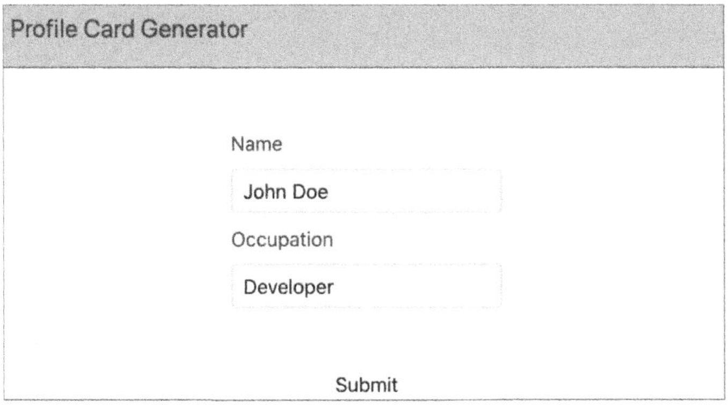

Figure 9.10 – AppProfileForm with the new Occupation field

2. To track the value of occupation with a two-way data binding, we will add a new instance of the ref() function:

```
<script setup>
// rest of component
const occupation = ref('');
// rest of component
}
```

3. We will now apply a two-way data binding from the occupation reactive data property to the occupation input using v-model:

```
<template>
  <!--rest of template -->
    <input
       id="occupation"
       type="text"
       name="occupation"
       v-model="occupation"
       class="border-2 border-solid border-blue-200
          rounded px-2 py-1"/>
  <!-- rest of template -->
</template>
```

4. For the occupation value to be transmitted when submit is clicked, we will need to add it to the submitForm method as a property of the submit event payload:

```
<script setup>
import { ref } from 'vue'
const emit = defineEmits(['submit'])

const name = ref('');
const occupation = ref('');

function submitForm() {
  emit('submit', {
    name: this.name,
    occupation: this.occupation
  });
}
</script>
```

5.   The final step of adding this field is to display it in the `AppProfileDisplay` component. We will add a paragraph with a couple of styling classes. We'll also take this opportunity to remove the `h-64` and `bg-blue-200` classes from the container (if they are present):

```
<template>
  <section class="md:w-1/3 flex flex-col p-12">
   <!-- rest of template -->
    <p class="mt-2">{{ formData.occupation }}</p>
  </section>
</template>
```

Our browser should look as follows:

Figure 9.11 – AppProfileForm

As we have just seen, adding a new field using the common ancestor to manage the state is a case of passing the data up in an event and back down in the props to the reading component.

We will now see how we can reset the form and profile display with a **Clear** button.

Exercise 9.02 – adding a Clear button to the profile card generator

When creating a new profile with our application, it is useful to be able to reset the profile. To this end, we will add a **Clear** button.

A **Clear** button should reset the data in the form but also in `AppProfileDisplay`. The complete code can be found at `https://github.com/PacktPublishing/Frontend-Development-Projects-with-Vue.js-3/tree/v2-edition/Chapter09/Exercise9.02`

Now let's look at the steps to perform this exercise:

1. We want a **Clear** button to be displayed. We will take this opportunity to improve the styling of both the **Clear** and **Submit** buttons (in `src/components/AppProfileForm.vue`):

    ```
    <template>
     <!-- rest of template -->
        <div class="w-1/2 flex md:flex-row mt-12">
          <button
            class="flex md:w-1/2 justify-center"
            type="button"
          >
            Clear
          </button>
          <button
            class="flex md:w-1/2 justify-center"
            type="submit"
            @click="submitForm()">
            Submit
          </button>
        </div>
     <!-- rest of template -->
    </template>
    ```

2. To clear the form, we need to reset the name and `occupation` fields. We can create a `clear` method that will do this (in `src/components/AppProfileForm.vue`):

    ```
    <script setup>
    // rest of the component
    function clear() {
      this.name = '';
      this.occupation = '';
    }
    // rest of the component
    </script>
    ```

3. We want to bind the `clear` method to `click` events on the `Clear` button to reset the form (in `src/components/AppProfileForm.vue`):

    ```
    <template>
     <!-- rest of template -->
        <button
    ```

```
        class="flex md:w-1/2 justify-center"
        type="button"
        @click="clear()">
        Clear
      </button>
  <!-- rest of template -->
</template>
```

Thus, we can now enter data into the form and submit it as per the following screenshot:

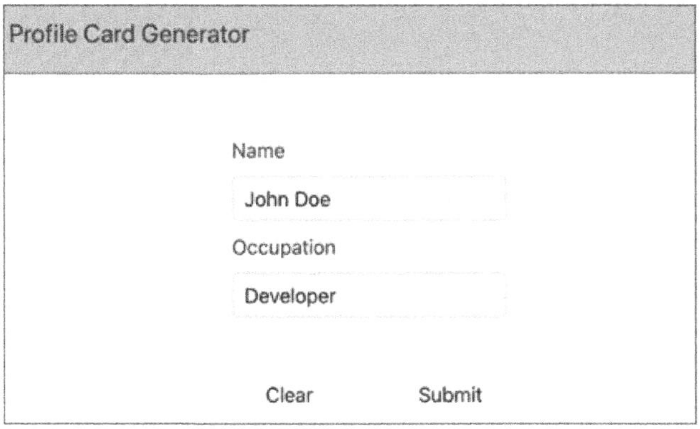

Figure 9.12 – AppProfileForm with the Name and Occupation fields filled in

On clicking the **Submit** button, it will propagate data to `AppProfileDisplay` as follows:

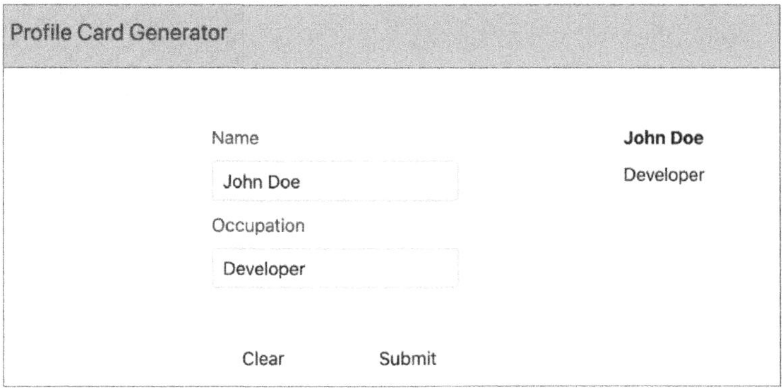

Figure 9.13 – AppProfileForm and AppProfileDisplay with data filled in
and submitted with a Clear button

Unfortunately, `AppProfileDisplay` still has stale data, as shown in the following screenshot:

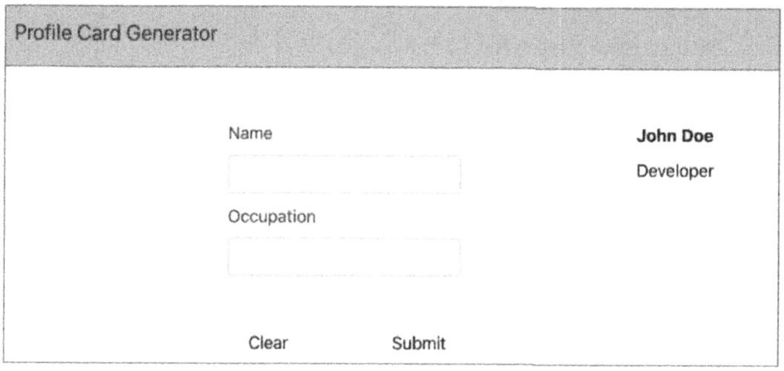

Figure 9.14 – AppProfileForm and AppProfileDisplay with only AppProfileForm
cleared while AppProfileDisplay still has stale data

4. To also clear the contents of `AppProfileDisplay`, we will need to update `formData` in `App.vue` by emitting a `submit` event with an empty payload in `src/components/AppProfileForm.vue`:

```
<script setup>
// rest of the component
function clear() {
  this.name = '';
  this.occupation = '';
  emit('submit', {});
}
// rest of the component
</script>
```

When we fill out the form and submit it, it will look as follows:

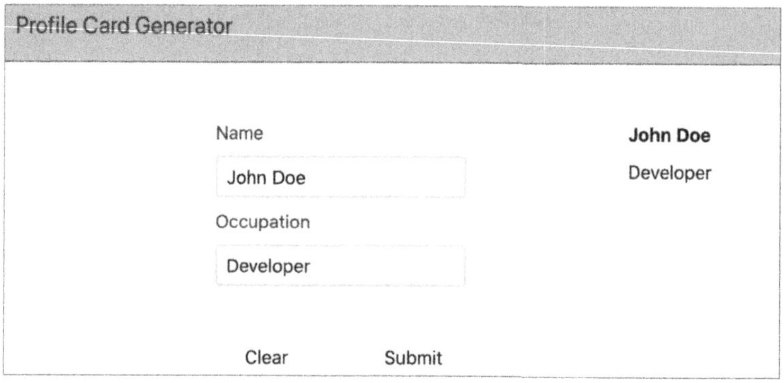

Figure 9.15 – AppProfileForm and AppProfileDisplay with data filled out
and submitted with a Clear button

We can click on **Clear** and reset the data displayed in both `AppProfileDisplay` and `AppProfileForm` as per the following screenshot:

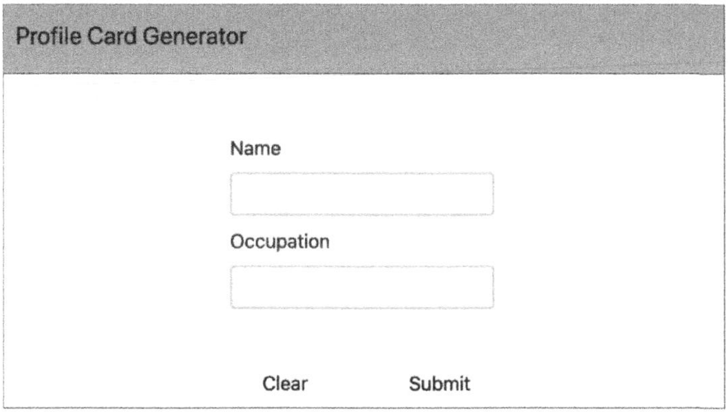

Figure 9.16 – AppProfileForm and AppProfileDisplay after data is cleared (using the Clear button)

We have now seen how to set up communication between sibling components through a common ancestor.

> **Note**
>
> There is quite a bit of bookkeeping and menial work required to keep track of all the bits of the state that need to stay in sync across the application.

In the next section, we will look at how Vue 3's built-in support for reactive data means we can roll our own simple state management.

Adding simple state management

For our simple application, we can replace a lot of the boilerplate code if we use the `reactive()` API to build a simple store:

1. Let's start by building a new file, `store.js`, that uses a `reactive` object for our profile values:

    ```
    import { reactive } from 'vue';

    export const store = reactive({
      name:'',
      occupation:''
    });
    ```

This *very* simple object will be very powerful due to the use of Vue 3's reactivity support. Any component making use of the values from here will be able to rely on knowing that when a value changes, it will instantly be reflected. Right away, we can see how this simplifies things as we switch to the store.

2. In `AppProfileForm`, let's import the store first:

```
<script setup>
import { store } from '@/store.js';
</script>
```

3. Next, update both fields to point to the store instead of local data. In the following code, the `v-model` value was changed and the **Submit** button is removed – it's no longer necessary:

```
<!-- rest of component -->
<div class="flex flex-col">
  <label class="flex text-gray-800 mb-2" for="name">
    Name
  </label>
  <input
    id="name"
    type="text"
    name="name"
    class="border-2 border-solid border-blue-200
      rounded px-2 py-1" v-model="store.name"/>
</div>

<div class="flex flex-col mt-2">
  <label class="flex text-gray-800 mb-2"
    for="occupation">Occupation</label>
  <input
    id="occupation"
    type="text"
    name="occupation"
    v-model="store.occupation"
    class="border-2 border-solid border-blue-200
      rounded px-2 py-1"
  />
</div>
```

4. Now, we can edit the script block to remove most of the previous logic. The `clear` method needs to be updated to change the store values:

```
<script setup>
import { store } from '@/store.js';

function clear() {
  store.name = '';
  store.occupation = '';
}
</script>
```

5. Next, we can make similar changes to `AppProfileDisplay`. First, import the store:

```
<script setup>
import { store } from '@/store.js';
</script>
```

Then, modify the template:

```
<template>
  <section class="md:w-1/3 flex flex-col p-12">
  <!-- Profile Card -->
  <h3 class="font-bold font-lg">{{ store.name }}</h3>
  <p class="mt-2">{{ store.occupation }}</p>
  </section>
</template>
```

We've now switched from a system of events being broadcasted from components to one of a simpler, shared state. Our code is simpler, which will make updates even easier.

Exercise 9.03 – moving the Clear button to the application header profile card generator and updating the Clear logic

In our profile card generator application, the **Clear** button clears the state in the whole application. Its presence inside the form makes the **Clear** button's functionality unclear since it looks as though it might only affect the form.

To reflect the fact that the **Clear** button has a global functionality, we will move it into the header.

We will also update our store to handle the logic of clearing the state. Our simple state utility not only can define variables but also methods. Since the script is handling keeping the values, it makes sense for it to handle logic related to those values.

You can also find the complete code at `https://github.com/PacktPublishing/Frontend-Development-Projects-with-Vue.js-3/trcc/v2-edition/Chapter09/Exercise9.03`

The following steps will help us perform this exercise:

1. We will start by creating a `button` component in `src/components/AppHeader.vue`:

```
<template>
  <header class="w-full flex flex-row p-4 border-b
    bg-blue-300 border-gray-700">
    <h2 class="text-xl flex text-gray-800">
      Profile Card Generator</h2>
    <button class="flex ml-auto text-gray-800
      items-center">
      Reset
    </button>
  </header>
</template>
```

2. In our store, let's add a new `clear` function in store.js. It is responsible for resetting both values back to their initial state:

```
import { reactive } from 'vue';

export const store = reactive({
    name:'',
    occupation:'',
    clear() {
        this.name = '';
        this.occupation = '';
    }
});
```

3. In AppHeader, we need to import the store:

```
<script setup>
import { store } from '@/store.js';
</script>
```

4. Now, we need to bind the Reset button to call the store clear method:

```
<!-- rest of template -->
<button class="flex ml-auto text-gray-800
  items-center" @click="store.clear()">
  Reset
</button>
<script>
```

5. The final step is to delete the Clear button and Submit button:

```
<template>
  <!-- rest of template -->
    <div class="w-1/2 flex md:flex-row mt-12">
    <button
      class="flex md:w-1/2 justify-center"
      type="submit"
      @click="submitForm()">
      Submit
    </button>
  </div>
    <!-- rest of template -->
</template>
```

The form looks as follows when it gets filled out and submitted:

Figure 9.17 – Filled-out and submitted form

Resetting the form now clears the form fields as well as `AppProfileDisplay`:

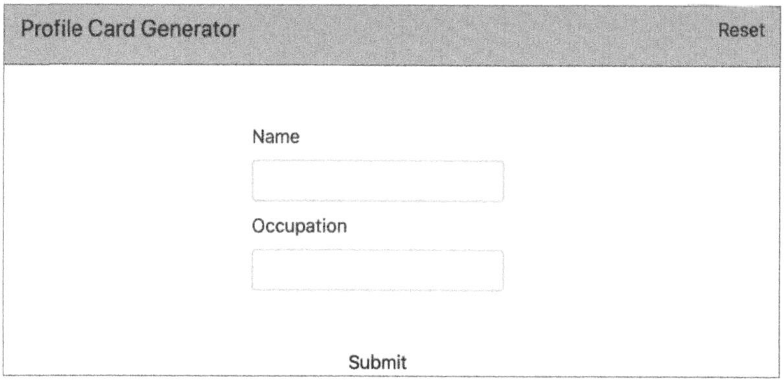

Figure 9.18 – Resetting the form and the display using the Reset button

You've now seen how Vue 3's built-in reactivity support makes it simple to handle state management in your components.

Activity 9.01 – adding Organization, Email, and Phone Number fields to a profile card generator

In a profile generator, you look at a profile to find some information about the individual. A person's organization, email, and phone number are often the most crucial pieces of information looked for on a profile card. This activity is about adding these details to a profile card generator.

To do this, we will add `Organization`, `Email`, and `Phone Number` fields in `AppProfileForm` and `AppProfileDisplay`:

1. Begin by adding the `organization` input field and label to `AppProfileForm`.

2. Next, add a new `email` input field and label to `AppProfileForm` for the `Email` field.

3. We can then add a new phone input field (of the `tel` type) and a label to `AppProfileForm` for the `Phone Number` field.

The new fields look as follows:

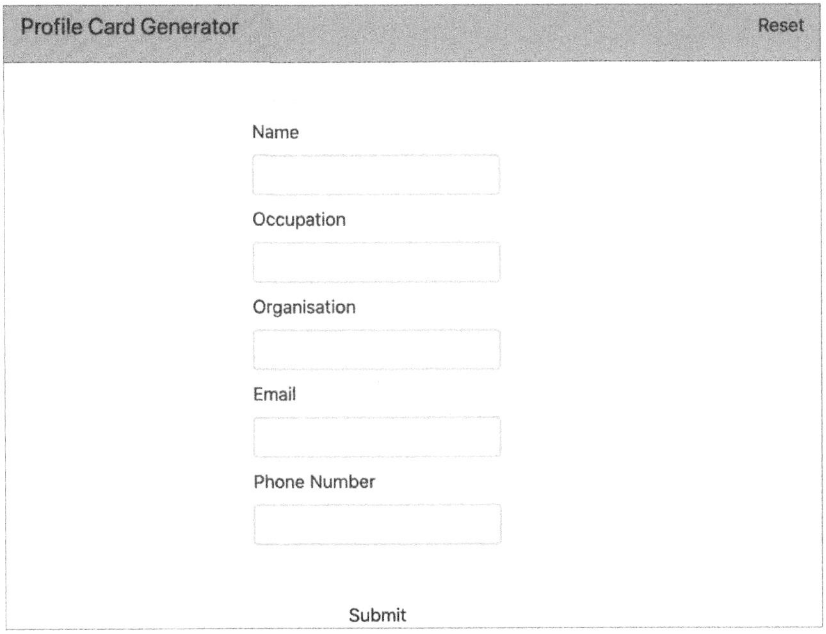

Figure 9.19 – Application with new Email and Phone Number fields

We can then add the organization, email, and phone fields to the initial state in src/store.js so that the values get set and then update clear to reset the new values.

4.   For organization to display, we add it after occupation in src/components/AppProfileDisplay.vue. We'll prefix it with the "at" literal string and only show it when there is a value. The end result is a paragraph that includes the occupation and organization.

5.   For email to display, we need to render it in src/components/AppProfileDisplay.vue using a conditional paragraph (to hide the Email label when there is no email set).

6.   For phone to display, we need to render it in src/components/AppProfileDisplay.vue using a conditional span (to hide the Phone Number label when there is no phone set).

The application should look as follows when the form is filled out and submitted:

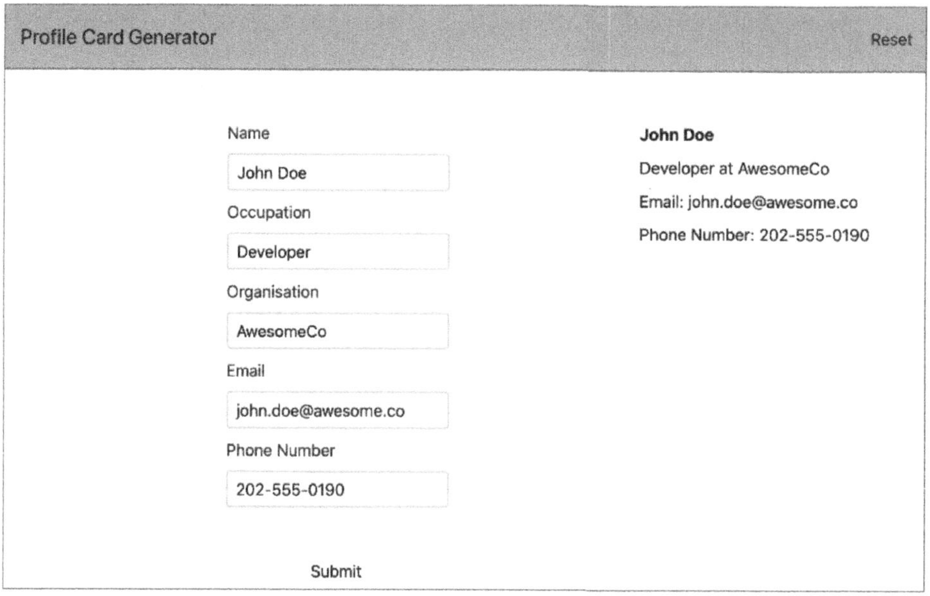

Figure 9.20 – Application with Email and Phone Number fields

> **Note**
>
> The solution for this activity can be found at https://github.com/PacktPublishing/ Frontend-Development-Projects-with-Vue.js-3/tree/v2-edition/ Chapter09/Activity9.01

You've now taken your application from a more complex event-driven state management system to one using a shared state that is far simpler to work with an update. Now that you've seen how to work with the global state, it's a good time to go over some thoughts on when it makes sense to use it.

Deciding when to use a local state or global state

As we have seen through the examples, the Vue.js ecosystem has solutions for managing shared and global states. What we will look at now is how to decide whether something belongs in a local state or global state.

A good rule of thumb is that *if a prop is passed through a depth of three components*, it is probably best to put that piece of state in a global state and access it that way – so for example, a value goes from a parent to a child, and then on to a grandchild. This could also apply to two siblings and a parent, with three components but less depth.

The second way to decide whether something is local or global is to ask the question *when the page reloads, does the user expect this information to persist?* Why does this matter? Well, a global state is a lot easier to save and persist than a local state. This is due to the nature of a global state *just being a JavaScript object* as opposed to a component state, which is more closely tied to the component tree and Vue.js. The browser supports powerful methods of persisting data on the client, from simpler web storage to the more complex IndexedDB. Either of these browser features could be used to store the state for a Vue application, restore them on load, and if used in a global state, then be applied to components across the app.

Another key idea to bear in mind is that it is very much possible to mix global states and local states in a component. Every component may use a mix of things that only apply to itself versus data that impacts the entire application.

As with most things, careful planning and thought into what data a component needs and what possibly needs to be shared can help with proper planning ahead of time.

Summary

This chapter was an introduction to the state management landscape in Vue.js. Throughout this chapter, we have looked at different approaches to shared and global state management in a Vue.js application.

We began by looking at storing a global state in one shared ancestor. This allows data sharing between sibling components through props and events. While this works, it does require extra code to handle the architecture of passing around data.

You then used Vue's built-in reactivity to create a simple, shared store. This resulted in a much simpler application, as much of the code from the previous version was able to be removed.

Finally, we have had a look at what criteria can be used to decide whether a state should live in a local component state or a more global or shared state solution.

The next chapter will be a deep dive into writing large-scale Vue.js applications with the new recommended way of handling shared state, the Pinia library.

10

State Management with Pinia

In the previous chapter, you were introduced to the idea of a *state* and how it can be used to synchronize data between multiple components in a Vue application. You first saw an example of handling states via event broadcasting and then improved upon that by including a simple state library.

In this chapter, you'll learn about the Pinia project and understand how it can help manage complex state interactions in your Vue applications. You'll learn how to install the library and start using it right away.

In this chapter, we will cover the following topics:

- What Pinia is
- Installing Pinia
- Using Pinia to create a store
- Adding and using getters in your Pinia store
- Working with Pinia actions
- Debugging Pinia in Devtools

Technical requirements

There are no technical requirements for this chapter outside of the `git` CLI that you will have already used by now.

The Node version has to be below v20 (preferable Yarn 1.22 and Node version above 16 and up to 19.x, and npm up to version 9.x.

You can find this chapter's source here: `https://github.com/PacktPublishing/Frontend-Development-Projects-with-Vue.js-3/tree/v2-edition/Chapter10`

What Pinia is

Pinia (`https://pinia.vuejs.org`) is a state management library for Vue.js applications. As you saw in *Chapter 9, The State of Vue State Management*, handling data that must be synchronized between multiple different components requires some form of management. Pinia helps with this by providing a simple method of setting up a central *store* that contains your application's state. Your components make use of this store to ensure they're all using the same information.

Pinia began as an experiment for Vue 3 but evolved to support Vue 2 as well. Pinia is now the *recommended* state management library for Vue applications, with the venerable Vuex (`https://vuex.vuejs.org/`) now in maintenance mode:

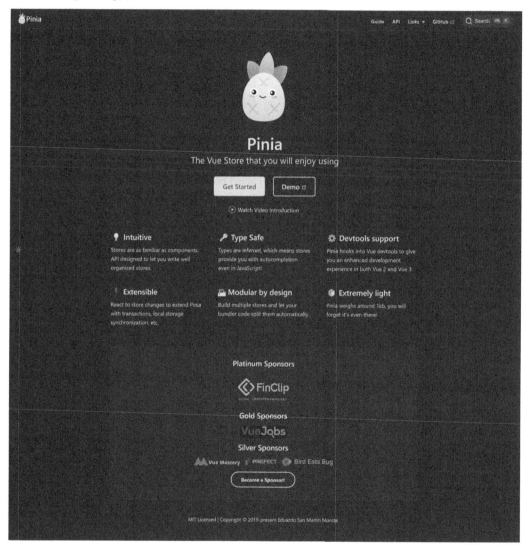

Figure 10.1 – The Pinia website

Along with state management, using Pinia also provides other benefits, including the following:

- Devtools support via the Vue extension. This extension supports Chrome, Edge, and Firefox. There's also a standalone Electron desktop application.
- **Hot Module Replacement** (**HMR**), which lets you edit your store and update it in your development environment without needing to reload the entire web page.
- Optional TypeScript support.
- **Server-Side Rendering** (**SSR**) support.
- Plugins to extend Pinia's functionality.

In general, there's a few core aspects of Pinia you need to be aware of. Developers with previous experience with Vuex will recognize these.

At a high level, a **store** is the combination of the data and logic that needs to be shared throughout an application. The **state** of a Pinia application is the data of your application's store. Pinia provides APIs to both read and write to this data. **Getters** act much like virtual properties in Vue applications. **Actions** let you define custom logic for a store – for example, using an AJAX call to validate changes to data before they are committed. While Pinia has more to it, these three core concepts will be our focus in this chapter and the meat of any use of Pinia.

Installing Pinia

To use Pinia in a Vue application, you've got two ways to add it. First, when creating a new Vue application via the standard method (npm init vue@latest), one of the questions asked will be whether you wish to include Pinia. Simply say *Yes* here:

```
ray@Mandalore:~/projects/testingzone/vue3stuff$ npm init vue@latest

Vue.js - The Progressive JavaScript Framework

✓ Project name: … vue-project
✓ Add TypeScript? … No / Yes
✓ Add JSX Support? … No / Yes
✓ Add Vue Router for Single Page Application development? … No / Yes
? Add Pinia for state management? › No / Yes
```

Figure 10.2 – Indicating whether you wish to add Pinia to a new Vue project

If you have an existing Vue 3 application, adding support is nearly as easy. First, in the project, add Pinia via npm: npm install pinia. Next, you need to include Pinia in the application. Your main.js file (located in the /src directory) will look like so:

```
import { createApp } from 'vue'
```

```
import App from './App.vue'

createApp(App).mount('#app')
```

Begin by importing Pinia:

```
import { createApp } from 'vue'
import { createPinia } from 'pinia'
import App from './App.vue'

createApp(App).mount('#app')
```

Then, modify the `createApp` line. We break it out into a few lines so that we can inject Pinia:

```
import { createApp } from 'vue'
import { createPinia } from 'pinia'

import App from './App.vue'

const app = createApp(App)

app.use(createPinia())

app.mount('#app')
```

Now that we've been introduced to the basic aspects of Pinia and how to include it in a Vue application, let's start working on our first example.

Using Pinia to create a store

Let's start using Pinia by demonstrating how to define a store within it and then use the state data in an application:

1. Create a new Vue application and enable Pinia, as shown in *Figure 10.2*. This will give you a Vue application with a store already created. You will find it under `src/stores/counter.js`:

    ```
    import { defineStore } from 'pinia'

    export const useCounterStore = defineStore({
      id: 'counter',
      state: () => ({
    ```

```
      counter: 1
    }),
    getters: {
      doubleCount: (state) => state.counter * 2
    },
    actions: {
      increment() {
        this.counter++
      }
    }
  })
```

This simple Pinia file demonstrates all three of the major aspects we defined previously – the state, getters, and actions. In this section, we're only concerned with the state. When installed, Pinia defined one piece of data, `counter`, with a value of `1`. How can we access this in our application?

2. Switch to the `App.vue` file and remove all the contents. We're going to greatly simplify it. First, let's define the layout to simply output the value of `counter`:

```
<template>
  <p>
  Counter: {{ store.counter }}
  </p>
</template>
```

3. Next, we need to make our store available to the component. We'll define this in a `script setup` block:

```
<script setup>
import { useCounterStore } from './stores/counter'
const store = useCounterStore()
</script>
```

4. We begin by importing the store. Once imported, we create an instance of the store so that it can be used in our template. While not terribly exciting, *Figure 10.3* demonstrates how this looks in the browser:

Counter: 1

Figure 10.3 – Our store value correctly displayed in the App component

5. To get any benefits from a shared state at all, we need at least one more component. In the
    `components` folder, create a new file, `EditCounter.vue`, and use the following short
    snippet of code:

```
<script setup>
import { useCounterStore } from '@/stores/counter';
const store = useCounterStore()
</script>

<template>
  <h2>Edit Counter</h2>
  <input type="text" v-model="store.counter">
</template>
```

6. As with the `App.vue` component, we use the `setup` block to import the store and create an
    instance. This time, we use a simple edit field and v-model to bind its value to the store's `counter`
    value. Return to `App.vue` and edit it to import and use the `EditCounter` component:

```
<script setup>
import EditCounter from './components/EditCounter.vue'

import { useCounterStore } from './stores/counter'
const store = useCounterStore();
</script>

<template>
  <p>
  Counter: {{ store.counter }}
  </p>
  <EditCounter></EditCounter>
</template>
```

Now, we're getting somewhere. We've got one component, App, simply rendering the shared
state, and another, `EditCounter`, which also displays it but in an editable fashion. Now, you
can edit the value and see it update:

Figure 10.4 – Multiple components using the same shared state

Now that we've seen how to install and initialize Pinia, and use a simple store, we can create a simple demonstration of it in action.

Exercise 10.01 – building a Color Preview app with a shared state

Now that we've seen a simple example of using a shared state with Pinia, let's build a simple application that will use it. Our application will let you use sliders to specify the red, green, and blue values of a color. One component will be used for the editor and another component will provide a preview.

The complete code for this exercise can be found at `https://github.com/PacktPublishing/Frontend-Development-Projects-with-Vue.js-3/tree/v2-edition/Chapter10/Exercise10.01`:

1. To begin, create a new Vue.js application and ensure Pinia support is selected. As prompted, change into the directory, run npm install, and then `npm run dev` to start the application running. Clear the contents of the App.vue component and enter the following:

```
<script setup>
import RGBEdit from './components/RGBEdit.vue'
import PreviewColor from './components/PreviewColor.vue'
</script>

<template>
<h1>Color Editor</h1>

<p>
Use the sliders below to set the red, green, and blue
values for a color.
</p>

<div class="twocol">
  <RGBEdit></RGBEdit>
  <PreviewColor></PreviewColor>
</div>
</template>

<style>
.twocol {
  display: grid;
  grid-template-columns: 1fr 1fr;
```

```
   column-gap: 10px;
 }
 </style>
```

We begin by importing two components (which we will define next). The template portion includes some simple explanatory text and then renders the two components. Finally, a bit of CSS is used to display these components in a grid. Note that App.vue doesn't make use of the store at all, but our two components will.

2. Now, let's define the child components. We're going to create them as essentially empty so that we can simply test that our application is working. In src/components, create RGBEdit.vue:

```
<template>
<div>
  <h2>Edit RGB</h2>
</div>
</template>
```

Next, create PreviewColor.vue:

```
<template>
<div>
  <h2>Preview Color</h2>
</div>
</template>
```

Note that you can remove the existing components the Vue initialization script created. We won't need those. At this point, you should see the following in your browser:

Figure 10.5 – The color application starting to come together

3. Now, let's define our sites store. In src/stores, make a new file (and feel free to remove the default one) named color.js:

```
import { defineStore } from 'pinia'

export const useColorStore = defineStore({
```

```
    id: 'color',
    state: () => ({
      red: 0,
      blue: 0,
      green: 0
    })
  })
```

Our store has three state values, each representing part of a color as defined in **Red, Green, and Blue (RGB)**. All three colors begin with a value of 0.

4. Next, let's flesh out our RGBEdit.vue. First, we'll import and create an instance of the store:

```
<script setup>
import { useColorStore } from '@/stores/color';
const store = useColorStore()
</script>
```

Next, we'll edit the template portion to add three range-style editing fields. This will make it much easier for the user to quickly preview colors:

```
<template>
<div>
  <h2>Edit RGB</h2>
  <label for="red">Red</label> <input type="range"
    min="0" max="255" id="red" v-model="store.red">
      <br/>
  <label for="green">Green</label>
    <input type="range" min="0" max="255" id="green"
      v-model="store.green"><br/>
  <label for="blue">Blue</label>
    <input type="range" min="0" max="255" id="blue"
      v-model="store.blue"><br/>
</div>
</template>
```

Each range control has a min of 0 and a max of 255, which represents the valid range for colors in web applications. Next, we will add a bit of styling to control the size of the label elements:

```
<style>
label {
```

```
        display: inline-block;
        width: 50px;
    }
    </style>
```

Save this and now confirm in the browser that you have editing controls for the color:

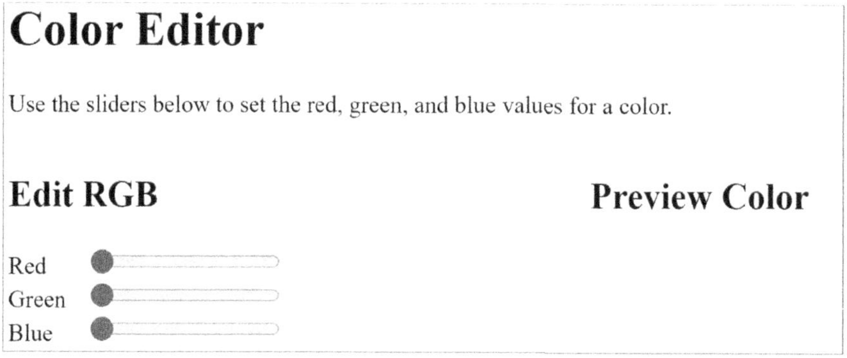

Color Editor

Use the sliders below to set the red, green, and blue values for a color.

Edit RGB   Preview Color

Red   ● ─────────────────
Green ● ─────────────────
Blue   ● ─────────────────

Figure 10.6 – Our application now has controls to edit the color

5. At this point, we've got an editing component, but we need to finish the preview component. Open PreviewColor.vue and first import the store:

```
<script setup>
import { useColorStore } from '@/stores/color';
const store = useColorStore()
</script>
```

In order to render a preview of the color, we need to convert the numerical colors to hex, which is how colors are defined on the web. Given that we have three numbers in our store, let's say 100, 50, and 100 for red, green, and blue respectively, we need to convert them into #64324.

We can write a computed property to handle this translation for us. Edit the script portion to include computed support and define the following computed property:

```
<script setup>
import { computed } from 'vue'
import { useColorStore } from '@/stores/color';
const store = useColorStore()
```

```
const previewRGB = computed(() => {

  return {
    backgroundColor: "#" + Number(store.red)
    .toString(16).padStart(2, '0') +
    Number(store.green).toString(16)
    .padStart(2, '0') + Number(store.blue)
    .toString(16).padStart(2, '0')
  }
});
</script>
```

Moving on to the `template` section, let's use this in the display:

```
<template>
<div>
  <h2>Preview Color</h2>
  <div class="previewColor" :style="previewRGB"></div>
  <p>
  CSS color string: {{ previewRGB.backgroundColor }}
  </p>
</div>
</template>
```

Note that the empty `div` is using the `computed` property to dynamically update the background color of the element. One last thing to add is a basic size for that `div` element:

```
<style>
.previewColor {
  width: 250px;
  height: 250px;
}
</style>
```

6. For the final step, simply play with the application and find a color that looks amazing!

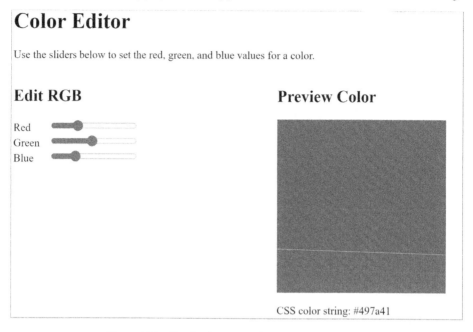

Figure 10.7 – The final version of the color application

In the next section, we'll introduce getters in Pinia and demonstrate how to use them.

Adding and using getters in your Pinia store

As stated earlier, getters in Pinia act just like computed properties. They allow you to request a simple value that's generated by custom logic written in a function.

If you go back to the original Pinia store created by default, you'll see it had a getter defined:

```
import { defineStore } from 'pinia'

export const useCounterStore = defineStore({
  id: 'counter',
  state: () => ({
    counter: 0
  }),
  getters: {
    doubleCount: (state) => state.counter * 2
  },
```

```
  // rest of file...
})
```

The doubleCount getter simply takes the current value of counter and returns the double of it. As demonstrated, getters are automatically passed the current state as an argument, which can then be used in whatever logic makes sense in your particular getter function.

Just like regular values defined in the state, getters can be addressed in your components, as shown here:

```
<template>
  <p>
  Counter: {{ store.counter }}
  </p>
  <p>
  Double Count: {{ store.doubleCount }}
  </p>
</template>
```

Let's build upon the last exercise and give this feature a try.

Exercise 10.02 – improving the Color Preview app with getters

In the previous exercise, you used Pinia to store the state of a color value comprising three components – red, green, and blue. In the application, the PreviewColor component displayed the hex value of the combined color. In this exercise, that custom logic will be removed from the component and stored within a getter in the store.

The complete code for this exercise can be found at https://github.com/PacktPublishing/Frontend-Development-Projects-with-Vue.js-3/tree/v2-edition/Chapter10/Exercise10.02

1. In the store, src/stores/color.js, add a new section for the getter:

```
import { defineStore } from 'pinia'

export const useColorStore = defineStore({
  id: 'color',
  state: () => ({
    red: 0,
    blue: 0,
    green: 0
```

```
    }),
    getters: {
      hex: (state) => {
        return  "#" + Number(state.red).toString(16)
          .padStart(2, '0') +
        Number(state.green).toString(16)
          .padStart(2, '0') +
        Number(state.blue).toString(16)
          .padStart(2, '0');
      }
    }
  })
```

The hex getter returns a string, starting with the pound symbol and followed by the hex values of the RGB numbers. Given that all values are 255 (the color white), the result would be #FFFFFF.

2. In PreviewColor.vue, we need to update the code to make use of the getter. Remove all the custom code used to translate the various values and simply use the getter:

```
<script setup>
import { computed } from 'vue'
import { useColorStore } from '@/stores/color';
const store = useColorStore()

const previewRGB = computed(() => {
  return {
    backgroundColor: store.hex
  }
});
</script>
// Rest of component, unchanged
```

As you can see, the component's code is much simpler now that the logic has moved into the Pinia store, and we get to reuse that logic elsewhere if we expand upon the application.

Additional getter features

Before moving on to actions, let's quickly discuss two additional things you can do with getters. The first is creating a getter that makes use of another getter. You can do this with arrow functions by simply using a state:

```
doubleCount: (state) => state.counter * 2,
superDuperState: (state) => state.doubleCount * 999,
```

If you are using regular function syntax, access the store via `this` or via a passed-in argument:

```
doubleCount: (state) => state.counter * 2,
superDuperState: (state) => state.doubleCount * 999,
doubleDoubleCount() {
  return this.doubleCount * 2;
},
```

Finally, while getters don't allow for additional arguments, you can create a getter that returns a function itself, not a regular value, such as the following:

```
countPlusN: (state) => x => Number(state.counter) + Number(x)
```

To use this within a component, you would pass a value to `countPlusN`, like so:

```
doublePlusN: {{ store.countPlusN(9) }}
```

Note that getters defined in this way will not have any caching applied to them.

Now that we've enhanced our store with getters, let's see how actions further add to the flexibility of Pinia.

Working with Pinia actions

Actions are the Pinia equivalent of component methods. They let you define custom logic for a store and can be asynchronous as well. This is useful for times when server-side logic needs to be called to validate a change to the state. Actions are defined with the `actions` block of a Pinia object, and you can see an example in the default store created by Pinia:

```
import { defineStore } from 'pinia'

export const useCounterStore = defineStore({
  id: 'counter',
  state: () => ({
    counter: 0
```

```
    }),
    // rest of store...
    actions: {
      increment() {
        this.counter++
      }
    }
  })
```

In this example, the increment action simply takes the counter value and adds one to it. Actions access state values by using the this scope and, as stated previously, can be asynchronous as well. An example of an action with a bit of logic could look like so:

```
decrement() {
  if(this.counter > 0) this.counter--
}
```

This action will apply a bit of validation before decreasing the value of counter and ensure that it never goes below zero.

Let's improve on our color editor by adding a few actions.

Exercise 10.03 – adding lightening and darkening features to the Color Preview app

The last exercise had you improve the Color Preview application by moving the logic of generating hex strings to a getter with the Pinia store. In this exercise, you're going to add two new features – buttons that either lighten and darken the current color.

The complete code for this exercise can be found at https://github.com/PacktPublishing/Frontend-Development-Projects-with-Vue.js-3/tree/v2-edition/Chapter10/Exercise10.03

1. We'll begin by using a third-party library to handle our color logic. The pSBC library was developed by a user helping out on Stack Overflow. The author took his Stack Overflow answer and turned it into a mini library that you can use for free.

    This code is documented on his GitHub at https://github.com/PimpTrizkit/PJs/wiki/12.-Shade,-Blend-and-Convert-a-Web-Color-(pSBC.js). If you scroll down to the **Code** section, you can copy and paste the entire library and insert it at the end of src/stores/color.js. Once copied into the store, the pSBC function can be used in the store.

To lighten a hex color, you pass a positive value – for example, pSBC(0.5, "#0022FF"). The number represents a percentage – in this case, 50 percent. To darken a color, you simply pass a negative value: pSBC(-0.5, "#0022FF").

2. With the pSBC library pasted into the store, add a new actions block to the store:

```
actions: {
}
```

3. Next, add the lighten function. This function will get the current hex value (which is much easier now with our getter!), pass it to the library, and then take the result and convert it back into decimal numbers:

```
lighten() {
  let newHex = pSBC(0.4, this.hex);
  // parse out hex back to dec
  this.red = parseInt(newHex.substring(1,3), 16);
  this.green = parseInt(newHex.substring(3,5), 16);
  this.blue = parseInt(newHex.substring(5,), 16);
},
```

4. Now, add the darken function:

```
darken() {
  let newHex = pSBC(-0.4, this.hex);
  // parse out hex back to dec
  this.red = parseInt(newHex.substring(1,3), 16);
  this.green = parseInt(newHex.substring(3,5), 16);
  this.blue = parseInt(newHex.substring(5,), 16);
}
```

5. Now that the store includes the actions we need, let's add the buttons to make use of them. In src/components/RGBEdit.vue, add the following beneath the last label:

```
<p>
<button @click="store.darken()">Darken</button>
<button @click="store.lighten()">Lighten</button>
</p>
```

Each button calls the respective action in the store. When run and viewed in the browser, you can see the new UI:

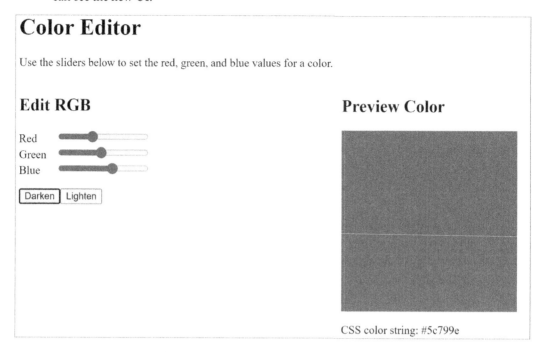

Figure 10.8 – The Color Preview app with new Darken and Lighten buttons

To test out the functionality, simply move the sliders around and then try clicking on the buttons.

Debugging Pinia in Devtools

Earlier in *Chapter 3, Vite and Vue Devtools*, you were introduced to Vue Devtools. **Devtools** are an incredibly powerful way to debug and optimize web applications, and the Vue plugin makes them even more vital for Vue developers. What makes Vue Devtools even more powerful is automatic recognition and support for applications using Pinia.

Let's take a quick tour of what this support looks like by using the Color Preview application last modified in *Exercise 10.03*. Run the application from the command line, open the URL in your browser, and open your developer tools. Note the **Pinia** tab on the right in *Figure 10.9*:

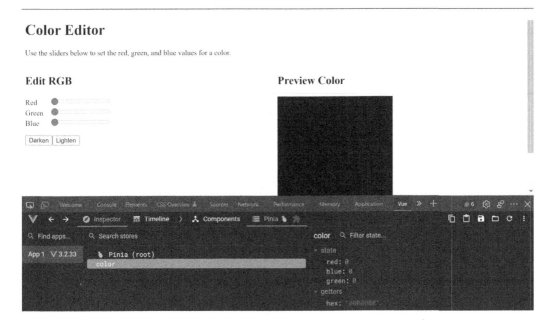

Figure 10.9 – Pinia support in Vue Devtools

Right away, you can see you've got access to the complete state as well as any getters. If you start modifying the RGB values, you can see them immediately reflected:

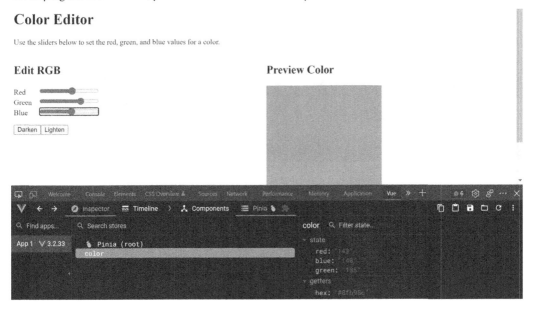

Figure 10.10 – The state values update as the user works with the app

If you hover the mouse over one of the values in the state, you will see both a pencil icon and a three-dot menu icon. The pencil icon lets you directly edit state values, while the three-dot menu gives you the ability to copy the value to the clipboard or the path:

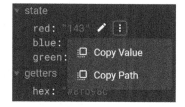

Figure 10.11 – Tools to edit or copy state values

The icons in the upper-right portion allow you to copy the entire state to your clipboard, replace the state with the contents of your state, save the state to the filesystem, or import a saved state. As an example, if you save the state to the filesystem, it will look like this:

```
{"color":{"red":0,"blue":"69","green":"217"}}
```

If you click the **Timeline** tab, you will get a history of changes related to your Pinia store:

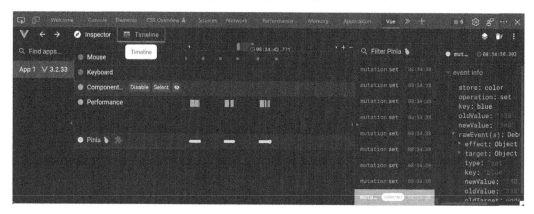

Figure 10.12 – Pinia modifications history

In *Figure 10.12*, you can see detailed information showing changes along with previous and new values. You can click on any of the previous mutations to see historical changes.

Hopefully, this demonstrates just how useful it is to use Vue Devtools and how nicely integrated Pinia is. Make sure to fully use it when trying to solve any gnarly bugs you run into in the future!

Activity 10.01 – creating a simple shopping cart and price calculator

Imagine a hypothetical corporate hardware site that lets employees select products they need to be shipped to their office. This cart is much simpler than a typical e-commerce site, as it doesn't need to process credit cards or even ask the person where they are (IT knows where you sit!).

It still needs to present you with a list of items, let you select how much you want, and then provide you with a total price that will be billed to your department.

In this activity, you need to build a Pinia store that represents the available products and their prices. You will need multiple components to handle the different aspects of the application and properly interact with the store data:

1. Begin by creating a new Pinia store. Your store should use two values in the state, an array of products with hardcoded names and values, and an empty cart array. Here's an example list of products:

```
products: [
    { name: "Widgets", price: 10 },
    { name: "Doodads", price: 8 },
    { name: "Roundtuits", price: 12 },
    { name: "Fluff", price: 4 },
    { name: "Goobers", price: 7 }
],
```

2. Your application will consist of three components. The first is a `Products` component to list products. The second is a `Cart` component that renders the current cart. Finally, there is a `Checkout` component, which renders the total along with a not-really-functional **Checkout** button.

3. The `Products.vue` component should render each product and have a button to add and remove it from the cart. These buttons should call actions in the Pinia store and either add or remove an item from the cart:

Products

Name	Price		
Widgets	10	Add to Cart	Remove from Cart
Doodads	8	Add to Cart	Remove from Cart
Roundtuits	12	Add to Cart	Remove from Cart
Fluff	4	Add to Cart	Remove from Cart
Goobers	7	Add to Cart	Remove from Cart

Figure 10.13 – The Products component

4.   The Cart.vue component renders a table of items in the cart. It should show the name of the product and the current quantity. If a line item ever goes to zero, it should not be displayed in the table. The following figure demonstrates this:

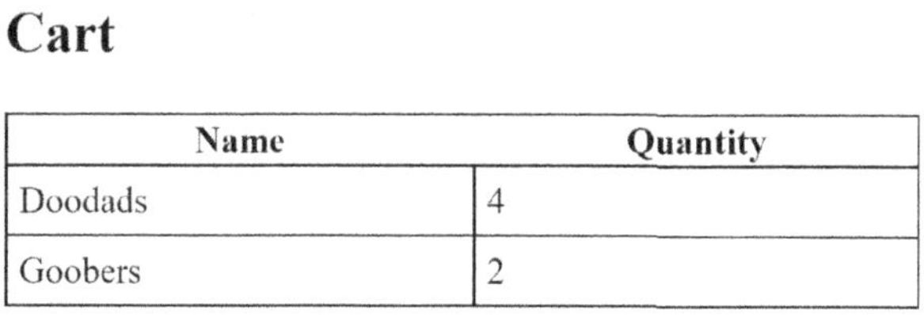

Cart

Name	Quantity
Doodads	4
Goobers	2

Figure 10.14 – The Cart component

5.   The Checkout.vue component will render two things. First, it will render a total cost. This is based on the products and quantity in the cart. Secondly, it will render a **Checkout** button but only if there is an actual cost. The **Checkout** button does not need to do anything:

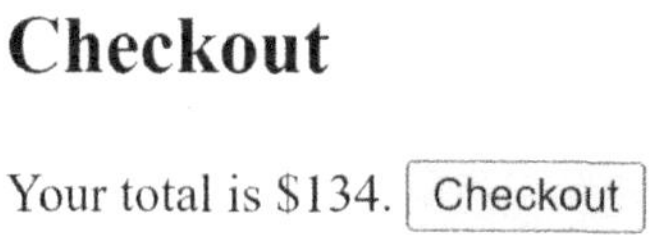

Checkout

Your total is $134. Checkout

Figure 10.15 – The Checkout component

> **Note**
> The solution for this activity can be found at https://github.com/PacktPublishing/ Frontend-Development-Projects-with-Vue.js-3/tree/v2-edition/ Chapter10/Activity10.01

Congratulations! You've now built a real, if simple, application making use of Pinia. Your application has three components kept perfectly in sync via Pinia's store, and you've gotten the hang of working with state management using the officially recommended library.

Summary

This chapter introduced you to Pinia, Vue's recommended library for handling a shared state in a complex, multi-component application.

We began by discussing how to install Pinia. Next, we introduced states and showed you how to use those values in your components.

You looked at getters as a way of handling *virtual* properties and encapsulating logic.

Finally, you saw how actions let you define custom methods for working with your state.

In the next chapter, you'll be introduced to testing with Vue, specifically unit testing, which will prepare you for end-to-end testing in the chapter after that.

Part 4:
Testing and Application Deployment

In the final part of the book, we will be going head first into the testing aspect of Vue.js applications. We will learn about the fundamentals of testing, different types of testing, and when and where it is required, and start testing our applications using the Jest testing framework for unit and snapshot tests and Cypress for End-to-End tests. By writing tests, we will be making sure that our applications behave in the intended way. The final chapter will cover how to deploy our Vue applications to the web.

We will cover the following chapters in this part:

- *Chapter 11, Unit Testing*
- *Chapter 12, End-to-End Testing*
- *Chapter 13, Deploying Your Code to the Web*

11

Unit Testing

In previous chapters, we saw how to build reasonably complex Vue.js applications. This chapter is about testing them to maintain code quality and prevent defects. We will look at approaches to unit testing Vue.js applications in order to improve the quality and speed of delivery of our applications.

We will also look at using tests to drive development using **Test-Driven Development** (**TDD**). As we proceed, we will gain an understanding of why code needs to be tested and what kinds of testing can be employed on different parts of a Vue.js application.

In this chapter, we will cover the following topics:

- Understanding testing and the need to test code
- Building your first test
- Testing components
- Testing methods
- Testing routing
- Testing state management with Pinia
- Snapshot testing

Technical requirements

There are no technical requirements for this chapter outside of the `git` CLI, which you will have already used by now.

The Node version has to be below v20 (preferable Yarn 1.22 and Node version above 16 and up to 19.x, and npm up to version 9.x.

You can find this chapter's source code here: `https://github.com/PacktPublishing/Frontend-Development-Projects-with-Vue.js-3/tree/v2-edition/Chapter11`

Understanding testing and the need to test code

Testing is a crucial process for ensuring that the code does what it's meant to do. Quality production software is empirically correct. That means that for the enumerated cases that developers and testers have found, the application behaves as expected.

This lies in contrast with software that has been proven to be correct, which is a very time-consuming endeavor and is usually part of academic research projects. We are still at the point where correct software (proven) is still being built to show what kinds of systems are possible to build with this constraint of correctness.

Testing prevents the introduction of defects such as bugs and regressions (that is, when a feature stops working as expected). In the next section, we will learn about the various types of testing.

Different types of testing

The testing spectrum spans from **end-to-end testing** (by manipulating the user interface) to **integration tests**, and finally to **unit tests**.

End-to-end testing

End-to-end tests test everything, including the user interface, the underlying HTTP services, and even database interactions; nothing is mocked. If you've got an e-commerce application, an end-to-end test might actually place a real order with a real credit card, or it might place a test order with a test credit card.

End-to-end tests are costly to run and maintain. They require the use of full-blown browsers controlled through programmatic drivers such as Selenium, WebdriverIO, or Cypress. This type of test platform is costly to run, and small changes in the application code can cause end-to-end tests to start failing.

Integration tests

Integration or system-level tests ensure that a set of systems is working as expected. This will usually involve deciding on a limit as to where the system under test lies and allowing it to run, usually against mocked or stubbed upstream services and systems (which are therefore not under test).

Since external data access is stubbed, a whole host of issues, such as timeouts and flakes, can be reduced (when compared to end-to-end tests). Integration test suites are usually fast enough to run as a continuous integration step, but the full test suite tends not to be run locally by engineers.

Unit tests

Unit tests are great at providing fast feedback during development. Unit testing paired with TDD is part of extreme programming practice. Unit tests are great at testing complicated logic or building a system from its expected output. Unit tests are usually fast enough to run a developer's code against before sending their code for review and continuous integration tests.

The following diagram is an interpretation of the pyramid of testing. It can be interpreted to mean that you should have a high number of cheap and fast unit tests, a reasonable number of system tests, and just a few end-to-end UI tests:

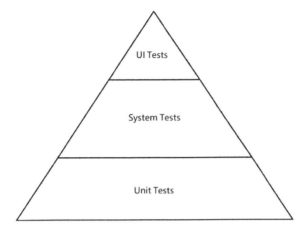

Figure 11.1 – Pyramid of testing diagram

Now that we've looked at why we should be testing applications, let's start writing some tests.

Building your first test

To illustrate how quick and easy it is to get started with automated tests in a Vue 3 project, we will start by creating a simple test using Vitest (https://vitest.dev/), the officially recommended testing framework for Vue 3 and the simplest to begin with as the installation steps of a new application let you select it right away.

In the following figure, you can see the prompt for installing Vitest:

```
ray@Hoth:~/projects/Front-End-Development-Projects-with-Vue.js/Chapter11$ npm init vue@latest
Need to install the following packages:
  create-vue@latest
Ok to proceed? (y)

Vue.js - The Progressive JavaScript Framework

✓ Project name: … test1
✓ Add TypeScript? … No / Yes
✓ Add JSX Support? … No / Yes
✓ Add Vue Router for Single Page Application development? … No / Yes
✓ Add Pinia for state management? … No / Yes
? Add Vitest for Unit Testing? › No / Yes
```

Figure 11.2 – Creating an application and selecting Yes to using Vitest

After the application is scaffolded, you will find it created a __tests__ folder under `components` and created a test already. For now though, delete the file (but not the folder) and create a new __tests__ folder directly under the root of you project. Next, create an `App.test.js` file.

We will use `shallowMount` to render the application and test whether it displays **The Vue.js Workshop Blog**. For the purposes of this example, we'll use the text `The Vue.js Workshop Blog`. `shallowMount` does a *shallow render*, which means that only the top level of a component is rendered; all the child components are stubbed.

This is useful for testing a component in isolation since the child components' implementations are not run:

```
import { describe, it, expect } from 'vitest'
import { shallowMount } from '@vue/test-utils'
import App from '../src/App.vue'
describe('App', () => {
  it('App renders blog title correctly', () => {
    const wrapper = shallowMount(App)
    expect(wrapper.text()).toContain('The Vue.js Workshop
                                      Blog')
  })
})
```

Save this file, and at the Terminal (ensure you've already run npm `install` to finish creating a new application), run npm `run test:unit`.

When you indicated in the installation prompt that you wanted to include Vitest, it added the following script to the `package.json` file:

```
"test:unit": "vitest --environment jsdom"
```

You will get a report on the test run and its immediate failure:

```
ray@Hoth:~/ ... /Chapter11/test1$ npm run test:unit

> test1@0.0.0 test:unit
> vitest --environment jsdom


 DEV  v0.13.1 /home/ray/projects/Front-End-Development-Projects-with-Vue.js/Chapter11/test1

 ❯ __tests__/App.test.js (1)
   ❯ App (1)
     × App renders blog title correctly
─────────────────────────────────── Failed Tests 1 ───────────────────────────────────

 FAIL  __tests__/App.test.js > App > App renders blog title correctly
AssertionError: expected 'Th Vue.js Workshop Blog' to include 'The Vue.js Workshop Blog'
 ❯ __tests__/App.test.js:9:28
      7|   it('App renders blog title correctly', () ⇒ {
      8|     const wrapper = shallowMount(App)
      9|     expect(wrapper.text()).toContain('The Vue.js Workshop Blog')
       |                            ^
     10|   })
     11| })

─────────────────────────────────────────────────────────────────────────────[1/1]─

 Test Files  1 failed (1)
      Tests  1 failed (1)
       Time  1.10s (in thread 15ms, 7325.89%)


 FAIL  Tests failed. Watching for file changes ...
       press h to show help, press q to quit
```

Figure 11.3 – The unit test running and failing

To make the test pass, we can edit our App.vue file to include the header we want (note that we also removed much of the code created by default):

```
<script setup>
</script>

<template>
  <header>
  <h1>The Vue.js Workshop Blog</h1>
  </header>
</template>

<style>
</style>
```

Save the file and you'll immediately see the result:

```
RERUN  src/App.vue

√ __tests__/App.test.js (1)

Test Files  1 passed (1)
      Tests  1 passed (1)
       Time  15ms

PASS  Waiting for file changes ...
      press h to show help, press q to quit
```

Figure 11.4 – The test passing!

You have just completed your first piece of TDD. This process started by writing a test that failed. This failure was followed by an update to the code under test (in this case the App.vue component), which made the failing test pass.

The TDD process gives us confidence that our features have been tested properly since we can see that tests fail before they pass when we update the code that drives our feature.

In the next section, we'll show how to take what we've learned and apply it to Vue components.

Testing components

Components are at the core Vue.js applications. Writing unit tests for them is straightforward with Vitest. Having tests that exercise the majority of your components gives you confidence that they behave as designed. Ideal unit tests for components run quickly and are simple.

We'll carry on building the blog application example. We have now built the heading, but a blog usually also needs a list of posts to display.

We'll create a PostList component. For now, it will just render a div wrapper and support a posts Array prop:

```
<script setup>
defineProps({
  posts: {
    type: Array,
      default: () => []
  }
})
```

```
</script>

<template>
  <div>
  </div>
</template>
```

We can add some data in the App component:

```
<script>
export default {
  data() {
    return {
      posts: [
        {
          title: 'Vue.js for React developers',
            description: 'React has massive popularity here
              are the key benefits of Vue.js over it.',
                tags: ['vue', 'react'],
        },
        {
          title: 'Migrating an AngularJS app to Vue.js',
            description: 'With many breaking changes,
              AngularJS developers have found it easier to
                retrain to Vue.js than Angular 2',
                tags: ['vue', 'angularjs']
        }
      ]
    }
  }
}
</script>
```

Now that we have some posts, we can pass them as a bound prop to the `PostList` component from the App component:

```
<script setup>
import PostList from './components/PostList.vue'
</script>

<template>
  <header>
  <h1>The Vue.js Workshop Blog</h1>
  </header>

  <PostList :posts="posts" />
</template>
```

Our `PostList` component will render out each post in a `PostListItem` component, which we'll create as follows.

`PostListItem` takes two props: `title` (which is a string) and `description` (also a string). It renders them in an h3 tag and a p tag, respectively:

```
<script setup>
defineProps({
  title: {
    type: String
  },
  description: {
    type: String
  }
})

</script>

<template>
  <div>
  <h3>{{ title }}</h3>
  <p>{{ description }}</p>
  </div>
</template>
```

We now need to loop through the posts and render out a `PostListItem` component with relevant props bound in the `PostList.vue` component:

```
<script setup>
import PostListItem from './PostListItem.vue';

defineProps({
  posts: {
    type: Array,
      default: () => []
  }
})
</script>

<template>
  <div>
    <PostListItem v-for="post in posts"
      :key="post.slug"
      :title="post.title"
      :description="post.description"/>
  </div>
</template>
```

To test the `PostListItem` component, we can do a shallow render with some arbitrary title and description props set, and check that they get rendered. Add a new file to `src/__tests__` named `PostListItem.test.js`:

```
import { describe, it, expect } from 'vitest'

import { shallowMount } from '@vue/test-utils';
import PostListItem from '../components/PostListItem.vue';

describe('PostListItem', () => {
  it('PostListItem renders title and description
  correctly', () => {

    const wrapper = shallowMount(PostListItem, {
      propsData: {
```

```
        title: "Blog post title",
        description: "Blog post description"
      }
    })
    expect(wrapper.text()).toMatch("Blog post title")
    expect(wrapper.text()).toMatch("Blog post description")
  })
})
```

This test can be run individually at the command line by using the npm run test:unit __ tests__/PostListItem.test.js command (as seen in *Figure 11.5*):

```
ray@Hoth:~/ ... /Chapter11/test1$ npm run test:unit __tests__/PostListItem.test.js

> test1@0.0.0 test:unit
> vitest --environment jsdom "__tests__/PostListItem.test.js"


 DEV  v0.13.1 /home/ray/projects/Front-End-Development-Projects-with-Vue.js/Chapter11/test1

 √ __tests__/PostListItem.test.js (1)

 Test Files  1 passed (1)
      Tests  1 passed (1)
       Time  1.12s (in thread 13ms, 8628.30%)


 PASS  Waiting for file changes...
       press h to show help, press q to quit
```

Figure 11.5 – PostListItem test output

Next, we'll see one of the pitfalls of shallow rendering. When testing the PostList component, all we can do is test the number of PostListItem components it's rendering.

Save this test as __tests__/PostList.test.js:

```
import { describe, it, expect } from 'vitest'

import { shallowMount } from '@vue/test-utils';
import PostList from '../src/components/PostList.vue';
import PostListItem from '../src/components/PostListItem.vue';

describe('PostList', () => {
  it('PostList renders the right number of PostListItem',
```

```
  () => {

    const wrapper = shallowMount(PostList, {
      propsData: {
        posts:  [
          {
            title: "Blog post title",
            description: "Blog post description"
          }
        ]
      }
    })
    expect(wrapper.findAllComponents(PostListItem))
      .toHaveLength(1);
  })
})
```

This passes, but we are testing something that the user will not directly interact with, the number of
PostListItem instances rendered in PostList, as shown in the following screenshot:

```
ray@Hoth:~/ ... /Chapter11/test1$ npm run test:unit __tests__/PostList.test.js

> test1@0.0.0 test:unit
> vitest --environment jsdom "__tests__/PostList.test.js"

 DEV  v0.13.1 /home/ray/projects/Front-End-Development-Projects-with-Vue.js/Chapter11/test1

 √ __tests__/PostList.test.js (1)

Test Files  1 passed (1)
     Tests  1 passed (1)
      Time  1.05s (in thread 15ms, 7020.23%)

 PASS  Waiting for file changes ...
       press h to show help, press q to quit
```

Figure 11.6 – PostList test output

A better solution is to use the mount function, which renders the full component tree, whereas the
shallowMount function would only render out the children of the component being rendered.
With mount, we can assert that the titles and descriptions are rendered to the page.

The drawback of this approach is that we're testing both the PostList component and the
PostListItem component since the PostList component doesn't render the title or description;
it renders a set of PostListItem components that in turn render the relevant title and description.

The code is as follows:

```
import { describe, it, expect } from 'vitest'

import { shallowMount, mount } from '@vue/test-utils';
import PostList from '../src/components/PostList.vue';
import PostListItem from '../src/components/PostListItem.vue';

describe('PostList', () => {

  // Previous test…

  it('PostList renders passed title and description for
  each passed post', () => {

    const wrapper = mount(PostList, {
      propsData: {
        posts: [
          {
            title: "Title 1",
            description: "Description 1"
          },
          {
            title: "Title 2",
            description: "Description 2"
          }
        ]
      }
    })

    const outputText = wrapper.text()
    expect(outputText).toContain('Title 1')
    expect(outputText).toContain('Description 1')
    expect(outputText).toContain('Title 2')
    expect(outputText).toContain('Description 2')
  })
})
```

The new tests pass as indicated by the following output of the npm run test:unit __tests__/ PostList.test.js command:

```
ray@Hoth:~/ ... /Chapter11/test1$ npm run test:unit __tests__/PostList.test.js

> test1@0.0.0 test:unit
> vitest --environment jsdom "__tests__/PostList.test.js"

 DEV  v0.13.1 /home/ray/projects/Front-End-Development-Projects-with-Vue.js/Chapter11/test1

 √ __tests__/PostList.test.js (2)

Test Files  1 passed (1)
     Tests  2 passed (2)
      Time  1.06s (in thread 19ms, 5603.15%)

 PASS  Waiting for file changes ...
       press h to show help, press q to quit
```

Figure 11.7 – Test run for PostList with both shallow and mounted tests

We have now seen how to write unit tests for Vue.js with Vitest and vue-test-utils. These tests can be run often and the test runs complete within seconds, which gives us near-immediate feedback while working on new or existing components.

Exercise 11.01: Building and unit testing a tag list component

When creating the fixture for posts, we populated a tags field with vue, angularjs, and react but did not display them.

The complete code for this exercise can be found at https://github.com/PacktPublishing/ Frontend-Development-Projects-with-Vue.js-3/tree/v2-edition/Chapter11/ Exercise11.01

To make tags useful, we will display the tags in the post list:

1. We can start by writing a unit test that will explain what we expect a PostListItem component to do when passed a set of tags as props. It expects that each tag will be rendered with a hashtag prepended to it.

    For example, the react tag will be shown as #react. In the __tests__/PostListItem. test.js file, we can add a new test:

    ```
    // rest of test and imports
    it('PostListItem renders tags with a # prepended to
    them', () => {

      const wrapper = shallowMount(PostListItem, {
        propsData: {
    ```

```
            tags: ['react', 'vue']
        }
    })
    expect(wrapper.text()).toMatch('#react')
    expect(wrapper.text()).toMatch('#vue')
})
```

This test fails when run with the `npm run test:unit __tests__/PostListItem.test.js` command, as shown in *Figure 11.8*:

```
ray@Hoth:~/ ... /Chapter11/Exercise11.01$ npm run test:unit __tests__/PostListItem.test.js

> Exercise11.01@0.0.0 test:unit
> vitest --environment jsdom "__tests__/PostListItem.test.js"

 DEV  v0.13.1 /home/ray/projects/Front-End-Development-Projects-with-Vue.js/Chapter11/Exercise11.01

 ❯ __tests__/PostListItem.test.js (2)
   ✓ PostListItem (1)
   ❯ PostListItem (1)
     × PostListItem renders tags with a # prepended to them
─────────────────────────── Failed Tests 1 ───────────────────────────

 FAIL  __tests__/PostListItem.test.js > PostListItem > PostListItem renders tags with a # prepended to them
AssertionError: expected '' to include '#react'
 ❯ __tests__/PostListItem.test.js:28:28
     26|      }
     27|    })
     28|    expect(wrapper.text()).toMatch('#react')
       |                           ^
     29|    expect(wrapper.text()).toMatch('#vue')
     30|  })
                                                                                                    ─[1/1]─

 Test Files  1 failed (1)
      Tests  1 failed | 1 passed (2)
       Time  983ms (in thread 17ms, 5784.07%)

 FAIL  Tests failed. Watching for file changes...
       press h to show help, press q to quit
```

Figure 11.8 – Tag test for PostListItem failing

2. Next, we should implement the tag list rendering in `src/components/PostListItem.vue`. We'll add tags as props of the `Array` type and use `v-for` to render out the tags:

```
<script setup>
defineProps({
  title: {
    type: String
  },
  description: {
    type: String
  },
```

```
  tags: {
    type: Array,
    default: () => []
  }
})

</script>

<template>
  <div>
  <h3>{{ title }}</h3>
  <p>{{ description }}</p>

  <ul>
    <li
    v-for="tag in tags"
    :key="tag">
    #{{ tag }}
    </li>
  </ul>

  </div>
</template>
```

With the `PostListItem` component implemented, the unit test should now pass:

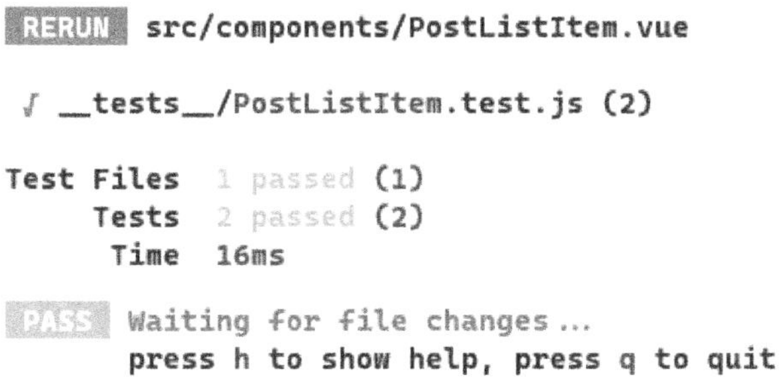

```
RERUN   src/components/PostListItem.vue

  √ __tests__/PostListItem.test.js (2)

Test Files   1 passed (1)
    Tests   2 passed (2)
     Time   16ms

  PASS   Waiting for file changes ...
         press h to show help, press q to quit
```

Figure 11.9 – PostListItem unit test passing

However, the tags are not displayed in the application:

The Vue.js Workshop Blog

Vue.js for React developers

React has massive popularity here are the key benefits of Vue.js over it.

Migrating an AngularJS app to Vue.js

With many breaking changes, AngularJS developers have found it easier to retrain to Vue.js than Angular 2

Figure 11.10 – PostList displaying without tags despite the correct PostListItem implementation

3.   We can write a unit test for `PostList` that would show this behavior. In essence, we'll be passing some tags in our `posts` list and running the same assertions as are already present in the `PostListItem.test.js` file.

We'll do this in `__tests__/PostList.test.js`:

```
it('PostList renders tags for each post', () => {

    const wrapper = mount(PostList, {
      propsData: {
        posts: [
              {
                tags: ['react', 'vue']
              },
              {
                tags: ['html', 'angularjs']
              }
              ]
        }
    })

    const outputText = wrapper.text()
    expect(outputText).toContain('#react')
    expect(outputText).toContain('#vue')
    expect(outputText).toContain('#html')
    expect(outputText).toContain('#angularjs')
  })
```

As per our application output shown in *Figure 11.11*, the test is failing when run with the npm run test:unit __tests__/PostList.test.js command:

```
> Exercise11.01@0.0.0 test:unit
> vitest --environment jsdom "__tests__/PostList.test.js"


 DEV  v0.13.1 /home/ray/projects/Front-End-Development-Projects-with-Vue.js/Chapter11/Exercise11.01

 ❯ __tests__/PostList.test.js (3)
   ❯ PostList (3)
     √ PostList renders the right number of PostListItem
     √ PostList renders passed title and description for each passed post
     × PostList renders tags for each post
```
―――――――――――――――――――――――― Failed Tests 1 ――――――――――――――――――――――――

```
 FAIL  __tests__/PostList.test.js > PostList > PostList renders tags for each post
AssertionError: expected '' to include '#react'
 ❯ __tests__/PostList.test.js:64:21
     62|
     63|          const outputText = wrapper.text()
     64|          expect(outputText).toContain('#react')
       |                             ^
     65|          expect(outputText).toContain('#vue')
     66|          expect(outputText).toContain('#html')
```
――[1/1]―

```
Test Files  1 failed (1)
     Tests  1 failed | 2 passed (3)
      Time  1.13s (in thread 22ms, 5145.37%)

 FAIL  Tests failed. Watching for file changes ...
       press h to show help, press q to quit
```

Figure 11.11 – PostList tags test failing

4. In order to fix this test, we can find the issue in src/components/PostList.vue, where the tags prop for PostListItem is not bound. By updating src/components/PostList.vue to bind the tags prop, we can fix the unit test:

```
<!-- rest of template -->
<PostListItem v-for="post in posts"
  :key="post.slug"
  :title="post.title"
  :description="post.description"
  :tags="post.tags"
/>
```

The failing unit test now passes, as shown in the following screenshot.

```
 RERUN  __tests__/PostList.test.js

 √ __tests__/PostList.test.js (3)

Test Files  1 passed (1)
     Tests  3 passed (3)
      Time  21ms

 PASS  Waiting for file changes ...
       press h to show help, press q to quit
```

Figure 11.12 – PostList tags test passing

We have now seen how we can test rendered component output with both the shallow rendering and mounting of components. Let's briefly understand what each of these terms means:

- **Shallow rendering**: This renders at a depth of 1, meaning that if children are components, they will just be rendered as the component tag; their template will not be run

- **Mounting**: This renders the full component tree in a similar fashion as would be rendered in the browser

Next, we'll look at how to test component methods.

Testing component methods

In the previous version of Vue, the recommendation would have been to do testing on filters and mixins, but typically avoid writing tests for methods as they aren't directly called by users.

In Vue 3, both filters and mixins are deprecated and replaced with *regular* methods and computed properties. That being said, finding the methods appropriate for tests may require some thought.

Consider a `computed` property that truncates its input to eight characters:

```
// rest of file...
import { computed } from 'vue';

const props = defineProps({
  title: {
    type: String
  },
  description: {
    type: String
  },
  tags: {
    type: Array,
    default: () => []
  }
})

const truncated = computed(() => {
  return props.description && props.description.slice(0,8)
})

defineExpose({ truncated })
```

In the preceding code sample, `truncated` is defined as a computed property based on the `description` value passed as a property. At the end, `defineExpose` is used to make the property available for testing. Items that are specified within `script setup` are considered *closed* and are not available outside the component itself. By using `defineExpose`, we can then write a test against `truncated`.

We can test the logic of the computed property in two ways. First, longer strings should be truncated. Secondly, shorter strings should be returned as is.

Here are the additional tests added to `PostListItem.test.js`:

```
it('truncated properly returns only the first 8 characters', ()
=> {

  const wrapper = shallowMount(PostListItem, {
    propsData: {
      title: "Blog post title",
      description: "Blog post description"
    }
  })
  expect(wrapper.vm.truncated).toMatch('Blog pos')
})

it('truncated properly doesnt change shorter values', () => {

  const wrapper = shallowMount(PostListItem, {
    propsData: {
      title: "Blog post title",
      description: "Test"
    }
  })
  expect(wrapper.vm.truncated).toMatch('Test')
})
```

The first new test passes a long value for description and confirms that the truncated version is shorter. Note the use of vm to access the Vue instance of the component and then the `truncated` computed property. The next test confirms that if a shorter value is used, truncated will not shorten it.

Remember that a user would not actually call `truncated` directly. As an alternative to directly testing the computed property, we could confirm that any template usage works properly as well. In that case, using `wrapper.text()` would make sense to return the rendered result.

Exercise 11.02: Building and testing an ellipsis method

We have seen how to test an arbitrary `truncated` computed method; we will now implement an `ellipsis` computed method and test it.

The complete code for this exercise can be found at `https://github.com/PacktPublishing/Frontend-Development-Projects-with-Vue.js-3/tree/v2-edition/Chapter11/Exercise11.02`

1. We can start by writing a set of tests for the `ellipsis` computed method (which will live in `src/components/PostListItem.vue`). One test should check that the filter does nothing if the passed value is less than 50 characters; another should check whether the passed value is more than 50 characters and if so, truncate the value to 50 and appends ....

    We will do this in a `__tests__/ellipsis.test.js` file:

    ```
    // rest of script
    describe('ellipsis', () => {

      it('ellipsis should do nothing if value is less
      than 50 characters', () => {

        const wrapper = shallowMount(PostListItem, {
          propsData: {
            title: "Blog post title",
            description: "Test"
          }
        })
        expect(wrapper.vm.truncated).toMatch('Test')

    })

      it('ellipsis should truncate to 50 and append "..."
      when longer than 50 characters', () => {

        const wrapper = shallowMount(PostListItem, {
          propsData: {
            title: "Blog post title",
            description: "Should be more than
            the 50 allowed characters by a small amount"
    ```

```
      }
    })
    expect(wrapper.vm.truncated).toMatch('Should be
      more than the 50 allowed characters by a...')


  })


})
```

2. We can now implement the logic for `ellipsis` in `src/components/PostListItem.vue`. We will add a `computed` object with `ellipsis`, which will use `String#slice` if the passed value is longer than 50 characters and do nothing otherwise:

```
<script setup>
// rest of script
const ellipsis = computed(() => {
  return props.description && props.description.length
    > 50 ? `${props.description.slice(0,50)}...` :
      props.description;
})

defineExpose({ truncated, ellipsis })
</script>
<template>
  <div>
  <h3>{{ title }}</h3>
  <p>{{ ellipsis }}</p>

  <ul>
    <li v-for="tag in tags" :key="tag">
    #{{ tag }}
    </li>
  </ul>

  </div>
</template>
```

As you can see, the `ellipsis` computed method works on the description prop and handles trimming values longer than 50 characters. The tests now pass as shown in *Figure 11.13*:

```
RERUN  __tests__/ellipsis.test.js

√ __tests__/ellipsis.test.js (2)

Test Files  4 passed (4)
     Tests  10 passed (10)
      Time  96ms

PASS  Waiting for file changes ...
      press h to show help, press q to quit
```

Figure 11.13 – Ellipsis tests now passing

We have now seen how to test methods and computed properties of a Vue.js component.

Next, we will see how to deal with an application that uses Vue.js routing.

Testing Vue routing

We have currently got an application that renders our blog home page or feed view.

Next, we should have post pages. To do this, we will use Vue Router, as covered in previous chapters, and ensure that our routing works as designed with unit tests.

Vue Router is installed using npm, specifically, npm `install vue-router@4`, and then wiring it up in the `main.js` file:

```
import { createApp } from 'vue'
import App from './App.vue'
import router from './router';


createApp(App).use(router).mount('#app')
```

Next, we can create a file to define our routes in `src/router/index.js`. This will instantiate the router and define our initial paths. We will begin with a root path (`/`) to display the `PostList` component:

```
import { createRouter, createWebHistory } from
'vue-router';
import PostList from '@/components/PostList.vue';

const routes = [
  {
```

```
      path: '/',
      component: PostList
    }
];
```

```
const router = createRouter({
  history: createWebHistory(),
  routes
});
```

```
export default router;
```

Now that we've got our initial route, we should update the App.vue file to leverage the component being rendered by the router. We'll render render-view instead of directly using PostList. The posts binding, however, stays the same:

```
<!—rest of file… -->
<template>
  <header>
  <h1>The Vue.js Workshop Blog</h1>
  </header>

  <router-view :posts="posts"></router-view>
</template>—-- rest of file... -->
```

Now, our posts in the App.vue file are missing a bit of core data to render a SinglePost component. We need to make sure to have the slug and content properties to render something useful on our SinglePost page:

```
<script>
export default {
  data() {
    return {
      posts: [
        {
          slug: 'vue-react',
          title: 'Vue.js for React developers',
          description: 'React has massive popularity here
                        are the key benefits of Vue.js over
```

```
                                    it.',
                content: 'This is the content of the Vue.js for
                            React developers post.',
                tags' ['vue', 'react'],
            },
            {
                slug: 'vue-angularjs',
                title: 'Migrating an AngularJS app to Vue'js',
                description: 'With many breaking changes,
                                AngularJS developers have found it
                                easier to retrain to Vue.js than
                                Angular 2',
                content: 'This is the content of the Vue.js for
                            AngularJS developers post.',
                tags' ['vue', 'angularjs']
            }
        ]
      }
    }
  }
</script>
```

We can now start working on a `SinglePost` component. For now, we'll just have some placeholders in the template. Also, `SinglePost` will receive posts as a prop, so we can fill that in as well:

```
<script setup>
defineProps({
  posts: {
    type: Array,
      default: () => []
  }
})
</script>

<template>
  <div>
```

```
  <h2>Post: RENDER ME</h2>
  <p>Placeholder for post.content.</p>
  </div>
</template>
```

Next, we will register SinglePost in router/index.js with the /:postId path (which will be available to the component under this.$route.params.postId):

```
import { createRouter, createWebHistory } from
'vue-router';
import PostList from '@/components/PostList.vue';
import SinglePost from '@/components/SinglePost.vue';

const routes = [
  {
    path: '/',
    component: PostList
  },
  {
    path: '/:postId',
    component: SinglePost
  }
];

const router = createRouter({
  history: createWebHistory(),
  routes
});


export default router;
```

If we switch back to implementing the SinglePost component, we've got access to postId, which will map to the slug in the posts array, and we've also got access to posts since it's being bound onto render-view by App.

Now we can create a computed property, post, which finds posts based on postId:

```
// other imports
import { useRoute } from 'vue-router';
```

```
// props code
const route = useRoute();

const post = computed(() => {
  const { postId } = route.params;
  return props.posts.find(p => p.slug === postId);
})
```

From this computed `post` property, we can extract `title` and `content` if `post` exists (we have to watch out for posts that don't exist). So, still in `SinglePost`, we can add the following computed properties:

```
const title = computed(() => {
  return post && post.value.title;
})

const content = computed(() => {
  return post && post.value.content;
})
```

We can then replace the placeholders in the template with the value of the computed properties. So, our template ends up as follows:

```
<template>
  <div>
  <h2>Post: {{ title }}</h2>
  <p>{{ content }}</p>
  </div>
</template>
```

Now let's update the application so that we can link to individual posts. In `PostList.vue`, pass the slug in as a new property:

```
<!-- rest of template -->
<PostListItem v-for="post in posts"
:key="post.slug"
:title="post.title"
:description="post.description"
:tags="post.tags"
:slug="post.slug"
/>
<!-- rest of template -->
```

Next, in `PostListItem`, we will first add a new `slug` property:

```
// rest of the props...
slug: {
  type: String
}
```

Then we edit the template to link with the `slug` property:

```
<template>
  <div>
  <router-link :to="`/${slug}`">
  <h3>{{ title }}</h3>
  </router-link>
  <p>{{ ellipsis }}</p>

  <ul>
    <li v-for="tag in tags" :key="tag">
    #{{ tag }}
    </li>
  </ul>
  </div>
</template>
```

`router-link` is a Vue Router-specific link, which means that on the `PostList` page, upon clicking on a post list item, we are taken to the correct post's URL, as shown in the following screenshot:

The Vue.js Workshop Blog

Vue.js for React developers

React has massive popularity here are the key bene...

- #vue
- #react

Migrating an AngularJS app to Vue.js

With many breaking changes, AngularJS developers h...

- #vue
- #angularjs

Figure 11.14 – Post list view displayed in the browser

After clicking on a title, the right post is displayed:

The Vue.js Workshop Blog

Post: Migrating an AngularJS app to Vue.js

This is the content of the Vue.js for AngularJS developers post.

Figure 11.15 – Single post view displaying in the browser

To test vue-router, we will need to build our tests to handle the asynchronous nature of the router. We'll begin by testing that clicking on a post properly loads just the information for a single post. We can do this by looking for all the blog posts on the initial page, and only one particular post when a route is clicked:

```
import { describe, it, expect } from 'vitest';
import { mount, flushPromises } from '@vue/test-utils'

import App from '../src/App.vue';
import router from "@/router";

describe('SinglePost', () => {

  it('Router renders single post page when clicking a post
  title', async () => {
    router.push('/');
    await router.isReady();

    const wrapper = mount(App, {
      global: {
        plugins: [router]
      }
    })

    expect(wrapper.text()).toMatch("Vue.js for React
                                    developers");
    expect(wrapper.text()).toMatch("Migrating an AngularJS
                                    app to Vue.js");
```

```
await wrapper.find('a').trigger('click');
await flushPromises();

expect(wrapper.text()).toMatch("Vue.js for React
                                developers");
expect(wrapper.text()).not.toMatch("Migrating an
                                    AngularJS app to
                                    Vue.js2");


    })


  })
```

On top, we import both `mount` and a new utility, `flushPromises`, that we'll use later. We also import our router. In the test, we begin by navigating to the root path and as stated earlier, due to the asynchronous nature of the router, we wait for it to finish.

We then check for both blog posts. After that, we trigger a click event on the first post, wait for it to finish with `flushPromises`, and then check to see that only our first post is rendered.

We should check that navigating directly to a valid post URL will yield the correct result. In order to this we'll use `router.replace('/')` to clear any state that's set and then use `router.push()` with a post slug. We will then use similar assertions to ensure we're rendering just one post:

```
It('Router renders single post page when a slug is set',
async () => {
  await router.replace('/');
  await router.push('/vue-react');

  const wrapper = mount(App, {
    global: {
      plugins: [router]
    }
  })


  expect(wrapper.text()).toMatch("Vue.js for React
                                developers");
  expect(wrapper.text()).not.toMatch("Migrating an
                                    AngularJS app to
```

```
                                               Vue.js");

    })
```

Those two tests work as expected when run with the npm run test:unit __tests__/
SinglePost.test.js command. The following screenshot displays the desired output:

```
ray@Hoth:~/ ... /Chapter11/Exercise11.03$ npm run test:unit __tests__/SinglePost.test.js

> Exercise11.02@0.0.0 test:unit
> vitest --environment jsdom "__tests__/SinglePost.test.js"

 DEV  v0.13.1 /home/ray/projects/Front-End-Development-Projects-with-Vue.js/Chapter11/Exercise11.03

 √ __tests__/SinglePost.test.js (2)

Test Files  1 passed (1)
     Tests  2 passed (2)
      Time  1.14s (in thread 36ms, 3154.10%)

 PASS  Waiting for file changes ...
       press h to show help, press q to quit
```

Figure 11.16 – Routing tests passing for SinglePost

Now that you've seen how to test your routes, let's practice it with an example.

Exercise 11.03: Building a tag page and testing its routing

Much like we built a single-post page, we'll now build a tag page, which is similar to the PostList
component except only posts with a certain tag are displayed and each post is a link to a relevant
single-post view.

You can find the complete code at https://github.com/PacktPublishing/Frontend-
Development-Projects-with-Vue.js-3/tree/v2-edition/Chapter11/
Exercise11.03

1. We can start by creating a new TagPage component in src/components/TagPage.vue.
    We know it will receive posts as a prop and that we want to render a PostList component:

    ```
    <script setup>
    import PostList from './PostList.vue';

    defineProps({
      posts: {
        type: Array,
        default: () => []
    ```

```
    }
  })

</script>

<template>
  <h3>#INSERT_TAG_NAME</h3>
</template>
```

2. Next, we want to wire the TagPage component to the router in src/router.js. We'll import it and add it as part of routes with the /tags/:tagName path:

```
// other imports
import TagPage from '@/components/TagPage.vue';

const routes = [
  // other routes
  {
    path:'/tags/:tagName',
    component: TagPage
  }
];

// router instantiation and export
```

3. Back in TagPage.vue, we can now use the tagName param and create a tagName computed property as well as a tagPosts computed property that filters based on the tag.

```
import { computed } from 'vue';
import { useRoute } from 'vue-router';

const props = defineProps({
  posts: {
    type: Array,
    default: () => []
  }
})

const route = useRoute();
```

```
const tagName = computed(() => {
  return route.params.tagName;
})

const tagPosts = computed(() => {
  return props.posts.filter(p =>
    p.tags.includes(route.params.tagName));
})
```

4. Now that we have access to `tagPosts` and `tagName`, we can replace the placeholders in the template. We will render #{{ tagName }} and bind `tagPosts` to the `posts` prop of `PostList`:

```
<template>
  <h3># {{ tagName }}</h3>
  <PostLists :posts="tagPosts" />
</template>
```

Now, the page displays something like the following if we navigate, for example, to /tags/angularjs:

The Vue.js Workshop Blog

angularjs

Migrating an AngularJS app to Vue.js

With many breaking changes, AngularJS developers h...

- #vue
- #angularjs

Figure 11.17 – Tag page for angularjs

5. The next step is to convert the tag anchors (a) in `PostListItem` to `router-link` that points to /tags/${tagName} (in `src/components/PostListItem.vue`):

```
<router-link :to="`/tags/${tag}`"
v-for="tag in tags" :key="tags">
#{{ tag }}
</router-link>
```

6. Now it is time to write some tests. We will first check that being on the home page and clicking on **#angularjs** puts us on the angularjs tag page. We'll write it as follows in __tests__/TagPage.test.js:

```
// rest of test...
describe('TagPage', () => {

  it('Router renders tag page when clicking a tag in
  the post list item', async () => {
    router.push('/');
    await router.isReady();

    const wrapper = mount(App, {
      global: {
      plugins: [router]
      }
    })
    expect(wrapper.text()).toMatch("Vue.js for React
                                    developers");
    expect(wrapper.text()).toMatch("Migrating an
                                    AngularJS app to
                                    Vue.js");

    await wrapper.find('a[href="/tags/angularjs"]')
      .trigger('click');
    await flushPromises();

    expect(wrapper.text()).toMatch("Migrating an
                                    AngularJS app to
                                    Vue.js");
    expect(wrapper.text()).not.toMatch("Vue.js for
                                        React
                                        developers");

  })

})
```

7. We should also test that going directly to the tag URL works as expected; that is, we do not see irrelevant content:

```
// rest of test...
  it('Router renders tag page when a URL is set',
  async () => {
    await router.replace('/');
    await router.push('/tags/angularjs');

    const wrapper = mount(App, {
      global: {
      plugins: [router]
      }
    })

    expect(wrapper.text()).toMatch("Migrating an
                                   AngularJS app to
                                   Vue.js");
    expect(wrapper.text()).not.toMatch("Vue.js for
                                       React
                                       developers");

  })
```

The tests pass since the application is working as expected. Therefore, the output will be as follows:

```
RERUN  __tests__/TagPage.test.js

√ __tests__/TagPage.test.js (2)

Test Files  6 passed (6)
     Tests  14 passed (14)
      Time  188ms

PASS  Waiting for file changes ...
      press h to show help, press q to quit
```

Figure 11.18 – TagPage routing tests passing on the command line

Before going on, however, let's run *all* our unit tests. You'll notice that while our tests pass, there are now various warnings:

```
stderr | __tests__/PostList.test.js > PostList > PostList renders tags for each post
[Vue warn]: Failed to resolve component: router-link
If this is a native custom element, make sure to exclude it from component resolution via compilerOptions.isCustomElemen
t.
  at <PostListItem key=undefined title=undefined description=undefined  ... >
  at <PostList posts= [ { tags: [ 'react', 'vue' ] }, { tags: [ 'html', 'angularjs' ] } ] ref="VTU_COMPONENT" >
  at <VTUROOT>
[Vue warn]: Failed to resolve component: router-link
If this is a native custom element, make sure to exclude it from component resolution via compilerOptions.isCustomElemen
t.
  at <PostListItem key=undefined title=undefined description=undefined  ... >
  at <PostList posts= [ { tags: [ 'react', 'vue' ] }, { tags: [ 'html', 'angularjs' ] } ] ref="VTU_COMPONENT" >
  at <VTUROOT>

stderr | __tests__/App.test.js > App > App renders blog title correctly
[Vue warn]: Failed to resolve component: router-view
If this is a native custom element, make sure to exclude it from component resolution via compilerOptions.isCustomElemen
t.
  at <App ref="VTU_COMPONENT" >
  at <VTUROOT>
```

Figure 11.19 – Warnings about router-link and router-view

As these warnings don't fail our tests, we should remove them. We've got a few options for how to do this.

One way is to simply stub out, or *fake*, the components we don't need. In this case, we want our tests to ignore the router components that we aren't testing at the time. We can address this by using an option supported by both `mount` and `shallowMount`, stubs. By using the `stubs` option, we tell Vue's test utilities to *stub*, or create an empty component of, a set of tags.

We add this option in a new global argument to either `mount` or `shallowMount`. Here's an example in `ellipsis.test.js`:

```
const wrapper = shallowMount(PostListItem, {
  propsData: {
    title: "Blog post title",
    description: "Test"
  },
  global: {
    stubs:['router-link'],
  }
})
```

Once added to both tests in `ellipsis.test.js`, those warnings go away. Next, we'll fix App. `test.js`:

```
describe('App', () => {
  it('App renders blog title correctly', () => {
```

```
        const wrapper = shallowMount(App, {
          global: {
            stubs:['router-link','router-view'],
          }
        })
        expect(wrapper.text()).toContain('The Vue.js Workshop
                                        Blog')
      })
    })
```

Notice we stub `router-view` as well. Next, we'll fix `PostList.test.js` and `PostListItem.test.js`. Both of these actually use `router-link` so we can't stub them, but we can provide them as plugins to `mount` and `shallowMount`. In `PostList.test.js`, we first import our router:

```
import router from '@/router';
```

Then in each of the three tests, pass the router as a plugin in the `global` object, for example:

```
const wrapper = mount(PostList, {
  propsData: {
    posts:  [
    {
      tags: ['react', 'vue']
    },
    {
      tags: ['html', 'angularjs']
    }
    ]
  },
  global: {
    plugins: [ router ]
  }
})
```

Next, we can update `PostListItem.test.js`, but we need to make another change here. Previously the test made use of `shallowMount`, but we need to switch to `mount` so `router-link` properly renders its output. Here's the entire test with both the plugin change and the switch to `mount`:

```
// rest of test...
describe('PostListItem', () => {
```

```
it('PostListItem renders title and description
correctly', () => {

  const wrapper = mount(PostListItem, {
    propsData: {
      title: "Blog post title",
      description: "Blog post description"
    },
    global: {
      plugins: [ router ]
    }
  })

  expect(wrapper.text()).toMatch("Blog post title")
  expect(wrapper.text()).toMatch("Blog post description")
})

it('PostListItem renders tags with a # prepended to
them', () => {

  const wrapper = mount(PostListItem, {
    propsData: {
      tags: ['react', 'vue']
    },
    global: {
      plugins: [ router ]
    }
  })
  expect(wrapper.text()).toMatch('#react')
  expect(wrapper.text()).toMatch('#vue')
})


})
```

At this point, our warnings have been resolved. We've now seen how to implement and test an application that includes vue-router. In the next section, we will learn about testing Pinia in detail.

Testing state management with Pinia

To show how to test a component that relies on Pinia (Vue's official global state management solution), we'll implement and test a newsletter subscription banner.

To start with, we should create the banner template. The banner will contain a **Subscribe to the newsletter** call to action and a close button.

```
<script setup>
</script>

<template>
  <div>
  <strong>Subscribe to the newsletter</strong>

    <button>Close</button>
    </div>
</template>

<style scoped>
div {
  background-color: #c0c0c0;
  size: 100%;
  padding: 10px;
}

div button {
  float: right;
}
</style>
```

We can display the `NewsletterBanner` component in the `App.vue` file as follows:

```
<script setup>
import NewsletterBanner from './components/NewsletterBanner.
vue';
</script>

<template>
```

```
  <NewsletterBanner />
  <header>
  <h1>The Vue.js Workshop Blog</h1>
  </header>

  <router-view :posts="posts"></router-view>
</template>
<!-- rest of template -->
```

We'll then install Pinia with the `npm install -save pinia` command. Once Pinia is installed, we can initialize our store in a `store.js` file as follows:

```
import { defineStore } from 'pinia'

export const userPreferencesStore = defineStore({
  id: 'userPreferences',
  state: () => ({
  }),
  getters: {
  },
  actions: {
  }
})
```

Our Pinia store is also registered in the `main.js` file:

```
import { createApp } from 'vue'
import { createPinia } from 'pinia'
import App from './App.vue'
import router from './router';

const app = createApp(App);
app.use(router);
app.use(createPinia());
app.mount('#app');
```

In order to decide whether the newsletter banner should be displayed or not, we need to add an initial state to our store:

```
state: () => ({
  dismissedSubscriberBanner: false
}),
```

To close the banner, we need an action that will set `dismissedSubscribeBanner` to `true`:

```
actions: {
  dismissSubscriberBanner() {
    this.dismissedSubscriberBanner = true;
  }
}
```

We can now use the store state and the `dismissSubscribeBanner` action to decide whether to show the banner (using `v-if`) and whether to close it (binding to a click on the close button):

```
<script setup>
import { computed } from 'vue';

import { userPreferencesStore } from '@/store.js';

const store = userPreferencesStore();

const showBanner = computed(() => {
  return !store.dismissedSubscriberBanner;
})
</script>

<template>
  <div v-if="showBanner">
  <strong>Subscribe to the newsletter</strong>

  <button @click="store.dismissSubscriberBanner()">
    Close</button>
  </div>
</template>

<!-- rest of template -->
```

At this point, the banner looks like this in a browser:

Figure 11.20 – Newsletter banner displayed in a browser

Before we write our unit test, it may be a good idea to see if our *existing* tests work. (And as you can probably guess, this is leading to something.) If you go ahead and run all the tests, you'll see a whole new set of issues.

In the first following figure, note the warnings:

```
stderr | __tests__/SinglePost.test.js > SinglePost > Router renders single post page when clicking a post title
[Vue warn]: injection "Symbol(pinia)" not found.
  at <NewsletterBanner>
  at <App ref="VTU_COMPONENT" >
  at <VTUROOT>
[Vue warn]: Unhandled error during execution of setup function
  at <NewsletterBanner>
  at <App ref="VTU_COMPONENT" >
  at <VTUROOT>

stderr | __tests__/TagPage.test.js > TagPage > Router renders tag page when clicking a tag in the post list item
[Vue warn]: injection "Symbol(pinia)" not found.
  at <NewsletterBanner>
  at <App ref="VTU_COMPONENT" >
  at <VTUROOT>
[Vue warn]: Unhandled error during execution of setup function
  at <NewsletterBanner>
  at <App ref="VTU_COMPONENT" >
  at <VTUROOT>

 √ __tests__/ellipsis.test.js (2)
 √ __tests__/App.test.js (1)
 √ __tests__/NewsletterBanner.test.js (1)
 √ __tests__/PostList.test.js (3)
 √ __tests__/PostListItem.test.js (2)
 ❯ __tests__/SinglePost.test.js (2)
   ❯ SinglePost (2)
     × Router renders single post page when clicking a post title
     √ Router renders single post page when a slug is set
 ❯ __tests__/TagPage.test.js (2)
   ❯ TagPage (2)
     × Router renders tag page when clicking a tag in the post list item
     √ Router renders tag page when a URL is set

──────────────────────────── Failed Tests 2 ────────────────────────────

 FAIL  __tests__/SinglePost.test.js > SinglePost > Router renders single post page when clicking a post title
 FAIL  __tests__/TagPage.test.js > TagPage > Router renders tag page when clicking a tag in the post list item
Error: [💩]: getActivePinia was called with no active Pinia. Did you forget to install pinia?
        const pinia = createPinia()
        app.use(pinia)
This will fail in production.
 ❯ Module.useStore file:/home/ray/projects/Front-End-Development-Projects-with-Vue.js/Chapter11/Exercise11.04/node_modul
es/pinia/dist/pinia.mjs:1692:19
```

Figure 11.21 – Test failures related to Pinia

As you can see, we now have two tests failing due to Pinia. As with the issues we saw with Vue Router, we need to do some work to ensure our tests don't throw an error just because we added in Pinia. To begin, we're going to install some Pinia-specific testing utilities via npm:

```
npm install --save @pinia/testing
```

This gives us the ability to then import a utility to help test Pinia stores, as well as helping with the new errors being thrown. In `SinglePost.test.js`, import Pinia's testing utility:

```
import { createTestingPinia } from '@pinia/testing'
```

Then, much like how we passed Vue Router as a plugin, we'll also pass a test-specific version of Pinia:

```
const wrapper = mount(App, {
  global: {
    plugins: [router,
      createTestingPinia({createSpy:vi.fn})]
  }
})
```

The `createSpy` parameter is used to stub action calls and uses `vi.fn`. In our first line in the unit test, we can modify the imports from `vitest` like so:

```
import { describe, it, expect, vi } from 'vitest';
```

Update the plugins attribute for all the wrappers in `SinglePost.test.js` and repeat the same fixes for `TagPage.test.js`.

The next check should be that if the store has `dismissedSubscriberBanner: true`, the banner should not be displayed. This is done by using the `initialState` feature of `createTestingPinia`. It lets you define initial state values based on the ID value of our store.

```
it('Newsletter Banner should not display if store is
initialised with it dismissed', () => {

  const wrapper = shallowMount(NewsletterBanner, {
    global: {
      plugins: [createTestingPinia({
        initialState: {
          userPreferences: {
```

```
                dismissedSubscriberBanner: true
            }
        },
        createSpy:vi.fn
    })]
    }
})


expect(wrapper.text()).not.toMatch("Subscribe to the
                                    newsletter");

})
```

The final test we'll write is to make sure that clicking the banner's **Close** button fires an action to the store. We can do this by checking that it is called when clicking the **Close** button:

```
it('Newsletter Banner should hide on "close" button
click', async () => {

    const wrapper = shallowMount(NewsletterBanner, {
        global: {
            plugins: [createTestingPinia(
                { createSpy:vi.fn })]
        }
    })

    const store = userPreferencesStore();
    await wrapper.find('button').trigger('click');

    expect(store.dismissSubscriberBanner)
        .toHaveBeenCalledTimes(1);

})
```

The tests will now pass when run with the `npm run test:unit __tests__/NewsletterBanner.test.js` command, as follows:

```
ray@Hoth:~/ ... /Chapter11/Exercise11.04$ npm run test:unit __tests__/NewsletterBanner.test.js

> Exercise11.02@0.0.0 test:unit
> vitest --environment jsdom "__tests__/NewsletterBanner.test.js"


  DEV  v0.13.1 /home/ray/projects/Front-End-Development-Projects-with-Vue.js/Chapter11/Exercise11.04

 √ __tests__/NewsletterBanner.test.js (3)

 Test Files  1 passed (1)
      Tests  3 passed (3)
       Time  1.12s (in thread 25ms, 4472.14%)

  PASS  Waiting for file changes ...
        press h to show help, press q to quit
```

Figure 11.22 – Unit tests for NewsLetterBanner passing on the command line

You've now had a chance to work with Pinia state management and testing, let's now work on an exercise to demonstrate what you've learned.

Exercise 11.04: Building and testing a cookie disclaimer banner

We'll now look at how to implement a cookie disclaimer banner using Pinia and how to test it. We will store whether the cookie banner is being shown in Pinia (the default is `true`); when the banner is closed, it will update to `false`.

You can find the complete code at `https://github.com/PacktPublishing/Frontend-Development-Projects-with-Vue.js-3/tree/v2-edition/Chapter11/Exercise11.04`

1. Create a green cookie banner with a `Cookies Disclaimer` title in bold, the disclaimer, and an `I agree` button. We will create this in `src/components/CookieBanner.vue`:

    ```
    <template>
      <div>
      <strong>Cookies Disclaimer</strong>
        We use cookies to improve our experience.
      <button>I agree</button>
      </div>
    </template>

    <style scoped>
    div {
    ```

```
      background-color: green;
      size: 100%;
      padding: 10px;
      margin-top: 50px;
    }

    div button {
      float: right;
    }
    </style>
```

2. Next, we will need to import and render `CookieBanner` below `router-view` in `src/App.vue`:

```
    <script setup>
    import NewsletterBanner from './components/
    NewsletterBanner.vue';
    import CookieBanner from './components/CookieBanner.vue';
    </script>

    <template>

      <NewsletterBanner />
      <header>
      <h1>The Vue.js Workshop Blog</h1>
      </header>

      <router-view :posts="posts"></router-view>

      <CookieBanner />
    </template>
    <!-- rest of template -->
```

3. Add a state value to control whether to display the cookie banner. In our Pinia store, we will initialize `acceptedCookie` to `false`:

```
    // rest of Pinia store...
    state: () => ({
      dismissedSubscriberBanner: false,
```

```
      acceptedCookie: false
  }),
  // rest of Pinia store...
```

4. We will also need an `acceptCookie` action to close the banner:

```
  // rest of Pinia store...
  actions: {
    dismissSubscriberBanner() {
      this.dismissedSubscriberBanner = true;
    },
    acceptCookie() {
      this.acceptedCookie = true;
    }
  }
  // rest of Pinia store...
```

5. Next, we will expose the store state as an `acceptedCookie` computed property:

```
<script setup>
import { computed } from 'vue';

import { userPreferencesStore } from '@/store.js';

const store = userPreferencesStore();

const acceptedCookie = computed((() => {
  return store.acceptedCookie;
})
</script>
```

6. We will use `v-if` to show the banner when cookies have not been accepted yet. The **I agree** button will close the banner when it's clicked by calling the store action:

```
<template>
  <div v-if="!acceptedCookie">
  <strong>Cookies Disclaimer</strong>
    We use cookies to improve our experience.
  <button @click="store.acceptCookie">I agree</button>
  </div>
</template>
```

We now have a cookie banner that is displayed until **I agree** is clicked, as shown in the following screenshot:

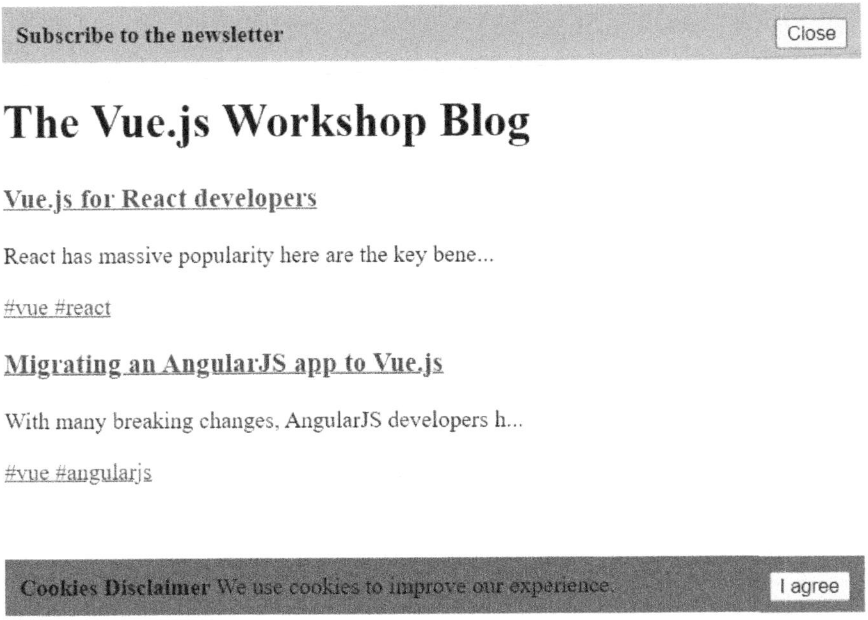

Subscribe to the newsletter   Close

The Vue.js Workshop Blog

Vue.js for React developers

React has massive popularity here are the key bene...

#vue #react

Migrating an AngularJS app to Vue.js

With many breaking changes, AngularJS developers h...

#vue #angularjs

Cookies Disclaimer We use cookies to improve our experience.   I agree

Figure 11.23 – Cookie banner displayed in the browser

7.   We will now write a test that checks that `CookieBanner` is displayed by default:

```
import { describe, it, expect, vi } from 'vitest'

import { shallowMount } from '@vue/test-utils';
import CookieBanner from '../src/components/CookieBanner.
vue';

import { createTestingPinia } from '@pinia/testing'
import { userPreferencesStore } from '@/store.js';

describe('CookieBanner', () => {
  it('Cookie Banner should display if store is
  initialized with it not dismissed', () => {

    const wrapper = shallowMount(CookieBanner, {
      global: {
```

```
        plugins:
          [createTestingPinia({createSpy:vi.fn})]
      }
    })


    expect(wrapper.text()).toMatch("Cookies
                                    Disclaimer");


  })


})
```

8. We will also write a test to check whether `acceptedCookie` is `true` in the store, and if so, the cookie banner won't be displayed:

```
it('Cookie Banner should not display if store is
initialised with it dismissed', () => {
  const wrapper = shallowMount(CookieBanner, {
    global: {
      plugins: [createTestingPinia({
        initialState: {
          userPreferences: {
            acceptedCookie: true
          }
        },
        createSpy:vi.fn
      })]
    }
  })


  expect(wrapper.text()).not.toMatch("Cookies
                                      Disclaimer");


})
```

9. Finally, we want to check that when the **I agree** button is clicked, the `acceptCookie` action is triggered:

```
it('Cookie Banner should hide on "I agree" button click',
async () => {
  const wrapper = shallowMount(CookieBanner, {
    global: {
      plugins:
        [createTestingPinia({ createSpy:vi.fn })]
    }
  })

  const store = userPreferencesStore();
  await wrapper.find('button').trigger('click');

  expect(store.acceptCookie)
    .toHaveBeenCalledTimes(1);

})
```

The three tests we wrote pass when run with `npm run test:unit __tests__/CookieBanner.test.js`, as follows:

```
ray@Hoth:~/ ... /Chapter11/Exercise11.04$ npm run test:unit __tests__/CookieBanner.test.js

> Exercise11.02@0.0.0 test:unit
> vitest --environment jsdom "__tests__/CookieBanner.test.js"


DEV  v0.13.1 /home/ray/projects/Front-End-Development-Projects-with-Vue.js/Chapter11/Exercise11.04

 ✓ __tests__/CookieBanner.test.js (3)

Test Files  1 passed (1)
     Tests  3 passed (3)
      Time  1.16s (in thread 25ms, 4633.61%)

PASS  Waiting for file changes ...
      press h to show help, press q to quit
```

Figure 11.24 – Tests for the cookie banner passing

We've now seen how to test components that rely on Pinia for state and updates. Next, we'll look at snapshot testing to see how it simplifies the testing of render output.

Snapshot testing

Snapshot tests provide a way to write tests for fast-changing pieces of code without keeping the assertion data inline with the test. Changes to a snapshot reflect changes to the output, which is quite useful for code reviews.

For example, we can add a snapshot test to the `PostList.test.js` file:

```
it('PostList renders correctly', () => {
  const wrapper = mount(PostList, {
    propsData: {
      posts: [
        {
          title: "Title 1",
          description: "Description 1"
        },
        {
          title: "Title 2",
          description: "Description 2"
        }
      ]
    },
    global: {
      plugins: [ router ]
    }
  })

  expect(wrapper.text()).toMatchSnapshot();
});
```

The first time this test is run, a snapshot file will be written to `__tests__/__snapshots__`:

```
// Vitest Snapshot v1

exports[`PostList > PostList renders tags for each post 2 1`] =
`"Title 1Description 1Title 2Description 2"`;
```

This makes it easy to quickly see what the changes mean in terms of concrete output.

We've now seen how to use snapshot tests. Next, we'll put all the tools we've learned about in this chapter together to add a new page.

Activity 11.01: Adding a simple search-by-title page with tests

We have already built a post list page, a single-post view page, and a posts-by-tag page. A great way to resurface old content on a blog is by implementing good search functionality. We will add search functionality to the `PostList` page:

1. Create the search form with an input and a button in a new file at `src/components/SearchForm.vue`.

2. We'll now get the form to display by importing and rendering it on `src/App.vue`.

   We are now able to search the search form in the application, as follows:

   Figure 11.25 – The post view with a search form

3. We're now ready to add a snapshot test for the search form. In `__tests__/SearchForm.test.js`, we should add `SearchForm should match expected HTML`.

4. We want to track the contents of the search form input using `v-model` to two-way bind the `searchTerm` instance variable and the contents of the input.

5. When the search form is submitted, we'll need to update the URL with the right parameter. This can be done with `this.$router.push()`. We will store the search in a q query parameter.

6. We will want to reflect the state of the q query parameter in the search form input. We can do this by reading q from `this.$route.query` and setting it as the initial value for the `searchTerm` data field in the `SearchForm` component state.

7. Next, we'll want to filter the posts passed to `PostList` on the home page. We'll use `route.query.q` in a computed property that filters posts by their title. This new computed property will then be used instead of posts in `src/App.vue`.

8. Next, we should add a test that changes the search query parameter and check that the app shows the right result. To do this, we can import `src/App.vue` and `@/router.js`, and render the app with the store and the router. We can then update the search field contents. Finally, we can submit the form by clicking the element where test ID is `Search` (which is the search button).

> **Note**
>
> The solution for this activity can be found at `https://github.com/PacktPublishing/` `Frontend-Development-Projects-with-Vue.js-3/tree/v2-edition/` `Chapter11/Activity11.01`

Summary

Throughout this chapter, we've looked at different approaches to testing different types of Vue.js applications.

Testing in general is useful for empirically showing that the system is working. Unit tests are the cheapest to build and maintain and should be the base of testing functionality. System tests are the next level up in the testing pyramid and allow you to gain confidence that the majority of features are working as expected. End-to-end tests show that the main flows of the full system work.

We've seen how to unit test components and methods, as well as testing through layers, and testing component output in a black-box fashion instead of inspecting component internals to test functionality. Using the Vitest testing library, we tested advanced functionality, such as routing and applications, that leverage Pinia.

Finally, we looked at snapshot testing and saw how it can be an effective way to write tests for template-heavy chunks of code.

In the next chapter, we will look at end-to-end testing techniques that can be applied to Vue.js applications.

12
End-to-End Testing

In this chapter, we will look at how to create an **End-to-End** (**E2E**) test suite for a Vue.js application with Cypress. In order to write robust tests, we'll look at common pitfalls and best practices, such as intercepting HTTP requests and waiting for elements to appear without timeouts.

As we proceed, you will gain an understanding of E2E testing and its use cases. You will see how Cypress can be configured to test a Vue.js application and also interact with and inspect a **User Interface** (**UI**) using it. Throughout the chapter, you will gain familiarity with the pitfalls of arbitrary timeouts and how to avoid them with Cypress' waiting functionality.

Toward the end of the chapter, you will also learn when, why, and how to intercept HTTP requests with Cypress.

In this chapter, we will cover the following topics:

- Understanding E2E testing and its use cases
- Configuring Cypress for a Vue.js application
- Using Cypress to interact with and inspect a Vue.js UI
- Triggering and waiting for UI updates with Cypress
- Intercepting HTTP requests

Technical requirements

There are no technical requirements for this chapter beyond the `git` CLI, which you will have already used by now.

The Node version has to be below v20 (preferable Yarn 1.22 and Node version above 16 and up to 19.x, and npm up to version 9.x.

You can find this chapter's source here: `https://github.com/PacktPublishing/Frontend-Development-Projects-with-Vue.js-3/tree/v2-edition/Chapter12`

Understanding E2E testing and its use cases

Most developers will have seen a version of the testing pyramid shown in the following figure:

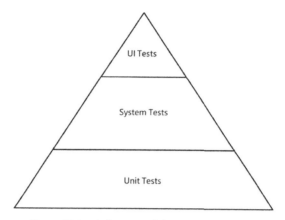

Figure 12.1 – A diagram of the testing pyramid

E2E tests fall under the UI testing category. The type of test we'll be looking at in this chapter is automated E2E tests using Cypress.

E2E and UI tests provide a level of confidence higher than unit or integration tests. They're testing the application as used by the end user. The end user doesn't care why or where a bug is happening, just that there is a bug.

The where and why of a bug tends to be the concern of unit and system-level tests. Unit and system-level tests check that the internals of a system work as the specification or code describes them. UI-level tests validate that application flows are working as expected.

A strong E2E test suite that runs quickly, has few false negatives (where a test fails but the application works), and even fewer false positives (where all tests pass but the application is broken) enables **Continuous Deployment (CD)**. CD, as its name suggests, involves deploying a project or application continuously.

In this kind of setup, an application version is validated by the E2E suite and is then automatically deployed to production.

Configuring Cypress for a Vue.js application

Cypress is a JavaScript E2E testing framework. It's designed to solve the very specific need of writing E2E tests using JavaScript. This is in contrast to other full-fledged browser automation solutions, such as WebdriverIO (https://webdriver.io/), Selenium WebDriver (https://www.selenium.dev/), Puppeteer (https://developers.google.com/web/tools/puppeteer/), and Playwright (https://github.com/microsoft/playwright), which are commonly used to write E2E tests.

The big difference with Cypress compared to these other solutions is its singular focus on writing E2E tests (as opposed to generic browser automation). Tests can only be written using JavaScript (Selenium supports other languages), and require Chrome, Edge, or Firefox (WebKit support is in development).

Cypress has a **Graphical User Interface** (**GUI**) to run and debug tests locally and comes with built-in assertion and stubbing/mocking libraries.

To add Cypress to a new Vue project, simply enable it when prompted:

```
ray@Hoth:~/ ... /Front-End-Development-Projects-with-Vue.js/Chapter12$ npm init vue@latest

Vue.js - The Progressive JavaScript Framework

✓ Project name: … vue-project
✓ Add TypeScript? … No / Yes
✓ Add JSX Support? … No / Yes
✓ Add Vue Router for Single Page Application development? … No / Yes
✓ Add Pinia for state management? … No / Yes
✓ Add Vitest for Unit Testing? … No / Yes
? Add Cypress for End-to-End testing? › No / Yes
```

Figure 12.2 – Enabling Cypress when creating a new Vue 3 project

To add Cypress to an existing project, use `npm install @cypress/vue@next --dev`.

The plugin adds a `test:e2e` script that we can run using the following two commands. The first prepares a build of the Vue application. The second actually starts the Cypress app:

```
npm run build
npm run test:e2e
```

You will be asked to use a browser for testing first, as shown in *Figure 12.3*:

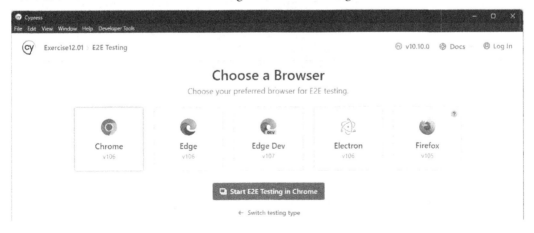

Figure 12.3 – Cypress asking for the preferred browser to use for testing

After selecting a browser, the main Cypress UI is displayed:

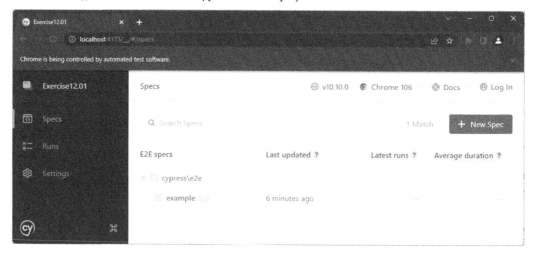

Figure 12.4 – Cypress testing UI

If you click on the example link, you'll see the test running and the output:

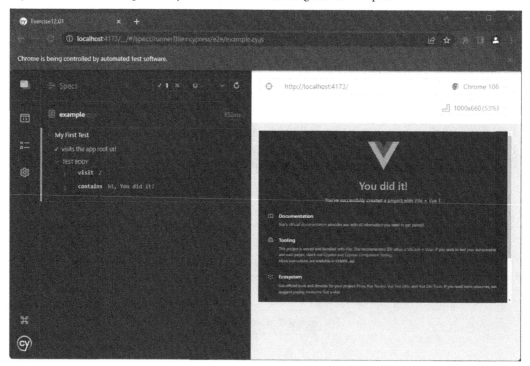

Figure 12.5 – Cypress running a test

Cypress creates a default test for us at `cypress/e2e/example.cy.js`. The test navigates to the root of the Vue application and looks for an `h1` tag that contains `You did it!`:

```
// https://docs.cypress.io/api/introduction/api.html

describe('My First Test', () => {
  it('visits the app root url', () => {
    cy.visit('/')
    cy.contains('h1', 'You did it!')
  })
})
```

This will work in a default Vue 3 project.

We can try visiting `google.com` using `cy.visit(url)` and check that the `input` element that's synonymous with the Google home page is there by selecting the input elements on the page with `cy.get('input')` first and then using the `.should('exist')` assertion:

```
describe('My First Test', () => {
  it('Opens an arbitrary URL', () => {
    cy.visit('https://google.com')
    cy.get('input').should('exist')
  })
})
```

The Cypress window will automatically load and run the new test:

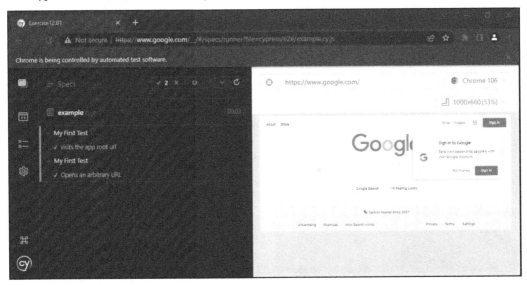

Figure 12.6 – Cypress tests running in Chrome while visiting the Google home page

We've now seen how to install and use Cypress to visit web pages. In the next section, we'll see how Cypress can be used to interact with and inspect a UI.

Using Cypress to interact with and inspect a Vue.js UI

In order to E2E test a new application, Commentator Pro, we should start by adding something to test. In this case, we'll have a heading (h2) with the name of the application. In the App.vue file, we'll have the following code:

```
<template>
<h2>Commentator Pro</h2>
</template>
```

In order to test this with Cypress, we can change the cypress/e2e/example.cy.js file with the following code. We'll go to the running application using cy.visit('/') and then check that the h2 on the page contains Commentator Pro using cy.contains('h2', 'Commentator Pro'). The cy.contains function is overloaded and can be used with one parameter (the text to match against) or two parameters (the selector for the container and the text to match against):

```
describe('Commentator Pro', () => {
  it('Has a h2 with "Commentator Pro"', () => {
    cy.visit('/')
    cy.contains('h2', 'Commentator Pro')
  })
})
```

We can then run example.cy.js using the Cypress UI, as shown in the following screenshot:

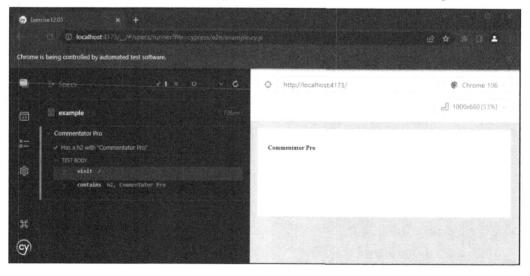

Figure 12.7 – A heading content test running successfully in Chrome

Now that we've seen how to visit a page and assert its content, we'll see how we can use Cypress to automate tests for a new feature in a Vue.js application.

Exercise 12.01 – adding a New Comment button and a corresponding E2E test

In order for the Commentator Pro application to be useful, we should have an **Add a New Comment** button to allow users to add comments.

We will add a blue jumbo button with **Add a New Comment** as text and write the corresponding E2E test with Cypress.

The complete code can be found at `https://github.com/PacktPublishing/Frontend-Development-Projects-with-Vue.js-3/tree/v2-edition/Chapter12/Exercise12.01`

To do this, perform the following steps:

1. To add a button in the app, we'll add a `button` element with some text in `src/App.vue`:

    ```
    <template>
    <h2>Commentator Pro</h2>

    <button>
    Add a New Comment
    </button>
    </template>
    ```

    The output should show as follows:

    Figure 12.8 – The Commentator Pro application with the Add a New Comment button

2. Next, we'll create a new E2E test at `cypress/e2e/add-new-comment.cy.js`. We'll set the name of the suite and description of the test to `Adding a New Comment`, and the home page should have a button with the right text:

    ```
    describe('Adding a New Comment', () => {
      it('the homepage should have a button with the right
      text', () => {
    ```

```
      // test will go here
    })
  })
```

3. In order to test the home page, we'll have to navigate to it using cy.visit('/'):

```
describe('Adding a New Comment', () => {
  it('the homepage should have a button with the right
  text', () => {
    cy.visit('/')
  })
})
```

4. Finally, we can write the assertion that a button instance containing the Add a New Comment text is on the page:

```
describe('Adding a New Comment', () => {
  it('the homepage should have a button with the right
  text', () => {
    cy.visit('/')
    cy.contains('button', 'Add a New Comment')
  })
})
```

5. We can run this test using the Cypress UI first by running a new build (npm run build), and then npm run test:e2e. If you already had Cypress running, you do not need to restart it. You can visit the list of tests by clicking on the **Specs** navigation item in the left-hand menu.

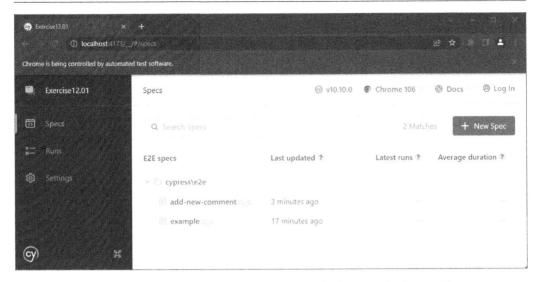

Figure 12.9 – The add-new-comment.cy.js test displaying in the Cypress UI

6. When we run the test (by clicking on it), we'll get the following output in Chrome. The test passes since there is a button with the relevant text on the home page:

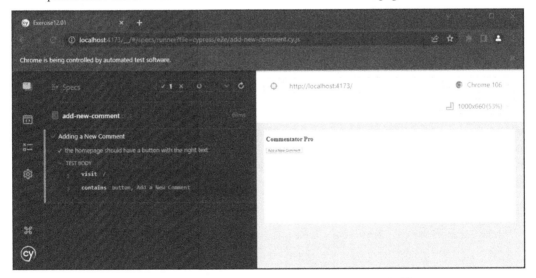

Figure 12.10 – Cypress running our add-new-comment test in Chrome

We've now seen how to visit pages and assert against their content.

In the next section, we will look at using Cypress to test interactive behavior. Cypress has automatic selector retries, which makes it a great fit for testing highly interactive Vue.js applications. We'll see how to use Cypress to interact with the UI and assert the effect of our interactions.

Triggering and waiting for UI updates with Cypress

The tests we've written up until now are quite simple and only check that the application isn't crashing on load in the browser.

One of the strengths of E2E tests is testing that the UI behaves as expected when a user interacts with it with high fidelity. We'll use Cypress' selection (the `.get()` function), event triggering (the `.click()` function), and assertion (the `.should()` function) functionality to test a Vue.js application in this section.

Cypress' automatic retries on DOM selection will allow us to write E2E tests without explicit wait or timeout conditions. Waits and timeouts are a staple of other E2E testing systems and tend to be a source of flakiness in tests.

To begin with, we will add a comment editor to our Commentator Pro application. Displaying the editor (a simple `textarea`) will be toggled by clicking on the **Add a New Comment** button.

In order to keep writing tests without wrangling complicated and brittle selectors, we'll start adding `data-test-id` attributes; to begin with, we can add one to the **Add a New Comment** button in the `App.vue` file:

```
<template>
<h2>Commentator Pro</h2>

<button data-test-id="new-comment-button">
Add a New Comment
</button>
</template>
```

Next, we'll add a `showEditor` property to the Vue.js `data()` method on the `App` component. We'll use this expression in `v-if` for the editor. We can also set the **Add a New Comment** button to toggle this instance property:

```
<template>
<h2>Commentator Pro</h2>

<button @click="showEditor = !showEditor"
  data-test-id="new-comment-button">
Add a New Comment
</button>
</template>
```

```
<script>
export default {

  data() {
    return {
      showEditor: false
    }
  }

}
</script>
```

We can add our editor with new-comment-editor data-test-id that is toggled by showEditor:

```
<template>
<!-- rest of template -->
<div v-if="showEditor">
  <p>
  <textarea data-test-id="new-comment-editor"></textarea>
  </p>
</div>
</template>
```

In order to test the toggling, we can add a test that opens that app and checks that the comment editor is not initially shown, as well as checking whether or not it is displayed depending on how many clicks are triggered on new-comment-button:

```
describe('Adding a New Comment', () => {
  // other tests
  it('the Add a New Comment button should toggle the editor
  display on and off', () => {
    cy.visit('/')
    cy.get('[data-test-id="new-comment-editor"]')
      .should('not.exist')

    cy.get('[data-test-id="new-comment-button"]').click()
    cy.get('[data-test-id="new-comment-editor"]')
      .should('be.visible')
```

```
    cy.get('[data-test-id="new-comment-button"]').click()
    cy.get('[data-test-id="new-comment-editor"]')
      .should('not.exist')
  })
})
```

The preceding code will generate the following result in Cypress:

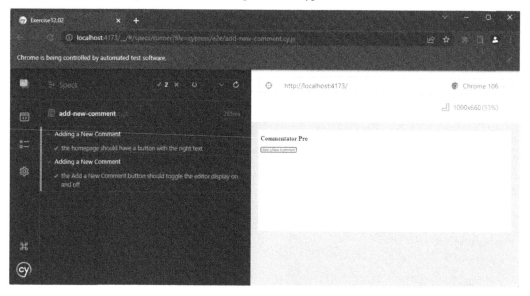

Figure 12.11 – Cypress running add-new-comment tests, including the new editor-toggling test

We've now seen how to write Cypress tests that select and assert over DOM elements.

> **Note**
>
> `data-test-id` instances, as a convention, are a way to decouple tests from application-specific and styling-specific selectors. This is especially useful if the people writing the tests aren't always the ones writing the code. In that situation, using `data-test-id` allows the markup structure and classes to change, but the tests will keep passing as long as the `test-id` instances remain on the correct element.

Exercise 12.02 – adding new comment editor input and a Submit functionality

To be able to send the new comment text to an API, we will need to store the text in a Vue.js state. The other prerequisite to adding a comment is to have a dummy **Submit** button.

The complete code can be found at `https://github.com/PacktPublishing/Frontend-Development-Projects-with-Vue.js-3/tree/v2-edition/Chapter12/Exercise12.02`

To accomplish this, perform the following steps:

1. To store the `textarea` (editor) content in memory, we'll use `v-model`. We'll create a new data (state) variable, `newComment`, that gets initialized to `""`. Now, `v-model` will two-way bind the `textarea` content and `newComment`:

    ```
    <template>
    <!-- rest of template -->
      <p>
      <textarea data-test-id="new-comment-editor"
        v-model="newComment"></textarea>
      </p>
    <!-- rest of template -->
    </template>

    <script>
    export default {
      data() {
        return {
          showEditor: false,
          newComment: ''
        }
      }
    }
    </script>
    ```

2. We'll add a `submit` button inside the editor, which should only appear when the editor is toggled on. We also make sure to include a `data-test-id="new-comment-submit"` attribute in order to be able to select it with Cypress later:

    ```
    <!-- rest of template -->
    <div v-if="showEditor">
      <p>
      <textarea data-test-id="new-comment-editor"
    ```

```
      v-model="newComment"></textarea>
    </p>
    <p>
    <button data-test-id="new-comment-submit">
      Submit
    </button>
    </p>
  </div>
  <!-- rest of template -->
```

3. It's now time to add an E2E test to test that new-comment-editor works as expected when we type text into it. In order to achieve this, we need to load up the application and click on the new-comment button so that the editor displays.

    We can then select new-comment-editor (by data-test-id) and use the Cypress .type function to add some text. We can chain .should('have.value', 'Just saying...') to validate that our interaction with textarea was successful. Remember to run npm run build when adding new tests:

```
describe('Adding a New Comment', () => {
  // other tests
  it('the new comment editor should support text
  input', () => {
    cy.visit('/')
    // Get the editor to show
    cy.get('[data-test-id="new-comment-button"]')
      .click()
    cy.get('[data-test-id="new-comment-editor"]')
      .should('be.visible')

    cy.get('[data-test-id="new-comment-editor"]')
      .type('Just saying...')
      .should('have.value', 'Just saying...')
  })
})
```

When run using the Cypress UI, this `add-new-comment` test suite should yield the following result:

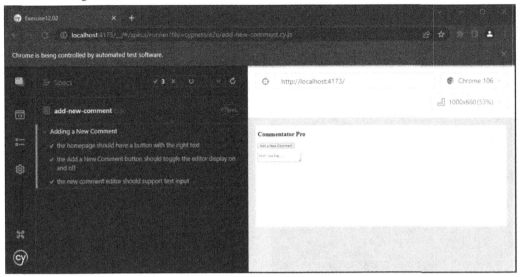

Figure 12.12 – Cypress running add-new-comment tests, including the new editor text input test

4. Finally, we can add an E2E test to check that the `submit` button does not appear by default but does appear when we click on the `new-comment` button. We can also check the text content of the `new-comment-submit` button:

```
describe('Adding a New Comment', () => {
  // other tests
  it('the new comment editor should have a submit
  button', () => {
    cy.visit('/')
    cy.get('[data-test-id="new-comment-submit"]')
      .should('not.exist')
    // Get the editor to show
    cy.get('[data-test-id="new-comment-button"]')
      .click()
    cy.get('[data-test-id="new-comment-submit"]')
      .should('be.visible')
    cy.contains('[data-test-id="new-comment-submit"]',
```

```
                                        'Submit')
            })
        })
```

When this test is run through the Cypress UI, we see the following result:

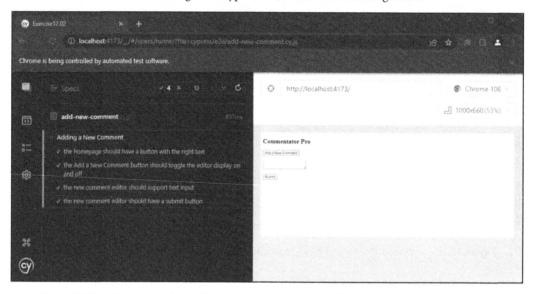

Figure 12.13 – Cypress running add-new-comment tests, including the new submit button test

5. One more feature we can add is to disable the `submit` button until there's text in the text editor. To do this, we can bind `:disabled` to `!newComment` on the `new-comment-submit` button. As an aside, one of the major reasons we added a two-way binding between `newComment` and `textarea` is to enable UI validations such as this one:

```
<button data-test-id="new-comment-submit"
  :disabled="!newComment">
  Submit
</button>
```

6. The relevant test will look at whether or not the `new-comment-submit` button is disabled when the text editor content is empty using Cypress' `should('be.disabled')` and `should('not.be.disabled')` assertions:

```
describe('Adding a New Comment', () => {
  // other tests
  it('the new comment submit button should be disabled
  based on "new comment" content', () => {
```

```
        cy.visit('/')
        // Get the editor to show
        cy.get('[data-test-id="new-comment-button"]')
          .click()
        cy.get('[data-test-id="new-comment-submit"]')
          .should('be.visible')

        cy.get('[data-test-id="new-comment-submit"]')
          .should('be.disabled')

        cy.get('[data-test-id="new-comment-editor"]')
          .type('Just saying...')

        cy.get('[data-test-id="new-comment-submit"]')
          .should('not.be.disabled')
    })
  })
```

This yields the following output when run through Cypress UI and Chrome automation:

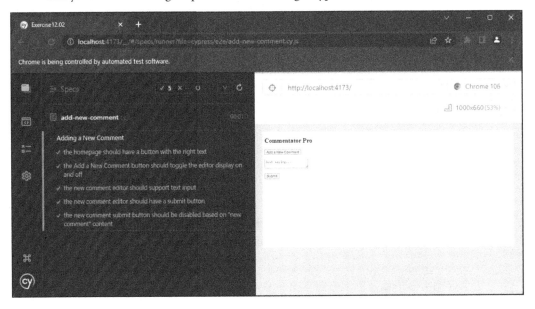

Figure 12.14 – Cypress running add-new-comment tests, including
the new-comment-submit button disabled test

We've now seen how to use Cypress to select, click, and input text. We've also seen approaches to check element visibility, text content, input values, and disabled states.

Anyone familiar with other automation frameworks will have noticed that in Cypress tests, there are no explicit waits or retries. This is because Cypress waits and retries assertions and selections automatically. Most of the tests we've written don't showcase this in a major way, but the next exercise, where we bring asynchronicity into the mix, will.

Exercise 12.03 – adding a submitting state to the new comment editor

In order to showcase Cypress's impressive, automatic retry/wait capability, we will look at adding and testing a `submitting` state for the new comment editor.

In effect, we'll be reacting to a click on the **Submit** button and showing a loading state for 2.5 seconds to simulate a reasonably slow HTTP request to a backend API. The loading state is simply a CSS class that makes the button have italic text.

This test will be an example that showcases Cypress' ability to automatically wait and retry selections. This feature reduces the need for arbitrary waits and the flakiness associated with them.

The complete code can be found at `https://github.com/PacktPublishing/Frontend-Development-Projects-with-Vue.js-3/tree/v2-edition/Chapter12/Exercise12.03`

Let's do this by following these steps:

1. In order to show a loading state, we add a new class to the component:

    ```
    <style scoped>
    .submitting {
      font-style: italic;
    }
    </style>
    ```

2. Next, we need to add an `isSubmitting` state to the Vue.js application in `data()`, which will allow us to toggle the state for the `submit` button. We will initialize it to `false` since we are not submitting anything until the user clicks on the **Submit** button:

    ```
    <script>
    export default {
      data() {
        return {
          // other properties
    ```

```
            isSubmitting: false
        }
      }
    }
</script>
```

3. Next, we will add a click handler for the submit button (as methods.submitNewComment).
   It will simulate a 2.5-second load time using setTimeout:

```
<script>
export default {
  // other component properties
  methods: {
    submitNewComment() {
      this.isSubmitting = true
      setTimeout(() => {
        this.isSubmitting = false;
        this.newComment = '';
      }, 2500)
    }
  }
}
</script>
```

4. Now that we've got a fake submit handler, we should bind it to click events on the
   new-comment-submit button:

```
<template>
  <!-- rest of template -->
  <div v-if="showEditor">
  <!-- rest of editor -->
  <button data-test-id="new-comment-submit"
    :disabled="!newComment"
      @click="submitNewComment()">Submit
  </button>
  </div>
</template>
```

5. Now comes the part where we need to react to the `submit` button. The `submitting` class will show when `isSubmitting` is `true`. To do this, we simply need to set the `submitting` class to be added when `isSubmitting` is `true`. In addition to this, we'll disable the button when `isSubmitting` is `true`:

```
<button data-test-id="new-comment-submit"
:disabled="!newComment || isSubmitting"
:class="{submitting:isSubmitting}"
@click="submitNewComment()">
Submit
</button>
```

6. Finally, we can add a test to check that the button applies the `submitting` class when the `submit` button is clicked. To begin with, we'll need to set up the text editor so that when clicking on the `add-new-comment` button and setting a text value for the comment, the text editor is shown and enabled.

Next, we can click on the enabled `new-comment-submit` button and check that it is disabled and has the `submitting` class (using the `should()` function). After that, we should write another assertion that the button does not show the `submitting` class:

```
it('the new comment editor should show a submitting
class on submit', () => {
  cy.visit('/')
  // Get the editor to show
  cy.get('[data-test-id="new-comment-button"]')
    .click()
  cy.get('[data-test-id="new-comment-submit"]')
    .should('be.visible')

  cy.get('[data-test-id="new-comment-editor"]')
    .type('Just saying...')

  cy.get('[data-test-id="new-comment-submit"]')
    .should('not.be.disabled')
    .click()
    .should('have.class', 'submitting')
    .should('be.disabled')
```

```
    // eventually, the submitting class should be
      removed
  cy.get('[data-test-id="new-comment-submit"]')
    .should('not.have.class', 'submitting')
})
```

Despite the 2.5 seconds during which the submitting class is shown, this test still passes due to Cypress' automatic retry/wait functionality:

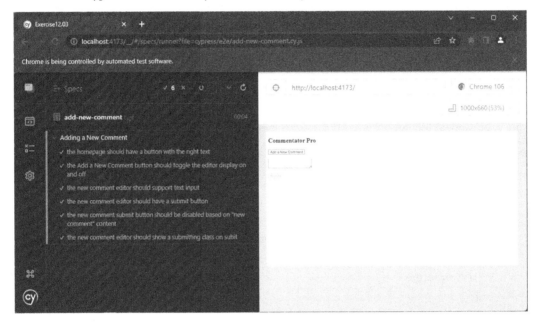

Figure 12.15 – Cypress running add-new-comment tests, including
the comment submission loading state test

We've now seen how Cypress allows us to seamlessly work around asynchronicity in the application by automatically waiting/retrying where an assertion or selection would fail.

Intercepting HTTP requests

As mentioned in previous sections, Cypress is designed as a JavaScript E2E testing solution. This means that it comes with built-ins such as assertions, automatic wait/retries, sane defaults for running the application, and extensive mocking functionality.

HTTP requests can be slow and tend to introduce flaky behavior into tests. What's meant by flaky is intermittent false negatives – that is, failures that are not caused by an application issue but rather by connectivity issues (for example, between the server running the tests and the backend hosts).

We would also be testing the implementation of the backend system. When using **Continuous Integration (CI)**, this would mean having to run the backend systems in whichever CI pipeline step needs to run E2E tests.

Usually, when the backend requests are intercepted and a mock response is sent, we also say that the HTTP requests are *stubbed* in order to avoid tests flaking (meaning intermittent failures not linked to application changes).

Seeing that the requests do not go all the way through the stack (including the backend API), this is technically not a full E2E test of the system anymore. We can, however, consider it an E2E test of the frontend application since the whole application is made up of separate exercises and is not implementation-specific.

In order to mock requests in Cypress, we'll need to use `cy.intercept()`.

To showcase HTTP interception, we'll fetch a list of comments from `JSONPlaceholder` and store them under a `comments` reactive instance variable. We can use `fetch` to do this in the `mounted()` life cycle event as follows:

```
<script>
// imports
export default {
  data() {
    return {
      // other data properties
      comments: []
    }
  },
  mounted() {
    fetch('https://jsonplaceholder.typicode.com/comments')
      .then(res => res.json())
      .then(comments => {
        this.comments = comments
      })
  }
  // other component properties
}
</script>
```

A sample comment includes an ID, a body, and an email, among other properties.

That means we can render the comments by creating a `div` container, which only shows if there are comments (`comments.length > 0`). Inside the `div` container, we can render a list of `div` elements using `v-for`. Each card will render the body of the comment and the author's email inside a `mailto:` link.

Note how we set `comments-list` and `comment-card` `data-test-ids` for the list container and the list items respectively:

```
<div v-if="comments.length > 0" data-test-id="comments-list">
<div v-for="(comment, index) in comments":key="comment.id +
index"data-test-id="comment">
  <p>{{ comment.body }}</p>
  <p><a :href="'mailto:' + comment.email">
    {{ comment.email }}</a>
  </p>
    </div>
</div>
```

If we were to test this without HTTP interception, we would have to keep the assertions quite generic. For example, we can check that `comments-list` is visible and that there is a number (greater than 0) of `comment-card` instances in a new E2E test file:

```
describe('Loading Existing Comments', () => {
  it('should load & display comments', () => {
    cy.visit('/')
    cy.get('[data-test-id="comments-list"]')
      .should('be.visible')

    cy.get('[data-test-id="comment-card"]')
      .should('have.length.gt', 0)
  })
})
```

The following test run using the Cypress GUI passes but the tests are quite generic. We can't make any assertions about the specific number of comments or their content:

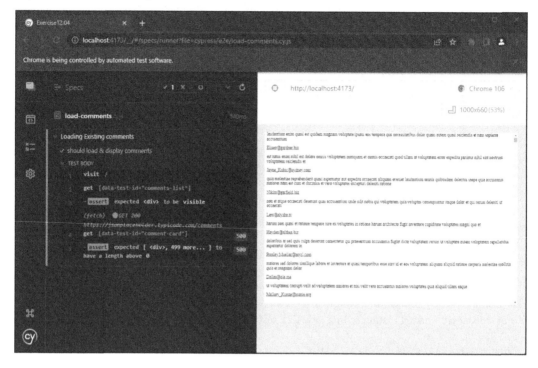

Figure 12.16 – Cypress running load-comments tests, including a generic load and display test

To intercept the request, we use `cy.intercept`. It lets us define a route and a static response – in our case, an array of comments. We'll use a fictitious email address in our stubs:

```
it('should load and display comments correctly', () => {
  cy.intercept('**/comments', [
    {
      body: 'Vue is getting great adoption',
      email: 'evan@vuejs.org',
      id: 100,
    },
    {
      body: 'Just saying...',
      email: 'evan@vuejs.org',
      id: 10
    },
```

```
    {
      body: 'The JS ecosystem is great',
      email: 'evan@vuejs.org',
      id: 1
    }
  ]).as('getComments')
}
```

Once we've got our stub route set up, we can visit the page and wait for the comment fetching to finish using `cy.wait('@getComments')`, since we've previously set the alias of the comments' `fetch` route to `getComments` with `.as('getComments')`:

```
describe('Loading Existing Comments', () => {
  // other tests
  it('should load and display comments correctly', () => {
    // test setup
    cy.visit('/')
    cy.wait('@getComments')

  })
})
```

We can then start asserting, first off, that `comments-list` is visible, and then assert the number of `comment-card` elements:

```
describe('Loading Existing Comments', () => {
  // other tests
  it('should load and display comments correctly', () => {
    // test setup
    cy.get('[data-test-id="comments-list"]')
      .should('be.visible')

    cy.get('[data-test-id="comment-card"]')
      .should('have.length', 3)
  })
})
```

We can also assert the specific contents of the cards using the `.contains()` function:

```
describe('Loading Existing Comments', () => {
  // other tests
  it('should load and display comments correctly', () => {
    // test setup
    cy.contains('[data-test-id="comment-card"]', 'Vue is
      getting great adoption').contains('evan@vuejs.org')
    cy.contains('[data-test-id="comment-card"]',
      'Just saying...').contains('evan@vuejs.org')
    cy.contains('[data-test-id="comment-card"]', 'The JS
      ecosystem is great').contains('evan@vuejs.org')
  })
})
```

We can then run the suite with the Cypress GUI and see it passing:

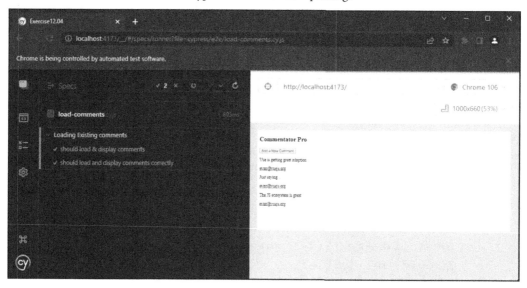

Figure 12.17 – Cypress running load-comments tests, including our stubbed comments test

We've now seen how and why we might stub HTTP requests using Cypress.

Exercise 12.04 – POST comment to the API on submission

The new-comment-submit button currently only sets a loading state for a few seconds and then resets – the comment is not actually being sent anywhere.

Let's use the JSONPlaceholder API as the place to send our new comment. When the POST request to the API succeeds, we'll add the comment to the top of the comment list.

The complete code can be found at https://github.com/PacktPublishing/Frontend-Development-Projects-with-Vue.js-3/tree/v2-edition/Chapter12/Exercise12.04

To complete the exercise, we will perform the following steps:

1. Start by making the submitNewComment method actually post data using fetch. New comments require an email address, which our application doesn't have, but we can set a fake email in our data as well:

```
<script>
// imports
export default {
  // other component properties
  data: {
    // other data
    email:'fakeemail@email.com'
  },
  methods: {
    submitNewComment() {
      this.isSubmitting = true

    fetch('https://jsonplaceholder.typicode.com/
comments ', {
        method: 'POST',
        headers: {
          'Content-Type': 'application/json'
        },
        body: JSON.stringify({
          email: this.email,
          body: this.newComment
        })
    })
  }
```

```
        }
    }
</script>
```

Unfortunately, the fetch() call doesn't update the data by itself or come out of the loading state. In order to do so, we need to chain some .then() function calls to handle the response, and a .catch function call in case we have an error.

On success (.then), we should get the JSON output of the request and add it to the front of a copy of the comments array. We should also reset isSubmitting, newComment, and showEditor. On error (.catch), we will just reset the loading state, isSubmitting, to false; we won't clear the editor or close it since the user might want to try to submit it again:

```
<script>
// imports
export default {
    // other component properties
    methods: {
        submitNewComment() {
            this.isSubmitting = true

            fetch(
                // fetch params
            ).then(res => res.json())
             .then(data => {
                this.comments = [
                data,
                ...this.comments,
                ]
                this.isSubmitting = false
                this.newComment = ''
            })
            .catch(() => {
                this.isSubmitting = false
            })
        }
    }
}
</script>
```

We should now add new tests to the cypress/e22/add-new-comment.js test suite.

2. First of all, to be good users of the JSON placeholder, we'll stub out all the GET requests to /comments for the add-new-comment suite. In order to do this, we'll use a beforeEach hook that will intercept requests matching the **/comments glob and return an empty array:

```
describe('Adding a New Comment', () => {
  beforeEach(() => {
    cy.intercept('GET','**/comments', []);
  })
  // tests
```

3. We can then proceed to update the the new comment editor should show a submitting class on submit test since we're not using setTimeout anymore but an HTTP request. To start with, we need to stub out the /comments POST request, for which we'll use the configuration object syntax for cy.intercept in order to introduce a delay into the HTTP request so that it doesn't respond immediately.

   We alias this request with .as('newComment'):

```
it('the new comment editor should show a submitting class
on submit', () => {
  cy.intercept('POST', '**/comments', (req) => {
    req.reply({
      delay: 1500, response: {}
    });
  }).as('newComment');
```

4. Instead of // eventually, the submitting class should be removed, we can now use cy.wait() to wait for the newComment HTTP request to complete before checking that the spinner is gone:

```
describe('Adding a New Comment', () => {
  // setup & tests
  it('the new comment editor should show a spinner on
  submit', () => {
    // test setup
    // click the "submit" button
    // check the submitting class appears
    cy.wait('@newComment')
    // check that the submitting class is gone
  })
})
```

5. Upon successfully posting a new comment, the comment text is cleared. We should test that this happens when a comment is posted. We'll use a similar skeleton to the updated loading state test, with the setup of the POST comments route stubbing `cy.intercept('POST', '**/comments', {}`, aliased as `.as('newComment')`.

We can then get the new comment editor to display, add some text, and submit the form. We'll then proceed to wait for the POST request to complete before checking that the comment has been cleared:

```
it('adding a new comment should clear the comment
text', () => {
  cy.intercept('POST', '**/comments', {
    body: {
      body: 'Just saying...',
      email: 'hi@raymondcamden.com'
    }
  }).as('newComment');

  cy.visit('/')

  // Get the editor to show
  cy.get('[data-test-id="new-comment-button"]')
    .click()
  cy.get('[data-test-id="new-comment-submit"]')
    .should('be.visible')

  cy.get('[data-test-id="new-comment-editor"]')
    .type('Just saying...')

  cy.get('[data-test-id="new-comment-submit"]')
    .should('not.be.disabled')
    .click()

  cy.wait('@newComment');
  cy.get('[data-test-id="new-comment-editor"]')
    .should('have.value', '')

});
```

This test can now be run with the Cypress GUI and will pass:

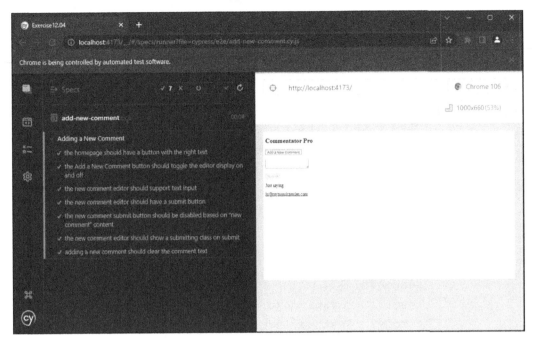

Figure 12.18 – Cypress running add-new-comment tests, including the editor comment text being cleared

6. The second bit of functionality that we've added is that on completion of the HTTP request, the new comment is added to the top of the comments list. To test this, it's better to change the response of the comments' GET request to have at least one element (so that we can check that the new comment is added to the top of the list):

```
describe('Adding a New Comment', () => {
  // setup & other tests
  it('submitting a new comment should POST to
  /comments and adds response to top of comments
  list', () => {
    cy.intercept('GET', '**/comments', [
      {
        email: 'evan@vuejs.org',
        body: 'Existing comment'
      }
```

```
      ]).as('newComment')
    })
  })
```

7. We can then stub the POST request with some mock data, add text to the editor, and submit
    the form:

```
describe('Adding a New Comment', () => {
  // setup & other tests
  it('submitting a new comment should POST to
  /comments and adds response to top of comments
  list', () => {
    // GET request stubbing
    cy.intercept({
      method: 'POST',
      url: '**/comments',
      response: {
        email: 'evan@vuejs.org',
        body: 'Just saying...',
      },
    }).as('newComment')
    cy.visit('/')

    cy.get('[data-test-id="comment-card"]').should
      ('have.length', 1)

    cy.get('[data-test-id="new-comment-button"]')
      .click()

    cy.get('[data-test-id="new-comment-editor"]')
      .type('Just saying...')

    cy.get('[data-test-id="new-comment-submit"]')
      .should('not.be.disabled')
```

```
        .click()

    cy.wait('@newComment')
  })
})
```

8. Finally, we can assert the fact that the first comment is the newly added comment using a combination of `cy.get()`, `.first()`, and `.contains()`:

```
describe('Adding a New Comment', () => {
  // setup & other tests
  it('submitting a new comment should POST to
  /comments and adds response to top of comments
  list', () => {
    // setup & wait for POST completion
    cy.get('[data-test-id="comments-list"]')
      .should('be.visible')

    cy.get('[data-test-id="comment-card"]')
      .should('have.length', 2).first()
      .contains('[data-test-id="comment-card"]',
      'Just saying...')
      .contains('fakeemail@email.com')
  })
})
```

When running the `add-new-comment` suite with the Cypress GUI, we can see the new test passing:

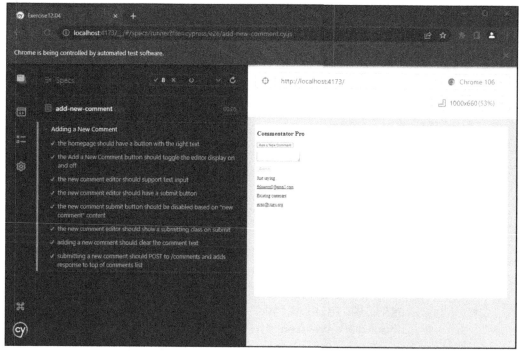

Figure 12.19 – Cypress running add-new-comment tests, including
the new comment added to the top of the list test

You've now seen how to handle network operations in your testing. As most applications make use of some sort of API call, this will be tremendously helpful in ensuring your tests cover as much ground as possible.

Activity 12.01 – adding the ability to set a user's email and test

You'll remember that we've hardcoded `fakeemail@email.com` as the email for any comments. What we'll do in this activity is add an email input that will set the `email` property on comments. We'll add the relevant tests in a new `cypress/e2e/enter-email.cy.js` suite:

1. In order to keep track of the email, we'll set it as a piece of reactive state in `data()` and add an email input to the page, which will be two-way bound to `email` using `v-model`. We also add a label and corresponding markup. Note that we'll have a `data-test-id` attribute on the email input set to `email-input`.

2. We'll now add a `beforeEach` hook to have Cypress intercept and stub out the GET comments (list) request. The comments list request should be aliased as `getComments`.

3. We'll add our first test, which checks whether typing into the email input works correctly. We'll go to the app, type an email, and check that what we typed is now the input value.

    When it is run using the Cypress UI, we should get the following passing test:

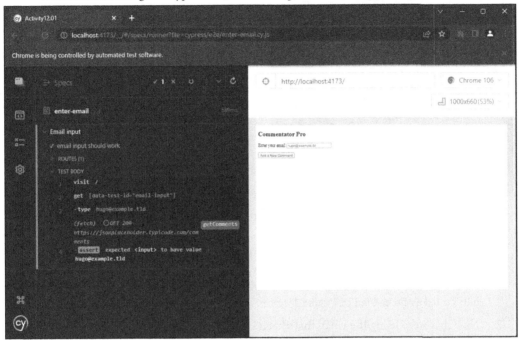

Figure 12.20 – Cypress running enter-email tests with the email input test

4. Having the `email` property is a pre-requisite to adding comments, so we'll disable the **Add a New Comment** button while `email` is empty (`!email`). We'll bind to the `disabled` attribute based on whether or not the email field is populated.

5. With this new `disable add new comment button while email is empty` functionality, we should add a new E2E test. We'll load up the page and on initial load, we'll check that the email input is empty and that the **Add a New Comment** button is disabled. We'll then type an email into the email input field and check that the **Add a New Comment** button is now `not` disabled, which means it is enabled.

When run using the Cypress UI, we should see the new test passing with the following output:

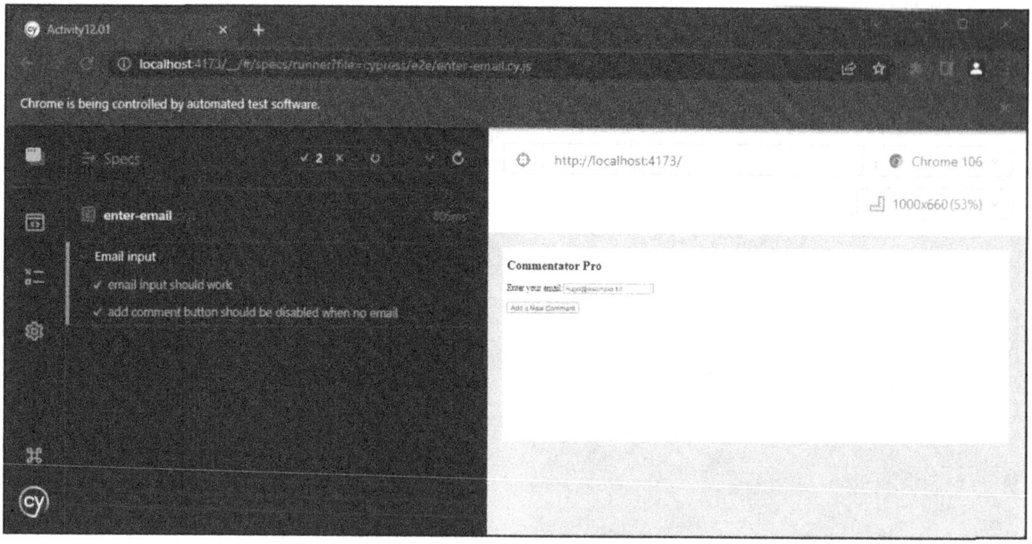

Figure 12.21 – Cypress running enter-email tests with the disabled add comment button test

6. Now that we've got a way to capture the email, we should pass it to the backend API when making the POST comments call (that is, when submitting a new comment). In order to do this, we should modify the spot in `methods.submitNewComment` where the email is hardcoded as `fakeemail@email.com`.

7. Now that we're using the email that's been input by the user, we should write an E2E test to check that it's being sent. We'll stub out the POST request, alias it to `newComment`, and send back an arbitrary value. We can then visit the page, fill out the email input, open the comment editor, fill that out, and submit it. We'll then wait on the `newComment` request and assert in the request body that the body and email are as they were when we completed them.

> **Note**
>
> We could also opt to not stub out the POST request and instead check that the new comment inserted on the page contains the right email and body.

When run using the Cypress UI, we get the following test run output:

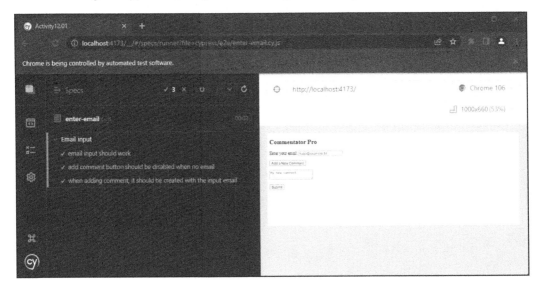

Figure 12.22 – Cypress running enter-email tests with the email input test

> **Note**
>
> The solution for this activity can be found at `https://github.com/PacktPublishing/`
> `Frontend-Development-Projects-with-Vue.js-3/tree/v2-edition/`
> `Chapter12/Activity12.01`

Summary

Throughout this chapter, we've looked at leveraging Cypress to test Vue.js applications E2E. E2E tests in general are useful to give us a high level of confidence that tested flows will work as expected, as opposed to unit or integration tests, which validate that our code works as expected at a much lower overhead.

We've seen how to use Cypress to inspect, interact with, and assert against a UI. We've also shown how Cypress' default wait/retry functionality is a great advantage when writing robust tests. We leveraged Cypress' HTTP interception library to stub out HTTP requests and make tests more predictable and faster.

Finally, we looked at how to set up visual regression testing with Cypress. In the next chapter, we'll look at how to deploy a Vue.js application to the web.

13
Deploying Your Code
to the Web

In the previous two chapters, you had an in-depth look at testing and how it can benefit your application. Now that you're confident in the stability and usability of your Vue.js application, it's time to take a deeper look at how to get that code up on the web.

In this chapter, you will be able to explain the benefits of a CI/CD workflow and how it ties into the release cycle, release cadence, and development workflows. To this end, you'll be able to articulate the differences between Vue.js development and production builds and what trade-offs are made.

To test and deploy a Vue.js application, you'll configure GitLab CI/CD with pipelines, jobs, and steps. You'll become familiar with Netlify, **Amazon Web Services Simple Storage Service (AWS S3)**, and AWS CloudFront, and their key similarities and differences.

In this chapter, we will cover the following topics:

- Exploring the benefits of CI/CD as part of an agile software development process
- Building our apps for production
- Using GitLab CI/CD to test our code
- Deploying to Netlify
- Deploying to AWS using S3 and CloudFront

Technical requirements

For this chapter, you will need the `git` CLI, which you will have already used. You will also need accounts with both Netlify and Amazon AWS.

The Node version has to be below v20 (preferable Yarn 1.22 and Node version above 16 and up to 19.x, and npm up to version 9.x.

You may find this chapter's source here: `https://github.com/PacktPublishing/Frontend-Development-Projects-with-Vue.js-3/tree/v2-edition/Chapter13`

Exploring the benefits of CI/CD as part of an agile software development process

Continuous integration (**CI**) is the practice of integrating code multiple times a day. To support this, a modern **version control system** (**VCS**), such as Git, which supports multiple working states (branches) in a single repository, is necessary to allow developers to work on code independently, while still allowing them to collaborate and integrate their changes safely.

To augment the abilities of the VCS, hosting and collaboration tools around repositories (such as GitLab or GitHub) have been created that allow developers to view and manage code changes more efficiently through a web **user interface** (**UI**).

As part of, or in addition to, these hosting platforms and the collaboration tools they provide, automated checks are crucial to maintaining high confidence in the quality of the code before, during, and after integration.

Adopting a CI approach often entails including additional code quality steps, such as unit or integration tests, coverage checks, and building artifacts on the mainline branches (branches into which changes are integrated) every time any new code is integrated. The convention that a team follows for using Git for code collaboration and CI is called a **Git workflow**, which is often shortened to **Git flow**.

A Git flow will predicate branch naming conventions, as well as how and when changes are integrated. For example, a team might decide that branches should be prefixed with ticket numbers followed by a short dash-cased description, such as `WRK-2334-fix-ie-11-scroll`.

Other examples of conventions that are decided on and adhered to as part of a Git flow are commit message lengths and titles, the automated checks that should pass or are allowed to fail, and the number of reviewers required to merge a change request, which is a pull request or merge request in GitHub and GitLab parlance, respectively.

Git flows fall under two rough categories: (feature) branch-based development and trunk-based development. We'll cover branch-based development first since its limitations have become quite clear and the majority of projects tend to use trunk-based development.

In a branch-based Git workflow, multiple working branches are kept in the repository. Branch-based flows can be used to keep branches that mirror the state of environments.

The following diagram shows three branches – production, staging, and develop:

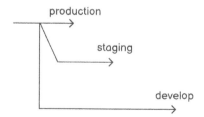

Figure 13.1 – A branch-based Git commit/branch tree with three environment branches

The *production* branch does not contain any changes from *staging* or *develop*. The *staging* is ahead of the *production* branch but has no changes in common with the *develop* branch other than the changes that are on the *production* branch. The *develop* branch is ahead of both the *staging* and *production* branches: it's branched off the *production* branch at the same commit as the *staging* branch, but it doesn't share any further commits with the *staging* branch.

A branch-based workflow can also be used to keep track of changes going into release lines. This is useful in cases where a project has to maintain two versions of an application or library, but bug fixes or security patches need to be applied to both versions.

In the following example, we have got a similar branching example as the environment branch one. Release 1.0.0 contains some changes that are not present in 1.0.1 and 1.1.0 but does not share any of the newer code. Releases 1.0.1 and 1.1.0 are branched off of 1.0.0 at the same time, but they do not share further changes:

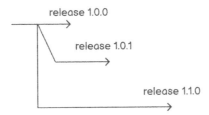

Figure 13.2 – A branch-based Git commit/branch tree with three release branches

In a trunk-based Git flow, each member of the team will create new branches off of a single branch, usually the *master* branch. This process is often referred to as **branching off of**:

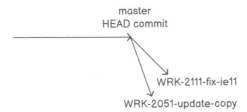

Figure 13.3 – A sample trunk-based Git commit/branch tree with
two feature branches branched off of the master

An extreme case of a trunk-based workflow is to have a *single* branch that everyone commits on.

> **Note**
>
> In a trunk-based environment, an alternative to *release branches* is to use Git tags to keep track of release snapshots. This gives the same advantages as maintaining branches but with reduced branch noise and the added benefit of immutability since tags cannot be changed once they're created.

Continuous delivery (CD) is the ability of a team to deploy every good build to a production environment.

A prerequisite to CD is CI since CI provides some initial confidence in the quality of a build. As part of CD, new systems, tools, and practices are required beyond CI.

The following diagram shows the tools and practices that relate more to CI and those that relate more to CD:

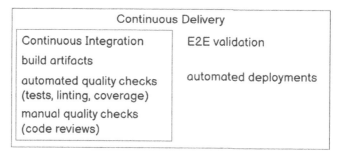

Figure 13.4 – The relationship between CI and CD practices

The extra ingredient required to adopt CD is a high level of confidence that the application is going to keep working as expected (for the end user) and that new defects have not been unwittingly introduced. This means an additional end-to-end testing step is needed during or after the CI checks, to validate the build before being able to deploy it.

These end-to-end tests can be conducted manually, or they can be automated. In an ideal CD setup, the latter (automated end-to-end tests) is preferred since it means deployments do not include manual interaction. If the end-to-end tests pass, the build can be deployed automatically.

To facilitate CD, systems that used to deploy software have had to be rethought. As part of CD, deployment cannot be a long-winded manual process. This has led to companies adopting cloud-native technologies, such as Docker, and **Infrastructure as Code (IaC)** tools, such as HashiCorp's **Terraform**.

The emphasis on moving toward CD practices has led to the inception of ideas such as **GitOps** and **ChatOps**. In GitOps and ChatOps, deployments and operational tasks are driven by the tools that developers and stakeholders interact with daily.

In GitOps, deployments can be done through GitHub/GitLab (or another Git-hosting provider), directly with GitHub Actions or GitLab CI/CD, or through CI/CD software (such as CircleCI or Jenkins), which have tight integrations and reporting with GitHub/GitLab.

In the case of ChatOps, conversational interfaces are used to deploy and operate the software. Some flavors of ChatOps can be considered a subset of GitOps – for example, interacting with tools such as **Dependabot** (a tool that keeps a project's dependencies up to date) through comments on a GitHub pull request.

ChatOps can also be implemented right into real-time chat tools, such as Slack or Microsoft Teams. Someone might send a message such as `deploy <service-name> <environment>`, which will deploy the service to the relevant environment. Note that chat interfaces are very reminiscent of command-line interfaces, which developers might be used to but other stakeholders might take some time to adopt them.

Now that we've looked at approaches to CI and CD, let's discuss the advantages of using CI and CD:

Continuous Integration	Continuous Delivery
Ensures the changeset being integrated is small (at most, a couple of days' worth of work)	Delivering value to production can be done more often and more safely
Reduces the chance of huge sweeping changes across the code base causing unforeseen bugs	A small changeset (a couple of days' worth of work) can be rolled back without any issue
Testing, code quality, and review steps give confidence in a clean integration	A larger changeset due to a longer fixed (monthly, weekly, or every sprint) release cadence (as opposed to CD) can have unforeseen consequences; the effect rollbacks have on a large release is complicated to grasp

Figure 13.5 – Advantages of CI and CD

Both practices also have an impact on the team's mindset and performance. Being able to see the changes you make integrated within a day and in production in less than a week means that contributors can see their work having an impact immediately.

CI/CD also helps promote agile principles, where changes are applied and deployed iteratively. This is as opposed to long timelines for projects, for which inaccuracies in estimations compound and can cause major delays.

With that, you've had a deep look at CI and CD. While both certainly imply more work in your process, the benefits will pay for themselves down the road with better stability and the ability to more nimbly respond to issues and add new features. Now, let's put this into practice.

Building our apps for production

Deploying applications to production starts with creating an artifact that can be deployed. In the case of Vue.js, we're building a client-side application, which means our build artifact will contain HTML, JavaScript, and CSS files.

A Vue project scaffolded with Vite will have a `build` command. As part of the build process, Vite will take JavaScript, Vue single-file components, and modules that are imported into each other and *bundle* them. **Bundling** means that related chunks of code that depend on each other will be output as a single JavaScript file.

The Vue CLI build step also includes a `dead code elimination` step. This means that it can analyze the code being generated and if any of it is never used – for example, a statement such as `if (false) { /* do something */}` – then it will not be present in the build output.

By default, the Vite builds for production when we call `vite build`, which, in Vue projects, is aliased to the `build` script, which can be run with `npm run build` or `yarn build`.

In a sample Vue project, we'll see something along these lines:

```
ray@Hoth:~/projects/testingzone/vue3stuff/vueproject1$ npm run build

> vueproject1@0.0.0 build
> vite build

vite v2.7.13 building for production ...
✓ 22 modules transformed.
dist/assets/logo.da9b9095.svg     0.30 KiB
dist/index.html                   0.48 KiB
dist/assets/index.de5eef59.js     10.14 KiB / gzip: 3.89 KiB
dist/assets/index.f3fa6de6.css    3.48 KiB / gzip: 1.15 KiB
dist/assets/vendor.7ed976ab.js    50.20 KiB / gzip: 20.25 KiB
```

Figure 13.6 – Output of "npm run build" in a fresh Vue project

The `dist` folder is now ready to deploy using a static hosting solution such as Netlify or AWS S3 and CloudFront.

With that, we've seen how to build a Vue.js application for production using the Vite CLI with the `npm run build` command. Next, we will learn how to use GitLab CI/CD to test our code (before deploying it).

Using GitLab CI/CD to test our code

GitLab has a built-in CI/CD tool called GitLab CI/CD. To use GitLab CI/CD, you'll need a GitLab account. To interact with Git repositories hosted on GitLab, you'll also need to associate an SSH key from your machine to your GitLab account.

> **Note**
> Instructions for adding an SSH key can be found in the GitLab documentation at `https://docs.gitlab.com/ee/ssh/index.html`.

Once you've created an account, you can create a new repository using the **Create blank project** action, as shown in the following screenshot. If you are an existing user, you can use the **Create new project** button at the top right of the **Projects** page.

Figure 13.7 – The GitLab Projects page with the New Project button

Regardless of your choice, you will be taken to the **New project** page, where you can create a project by giving it a name and a slug, as seen in the following screenshot:

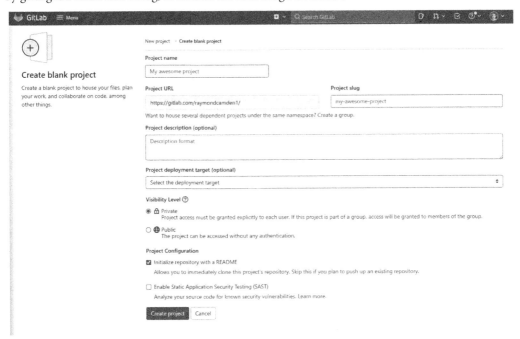

Figure 13.8 – The GitLab New project page

Once you click **Create project**, the GitLab project page will appear in an empty state that displays instructions on how to clone it. You should run the commands required to clone the repository, which probably boils down to something similar to the following (which you are expected to run on your machine):

```
git clone <repository-url>
```

You can find the proper URL by clicking on the blue **Clone** button.

On your machine, open the directory into which the repository was cloned. To add GitLab CI/CD, we need to add a `.gitlab-ci.yml` file to the root of the project. A sample `.gitlab-ci.yml` file that adds a `build` job to the `build` stage of the pipeline, installs dependencies (using `npm ci`), runs the production build (`npm run build`), and caches the output artifact is defined as follows.

It will begin with a job name that is defined by setting a top-level key in the YAML file – in this case, `build:`. In YAML syntax, we must increase the indent to denote that the `build` key points to an object.

In the `build job` object, we will define which Docker image is used to run the job, using `image: node:lts`. This means we want this job to run on a Node.js **Long-Term Support** (**LTS**) image, which will be Node.js 16 as of early 2022.

> **Note**
>
> You can access the up-to-date Node.js LTS schedule at `https://nodejs.org/en/about/releases/`.

The other property we can define in our job is the stage. By default, GitLab CI/CD pipelines have three stages: **Build**, **Test**, and **Deploy**. These stages can be replaced using custom stages when a team's workflow doesn't fit into these three categories (for example, if there is more than one environment to deploy to). Our pipeline only has one stage and one job at the moment, so most of the preceding doesn't apply to us.

> **Note**
>
> If you're curious, `stages` is used to define stages that can be used by jobs, and it is defined globally (`https://docs.gitlab.com/ee/ci/yaml/#stages`).
>
> The specification of `stages` allows for flexible multistage pipelines. The ordering of elements in stages defines the ordering of jobs' execution:
>
> a) Jobs of the same stage are run in parallel
>
> b) Jobs of the next stage are run after the jobs from the previous stage have been completed successfully
>
> See the documentation for more information: `https://docs.gitlab.com/ee/ci/yaml/#stages`.

The final properties we set are `script`, which defines steps that should be run when the job is running, and `artifacts`, which configures artifact storage. In our case, we'll run `npm ci` to install all the dependencies, followed by `npm run build`, which will run the production Vue.js build. Our artifact has been set up to be held for a week and to contain the `dist` folder (which is where the Vite CLI `build` output is stored).

In full, we have the following:

```
build:
  image: node:lts
  stage: build
  script:
    - npm ci
    - npm run build
  artifacts:
    expire_in: 1 week
    paths:
      - dist
```

Once we push this `.gitlab-ci.yml` file to a repository containing a Vue CLI project, we will see the following in the repository view, where a pipeline with one step is running on the latest commit:

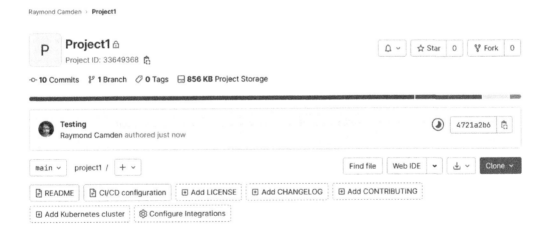

Figure 13.9 – GitLab repository view with the build job running on the latest commit

Note

GitLab now requires user verification before running pipelines. This can be done with a credit card; GitLab will *not* charge your card. It is only used as part of the validation process.

If we click on the **Pipeline** icon (the green checkmark), we will get the pipeline view. In the pipeline view, Build represents the state pipeline (which we set as build), which represents the job name (which we defined as build). We will see the same in-progress indicator until the job completes, as follows:

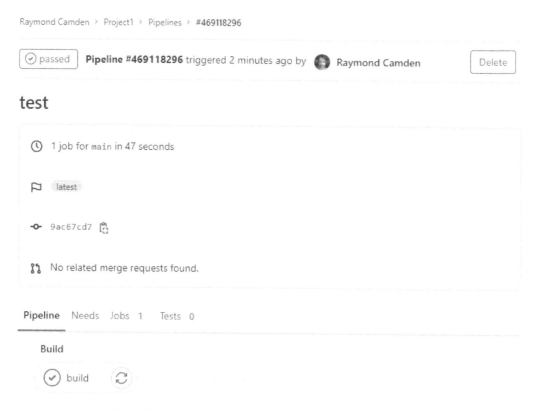

Figure 13.10 – GitLab CI pipeline view with the build job complete

Once the job completes, we will see a **Success** icon (green checkmark). We can click this icon or the job name to access the **Job** view while the job is running or after it has been completed (whether it has failed or succeeded). When a job has been completed, we will also see a **Retry** icon, which can be useful if we wish to retry a failed pipeline step.

The following screenshot shows that the job ran successfully:

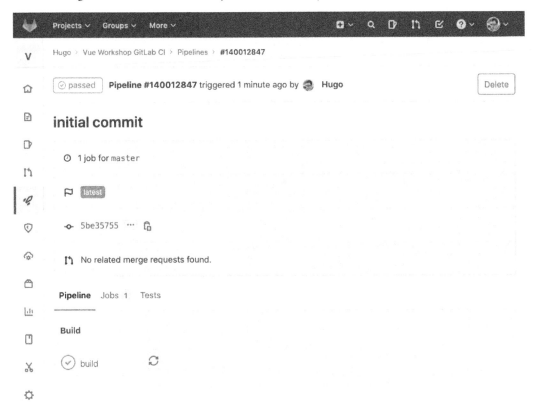

Figure 13.11 – GitLab CI pipeline view with the build job passing

After clicking the job, we will see the **Job** view, which shows us a detailed breakdown of all the steps in the job. Starting with the steps for preparing the `docker_machine` executor, which load up the Node.js Docker image, we can see the steps for running the script, as well as cache and artifact restores, as follows:

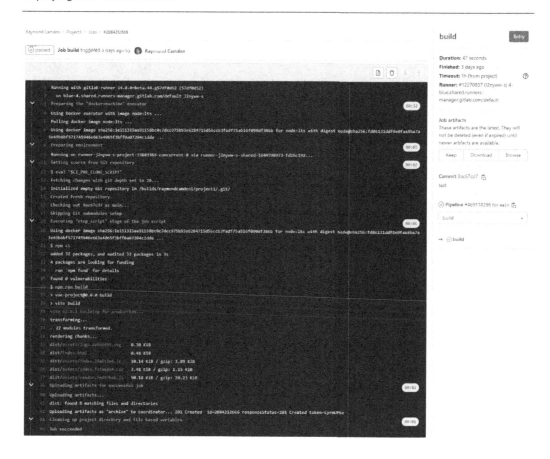

Figure 13.12 – The GitLab CI job view with the successful build job

If we want to add a `test` step to our GitLab CI/CD runs, we need to be in a project that supports unit testing. Installing and adding unit tests was covered in depth in *Chapter 11, Unit Testing.*

We will need to add a new job to the `.gitlab-ci.yml` file; we will call it `test`, use the `node:lts` image, and assign the job to the `test` state. In the job, we must run `npm ci`, followed by `npm run test:unit` (which is the npm script added by the `unit-jest` CLI plugin):

```
# rest of .gitlab-ci.yml
test:
  image: node:lts
  stage: test
  script:
    - npm ci
    - npm run test
```

Once we push this new `.gitlab-ci.yml` file up, we will get the following view on the main repository page:

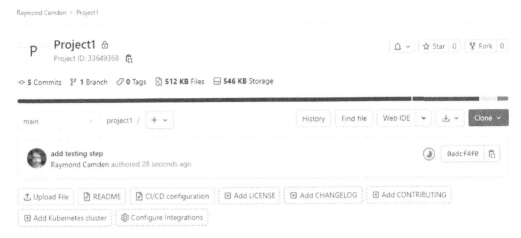

Figure 13.13 – Repository view with GitLab CI/CD running the pipeline with the new test step

We can click through to the pipeline view. The reason GitLab CI/CD uses pipelines is that a failing step at a certain stage will mean steps in any subsequent stages will not run. For example, if we get a failing `build` job, the jobs that are part of the `test` stage will not run:

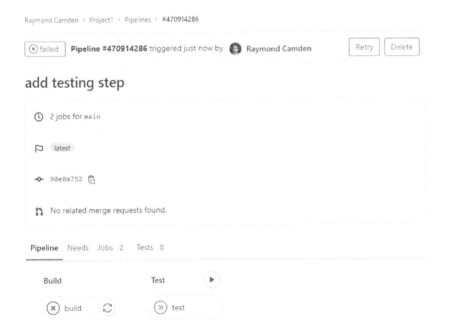

Figure 13.14 – GitLab CI/CD pipeline view with a failed build job that stops the test job/stage from running

If we push another commit or retry the build step (if the failure is not caused by changes) and navigate to the pipeline view again, we'll see the following:

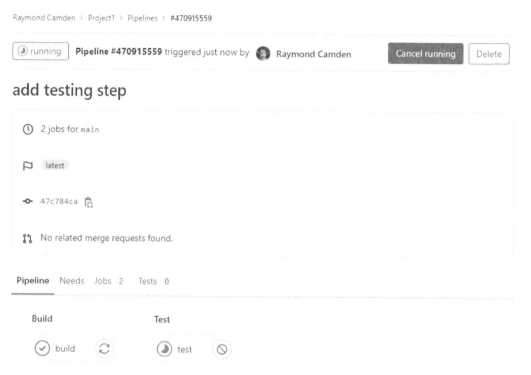

Figure 13.15 – GitLab CI/CD pipeline view with the test job running
after the build stage jobs have all succeeded

Once the `test` job has succeeded, we'll see the following pipeline:

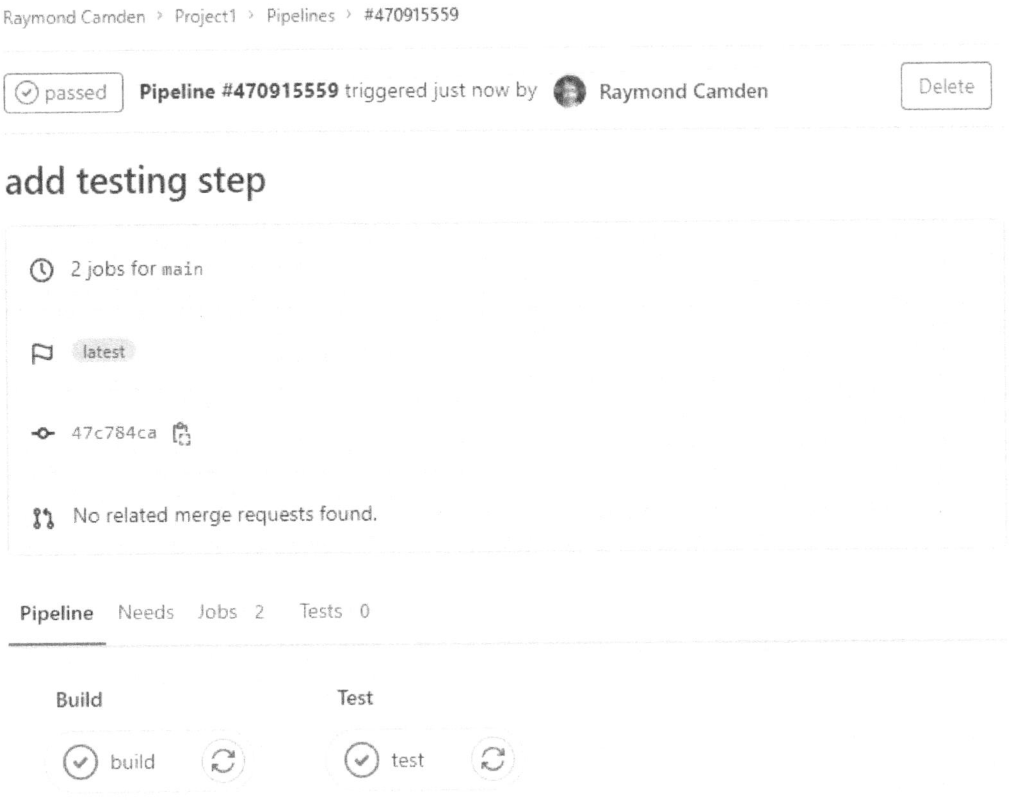

Raymond Camden > Project1 > Pipelines > #470915559

| ⊘ passed | **Pipeline #470915559** triggered just now by 🔘 Raymond Camden | Delete |

add testing step

🕐 2 jobs for main

🏳 latest

⦿ 47c784ca 📋

⥮ No related merge requests found.

Pipeline Needs Jobs 2 Tests 0

Build   Test

(✓) build (↻)   (✓) test (↻)

Figure 13.16 – GitLab CI/CD pipeline view with all jobs succeeding in the build and test stages

We've now added a GitLab CI/CD pipeline with the `build` and `test` stages that will validate that, on every push to the GitLab repository, the code still integrates as expected.

Exercise 13.01 – adding a lint step to our GitLab CI/CD pipeline

Linting is a way to get automated formatting and code style checks. Integrating it as part of CI makes sure that all code merged into the mainline branches adheres to a team's code style guide. It also reduces the number of code style review comments, which can be noisy and might detract from fundamental issues with the change request.

You can find the complete code for this exercise at `https://github.com/PacktPublishing/ Frontend-Development-Projects-with-Vue.js-3/tree/v2-edition/Chapter13/ Exercise13.01`

To add linting, follow these steps:

1. First, we need to ensure that our `package.json` file includes the `lint` script. If it's missing, we'll need to add it. The `eslint-plugin-vue` website (`https://eslint.vuejs.org/`) documents this. Once installed, use it in the lint script, like so:

    ```
    {
      "// other": "properties",
      "scripts": {
        "// other": "scripts",
        "lint": "eslint --ext .js,.vue src",
        "// other": "scripts"
      },
      "// more": "properties"
    }
    ```

2. To run the lint on GitLab CI/CD, add a new `lint` job that will run in a Node.js LTS Docker image at the `test` stage of the GitLab CI/CD pipeline. We will do this in `.gitlab-ci.yml`:

    ```
    lint:
      image: node:lts
      stage: test
    ```

3. For the `lint` job to run the `lint` script as per `package.json`, we need to add a `script` section in the `.gitlab-ci.yml` file. First, it needs to run `npm ci` to install the dependencies, and then `npm run lint` to start the linting process:

    ```
    lint:
      image: node:lts
      stage: test
      script:
        - npm ci
        - npm run lint
    ```

4. Finally, `commit` and `push` the code to GitLab using the following commands:

    ```
    git add .
    git commit -m "add linting"
    git push
    ```

Once the code has been pushed, we will see the pipeline run using the GitLab CI/CD UI, as follows (note how all the jobs at the test stage are run in parallel):

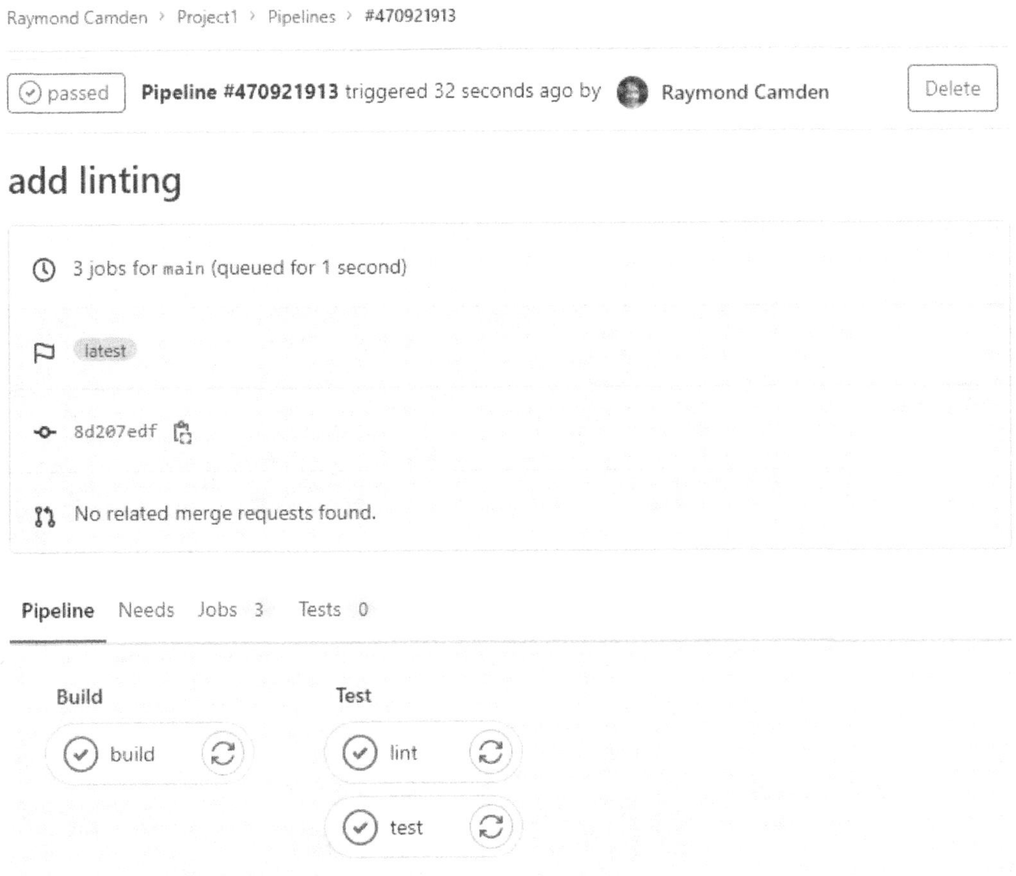

Raymond Camden › Project1 › Pipelines › #470921913

| ⊘ passed | **Pipeline #470921913** triggered 32 seconds ago by   Raymond Camden | Delete |

add linting

🕐 3 jobs for main (queued for 1 second)

🏳 latest

⦿ 8d207edf

⑁ No related merge requests found.

Pipeline   Needs   Jobs 3   Tests 0

Build

(✓) build   ↻

Test

(✓) lint   ↻

(✓) test   ↻

Figure 13.17 – The GitLab CI/CD pipeline view with all the jobs
succeeding, including "test" and "lint" running in parallel

We've now seen how to use GitLab CI/CD to run builds and tests on every commit. Next, we'll learn how to deploy a Vue.js application to Netlify.

Deploying to Netlify

Netlify is a hosting provider that specializes in static hosting and relevant supporting services to provide a fully interactive site that uses static hosting. This includes offerings such as Netlify Functions (serverless functions), Netlify Forms (a no-backend form submission system), and Netlify Identity (an identity/authentication provider).

The following sections require you to have a free Netlify account (you can sign up for one at `https://app.netlify.com/signup`).

The simplest way to deploy a site to Netlify is to use the drag-and-drop interface. You'll find this at the bottom of the **Sites** page in the logged-in view, as follows:

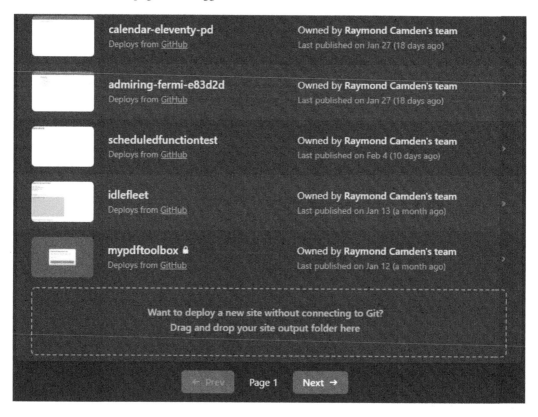

Figure 13.18 – Netlify's drag-and-drop deployment section at the bottom of the App home page

Now, we can choose a project where we've run the `npm run build` command and deploy the `dist` folder by simply dragging it to the drag-and-drop deployment section, as shown in the following screenshot:

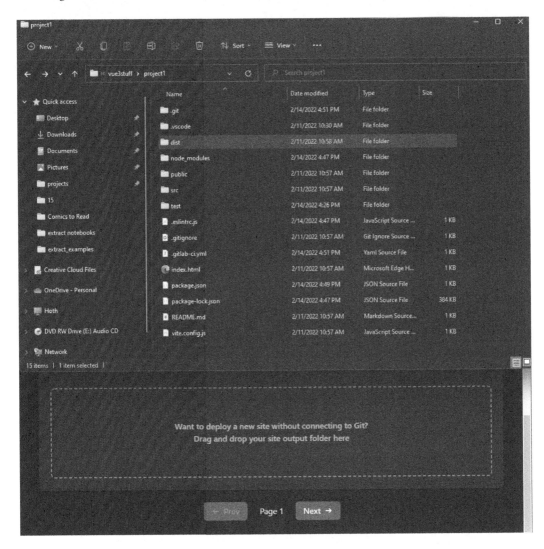

Figure 13.19 – Dragging and dropping the dist folder into the Netlify drag-and-drop deployment section

Once the upload has succeeded, Netlify will redirect you to your new website's administration page:

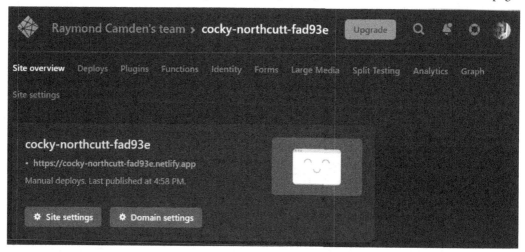

Figure 13.20 – The Netlify new app page for the drag-and-drop site

We can click on the link to the site. We'll see the default Vue CLI home page template, as follows:

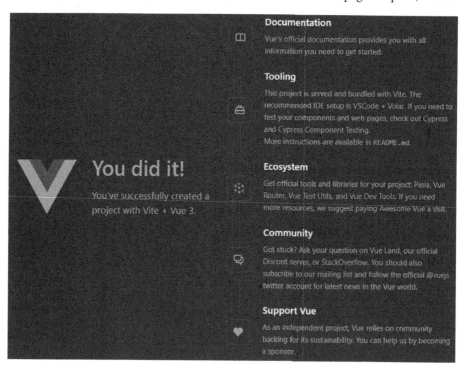

Figure 13.21 – Netlify new app displaying a greeting message

With that, we've learned how to manually deploy a site to Netlify using the drag-and-drop interface.

Next, we will learn how to deploy our site from GitLab to Netlify.

On the Netlify app's **Sites** page, we need to click the **Add new site** button, as shown in the following screenshot:

Figure 13.22 – Netlify home page with the New site from Git button

In the dropdown, select **Import an existing project**. We'll see a page asking us to choose a Git provider to connect to. For this example, we will use **GitLab**. The following screenshot shows what the screen will look like:

Figure 13.23 – Netlify – Create a new site | Connect to Git provider

Upon clicking **GitLab**, we will get an OAuth authorization challenge from GitLab, which we need to accept by clicking on the **Authorize** button, as shown in the following screenshot:

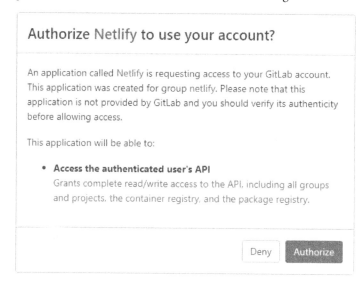

Figure 13.24 – GitLab OAuth authorization modal

We will then be redirected to Netlify and asked to choose a repository to deploy, as follows:

Figure 13.25 – Selecting a GitLab repository to deploy

After selecting the repository we want to deploy, we will be met with a configuration page. Since we're now building on Netlify's build servers, we need to configure Netlify to build the application and deploy the correct folder.

By default, Netlify figures out both the proper build command (`npm run build`) and publish directory (`dist`). If you need to change these values for some reason, you can, but the defaults should work for you.

Then, we must click the **Deploy site** button, which will start the deployment process, as follows:

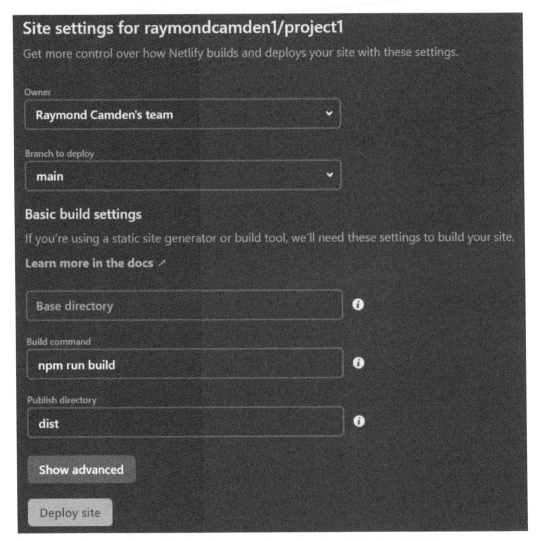

Figure 13.26 – The Netlify build configuration tab with configured settings

We will then be redirected to the newly created app's page, as shown here:

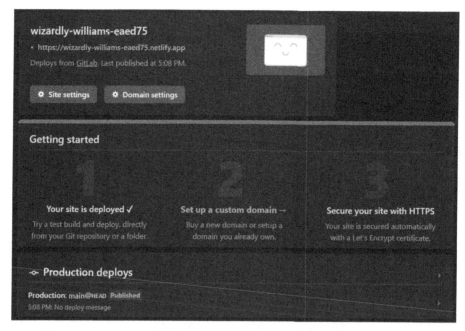

Figure 13.27 – New Netlify app

We have now seen how to deploy an application to Netlify using the manual upload method while using GitLab as the Git hosting provider.

Exercise 13.02 – deploying a site to Netlify from GitHub

In the previous exercise, you saw how to deploy a site to Netlify from GitLab. In this exercise, we'll modify that process to deploy from GitHub. How different is it from deploying it from GitLab? The answer is that they are very similar; the only notable difference is the first step in the **Connect to Git provider** tab:

1. Begin by clicking the **Add new site** button on the **Sites** page, as follows:

Figure 13.28 – Add new site on the Netlify dashboard

2. Select **Import an existing project** and choose **GitHub** as the Git hosting provider, as shown in the following screenshot:

Figure 13.29 – Continuous deployment

3. When we get the GitHub OAuth authorization challenge, as shown in the following screenshot, we must authorize Netlify:

Figure 13.30 – GitHub authorization challenge

4.   Select the Vue CLI project we want to deploy from the repository list, as follows:

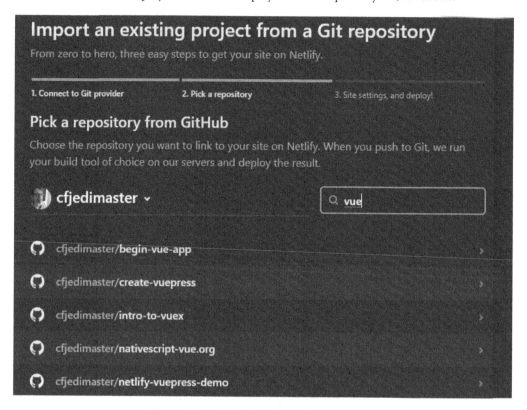

Figure 13.31 – Selecting the correct repository

5.   On the **Deployment options** tab, do the following:

I.   Select master (or main, depending on your repository) as the branch to deploy.

II.   Set **Build command** to npm run build.

III. Set **Publish directory** to dist.

The last two points look as follows:

Build settings

Repository:	**Link to a different repository** →
Base directory:	
	For monorepos or sites built from a subdirectory of a repository, the directory to change to before starting a build.
Build command:	**npm run build**
Publish directory:	**dist**

Figure 13.32 – The Netlify build configuration tab has been filled in with the proper settings

6.   Click **Deploy site** to start the deployment process.

We've now seen how to deploy an application to Netlify using the manual upload method and using GitLab or GitHub as the Git hosting provider. Next, we will learn how to use AWS S3 and AWS CloudFront to deploy a Vue.js application.

Deploying to AWS using S3 and CloudFront

Amazon S3 is a static storage offering that can be used as a host for static files, such as what is generated by the Vue CLI's `build` script.

CloudFront is AWS's **Content Delivery Network** (**CDN**) offering. A CDN can improve a web application's performance by serving static content from an **edge** location. These servers are positioned around the world and are more likely to be geographically located close to the end user than the **origin** servers (the ones that serve the content). The edge servers in a CDN request resources from the origin if they don't have them cached but will serve subsequent requests.

Let's learn how to configure S3 to host a Vue.js application (to do this, make sure that you have an AWS account):

1. Start by creating and configuring an S3 bucket.

    To do this, head to the S3 product page. It will look similar to the following:

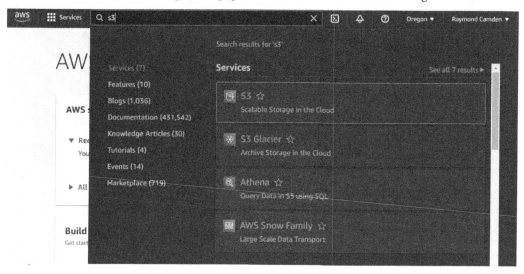

Figure 13.33 – Selecting S3 from the AWS service list

2. On the S3 console home page, click the **Create bucket** button, which will take us to the bucket creation page, as seen here:

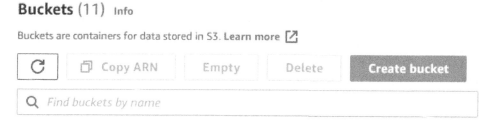

Figure 13.34 – The Create bucket button in the AWS S3 console

3. To begin, we will start by naming our bucket. Bucket names must be unique, so consider using `vue-workshop-yourname`. For this example, we've called it `vue-workshop-ray`:

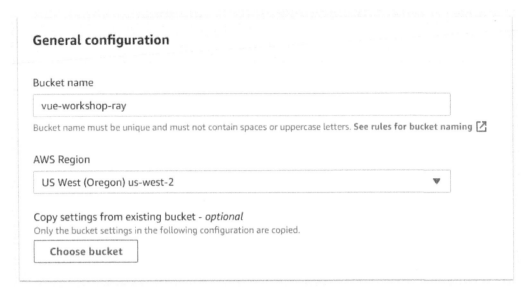

Figure 13.35 – Entering the bucket name on the bucket creation page

4. We will also need to set the S3 bucket to be public. This can be done by unselecting the **Block all public access** checkbox. Once this is done, we must check the acknowledgment checkbox, as seen here:

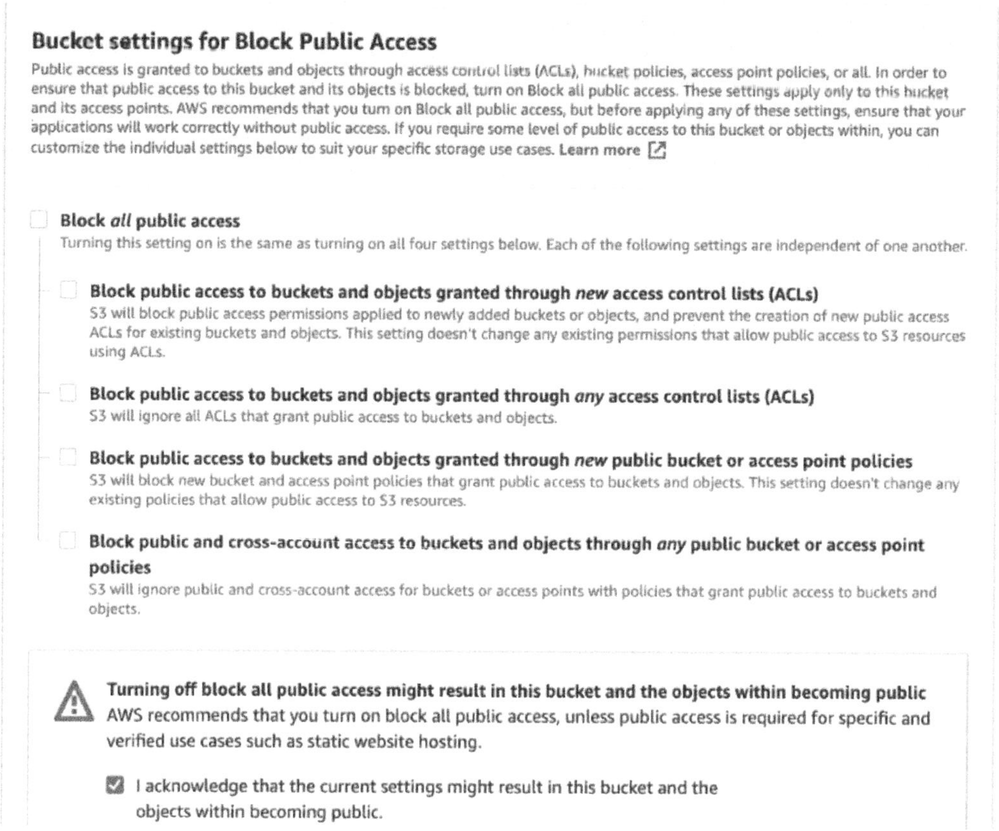

Bucket settings for Block Public Access

Public access is granted to buckets and objects through access control lists (ACLs), bucket policies, access point policies, or all. In order to ensure that public access to this bucket and its objects is blocked, turn on Block all public access. These settings apply only to this bucket and its access points. AWS recommends that you turn on Block all public access, but before applying any of these settings, ensure that your applications will work correctly without public access. If you require some level of public access to this bucket or objects within, you can customize the individual settings below to suit your specific storage use cases. **Learn more** 🗗

☐ **Block *all* public access**

Turning this setting on is the same as turning on all four settings below. Each of the following settings are independent of one another.

☐ **Block public access to buckets and objects granted through *new* access control lists (ACLs)**

S3 will block public access permissions applied to newly added buckets or objects, and prevent the creation of new public access ACLs for existing buckets and objects. This setting doesn't change any existing permissions that allow public access to S3 resources using ACLs.

☐ **Block public access to buckets and objects granted through *any* access control lists (ACLs)**

S3 will ignore all ACLs that grant public access to buckets and objects.

☐ **Block public access to buckets and objects granted through *new* public bucket or access point policies**

S3 will block new bucket and access point policies that grant public access to buckets and objects. This setting doesn't change any existing policies that allow public access to S3 resources.

☐ **Block public and cross-account access to buckets and objects through *any* public bucket or access point policies**

S3 will ignore public and cross-account access for buckets or access points with policies that grant public access to buckets and objects.

⚠ **Turning off block all public access might result in this bucket and the objects within becoming public**

AWS recommends that you turn on block all public access, unless public access is required for specific and verified use cases such as static website hosting.

☑ I acknowledge that the current settings might result in this bucket and the objects within becoming public.

Figure 13.36 – Setting the S3 bucket to be public and acknowledging the warning

5.   Once this is done, we will be redirected to the bucket list page. We want to click into our new bucket. Then, we need to access the **Properties** tag to find the **Static website hosting** option:

Static website hosting

Use this bucket to host a website or redirect requests. **Learn more** 🗗

Edit

Static website hosting

Disabled

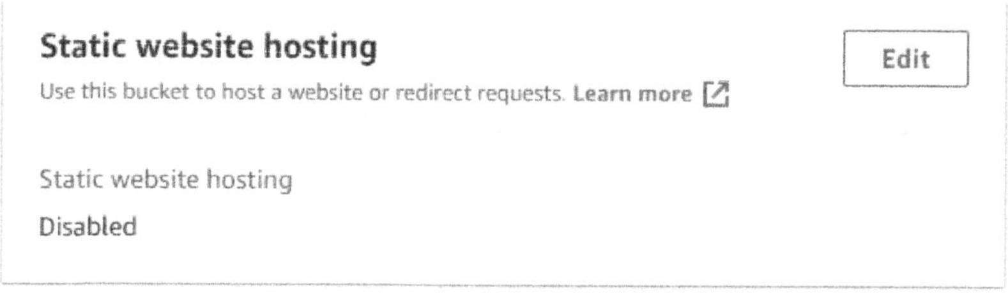

Figure 13.37 – The Static website hosting option in the S3 bucket's Properties tab

6. We can fill in the **Static website hosting** S3 property by selecting **Use this bucket to host a website** and setting the index document and error document to `index.html`:

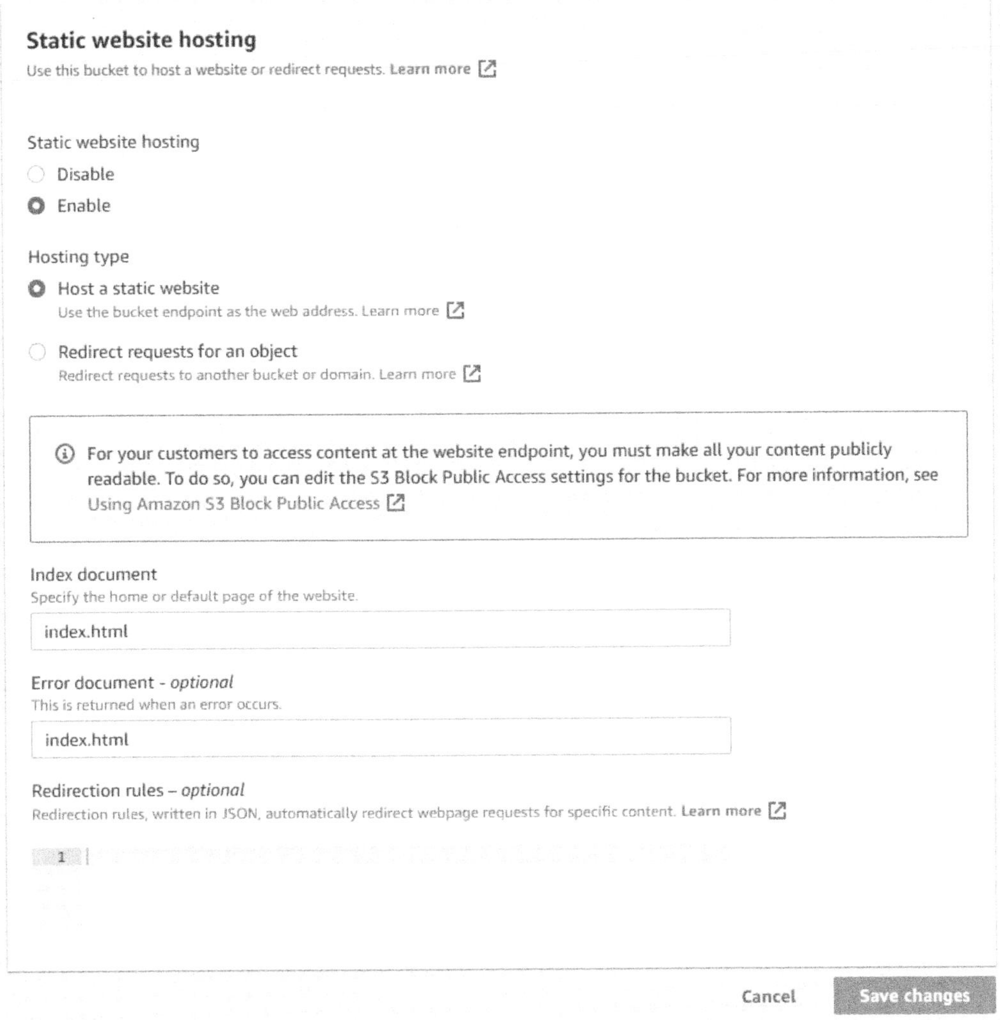

Static website hosting
Use this bucket to host a website or redirect requests. **Learn more** [↗]

Static website hosting
- ○ Disable
- ◉ Enable

Hosting type
- ◉ Host a static website
  Use the bucket endpoint as the web address. **Learn more** [↗]
- ○ Redirect requests for an object
  Redirect requests to another bucket or domain. **Learn more** [↗]

> ⓘ For your customers to access content at the website endpoint, you must make all your content publicly readable. To do so, you can edit the S3 Block Public Access settings for the bucket. For more information, see Using Amazon S3 Block Public Access [↗]

Index document
Specify the home or default page of the website.

    index.html

Error document - *optional*
This is returned when an error occurs.

    index.html

Redirection rules – *optional*
Redirection rules, written in JSON, automatically redirect webpage requests for specific content. **Learn more** [↗]

    1 |

Cancel   **Save changes**

Figure 13.38 – Filling out the Static website hosting S3 property

7.   After saving your changes, note the endpoint URL, which you will need for CloudFront:

Figure 13.39 – Noting the endpoint URL

8.   We can now go back to the **Objects** tab of the S3 bucket page, click **Upload**, and drag and drop the files from one of our dist folders, as seen in the following screenshot:

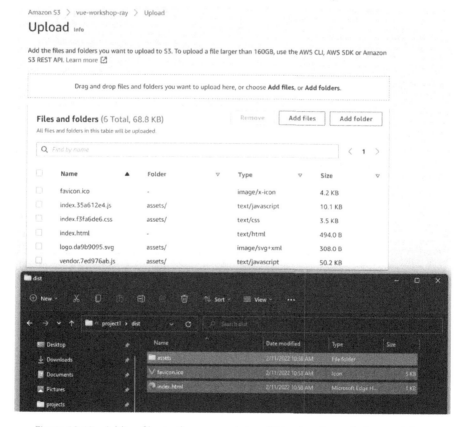

Figure 13.40 – Adding files to the vue-workshop S3 bucket through drag and drop

9. Once the files have been dropped onto the **Overview** page, we must click **Upload** to complete the process.

10. Next, we need to set a bucket policy to allow for read access to the files we've just uploaded. To do this, click the **Permissions** tab, and then **Edit** in the **Bucket policy** section. In the **Policy editor** area, paste the following JSON:

```
{
    "Version": "2012-10-17",
    "Statement": [
        {
            "Sid": "PublicReadGetObject",
            "Effect": "Allow",
            "Principal": "*",
            "Action": [
                "s3:GetObject"
            ],
            "Resource": [
                "arn:aws:s3:::vue-workshop-ray/*"
            ]
        }
    ]
}
```

Be sure to change `vue-workshop-ray` to the bucket name you chose and click **Save changes**:

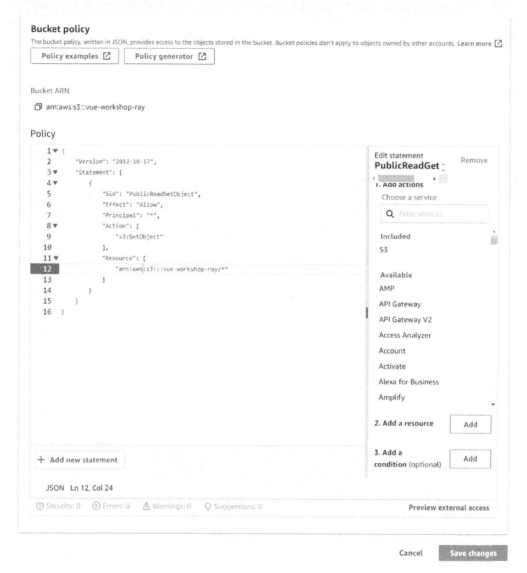

Figure 13.41 – Setting file permissions to public on files being uploaded to the S3 bucket

11. Our S3 bucket should now be configured to host static content. By visiting the website endpoint (available under **Properties | Static website hosting**), we will see the following Vue.js application (which is what we uploaded):

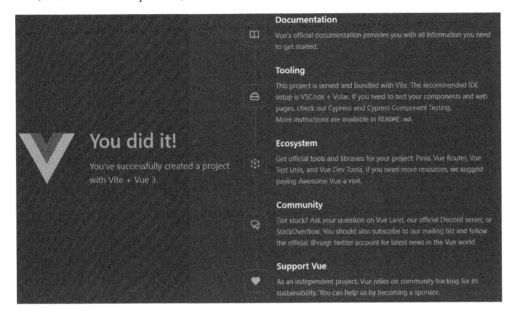

Figure 13.42 – The Vue.js application being served from our AWS S3 bucket

Note that S3 can only serve sites over HTTP, and domain names cannot be configured directly from S3 buckets. Beyond performance and robustness, being able to set custom domain names and HTTPS support are other reasons to set up AWS CloudFront as a CDN for our website.

12. We will start by navigating to the CloudFront console and clicking the **Create distribution** button, as follows:

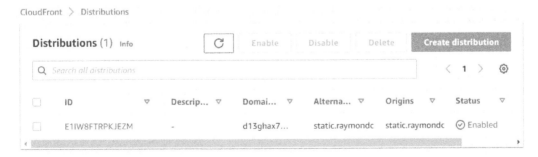

Figure 13.43 – Selecting CloudFront from the AWS service list

13. Now, we must fill out the **Origin** details. The **Origin domain** property should be the S3 bucket website endpoint domain – in other words, the domain of the URL we used to access it earlier. It looks something like `example.s3-website.us-west-1.amazonaws.com` for the `example` bucket in the `us-westwest-1` region. The following screenshot displays this:

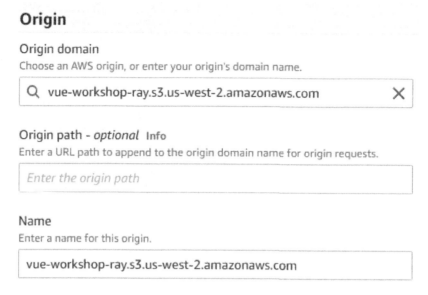

Figure 13.44 – Entering the website's endpoint domain
in the CloudFront distribution's Origin domain field

14. While we are setting up the distribution, it's a good idea to select the **Redirect HTTP to HTTPS** option for the **Viewer protocol policy** field; this can be found in the **Default cache behavior** section, as follows:

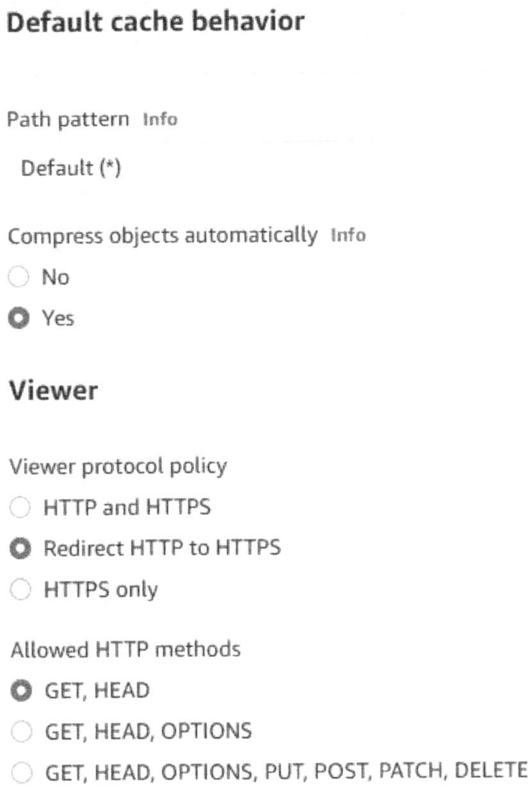

Default cache behavior

Path pattern Info

  Default (*)

Compress objects automatically Info

  ○ No

  ● Yes

Viewer

Viewer protocol policy

  ○ HTTP and HTTPS

  ● Redirect HTTP to HTTPS

  ○ HTTPS only

Allowed HTTP methods

  ● GET, HEAD

  ○ GET, HEAD, OPTIONS

  ○ GET, HEAD, OPTIONS, PUT, POST, PATCH, DELETE

Figure 13.45 – Selecting Redirect HTTP to HTTPS for the Viewer protocol policy field

Once done, we are now ready to click the **Create distribution** button and wait for the changes to propagate.

> **Note**
> CloudFront distribution changes take a while to propagate since they are being deployed to servers around the world.

We can open the domain name for the CloudFront distribution once the console's status is **Deployed**. With that, we have seen how to set up S3 and CloudFront to serve a static website. We will now learn how to use the AWS CLI to synchronize a local directory to the S3 bucket.

A prerequisite for the next section is to have a shell instance that has AWS credentials that have been injected using the AWS_ACCESS_KEY_ID, AWS_SECRET_ACCESS_KEY, and AWS_DEFAULT_ REGION environment variables. The access key and secret key need to be generated from the **Account** dropdown by selecting **My Security Credentials | Access Keys**. It also requires version 2 of the AWS CLI.

If we're in a Vue CLI project, we can deploy the dist folder (which can be built using npm run build) to our vue-workshop bucket using an AWS S3 CLI command. We want to update an s3 resource so that our command will start with aws s3. The command we want to issue is to synchronize files, so we will use the aws s3 sync command.

We will sync ./dist to the vue-workshop S3 bucket using the AWS URI syntax – that is, s3:// vue-workshop. We also want to make sure that the files we upload, just like the bucket configuration, allow public-read. In full, the command looks as follows:

```
aws s3 sync ./dist s3://vue-workshop --acl=public-read
```

Now, let's take what we've learned and apply it to our GitLab process.

Exercise 13.03 – deploying to S3 from GitLab CI/CD

S3 is a very cost-effective and performant solution for storing static files at scale. In this exercise, we'll learn how to integrate GitLab CI/CD and AWS S3 to deploy a Vue.js application. This automates the deployment of the Vue.js application. The deployment will run on every push to GitLab without any manual intervention.

You can find the complete code for this exercise at https://github.com/PacktPublishing/ Frontend-Development-Projects-with-Vue.js-3/tree/v2-edition/Chapter13/ Exercise13.03

To deploy to the S3 bucket from GitLab CI/CD, we will need to set up credential management:

1. Navigate to **CI/CD** in the **Settings** section of GitLab, as follows:

Figure 13.46 – CI/CD in the Settings menu

2. We will want to add variables, so let's expand that section. You will see an empty list of variables, as shown in the following screenshot:

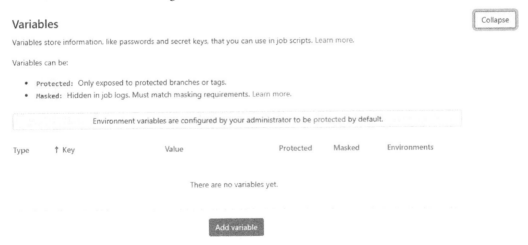

Figure 13.47 – The Variables section of the GitLab CI/CD settings expanded

3.   Next, we'll add two variables, `AWS_ACCESS_KEY_ID` and `AWS_SECRET_ACCESS_KEY`, using the UI (the values of these are not shown since they're sensitive API keys), as follows:

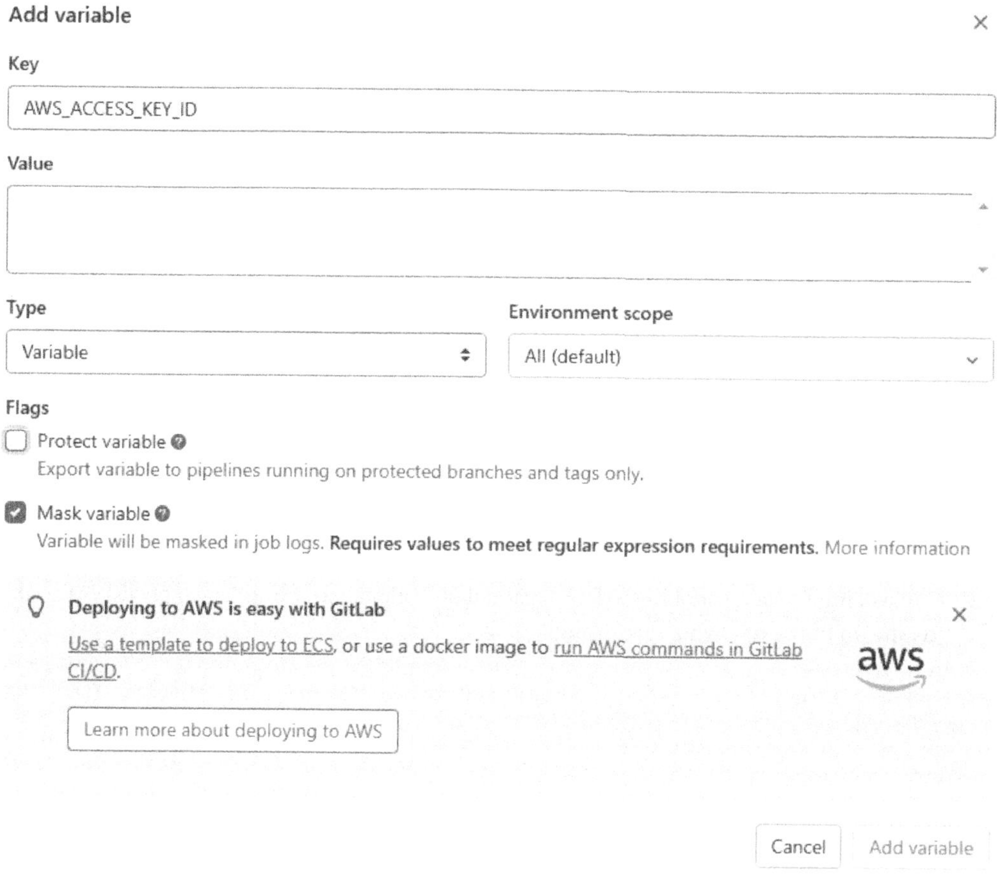

Add variable   ✕

Key

```
AWS_ACCESS_KEY_ID
```

Value

```


```

Type   Environment scope

```
Variable                                    ⬍
```      ```
All (default)   ⌄
```

Flags

☐ Protect variable ❓
  Export variable to pipelines running on protected branches and tags only.

☑ Mask variable ❓
  Variable will be masked in job logs. **Requires values to meet regular expression requirements.** More information

  💡 **Deploying to AWS is easy with GitLab**                                   ✕

     Use a template to deploy to ECS, or use a docker image to run AWS commands in GitLab
     CI/CD.                                                              **aws**

     ```
     Learn more about deploying to AWS
     ```

                                                          Cancel   Add variable

Figure 13.48 – Entering the AWS_ACCESS_KEY_ID environment variable
     ```

4. Now, we can add the default `AWS_REGION` variable using the UI (this isn't so sensitive, so its value is shown in the following screenshot):

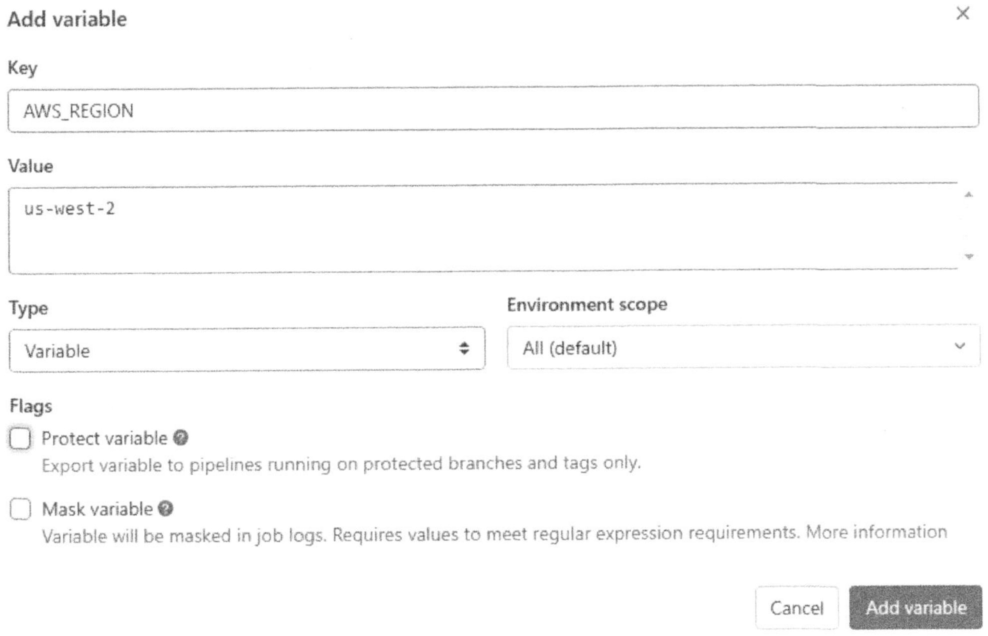

Add variable   ✕

Key

AWS_REGION

Value

us-west-2

Type   Environment scope

Variable   ⇕   All (default)   ⌄

Flags

☐ Protect variable ❷
Export variable to pipelines running on protected branches and tags only.

☐ Mask variable ❷
Variable will be masked in job logs. Requires values to meet regular expression requirements. More information

Cancel   Add variable

Figure 13.49 – Entering the AWS_DEFAULT_REGION environment variable

Now that we have set up our environment variables on GitLab CI/CD, we can start updating our `.gitlab-ci.yml` file.

5. First, we want to start caching the `dist` directory after our `build` step. To do this, we need to add a `cache` property to the `build` job:

```
build:
  # other properties
  cache:
    key: $CI_COMMIT_REF_SLUG
    paths:
      - dist
  # other properties

# other jobs
```

6. We can now add our `deploy` job, which will be a part of the `deploy` stage. To access the AWS CLI, we will use a Python image (`python:latest`) and install the AWS CLI using `pip` (a Python package manager) in our `before_script` step. Once we've installed the AWS CLI, we will run the deployment in the `script` step using the `aws s3 sync` command we used to deploy from our local machine:

```
# other jobs
deploy:
  image: python:latest
  stage: deploy
  cache:
    key: $CI_COMMIT_REF_SLUG
    paths:
      - dist
  before_script:
    - pip install awscli
  script:
    - aws s3 sync ./dist s3://vue-workshop-ray
--acl=public-read
```

> **Note**
>
> We don't need to invalidate caches since the Vite `build` command has built-in cache-busting, which it does by fingerprinting the contents of a file in the filename. Fingerprinting means that if the contents of a file change, its name/URL will change accordingly. When this new file is requested, it will be loaded from an uncached URL and will therefore get the latest version of the file.

Once this update to the configuration is pushed to the GitLab repository, we will see the pipeline running three stages that all pass, as follows:

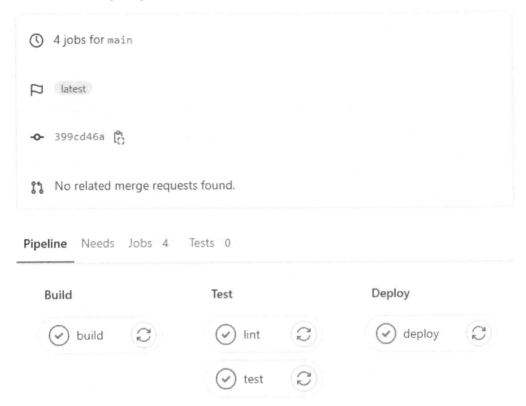

Figure 13.50 – Passing the build, test, and deploy jobs

We have now seen how to configure and deploy a Vue.js application to S3 and CloudFront using the AWS CLI and GitLab CI/CD.

Activity 13.01 – adding CI/CD to a Book Search app with GitLab and deploying it to Netlify

Now, let's take a fully built Book Search Vue.js application that loads data from the Google Books API and deploy it to GitLab CI/CD and Netlify. We will start by running the production build locally and checking the output.

Then, we will switch to running the build and code quality steps (linting) on GitLab CI/CD. Finally, we will set up a new Netlify application sourced to the GitLab repository.

The starting code for this activity can be found at https://github.com/PacktPublishing/ Frontend-Development-Projects-with-Vue.js-3/tree/v2-edition/Chapter13/ Activity13.01_initial; we will start with a **Book Search** application built with the Vue CLI. The solution can be found at https://github.com/PacktPublishing/Frontend-Development-Projects-with-Vue.js-3/tree/v2-edition/Chapter13/ Activity13.01_solution.

To start, follow these steps:

1. We will run a production build locally. We can use the command used to build all Vue CLI projects for production. We will also want to check that the relevant assets (JavaScript, CSS, and HTML) are generated correctly.

    We expect the dist folder to contain a similar structure, as follows:

Figure 13.51 – Sample contents of the dist folder (generated using
the tree command) after a production build run

2. To run GitLab CI/CD, we will need a .gitlab-ci.yml file. We will add a job to .gitlab-ci. yml in which we will install the packages followed by the production build into a Node.js LTS Docker container, at the build stage. We will also make sure to cache the output of the production build.

    Once we use git add .gitlab-ci.yml and commit and push the changes, we should see the following GitLab CI/CD pipeline run, which includes the build job while it is running (note the moon-like icon):

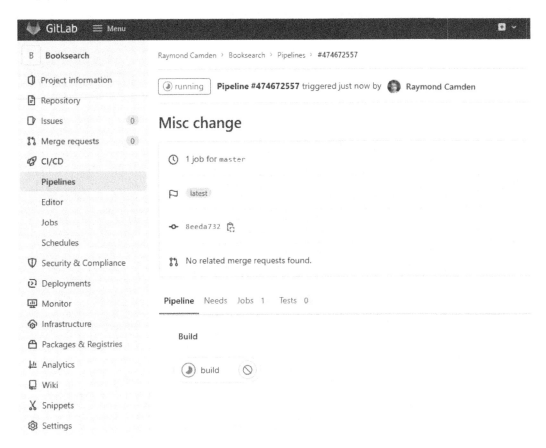

Figure 13.52 – The GitLab CI/CD pipeline with the build job running

The following screenshot, on the other hand, shows the GitLab CI/CD pipeline when the `build` job has been completed and is in the `passed` state (look for the green check):

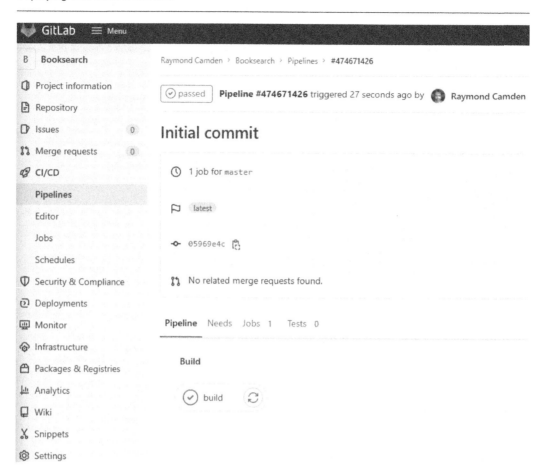

Figure 13.53 – GitLab CI/CD pipeline with the build job passed

3. Next, we will want to add a code quality job to the test stage on GitLab CI/CD (by updating
    .gitlab-ci.yml). We'll call the job lint and it will run an install of the dependencies as
    well as linting through the Vue CLI.

4. Once we use `git add .gitlab-ci.yml` and commit and push the changes, we should see the following GitLab CI/CD pipeline run, which includes the `lint` job while it is running:

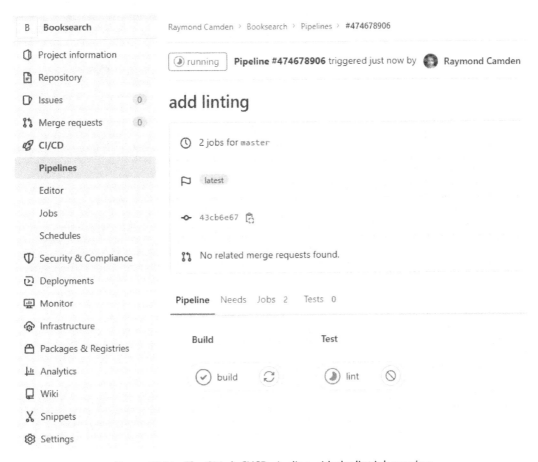

Figure 13.54 – The GitLab CI/CD pipeline with the lint job running

The following screenshot shows the GitLab CI/CD pipeline with the `lint` job completed:

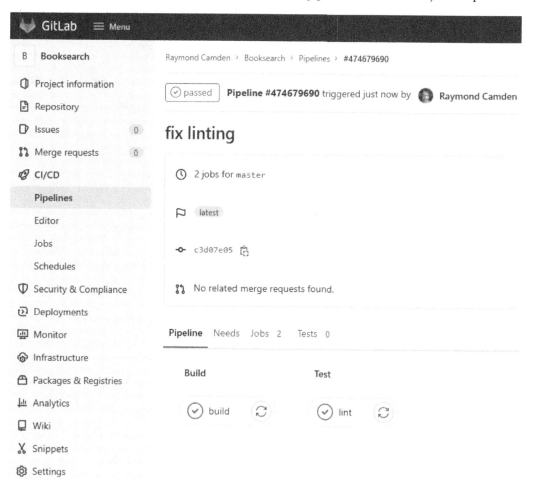

Figure 13.55 – GitLab CI/CD pipeline with the lint job completed

5. To deploy our application, we'll need to create a new Netlify application. From the **Sites** menu, add a new site and select **GitLab** as the provider. You should see your repository in the list of repos:

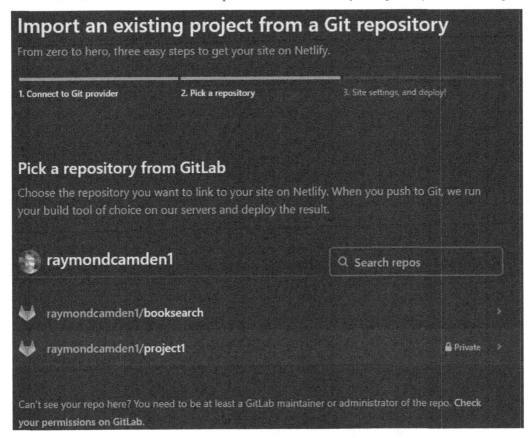

Figure 13.56 – Selecting the repository for the Netlify site

6.   In the next step, you can confirm that Netlify automatically recognizes how to build and deploy your site. Both the `build` command and `publish` directory should be set as follows.

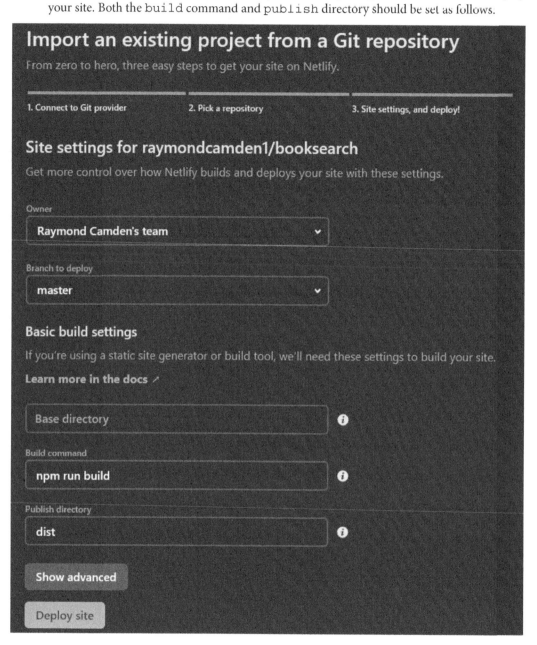

Figure 13.57 – The S3 bucket properties page with web hosting enabled
and configured with the index and error page set to index.html

7. Then, click **Deploy site**. Netlify will fetch the code from GitLab and run its build script:

gallant-bohr-539787
• Site deploy in progress
Deploys from GitLab. Created at 3:54 PM.
Site settings
Domain settings

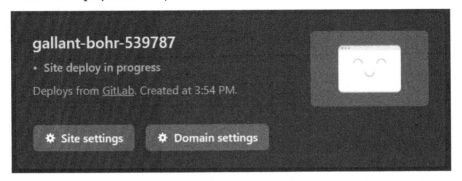

Figure 13.58 – Netlify running its deploy process

8. When done, you can click the URL for the site Netlify created and see the app running:

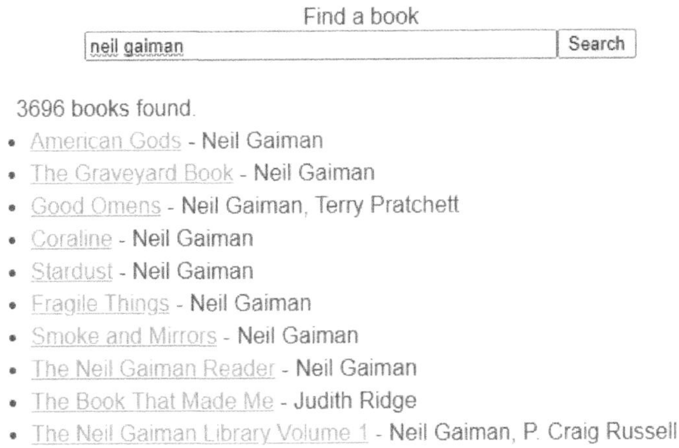

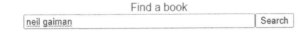

Find a book
neil gaiman
Search
3696 books found.
American Gods - Neil Gaiman
The Graveyard Book - Neil Gaiman
Good Omens - Neil Gaiman, Terry Pratchett
Coraline - Neil Gaiman
Stardust - Neil Gaiman
Fragile Things - Neil Gaiman
Smoke and Mirrors - Neil Gaiman
The Neil Gaiman Reader - Neil Gaiman
The Book That Made Me - Judith Ridge
The Neil Gaiman Library Volume 1 - Neil Gaiman, P. Craig Russell

Figure 13.59 – The Vue application running on Netlify

You've now walked through the process of taking a real (if simple) Vue application and creating a CI/CD process that lets you go from development to production in an automated and safe manner. Congratulations!

Summary

Throughout this chapter, we've looked at how to introduce CI and CD practices to Vue.js projects so that we can deploy to production safely and efficiently. We've also seen how CI and CD are beneficial in the context of an agile delivery process.

We used GitLab's CI/CD features to run tests, linting, and builds on every commit. We also learned how to leverage Netlify to host a static website by connecting Netlify to our hosting provider. Finally, we looked at how to set up and deploy to AWS S3 and CloudFront.

Throughout this book, you have learned how to use Vue.js to successfully build powerful, yet easy-to-build, web applications. You've worked with data, animations, forms, and more to build multiple different types of applications with various styles of user interaction. You also learned how to test all aspects of the application and finally took the steps to get your application into a live, production environment!

Index

Subscribe to our online digital library for full access to over 7,000 books and videos, as well as industry leading tools to help you plan your personal development and advance your career. For more information, please visit our website.

Why subscribe?

- Spend less time learning and more time coding with practical eBooks and Videos from over 4,000 industry professionals

- Improve your learning with Skill Plans built especially for you

- Get a free eBook or video every month

- Fully searchable for easy access to vital information

- Copy and paste, print, and bookmark content

Did you know that Packt offers eBook versions of every book published, with PDF and ePub files available? You can upgrade to the eBook version at packtpub.com and as a print book customer, you are entitled to a discount on the eBook copy. Get in touch with us at customercare@packtpub.com for more details.

At www.packtpub.com, you can also read a collection of free technical articles, sign up for a range of free newsletters, and receive exclusive discounts and offers on Packt books and eBooks.

Other Books You May Enjoy

If you enjoyed this book, you may be interested in these other books by Packt:

ASP.NET Core and Vue.js

Devlin Basilan Duldulao

ISBN: 978-1-80020-669-4

- Discover CQRS and mediator pattern in the ASP.NET Core 5 Web API

- Use Serilog, MediatR, FluentValidation, and Redis in ASP.NET

- Explore common Vue.js packages such as Vuelidate, Vuetify, and Vuex

- Manage complex app states using the Vuex state management library

- Write integration tests in ASP.NET Core using xUnit and FluentAssertions

- Deploy your app to Microsoft Azure using the new GitHub Actions for continuous integration and continuous deployment (CI/CD)

Vue.js 3 Cookbook

Heitor Ramon Ribeiro

ISBN: 978-1-83882-622-2

- Design and develop large-scale web applications using Vue.js 3's latest features
- Create impressive UI layouts and pages using Vuetify, Buefy, and Ant Design
- Extend your Vue.js applications with dynamic form and custom rules validation
- Add state management, routing, and navigation to your web apps
- Extend Vue.js apps to the server-side with Nuxt.js
- Discover effective techniques to deploy your web applications with Netlify
- Develop web applications, mobile applications, and desktop applications with a single code base using the Quasar framework

Packt is searching for authors like you

If you're interested in becoming an author for Packt, please visit `authors.packtpub.com` and apply today. We have worked with thousands of developers and tech professionals, just like you, to help them share their insight with the global tech community. You can make a general application, apply for a specific hot topic that we are recruiting an author for, or submit your own idea.

Share Your Thoughts

Now you've finished *Frontend Development Projects with Vue.js 3*, we'd love to hear your thoughts! Scan the QR code below to go straight to the Amazon review page for this book and share your feedback or leave a review on the site that you purchased it from.

`https://www.amazon.in/review/create-review/error?asin=1803234997`

Your review is important to us and the tech community and will help us make sure we're delivering excellent quality content.

Download a free PDF copy of this book

Thanks for purchasing this book!

Do you like to read on the go but are unable to carry your print books everywhere? Is your eBook purchase not compatible with the device of your choice?

Don't worry, now with every Packt book you get a DRM-free PDF version of that book at no cost.

Read anywhere, any place, on any device. Search, copy, and paste code from your favorite technical books directly into your application.

The perks don't stop there, you can get exclusive access to discounts, newsletters, and great free content in your inbox daily

Follow these simple steps to get the benefits:

1. Scan the QR code or visit the link below

https://packt.link/free-ebook/9781803234991

2. Submit your proof of purchase
3. That's it! We'll send your free PDF and other benefits to your email directly

Made in United States
North Haven, CT
06 June 2023

37428396R00343